Strategy in Informa[tion and] Influence Campaig[ns]

Information and influence campaigns are a particularly cogent example of the broader phenomenon we now term strategic political communication. If we think of political communication as encompassing the creation, distribution, control, use, processing and effects of information as a political resource, then we can characterize strategic political communication as the purposeful management of such information to achieve a stated objective based on the science of individual, organizational, and governmental decision-making. IICs are more or less centralized, highly structured, systematic, and carefully managed efforts to do just that.

Strategy in Information and Influence Campaigns sets out in comprehensive detail the underlying assumptions, unifying strategy, and panoply of tactics of the IIC, both from the perspective of the protagonist who initiates the action and from that of the target who must defend against it. Jarol Manheim's forward-looking, broad, and systematic analysis is a must-have resource for scholars and students of political and strategic communication, as well as practitioners in both the public and private sectors.

Jarol B. Manheim is Professor of Media and Public Affairs, and of Political Science, at The George Washington University, where he was the founding director of the School of Media and Public Affairs.

Strategy in Information and Influence Campaigns

How Policy Advocates, Social Movements, Insurgent Groups, Corporations, Governments and Others Get What They Want

Jarol B. Manheim

NEW YORK AND LONDON

First published 2011
by Routledge
270 Madison Avenue, New York, NY 10016

Simultaneously published in the UK
by Routledge
2 Park Square, Milton Park, Abingdon, Oxon OX14 4RN

Routledge is an imprint of the Taylor & Francis Group, an informa business

Typeset in Adobe Garamond by
RefineCatch Limited, Bungay, Suffolk
Printed and bound in the United States of America on acid-free paper by Walsworth Publishing Company, Marceline, MO.

Library of Congress Cataloging in Publication Data
Manheim, Jarol B., 1946–
Strategy in information and influence campaigns : how policy advocates, social movements, insurgent groups, corporations, governments, and others get what they want / Jarol B. Manheim.
p. cm.
Includes bibliographical references and index.
1. Communication in politics–United States. 2. Public relations and politics–United States. 3. Lobbying–United States. I. Title.
JA85.2.U6M373 2011
322.40973–dc22

2010029799

ISBN13: 978–0–415–88728–1 (hbk)
ISBN13: 978–0–415–88729–8 (pbk)
ISBN13: 978–0–203–83328–5 (ebk)

Contents

	List of Figures, Tables and Boxes	vi
	Preface	ix
	Acknowledgements	xiii
1	Points of Origin	3
2	Information and Influence Campaigns	18
3	Strategy and Tactics in Campaign Communication I: Winning the Argument	38
4	Strategy and Tactics in Campaign Communication II: Shaping the Decision	65
5	Networks and Netwaves: Organizing for Influence	85
6	Riding the Waves: Strategy and Tactics in Network Activation	123
7	Feeling the Pressure: The Dimensionality of Targets	141
8	Guarding the Castle: Deterring, Deflecting, Minimizing or Defeating Information and Influence Campaigns	153
9	Information, and Influence	170
	Appendix A. Need to Know: Strategic Intelligence and Research in the Campaign	185
	Appendix B. The IIC Knowledge Base: A Selective Bibliographic Inventory	194
	Notes	274
	Appendix C. A Bibliography for IIC Strategy (Including Sources Cited)	275
	Author Index	305
	Subject Index	313

Figures, Tables, and Boxes

Figures

2.1	From Information to Influence: The IIC Continuum	20
2.2	Directionality in Campaigns	35
3.1	Framework for Identifying Components of Persuasive Communications	42
3.2	Segmentation and Market Structures	52
3.3	Temporal Sequencing of Advertising Recall	62
4.1(a)	Dimensions of Information Space	80
4.1(b)	Dimensions of Cognitive Space	81
4.2	Content–Cognitive Interactions	82
5.1	Dimensions of Target Decision-Making Space	87
5.2	Power Structure Analysis	89
5.3(a)	Power Structure Analysis: Environmental Regulatory Agency	90
5.3(b)	Power Structure Analysis: Mining Company	91
5.3(c)	Power Structure Analysis: Environmental Advocacy Group	92
5.4	Classes of Stakeholders, by Key Attributes	94
5.5	Role Specialization within Campaigns	97
5.6	Channeling of Campaign Through Extra-Systemic Intermediaries	108
5.7	Map of Hypothetical Campaign Network	115
5.8	Basic Forms of Network Architecture	116
5.9	Sequencing of Campaign Intermediaries	117
5.10	Network Structure Arising from Sequencing of Intermediaries	118
6.1	Dynamics and Flow of Influence in Information and Influence Campaigns	135
6.2	Attributes, Strategic Requirements, and Campaign Tactics	136
6.3	The Interaction of Communications, Actions, and Relationships in the Campaign	138

7.1 Strategy, Tactics, Objectives, and Outcomes 144
8.1 Network Structure Arising from Sequencing of Intermediaries 158
8.2 Reverse Engineering of the Campaign Network Structure 159
9.1 The IIC Continuum Revisited 174
9.2 The Ethics Decision Tree 176
B.1 Schematic Representation of the Process of Protest by Relatively Powerless Groups 197
B.2 Social Amplification and Attenuation of Risk 231
B.3 Daisy Wheel Model of Brand Equities 269

Tables

5.1 Strategies and Tactics Directed at Selected Stakeholders 100
6.1 Classification of Protagonists by Attributes 124
6.2 Classification of Campaign Styles Associated with Protagonist Attributes 127
6.3 Likely Use of Third Parties Associated with Protagonist Attributes 133
A.1 Utility of Research in Information and Influence Campaigns, by Method and Research Question 186

Boxes

2.1 Redefining the Target to Advance the Campaign 24
2.2 Who's on First? No, Who's *Really* on First? 27
2.3 The Strategist as Storyteller 29
2.4 Reducing Access to Information to Improve News Coverage 30
2.5 Moving Up the Food Chain 34
2.6 A Battle of Co-Equals 36
3.1 Appealing to Pro-Social Values in PICs 41
3.2 Effective Core Messages Connect the Protagonist with the Audience 44
3.3 Defining the Moral High Ground 46
3.4 Uses of Digital Media in Campaigns 49
3.5 Strategic Audience Segmentation 54
3.6 The Name of the Game is the Name 59
3.7 Managing Information Flows to Control Agendas and Frames 60
4.1 Listen Up! 70
4.2 Dissonance Reduction Or Else! 73
4.3 Elements of Information Operations 77
5.1 Google This! 90
5.2 Leverage for the Environment 92
5.3 Personalization, Pejoratives, Power 95

5.4 Intermediaries Act in Their Own Self-Interest 98
5.5 The Perils of Leveraging Celebrity 102
5.6 The Compleat Sit-In 103
5.7 Throwing a Boomerang 109
5.8 Network-Building in Mexico 112
6.1 Different Strokes for Different Folks 125
6.2 Packaging the Protagonist to Fund and Legitimize the Campaign 130
6.3 Who Really Hates Wal-Mart? 131
7.1 Exploiting the Perceived Illegitimacy of the Target 145
7.2 Buried Treasure 147
8.1 Reverse Engineering the Corporation 156
8.2 Co-opting the Protagonist 161
8.3 Outsourcing the Counterattack 163
8.4 Anticipating and Resisting Demands for Information 165
9.1 The Ultimate "*Washington Post* Test" 179

Preface

Three guys walk into a bar—Sun Tzu, Niccolò Machiavelli, and Saul Alinsky. It sounds like the starting point of a bad joke, but, aside from the setting, it is actually the starting point for understanding a ubiquitous element of contemporary politics and political communication. Take the vision and discipline of the best-known military thinker of all time. Supplement that with the hard-nosed pragmatism, dedication and insight of the legendary sixteenth-century political advisor to the Medici. Then add the imagination, street smarts, and sheer audacity of the dean of twentieth-century community organizers. Throw in the last hundred years or so of knowledge gain in the social sciences, sprinkle with the latest information and communication technologies and techniques, and the mix is complete. Welcome to the exciting world of twenty-first-century information and influence campaigns.

Information and influence campaigns (IICs) are a particularly cogent example of the broader phenomenon we now term strategic political communication. If we think of political communication as encompassing the creation, distribution, control, use, processing and effects of information as a political resource, whether by governments, organizations, groups, or individuals, we can characterize *strategic* political communication as the purposeful management of such information to achieve a stated objective based on a sophisticated knowledge of underlying attributes and tendencies of people and institutions—which is to say, based on the science of individual, organizational, and governmental decision-making—and of the uses and effects of communication as a means of influencing them. IICs are more or less centralized, highly structured, systematic, and carefully managed efforts to do just that.

In several earlier books (Manheim 1991, 1994a, 2001, 2004), I have provided extended examples of these multifaceted, large-scale, and systematic efforts at influence, and of the motivations and strategies that drive them. While I will provide a number of illustrative examples in the present volume, the objective here is to extract from the full range of these campaigns in rather more abstract terms the underlying strategy that is common to them all—to examine the decisions that confront the campaign strategist and the criteria that are employed in making them. Some of these decisions are explicit in character, others implicit. Some are simple and straightforward, others complex and far from clear-cut. Some are based on gut instinct, others on highly sophisticated underlying knowledge. Some are opportunistic, others highly creative and original.

To my knowledge, there has never been a "perfect" information and influence campaign, one in which a strategist has sat down and literally worked through all of the elements we will delineate here. Doing so would require perfect knowledge, perfect information, perfect resources, perfect command of those resources, and perfect control of the campaign environment. Not a single one of those conditions is likely. So in that sense, we will over-describe campaign strategy in this book. On the other hand, most or all of the elements of strategy we will develop here have, in fact, been employed in one campaign or another—they are present in the strategic toolbox and available for use. So the world of decisions we are about to tour is a real world.

The book opens with a brief history lesson. Though its form is contemporary, as we'll see the information and influence campaign has deep roots in the Western political experience, whether in pursuit of the public interest or of something much narrower. In that sense, everything old really is new again. And yet, there is something new in the campaigns that we see today. Over the last century or so, whole new fields of study—the social sciences—have emerged from the mother ship of Philosophy to claim their space in human knowledge. And, because of their observational and experimental methodologies, along with them have come new, empirically supported theories about many aspects of human behavior, and vast bodies of supporting research and data. All of this, or at least much of it, is grist for the mill of the campaign strategist. Indeed, we can think of campaign strategy at the highest level as the systematic exploitation of the available theory and research in the design and implementation of information and influence campaigns. Where once the best campaign strategist could afford to render seat-of-the-pants judgments about what to do, when, where, how and why, today anyone running a seat-of-the-pants campaign is most likely to lose his shirt. Original thinking and good judgment are still requisites of the successful strategist, but so are good data and solid conceptual grounding.

With that in mind, the main body of the book is devoted to identifying and delineating key elements of strategy. The model here is not that of a cookbook offering recipes for campaign success, but more that of an introductory physics book. Just as in physics, I would argue, there are certain basic principles and tendencies (not laws) that explain how and why things work in information and influence campaigns. And just as in physics, if one wants to understand the operations of a system of action like the campaign, one must first master the basic rules. The purpose of this volume is to delineate the rules. Campaign specifics are of secondary, or even tertiary, importance at best. So buckle up.

In Chapter 1, we'll look back in history to the origins of the information and influence campaign, but end with a contemporary example that should help place in context the more abstract discussion to follow. Chapter 2 serves as a general introduction to the information and influence campaign, its elements and its applications. Chapters 3 and 4 focus on information and its role in campaigns. The first of these chapters looks in a relatively traditional way at content—at persuasion based on substantive argument. The second employs some leading theories of attitudes and other psychological states to look at persuasion in more structural terms. Chapters 5 and 6 make the turn from information to influence through the mechanism of social network analysis. They examine the relationship between protagonist and target, the benefits to be derived from recruiting various types of intermediaries to carry the campaign from the former to the latter, and some of the important strategic considerations that come into play in identifying, mobilizing and exploiting these third parties. Chapter 7 closes this portion of the argument with a strategic look at the targets themselves, and the use of strategic communication and relationship management that can be employed to influence them.

Chapter 8 looks at the campaign as a whole, but from the perspective of the target, and asks the question: How does one defend against this? The answer, I will suggest, derives from reverse engineering the campaign itself. Chapter 9 steps back to gain perspective through a consideration of the campaign as a social phenomenon and its implications for democratic systems, for political dialogue, and for daily political life. Appendix A discusses the uses of research in developing, implementing and assessing campaign strategy.

That brings us to Appendix B. The architecture I have selected for this book is a bit out of the ordinary, and I want to make it explicit. The core of the argument here is that campaign strategy has been greatly impacted by developments in the social sciences. Yet as you read the core chapters that follow, you will find very few references to the literature in which these developments are, well, developed. That is by choice, in part to facilitate making the argument of the book, which is complicated enough in its own right, and in part to serve the interests of non-scholarly readers. However, this argument about the grounding of campaign strategy in theory and research is not only real, but it is central to the thesis of this volume. Accordingly, the interested reader will find, in Appendix B and in the list of sources that follows it in Appendix C, an overview of representative literature that relates to and underlies many of the points made in the main body of the book. In effect, this is a review of strategy-related or strategy-applicable scholarly literature organized around the thematic outline of the book. My hope is that this will serve as both a validation of the assertion of the intellectual grounding of campaign strategy and a gateway to the relevant literatures.

All authors benefit, not only from the kindness of strangers in the form of anonymous referees, but from the generosity and insights of friends and colleagues who take the time to read and critique their work while it is still in progress. For my part, I express my sincere gratitude to Lance Bennett, Nick Cull, Tony Dyson, Bob Entman, and Bruce Gregory for their excellent suggestions, advice, and counsel, which have combined to make this volume better than anything I could have produced without them. And I thank the editorial crew at Routledge, starting with my editor, Michael Kerns, and including as well Mary Altman, Sioned Jones, Donna White, and Belinda Cunnison for their invaluable assistance in bring this project to fruition.

Writing this book has been both a pleasure and a challenge. The pleasure has come from having the opportunity to draw together into one, unified argument a wide array of facts, theories, ideas, trends and interpretations with which I—along with many others—have wrestled for a long time. The challenge has come from the need, incumbent on any author, to do so effectively. I hope that you will find reading the book, too, to be both a pleasure and a challenge. The pleasure will come if, having shown a modicum of interest in the topic, you find its presentation here both lucid and illuminating. The challenge will come when, having completed your journey, you take a few moments—or perhaps longer—to consider the implications of what you have read. As any author should, I accept full responsibility for what I have written. I hope, in return, that you will take full responsibility for what you have read. And for that, I thank you.

Acknowledgements

I acknowledge with gratitude the support of The George Washington University, which provided a year-long sabbatical leave that permitted the substantial completion of this book. I also acknowledge, with deep admiration, an intellectual debt to R. Edward Freeman, whose 1984 book, *Strategic Management: A Stakeholder Approach*, was decades ahead of its time, the coming of which it both presaged and hastened.

Figure 3.3 combines two figures from "The Remembering and Forgetting of Advertising," reprinted with permission from *Journal of Marketing*, published by the American Marketing Association, Hubert A. Zielske, volume 23 (1959), pp. 240, 242. Figures 4.1(a), 4.1(b), and 5.1 are reproduced from Jarol B. Manheim, "A Model of Agenda Dynamics," in Margaret L. McLaughlin, ed., *Communication Yearbook 10* (Beverly Hills: Sage, 1987); reproduced with permission. Figure 5.4 is adapted from Ronald K. Mitchell, Bradley R. Agle, and Donna J. Wood, "Toward a Theory of Stakeholder Identification and Salience: Defining the Principle of Who and What Really Counts," *Academy of Management Review* 22 (1997), p. 874; reproduced with permission. Figure 5.5 is adapted from Jarol B. Manheim, *The Death of a Thousand Cuts: Corporate Campaigns and the Attack on the Corporation* (Mahwah, NJ: Lawrence Erlbaum Associates, 2001). Figure 5.6 is based on the boomerang model developed by Margaret Keck and Kathryn Sikkink in *Activists Beyond Borders: Advocacy Networks in International Politics* (Ithaca, NY: Cornell University Press, 1998), p. 13. Portions of Figure 5.8 are based on a similar characterization in John Arquilla and David Ronfeldt, eds., *Networks and Netwars* (Santa Monica, CA: RAND, 2001). Figures 6.1–6.3, and Figure 7.1, and portions of the related discussion, were produced with US Government sponsorship; the judgments do not necessarily reflect the opinions or policies of the research sponsors. Figure B.1 is reproduced in modified form from Michael Lipsky, "Protest as a Political Resource," in *American Political Science Review* 62 (1968), p. 1147; reproduced with permission. Figure B.2 is reproduced in modified form from Roger E. Kasperson and Jeanne X. Kasperson, "Social Amplification and Attenuation of Risk," in *Annals of the American Academy of Political and Social Science* 545 (1996), p. 97; reproduced with permission. Figure B.3 is reproduced from Richard Jones, "Finding Sources of Brand Value: Developing a Stakeholder Model of Brand Equity," in *Journal of Brand Management* 13 (2005), p. 18; reproduced with permission.

You have to learn the rules of the game. And then you have to play better than anyone else.

Albert Einstein

1 Points of Origin

The government of one country trying to influence the economic, military or other policies of another. Environmentalists trying to influence the practices of a corporation. A labor union trying to influence the behaviors of an employer. An insurgent movement trying to gain supporters by legitimizing itself. A company trying to gain an advantage over a competitor in the marketplace. An advocacy group trying to influence legislators to change public policy. In these and many other efforts, one of the most common forms of engagement is through the conduct of some form of information and influence campaign.

For the moment, let us define the information and influence campaign (IIC) as an effort by one party, through some combination of communication and action, to change the behavior of another party to its advantage. Such campaigns are commonplace these days—they are undertaken by, or targeted against, such diverse entities as governments, international organizations, labor unions, nongovernmental advocacy organizations, corporations, or even insurgent groups—and they have about them the feel of a distinctly contemporary phenomenon. But like all such complex and sophisticated patterns of human behavior, the campaigns we observe today are the products of evolution. They build on a history of innovation, trial and error, redesign, adaptation to events and new technologies, responses to changing expectations, and all the other factors that make politics so much fun, whether as a spectator sport or as a profession. Before turning our attention to the principal focus in this volume, the strategies and tactics that characterize contemporary IICs, then, let us pause to consider these points of origin. We'll do that by looking at three examples that happen to fall at 100-year intervals.

The World's First Social Justice Campaign, 1787–1807[1]

On the afternoon of Tuesday, May 22, 1787—precisely three days before delegates across the ocean convened the Philadelphia Convention or, as it is known today, the Constitutional Convention, to draft the eponymous document—another group came together at a printing shop in London.

These twelve men, too, had a mission. Spearheaded by a young clergyman, Thomas Clarkson, who remained a driving force throughout, they met to form the first national advocacy association, the Society to Effect the Abolition of the Slave Trade, and in the process to initiate a grassroots social movement of a sort unknown in its time, and whose innovations resound to this day.

At the time, the trade in human beings was more rule than exception, and though moral outrage was oft expressed, it generally had little practical impact. That was about to change. Those at the May meeting, and others who soon joined their cause, launched one of the world's first comprehensive information and influence campaigns. Among them were Clarkson, who traveled widely in the following years organizing and agitating for change; Olaudah Equiano, an articulate former slave whose testimony regarding his personal experiences gave a face to the issue; John Newton, a repentant slave ship captain best remembered today as the composer of the hymn "Amazing Grace"; Granville Sharp, propagandist and pamphleteer; budding young industrialist and designer Josiah Wedgwood; and parliamentarian and eventual front-man for the movement William Wilberforce.

Their campaign—and that's what it was—was remarkable for its imagination, its organization, its breadth, its diversity, and its sheer inventiveness. The campaign was a faith-based effort, finding early and continuing support among Quaker communities, which lent it an immediate aura of moral authority. While one might assume today that an anti-slavery movement would hardly need additional moral garb, social values were different in the eighteenth century and this religious grounding, eventually to be augmented with support by other faiths, was an important anchor point. Though many persons at the time did, in fact, regard slavery as a moral evil, it was nonetheless an evil in the abstract and thus easily opposed in principle without requiring action. By recruiting and lending prominence to the aforementioned Olaudah Equiano, the Society personified slavery as a real, concrete evil, and one requiring remediation.

To gain legitimacy and influence in the political sphere, the Society recruited Wilberforce, a prominent and respected Member of Parliament, who became its principal legislative voice. Not coincidentally, Wilberforce, a close friend of William Pitt, who served as Prime Minister during much of the period in question and encouraged his engagement with the issue, was an Anglican, and his involvement also served to insulate the movement against marginalization as a purely Quaker undertaking. The Society initiated petition drives—an accepted expression of public opinion in an era that lacked polling—eventually producing an estimated 103 such documents signed by somewhere between 60,000 and 100,000 people that were submitted to Parliament in 1788 alone.

The slave trade was at heart an economic issue, driven by the demand for labor to produce agricultural products, principal among them sugar. The abolitionists took this head on, launching a consumer boycott in which some 300,000 Britons refused to purchase or eat slave-grown sugar. Other tactics included:

- research and fact-finding, primarily by Clarkson at the outset of the campaign, in anticipation of a Parliamentary inquiry into the question of slavery, and the development of narratives based on the horrors uncovered thereby,
- newspaper and magazine story placements,
- participation in commercial debating hall programs, the contemporaneous equivalent of talk radio (half of all advertised debates in 1788 dealt with the slave trade),
- cartoons and other forms of ridicule intended to demonize and reduce the acceptance of slave traders,
- publication of a children's book about the evils of slavery, *Little Truths Better than Great Fables*, by William Darton,
- publication of books and essays on the moral and practical aspects of the issue by Clarkson and others, their translation into the principal languages of the slave-trade—French, Portuguese, Danish, Dutch, Spanish—and their international distribution to key markets,
- campaigns of correspondence including the production of 500–1000 copies of letters that amounted to a prototype for the contemporary newsletter, ongoing exchanges with American supporters of the movement (important since the emerging new nation across the Atlantic was a primary market for the slave trade), as well as personal letters to the kings of Sweden and Spain,
- display of the first anti-slavery painting (*Execrable Human Traffick* by George Morland) at the Royal Academy in London,
- design and printing of wall posters and their display in public houses across Britain (the best known being a portrayal of the accommodations on the slave ship *Brookes*, an image that is still widely used today),
- the production of medallions (precursors of today's campaign buttons), used on snuff boxes and cufflinks by men and on hatpins by women, featuring a logo, designed by Josiah Wedgewood and praised by Benjamin Franklin, showing an African kneeling in chains, circled by the slogan, "Am I Not a Man and a Brother?",
- celebrity endorsements,
- fundraising correspondence, the forerunner of today's direct-mail appeals,
- lobbying Parliament, and, throughout the campaign
- meticulous scheduling, organization, and record-keeping, which has allowed historians to reconstruct the Society's activities.

The result? In early 1807, after a twenty-year campaign, Parliament passed a bill abolishing the British slave trade by forbidding slave ships from departing British ports after May 1 of that year. On March 25, King George III assented, and the bill became law. The problem of slavery was by no means solved, but in fairly short order the slave trade, the object of the Society and its campaign, was greatly diminished.

A Justice Campaign of a Different Sort, 1887–1890[2]

In November 1887, Thomas Alva Edison wrote a letter to the New York State Death Penalty Commission, charged at the time with finding the most humane means of executing criminals, urging that the state adopt the electric chair for this purpose. Edison wrote, in part:

> The best appliance in this connection is to my mind the one which will perform its work in the shortest space of time, and inflict the least amount of suffering upon its victim. This I believe can be accomplished by the use of electricity and the most suitable apparatus for the purpose is that class of dynamo-electric machine which employs intermittent currents. The most effective of these are known as "alternating machines," manufactured principally in this country by Mr. Geo. Westinghouse, Pittsburgh.
>
> (Essig, 2003: 117)

With this letter, America's most famous inventor launched his latest innovation, a version of the information and influence campaign tuned to advance a set of private interests in a competitive environment.

In point of fact, Edison was an opponent of capital punishment, and he wrote reluctantly, and only after the repeated urgings of Commissioner Alfred Porter Southwick, a Buffalo dentist and death penalty advocate. Southwick had qualified for membership on the Commission based in part on his own experiments, in which he gathered up many of the stray dogs that were at the time causing trouble in his home town and executed them with jolts of electricity, and in part on the fact that he had initiated, through a friend in the State Senate, the legislation establishing the Commission. Other members of the Commission included Elbridge T. Gerry, whose grandfather was a signer of the Declaration of Independence and attended the Constitutional Convention in 1787, and who himself was a prominent philanthropist and served as legal counsel to the American Society for the Prevention of Cruelty to Animals, and an obscure Albany lawyer named Matthew Hale. This august group began with a consideration of all of the ways that deserving criminals might be put to death. Their list included, *among others*:

- Beating with clubs
- Beheading
- Boiling in water

- Boiling in oil
- Boiling in melted sulfur
- Breaking on a wheel
- Burning
- Body illumination (tying the victim down, boring holes in his body, filling these with oil, and setting the oil alight)
- Burying alive
- Cannon, as in shooting from
- Crucifixion
- Dismemberment
- Drowning
- Exposure to wild beasts or snakes
- Flaying alive
- Garrote
- Guillotine
- Hanging
- Impalement
- Piercing with spikes in a device known as an iron maiden
- Poisoning
- Pressing to death
- Shooting, as by a firing squad
- Stabbing
- Stretching on the rack
- Stoning
- Strangling
- Suffocation
- Throwing from a cliff. (Essig, 2003: 91–96)

Perhaps not surprisingly, the Commission judged all of these methods to be inhumane to one degree or another, and cast about for some new means of execution. It considered, but then rejected, lethal injection with a hypodermic needle, on grounds that this might prejudice the public against the then emergent potential for delivering helpful medications by injection. (It was during the debate over this method that Dr. Southwick wrote to Edison asking his views of electrocution, the good doctor's preferred methodology, so that he could buttress his views against the objections of Gerry, who favored the needle.) Then, and perhaps not surprisingly, since it had been constituted for precisely this purpose, the Commission settled on a high-tech solution to the problem: death by electrocution.

As the Wizard of Menlo Park weighed Southwick's request, the soon-to-be-proverbial light bulb clicked on in his head. For Southwick had just presented Edison with a possible solution to his own most vexing problem, the competition posed by Westinghouse and his alternating-current electrical systems. If Edison could establish in the public mind the perception that Westinghouse's alternating current system was dangerous to use, and hardly something one would want to introduce into one's home, while his own direct current system was safe as could be, he stood to gain the upper hand in the emerging competition to electrify the country. And what better proof could there be than the decision by the State of New York to employ alternating current to kill?

Like many subsequent campaigns, this one was constructed on a body of belief and expectation that was already established in the public mind, and sought to position the protagonist—in this case, Mr. Edison—squarely atop the moral high ground, even as he moved to gain a tangible advantage.

On New Year's Eve 1879 Edison had stirred the public imagination, not to mention generated quite a bit of excitement, with his legendary demonstration of electric lighting at his Menlo Park, New Jersey, laboratory. Less than two years later, he had established a generating station and was laying conduit under Lower Manhattan, and on September 4, 1882, he flipped a switch that served only fifty-nine customers but lit the world. By 1887, he had 121 central generating stations in place.

But Edison had a problem. His entire system operated on direct current (DC), which had the advantage of being relatively safe, but the disadvantage of dissipating after traveling a very short distance—only about a mile. As a result, Edison's power grid required the building of generating stations at the rate of approximately one per square mile—an expensive undertaking to say the least. That created an opening for competitors, and one principal adversary did emerge in the person of George Westinghouse. Westinghouse's system employed a different technology, alternating current (AC), which had a keen advantage in that it could travel through miles of wire and still turn on the lights. This was the case because alternating current could be distributed at very high voltages—essentially higher pressure that would push it further through the wires—then, through electrical induction, stepped down to the much lower voltages required to power lighting and other applications. This is the function performed today by transformers, from the large oval boxes that hang on power poles and convert transmission voltages to household voltages, to the small plastic boxes we plug into the wall to further reduce the flow before it reaches laptop computers, cellular phones or other delicate electronic devices. Unfortunately for Mr. Edison, however, direct current does not work the same way, and cannot so easily be stepped up and down. The Westinghouse system thus required far fewer generating stations than the Edison system, and that made it potentially far more economical. By April 1887, the two men were in direct competition and cutting prices to win business, and by the fall of the year, Edison's sales agents were clamoring for assistance. It was at that moment that Mr. Southwick's request arrived.

As it turned out, Edison had a card to play. From the outset, he had laid his electrical cables underground. But the same could not be said of some competitors who employed alternating current and saved money by stretching their high-voltage distribution cables on poles that crisscrossed city streets. These overhead wires were genuinely dangerous, and they were everywhere. Edison realized, as he once put it, that "If we ever kill a customer, it would be a bad blow to the business." And he saw both value and urgency in helping the public to distinguish between safe (DC) and unsafe (AC) electricity. He was also growing to dislike Mr. Westinghouse, with whom he became involved in a series of patent disputes.

Sometimes a problem is an opportunity in disguise. Edison believed that, if he could play on the public's growing concern about electrical safety in such a way that people made a distinction between the two generating systems, he could drive demand toward the DC system that he largely controlled. The solution? An electric chair—a high profile, high-tech solution to a contemporaneous controversy—operating on the most effective form of electricity for killing a human being: alternating current. Game on.

Elements of the campaign included the following. In 1888, the Death Penalty Commission delivered its report to the legislature, along with a draft bill providing for death by electrocution. Later in the year, that bill became law. Along the way, Mr. Edison was asked by a reporter from the *New York World* how death by electrocution might be accomplished. Edison obliged by building and demonstrating (using a dog) an electric chair. "The current," Edison noted, "should come from an alternating machine." And when asked his opinion about what term should be applied to death by electrocution, Edison turned the problem over to his lawyers, one of whom proposed privately that an executed criminal should be said to have been "westinghoused" or have been sent "to the westinghouse."

Early in 1888, Edward Johnson, who headed the Edison Electric Light Company, published an 84-page pamphlet—what today we would term a white paper—titled *A Warning*, in which he set forth the technical and business advantages of the Edison system, before moving on to highlight the destructive power of AC systems with their accompanying high voltages. This document was organized around five so-called "cautions" and 21 appendices. Of the latter, Appendix J cited press accounts of deaths and injuries attributed to electrical shock, while Appendix K focused on technical aspects of the threat posed by "High Electrical Pressure." Per the document: "It is a matter of fact that any system employing high pressure . . . jeopardizes life . . . Any interruption of the flow of the current [i.e., by touching a wire] adds to its destructive property, whilst its complete reversal, as in the Alternating (Westinghouse) system increases this destructiveness enormously" (quoted in Klein, 2008: 262).

Also in 1888, Edison Electric hired a surrogate, one Harold Brown, who set about killing all manner of animals, from dogs to horses, using Westinghouse electrical generators, and publicizing his "experiments." Both Brown and Edison long denied that the former was an agent of the latter. Mr. Brown also became a regular contributor to the newspapers and journals of the day, where he advocated for the superior safety of DC systems. He wrote in the *New York Evening Post*, in a letter dated May 24 but published June 5, 1889, that "The only excuse for the use of the fatal 'alternating' current is that it saves the company operating it from spending a larger sum of money for the heavier copper wires, which are required by the safe [DC] systems. That is, the public must submit to *constant danger from sudden death* in order that a corporation may pay a *little larger dividend*" (quoted in Klein: 263–264). Brown then attended a meeting of the New York Board of Electrical Control to insist that his letter be read into the record. That same year, both Edison and Brown, who was identified as a "New York State Expert on Electrical Execution," published articles in the *North American Review* pointing out the dangers of alternating current. Later in 1889, Mr. Edison attacked his opponent's character, most notably in telling the *New York Herald*, "Westinghouse used to be a pretty solid fellow, but he has lately taken to shystering."

That same year, after three New York City workers lost their lives by electrocution in separate accidents involving overhead high-voltage wires owned, through subsidiaries, by Westinghouse, Edison noted dryly to a reporter, "They say I am prejudiced, but if I had anything to say I would abolish the alternating current." To another, he posed a simple question: "Have they killed anyone there today?" In February 1890, Mr. Edison testified before a committee of the Virginia State Senate that was considering a bill to limit AC transmission to not more than 200 volts, which, as we have seen, would make it far less competitive. The bill died in committee. And later in the year, when Ohio considered legislation imposing similar restrictions, rather than testify, Edison dispatched a team with an AC generator to Columbus, where they conducted a demonstration of the dangers of AC by electrocuting a calf and a horse.

Through all of this, Mr. Westinghouse declined to acknowledge the dangers of high-voltage AC, and when, after a particularly egregious electrocution death, the Mayor of New York convened the city's Board of Electrical Control and ordered the removal of unsafe wires, Westinghouse obtained a court injunction preventing the city from touching the wires of his companies. Advantage Edison.

Of course, in the end, that advantage was lost. Not only was alternating current more economical to distribute than direct current, but it also proved to be far more flexible in its applications. That, and the economic exigencies of the day, led to a series of reorganizations and mergers through which, in 1892, Mr. Edison's interests came to be known by the name they bear today—General Electric—and began to engage in a serious competition with Westinghouse . . . to provide alternating-current and related technologies.

Though he did not likely see his efforts as any sort of formal campaign, Edison's actions through this period were, in fact, prototypical of that latter-day phenomenon in many respects. He had a clear objective—to repel the challenge to his budding electrical empire posed by alternating current. He had a defined enemy—Westinghouse—whom he sought to demonize. He had a strategy—linking alternating current in the public mind with death and danger. He identified an opportunity in the controversy over implementation of the death penalty, defined the moral high ground of maximally humane execution, and reified this in the form of the electric chair. He did this, incidentally, despite his own objections to capital punishment, and in the face of evidence that death by electrocution was not all that humane. He remained focused on his message—alternating current kills—and considered, though he ultimately rejected, creating terms of art that explicitly linked death by electricity with his opponent. He employed surrogates to provide seemingly neutral and independent confirmation of his arguments. He supported legislative actions that advanced his cause, and did his best to generate public interest and support for them. He was opportunistic when events occurred that could be turned to advantage. He was an active publicist for his cause, he was adept at working the media, which he did systematically, and he knew how to leverage his personal fame and standing to lend credence to his arguments. A century and a quarter later, that playbook, though greatly augmented and refined, retains a familiar look and feel.

Sweatshop Days and Philip Knight, 1987 (okay, 1989) to the present[3]

Our third example represents an extension and an amalgam of the first two in that it was designed around a public-regarding objective—the abolition of sweatshop working conditions around the world—and gave rise to a social movement targeting this evil, but at the same time was intended to advance a much narrower set of interests, those of organized labor in the United States. A full appreciation of the campaign requires a bit of background.

The labor movement in the United States reached its greatest market share of the American workforce, and hence its peak of influence, in 1954, following which, for a variety of reasons that lie outside of our discussion here, it began upon more than a half-century of nearly unbroken decline. By the midpoint of this reversal, around the mid- to late-1970s, some of the movement's more insightful leaders began casting about for an organizing methodology by which they might reverse the trend. As it happened, just such a methodology was at hand. It derived from an approach called "power structure analysis" that was being developed around that same time by a number of activists on the political left, among them several alumni of a 1960s student organization, the Students for a Democratic Society (SDS). Power structure analysis plays a central role in IIC strategy today, and we will have a great deal more to say about it later in this volume. For the present, let me summarize the core concept thus: The way to force a change in the behavior of an opponent is to find ways to leverage against that opponent the interests of its own friends and allies, so that they become, in effect, the agents of the campaign. Labor unions began to experiment with this approach in a prototypical campaign against a clothing manufacturer, Farah Manufacturing, in 1972, and it soon evolved into a common instrument in labor's toolkit known as the "corporate campaign." By 1989 there had been perhaps two dozen such efforts.

One of the reasons that American unions were in decline had to do with the off-shoring of jobs. These were the early days of the phenomenon we now term globalization, and there was a race, driven by competition with Japanese companies, to maintain market share in the manufacture of price-sensitive goods like shoes and clothing by transferring production to those countries with the lowest labor costs. The U.S. balance of trade with countries such as South Korea and Indonesia was hemorrhaging, and for companies on the losing end, the choice was simple: control this flow of goods, or be displaced by it. They chose the former, and began moving their production to these new East Asian markets and, as a consequence, reducing their workforces in the U.S. This was a large-scale trend, and one that developed fairly quickly, but even within the overall trend, still more change was underway. By 1990, much of the low-cost production had come to rest in a single country, Indonesia, where the government went out of its way to attract foreign investment.

Riding this trend-within-a-trend, three shoe companies—Nike, Reebok, and Adidas—began shifting their manufacturing capacity to Indonesia. By the spring of 1990, Nike and Reebok were each ordering approximately 400,000 pairs of shoes each month from contractors based in that country. For Nike, the result was dramatic. Through the 1980s, the company had struggled to hold its own. But from 1989 forward, its profits soared. It came to dominate the market for athletic shoes, and it attracted a great deal of attention on Wall Street, where Nike stock became a favorite. But it also attracted unwanted attention in another quarter.

Jeff Ballinger was a young labor lawyer who had played a minor role in the Farah campaign before doing a stint as a labor educator and organizer in Turkey. In 1989, Ballinger was dispatched by the AFL-CIO to Jakarta to see what might be done about Nike and other companies that were, in the eyes of the labor federation, profiting at the expense of its membership. Ballinger focused on what he saw as the abuse of Indonesian workers, who tended to be young and mostly female. He worked through local social and religious groups to meet with them secretly and to collect anecdotes, which he then packaged, together with observations by religious and human rights NGOs, into a series of reports on working conditions in Indonesia. He distributed these reports to labor organizations, the media, Nike, and many of the athletes who endorsed its products. In 1993 Ballinger returned to the United States, where he founded a one-man organization, Press for Change, to carry forward his efforts. He did, however, return to Indonesia briefly that year, accompanied by a crew from CBS News that interviewed a number of Nike's contract workers and, in the ensuing report, gave both visibility and legitimacy to Ballinger's allegations. At that same point in time, a number of other organizations sprang forth or redirected their efforts to pressure Nike, which became for a time a pariah, or in the term often used in the corporate campaign, a corporate outlaw. In May 1998, Nike CEO Phil Knight, in a speech at the National Press Club in Washington, went so far as to apologize for his company's practices and to agree to a principal demand of his critics, that Nike accede to third-party review of its Indonesian producers.

In fact, however, there was a level at which Nike's labor practices in Indonesia were never really the issue. Just ten days after Knight's mea culpa, AFL-CIO President John Sweeney dismissed the company's concessions as "meaningless," and labor resumed its attack. Nike, it seems, was useful primarily as an iconic target around which could be consolidated symbolically a much more general, and a much higher-level, campaign effort, and the cost of letting the company off the hook was too high.

Recall that Nike came to labor's attention initially not on its own "merits," but as a prominent example of a fundamental and threatening trend, the off-shoring of unionized American manufacturing jobs to the detriment of the labor movement. Another factor contributing to labor's loss of influence was its loss of popular support. Again, the reasons for this lie beyond our scope here. But by the 1980s, and most especially among younger age cohorts, the movement was losing its legitimacy. That's where the Nike campaign and all that followed it came in.

In the early years of the last century, organized labor was generally held in low esteem, and labor leaders were widely seen as hoodlums, anarchists, or worse. Though the term would never have occurred to anyone at the time, an image makeover was in order. One of the events that contributed to that makeover, albeit a tragic one, was a deadly 1911 fire in a New York City clothing sweatshop, the Triangle Shirtwaist Factory. The fire, the photos of the burned bodies of women and girls who had worked at the factory and been trapped inside, and the appalling working conditions that contributed to the toll seared into the public consciousness a set of images that surely impacted greatly on the mainstreaming of the labor movement under the New Deal two decades hence. They also provided the movement itself with a visualization of its soul, the fight against sweatshops.

But with social and political acceptance, with the recognition of its collective bargaining rights, and with genuine gains in wages, hours, and working conditions, labor rapidly evolved away from its social-movement roots and toward its future as an economic powerhouse. It then went on to demonstrate its power through the strike and at the ballot box. At its peak, labor was a major player in both arenas—economic and political—and had to be accorded due respect. That's when things began to fall apart. Fast forward to 1989, and we can see that the campaign against Nike was in many ways a surrogate for a broader, and relatively explicit, effort to reclaim the soul of organized labor as a social movement, and to restore its public standing. Nike was useful in that regard, not only because it was the Wall Street darling de jour, but because its primary clientele—high school and college students—was exactly the target market for the unions' effort to rebuild a basic social constituency, by generation, from the ground up. Nike, then, became the index case for a new and much more extensive movement-building campaign that echoed in both theme and intent the efforts of the Society to Effect the Abolition of the Slave Trade. The goal was nothing less than restoration of the labor movement; the means was through a morally irrefutable and broadly attractive movement to bring an end to sweatshops.

That campaign today continues to expand in breadth and depth, across boundaries, across industries, and even across divergent working conditions, and even a dedicated volume might not do it justice. Instead, and in keeping with the purpose at hand, let us simply list some of its salient elements. They would include:

- *Enemy construction*. Mr. Knight and his company are but one example, and in many ways it is industrialism itself that is demonized in this campaign as a system that encourages the egregious exploitation of workers.
- *Selective targeting*. There is reason to believe, as an example, that all three companies operating in Indonesia at the time of Mr. Ballinger's visit (and since) had very similar production practices. Adidas, however, did not export from Indonesia to the United States, and was thus neither a threat to American labor nor an easy target, and Reebok was less prominent and, initially, took a more cooperative position with respect to the demands that were being made. So Nike was "It."
- *Demographic market segmentation*. The new-generation-centered appeal of the anti-sweatshop campaign, focused on college and HS students, has been accompanied by other, more instrumental initiatives such as internship and training programs designed for the same groups.
- *Unassailable moral high-ground framing*. The sweatshop thematic has not only deep and reverential historic resonance in the labor movement, but it has a natural appeal, especially to the target demographic.
- *Graphic imagery*. Think Josiah Wedgewood on steroids. The contemporary emphasis on institutional icons, logos, talking points and sloganeering, and drive-by, image-intensive media coverage, combined with the newly available (in historic terms) design capabilities of graphics software and the easy access for producers and consumers of such images alike to Internet-based distribution systems, have all developed largely during the same period as that in which the anti-sweatshop movement has matured. Every one of these new capabilities has been fully exploited, if only because the target cohort of the campaign is the very same cohort that has generated these technological innovations.

- *Targeting of influential stakeholders*. Because it is directed primarily at university students, and because the universities they attend are both prominent direct customers of Nike and other targeted manufacturers *and*, through their selection of logo-wear, aggregators of student demand, the anti-sweatshop campaign has generated pressure on universities themselves, as key corporate stakeholders, to disassociate themselves from producers whom labor deems to condone sweatshops. Two facts, that university endowment funds may also be invested in the stock of such companies, and that universities themselves tend to be open communities with large and influential pro-labor internal constituencies, provide additional inducements to focus the campaign here.
- *Ease of action to generate identity with campaign*. While the anti-sweatshop campaign welcomes and encourages student activism, its real objective is to generate identity with the labor movement. The campaign is positioned to accomplish this with ease, because all it takes to participate, and hence to identify with the cause and feel that one is a contributor, is to forgo purchasing a particular piece of logo wear from a particular manufacturer.
- *Grassroots organizing*. At the same time, organizing is essential in so long-lasting a campaign, and it is extensively present in this one. United Students Against Sweatshops, a nationwide organization with regional and campus chapters, is one case in point, but there are many others.
- *Coalition and alliance formation*. Even as it draws in its targeted demographic on university (and high school) campuses, the morality play that unfolds through the anti-sweatshop campaign has a natural appeal to others as well. Most notable among these are the clergy and other faith-based activists, particularly toward the left and center of the political spectrum, and such persons and groups have lent their own moral authority to the campaign in many ways. Similarly, the imagery of sweatshop labor appeals to consumers and organizations that represent them, though it is also the case that many of the latter have their own ties to the labor movement and can thus be seen primarily as advancing the interests of an ally.
- *Consumer boycotts and demonstrations*. As an extension of these alliances, the campaign has included demonstrations and some explicit boycott efforts, as, for example, at factory-owned Nike stores.
- *Media/news management*. In the tradition of Mr. Edison, this is a mainstay of all contemporary campaigns. Recall that the initial public impetus for the pressure on Nike came from media coverage of Mr. Ballinger's reports from Indonesia and from CBS's Indonesian tour.
- *Massive web activism*. As noted, the anti-sweatshop campaign has developed in tandem with the advent of Internet activism. If one had looked for campaign-related websites in the earliest days of the World Wide

Web circa 1995, as the author did, one would have found a mere handful—literally less than ten. The same search via Google in 2009 produced 745,000 hits. A refined search using the term "stop sweatshops" reduced the total to 574,000 hits.

- *Pressure for industry self-regulation.* There is an extensive story to be told about the role of demands for standards of conduct in the anti-sweatshop campaign. Here let me simply note that the manufacturers of shoes and clothing came under great political pressure to establish a code of conduct, which they did in consultation with labor and other activists. Immediately thereupon, the unions and other critics disavowed the code and established a rival standard-setting organization, with which they have since pressured universities to affiliate. The contest between these two rival organizations has emerged as one of the key institutional dimensions of the campaign.
- *Political engagement.* Opposition to sweatshops is a political lodestone, drawing politicians to the cause like so many metal filings. In addition to congressional hearings on the issue, at least one U.S. President, Bill Clinton, has personally intervened to pressure manufacturers. Various state and local legislative bodies have also become engaged, generally in the form of disinvestment initiatives or the prohibition of governmental procurement from offending companies.
- *Continuity of action over decades.* As we have seen, the anti-sweatshop campaign, and the parallel effort to revitalize the labor movement, took root in the 1980s. Today, it is almost a part of the U.S., and global, political culture.
- *Generalization to other industries.* The campaign, or at least the core theme, has not been limited to the industries that are generally thought to employ sweatshops. It has been common in recent years, for example, to encounter references to "high-tech sweatshops" in which, the verbal imagery suggests, highly educated software writers cluster together in dimly lit rooms to write code. There may be limits to how well this metaphor travels across industry boundaries, but it is, nonetheless, a powerful one that garners attention and communicates succinctly an essential point.

Everything Old Is New Again

By now it should be clear that the focus of this book, the information and influence campaign, has been with us in one form or another for at least a couple of centuries. In that sense, it is old news. And yet, there is something different about today's campaigns. For while all of that social movement organizing and self-interest pursuing was going on in the real world, there was great ferment in the halls of academe. During this same period, and most especially over the last century or so, a revolution has occurred in the ways that scholars study and understand human behavior. The social sciences—social psychology, sociology, political science, economics, mass communication, geography, and the rest—are the product of that revolution. For more than a century now, social scientists have been asking, in ever more sophisticated ways and with ever more empowering methods, questions about how individuals process information and make choices, about how organizations and governments function, about how individuals and organizations interact with technology, and about a host of other topics. And they have been finding answers—not always good or enduring ones, not always insightful ones, but answers nonetheless. Today, the mass of questions and answers in some fields is nearly 100 years deep, in others less so. But in sum, we know a great deal more about the behavior of humans and their social creations than we ever have before, and that knowledge base is growing daily.

More and more, the fruits of that knowledge have found their way into the development and implementation of campaign strategy. They represent, after all, the most advanced state of human knowledge regarding things of great strategic importance to any campaign—information and its effects, attitudes and their dynamics, institutional actors and their motivations, and the like. The campaign that does *not* do its best to incorporate this new knowledge into its strategy and tactics is consigning itself to disadvantage. All of the incentives clearly cut the other way.

It follows that the bridge between theory and practice in information and influence campaigns is of necessity much traveled. And yet, it is not well marked. The literature of campaigns tends to be anecdotal and a-conceptual, while the literature of social scientific inquiry tends to be unconcerned with real-world applications and implications of the discoveries reported there. Neither trend is surprising or unnatural; taken together they explain why the translation and exploitation of the knowledge base in campaigns is incomplete, inconsistent, and unequally distributed. It is my purpose in this book to mark the bridge—to identify the areas of social scientific inquiry of greatest relevance to those engaged in information and influence campaigns, and to suggest some of the ways this knowledge can be applied. We will turn to that task in the next chapter.

2 Information and Influence Campaigns

Nothing just happens in politics. If something happens, you can be sure it was planned that way.

Franklin D. Roosevelt

The United States is par excellence a country where public opinion plays an important role, inspiring, orienting, and controlling the policy of the nation. Nothing can be achieved or endure without it, and its veto is final. It is characterized by the fact that it is both more spontaneous than anywhere else in the world and also more easily directed by efficient propaganda technique than in any other country.

André Siegfried

One approach to mass media is to look not for reality, but for purposes which underlie the strategies of creating one reality instead of another.

Harvey Molotch and Marilyn Lester (1974: 111)

It is true that people win politically because they have induced other people to join them in alliances and coalitions. But the winners induce by more than rhetorical attraction. Typically they win because they have set up the situation in such a way that other people will want to join them—or will feel forced by circumstances to join them—even without any persuasion at all.

William H. Riker (1986: ix)

An information and influence campaign is a systematic, sequential and multifaceted effort by one actor to inform, or to influence the perceptions, preferences or actions of, some other actor or actors. By definition, then, campaigns are, at their hearts, complex, longitudinal acts of communication—exchanges of information designed to accomplish a specific objective. As we shall see, they can involve many other forms of exchange as well.

Each of these elements is central to the nature of a campaign, and critical to its potential success. To begin with, information and influence campaigns are not, and cannot succeed as, collections of random acts of communication. Absent thoughtful selection, guidance and control of their form and content, their channels and messages, any such collection will necessarily be inefficient, and occasionally, if not generally, self-contradictory. Messages will reach unintended audiences for which they are potentially counter-productive, even as they fail to reach intended audiences or, when they do so, may have minimal or contrary effect. Absent organization and logic, such bundles of information would seem to have as much potential to undermine the achievement of any given objective as to advance it.

Second, the need for a campaign in the first place would seem to suggest a stipulation on the part of the campaigner, whom we will hereafter term the protagonist, either that a given target requires some encouragement to adopt a change, or that the target requires reinforcement to prevent it from doing so in the face of contrary pressures that may arise from changing circumstances of the target, changes in the social, political or economic environment, or competing campaigns waged by the protagonist's own adversaries. Given that change is a longitudinal phenomenon—it can only be understood by a comparison of preferences or behaviors or the like across multiple time points—campaigns must comprise progressions of messages, message effects and observed changes in the target. They are, then, inherently sequential. It is the case that, on rare occasions, singular events can alter the psychological states or behaviors of individuals, organizations, or even governments. But it does not follow that singular, purposeful bursts of information *per se*, which is to say an intensive single-time-point communication campaign, can have the same effect.

Third, campaigns typically incorporate messaging schemes that are layered and subdivided, employing variations in timing, distribution channels, near- and long-term objectives, and other characteristics that render them complex rather than simple affairs. The more sophisticated the campaign, the more it employs the differentiation of messages, the segmentation of audiences and other techniques, the result of which is that the campaign may take on a very different appearance depending upon the social location and perspective of the observer. Different observers, or targets, will quite literally experience the campaign differently. And yet all of these partial views of the campaign will—should—be woven together through common and overlapping elements so that, even as an observer may encounter elements of the effort with which he or she may not be directly familiar, these will nevertheless demonstrate a sufficiency of continuity and touch points to lend them an air of familiarity.

When most people think about campaigns in politics, they focus on electoral campaigns—those designed to influence the selection of candidates for public office. That is quite natural, if for no other reason than the fact that these electoral campaigns are regular, frequent, and *designed* to be noticed. Visibility is an essential component of electoral campaign strategy. In addition, electoral campaigns are primarily directed at the public, or at least at the voting public, in an effort to influence votes on election day. Electoral campaigns are accepted as legitimate. Electoral campaigns focus on a specific, publicly regarded behavior that must be undertaken on a date certain, after which the campaign ends. Electoral campaigns are more or less transparent—we know who is running them, who is funding them, who is supporting them, how much money has been spent, and often how it has been spent. But not all campaigns seek visibility, and some pointedly eschew it. Not all campaigns target the general public. Not all campaigns, were they to become known, would be generally regarded as appropriate. Not all campaigns have clear and specified end dates, and some continue for a very long time. And not all campaigns are transparent in any of the regards just listed. In fact, there are many other kinds of campaigns, with diverse objectives, tactics and strategies, that have the potential to determine political outcomes or to influence the political life of a community, a nation, or the international system. They include, among others, public information and educational campaigns, image and product advertising campaigns, social marketing campaigns, public policy and lobbying campaigns, union organizing campaigns, reputation management campaigns, public diplomacy campaigns, propaganda campaigns, nation- or movement-building campaigns, insurgencies, and psychological or information warfare campaigns. In this book, we employ the term "information and influence campaigns"—and the shorthand acronym "IIC"—to reference *all* of these variants.

From Information to Influence

Though information and influence campaigns are, by definition, hybrid phenomena, Figure 2.1 suggests that the term IIC actually masks a continuum of differentiation between campaigns that are primarily

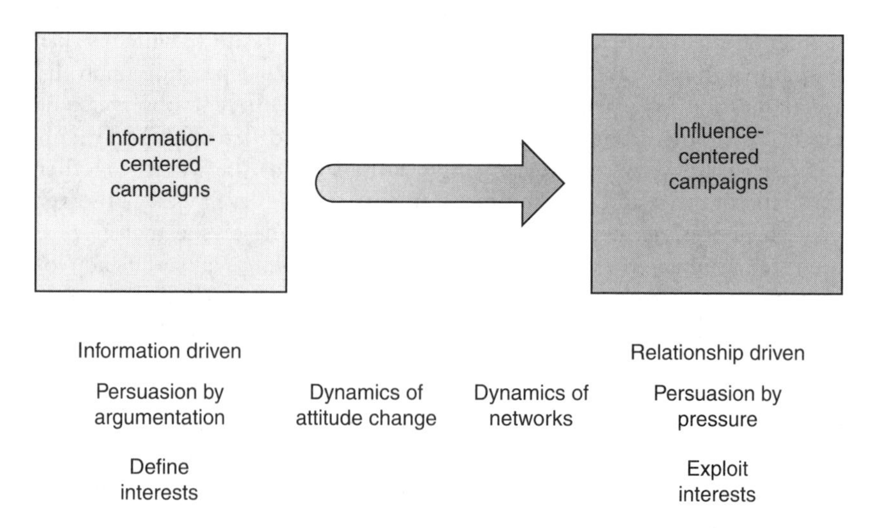

Figure 2.1 From Information to Influence: The IIC Continuum.

informational in content and objective, and those that focus mainly on exercising influence. The differences relate to the style of the campaign—whether it is centered primarily in managing information or managing relationships—the mechanisms of the campaign—which can range from the power of one's arguments to the power of one's alliances—and to the relationship of the campaign to the interests of the actor or actors whom it targets. Information-centered campaigns are often designed to define these interests, while influence-centered campaigns are often designed to exploit those that already exist. This is an argument to which we will return later in this chapter, and at length over the course of this book.

As Figure 2.1 suggests, part of our purpose here will be to examine the nature and extent of strategy-driven variations across different classes of campaigns and to extract their common elements. And as we will see, these campaigns do vary quite widely with respect to their scope and duration, their targets, their objectives or desired outcomes, their tactics, and their visibility, to name but a few key factors. Some will be directed at the general public or at major segments thereof, others at economic or political elites. Some will seek broad policy change, others narrow behavior change. Some will be highly aggressive and confrontational, others less so. And so forth.

Though we will draw on all of the aforementioned campaign types and still others in this book, we will focus on none of them. Rather, our emphasis here will be on a central underlying component that is common to *every* campaign, regardless of scope, focus, style or objective. That commonality is the development and application of a campaign *strategy*—an underlying idea of *how* to bring about the desired outcome of the campaign, whatever that may be. It is through the medium of strategy that we will bring together the diversity of campaign decisions, actions, applications, and outcomes into a single, more or less unified argument about the campaign phenomenon *per se*.

In general, a campaign strategy is an overarching directional framework for action, a concept or idea that integrates the many diverse parts of the campaign into a more or less unified whole. It is the ideational tapestry that weaves together, and makes sense of, the tactics through which the campaign is implemented. At its most effective, this strategy will be knowledge-based and responsive to changes in both the social environment of the campaign and the cognitive frames by which it is processed by those it touches. A *smart* strategy, then, will be one that is enlightened and unified by governing theories about such matters as the then-current psychological states (perceptions, preferences, identifications, etc.) and behavioral propensities of the target audiences and of any likely effects of the campaign itself on them, one that monitors and recognizes changes in the target(s) and in any other salient actors (such as opponents or counter-campaigners), one that routinely senses and adjusts to changes in the external campaign environment, and one that demonstrates dexterity in identifying and using the available toolkit of campaign techniques and channels. Let us postpone for the moment a discussion of underlying theories, and focus our attention on the remainder of these elements.

Elements of the Campaign

A campaign is generally built around a purposeful bringing together of three elements—the protagonist or its interests; the perceptions, wants and needs of the target; and the perceptions, wants and needs of any intermediaries whose participation is required to channel the campaign from the protagonist to the target. The first of these will drive the campaign, rather like an engine; the second will steer the campaign to its objective; the third will fuel the campaign at essential points along the way.

The protagonist will engage in campaign activity by positioning, or repositioning, itself either as aligned with the interests *of* the target or of sufficient import to justify some moderation of those interests *by* the target. That is to say, the protagonist will use campaign communication to demonstrate either its direct affinity with and support for the target, or its ability to impose some sort of costs or disadvantages on the target. The campaign for cessation of smoking will position the protagonist as an ally of the smoker determined to preserve his/her health. The campaign to impose environmental reforms on a polluting industry will position the protagonist as able to impose political or regulatory costs on the industry that would far exceed the price of voluntary compliance.

In general, portrayal of the protagonist in a campaign will comprise two sets of elements, which we can think of as substance and style. Substantive elements would include such items as the protagonist's personal or organizational traits—such things as trustworthiness, candor, representativeness, continuity, reach, power and influence—any relevant expertise or experience, issue or policy preferences, objectives, and an indication of the constituencies the protagonist purports to serve. It often incorporates some reference to the protagonist's allies, or those other actors who can be expected to rally to its side, as well as its enemies, who can be expected to rise in opposition. This could be done through the expedient of appropriate naming, for example, of the group or coalition of groups that is waging the campaign—think of the many entities that position themselves on the abortion controversy with reference to the words "life" and "choice"—or more subtly, as through the listing of one's allies or coalition members on a website or in a brochure or news release. And of course, where strategy dictates, such pro–con alliances can also be masked in ambiguity. Finally, and perhaps most importantly, the portrayal of the protagonist must incorporate some indication of the status or degree of its legitimacy and the sources from which that legitimacy derives.

Legitimacy is the acceptance on the part of a given audience that a particular actor—in our context this could be a protagonist, an intermediary, or a target—is generally seen to be acting properly toward pro-social objectives within an established set of values, norms, and expectations. Writing for an audience of business scholars, sociologist Mark Suchman (1995) suggested that legitimacy might be pragmatic in origin, arising from the self-interest of key stakeholders; moral, reflecting a normative acceptance of the actor and its behaviors; or cognitive, or, in effect, simply taken for granted. Within this framework, he proposed a variety of strategic mechanisms for gaining and maintaining legitimacy, and for restoring it when lost or damaged. With respect to gaining legitimacy, for example, he noted, "Legitimacy-building strategies fall into three clusters: (a) efforts to conform to the dictates of pre-existing audiences within the organization's current environment, (b) efforts to select among multiple environments in pursuit of an audience that will support current practices, and (c) efforts to manipulate environmental structure by creating new audiences and new legitimating beliefs" (587).

Stylistic elements of the portrayal of the protagonist in the campaign include such things as its appearance and mannerisms, its real or apparent accessibility or transparency, the issues and other actors with which it is associated (including linkages to other situations or campaigns where it has been visible to the target or to third parties that are expected to play roles in a given campaign), and even its communication skills. Most important here is the lexicon employed by the protagonist—the verbal language and nonverbal imagery by which it chooses to communicate. This has an effect on the perceptions that come to be associated with the protagonist, but it also has the far more fundamental potential literally to define just what is at stake in the campaign.

Though it is tempting to assume that substance trumps style, that is not necessarily the case, and it may actually be the exception. Take, for example, the selection of language. What one calls a thing matters greatly. Is an act of violence in the Middle East one of terror, or one of liberation? Is a legislative initiative that pumps money into the financial services industry a bailout of Wall Street banks, or a rescue of Main Street businesses? Is a popular, freely elected leader who maintains power by changing his nation's constitution to extend his term indefinitely a populist democrat, or an antidemocratic autocrat? The fate of nations turns on such matters of definition. But those definitions are seldom naturally occurring phenomena. They are grounded in existing cultural and social perspectives that may themselves be differentially distributed, but they are energized and rendered significant through systematic efforts to mobilize, shape, direct, and generally control the projection of those existing perspectives into contemporary disputes. Common understandings of many actors, events, and circumstances—the building blocks of definitions—exist in potentiality; it is campaigns that may cause them to resonate in reality. And they affect the full array of intermediaries and targets, from public opinion and the media to political leaders and governments.

In the context of campaigns, the interplay of substance and style is perhaps at its zenith when the lexicon that defines the issues and actors in the campaign—that literally shapes the common understanding of what the campaign is about—simultaneously defines, acknowledges or reifies the legitimacy of the campaign protagonist. Think of the campaign as a complicated and protracted morality play in which one side represents good, the other evil. Many campaigns play out in just this way. Now, consider the value of being the protagonist who gets to determine from the outset just what it is that constitutes good, and what constitutes evil. Chances are, those definitions would establish the moral superiority of the protagonist and, quite possibly, the moral inferiority of the target. Healthcare professionals good; smoking bad. Public interest good; corporations bad. Freedom fighters good; terrorists bad. Freedom fighters good; extant regime bad. Preferred position constitutional; opposing position unconstitutional. Add to that some other stylistic elements, such as associations between the key players and other social actors of high or low esteem—religious institutions, first responders, or the middle class versus greedy executives, corrupt politicians, or child pornographers—and one begins to see how substance and style interact in establishing the strength of the protagonist's positioning.

Box 2.1 Redefining the Target to Advance the Campaign

In their 2003 book, *Insurrection*, Global Exchange corporate accountability activists Kevin Danaher and Jason Mark pointed to a vulnerability of the corporation as an institution. They wrote:

> The idea that the corporation has rights apart from what is granted by the state has led to a series of judicial rulings giving corporations many of the same protections as flesh-and-blood persons. Courts have ruled that corporations enjoy freedom of speech rights as well as due process protections and freedom from unreasonable search and seizure. But there is virtually no popular support for the notion that corporations are the same as people. The idea violates common sense: Ask anyone on the street if they think a corporation is a person, and most people will say "no".
>
> (Danaher and Mark, 2003: 299)

They proposed that accountability activists leverage this discontinuity to redefine the boundaries of proper corporate behavior. The idea was to argue the absurdity of corporate personhood, using that argument to justify campaigns focused on rewriting the laws under which corporations are chartered and those that define the fiduciary responsibility of corporate executives, thereby converting these powerful centers of private interests into servants of the public interest.

The perceptions, wants and needs of the target can be of several different types—psychological, cultural, sociological, economic, political, ideological or programmatic among them. Psychological attributes of potential significance to a protagonist might include the target's worldview or perceptions of the issues that are in play; its relevant preferences and beliefs (and, if the target is an individual or an assemblage of individuals, its attitudes); its emotional state or tendencies, or in the case of an organization or a government, its inclination toward rational or irrational action; and its identities or associations. Cultural attributes might include its identification with a particular nation or region, an ethnic group or cluster, or perhaps a linguistic or other bloc. Sociological identifications, such as with a particular social class, group or community, can similarly be brought into play, or, in different circumstances, can restrict the range of play. Political considerations might include partisanship, either on the part of the target itself or as a factor in the campaign environment, but more generally would include the system dynamics and/or the existing body of public policies that serve either to advantage or to disadvantage the target—especially vis-à-vis the protagonist. Closely related to those, of course, would be any ideological or programmatic preferences or commitments associated with the target.

Some of these target attributes are visible to all or some of the participants in the campaign. The target will be, in some measure, self-aware, and will know and understand certain things about itself. And through experience or simple observation, the protagonist will also be aware of these attributes. We can think of these visible traits as the *manifest* attributes of the target. At the same time, a given target—whether an individual, group, organization, institution or government—may have certain attributes of which it is largely unaware, or which it has not associated with the setting in which the campaign occurs. For its part, the antagonist may also be unaware of these attributes, though it may also uncover some or all of them through research. We can think of these less apparent traits as the *latent* attributes of the target. There are some potential differences between the role played by manifest and latent attributes in a campaign. For example, *making* a particular attribute manifest as a way of locking in the target's preferences, as, for example, in applying a strategy of social or psychological inoculation (to be discussed in Chapter 8), can be an effective campaign tactic. But by and large, the two sets of attributes tend to occupy the same dimensions, and may, more often than not, be parallel and complementary.

That brings us to the perceptions, wants and needs of prospective campaign intermediaries, or third parties. Here we risk getting ahead of our argument, but it is worth characterizing briefly the most salient considerations. In IICs, there tend to be six principal types of intermediaries, any one or more of which may play a vital role. These include allies of the protagonist, surrogates for the protagonist, grassroots supporters of the protagonist, allies or constituents of the target, journalists, and the media organizations for which they work. Each of these prospective campaign participants has an array of wants and needs that must be addressed in a campaign that defines a role for them, and that can be used by the campaign to recruit and motivate their participation.

Allies of the campaign protagonist are independent actors whose existence generally predates the initiation of the campaign, who maintain their own agendas, which may overlap in greater or lesser degree with the agenda of the protagonist, and who have, for reasons of their own, chosen to join forces with the protagonist in some number of its past or present undertakings, or who might be induced to do so. There are a great many potential such inducements of a material nature—money or other resources, promises of future support, access to important contacts or associates of the protagonist, and so forth—and each of these may meet a want or need of the ally in question. But there are as well certain psychological inducements—a sense of common purpose, a feeling of being valued—that can prove to be equally, or even more, important.

Where natural and pre-existing allies of the protagonist do not exist or cannot be recruited, it is commonplace for a campaign to create them in the form of surrogates. A surrogate is a seemingly independent actor that rallies to the support of the campaign, and that may, in some circumstances, play a central role in it, but that exists only at the initiative of the protagonist, and may well cease to exist either during or at the conclusion of the campaign when the need for it dissipates. The typical surrogate is a shell organization with a high-sounding name and a presence that is centered primarily in the media, online, or in some other virtual space. The idea is to portray the surrogate as if it were a real ally. So in this instance, while the protagonist must supply sufficient material supports (including leadership and staffing) to allow the surrogate to function, it is the *appearance* of common purpose and the *appearance* of being valued that are essential to empowering such entities.

In campaigns that rely on public support or that assign some other role to members of the general public, or an issue-public, demographic grouping, or other subset thereof—and not all campaigns do so—the wants and needs of that public must also be taken into account in the development of campaign strategy. This set of requirements operates at two distinct levels, recruiting popular support and, when it is in hand, exploiting it to greatest effect. For a public to engage with and support a given campaign, the protagonist must generate in that public some combination of the following: a sense of identification with the protagonist or its cause, a sense that the public has been consulted, a sense of participation in the campaign, and a sense of representation. Allies and surrogates can be helpful in generating public identification with the campaign, either by expanding its apparent support in the first instance, or by helping to define or focus its objectives in the second. A sense of consultation can be achieved

Box 2.2 Who's on First? No, Who's *Really* on First?

As the 2009–2010 debate over healthcare reform made clear—and it may have been the only thing that debate made clear—it is not always easy to tell just whose voice is being heard. Among the many coalitions and surrogate groups that represented underlying interests: the Institute for Liberty, which went from a one-man interest group with a $25,000 budget and a post office box in 2008 to a downtown Washington office and a $1 million advocacy campaign in 2009 while declining to name its donors; Health Care for America Now, a consortium of unions and other groups with a $42 million budget; the Partnership to Improve Patient Care (pharmaceuticals industry); American Council on Science and Health (also an industry-friendly group); Center for Medicine in the Public Interest, funded by a research institute that is, in turn, funded by industry grants, and headed by the global healthcare chief at Porter Novelli, a public relations firm whose clients include such major companies as Pfizer and Wyeth; and the 60 Plus Association, which positions itself as an alternative to AARP, the powerful seniors' lobby, but has no members and declines to name its donors, though it says they do not include drug or insurance companies (Eggen, 2010).

by establishing any visible mechanisms of public expression or feedback *to* the campaign or the protagonist. Examples would be requests for advice, opportunities and encouragement to comment (as, for example, in response to blog entries or webpage content), or some applications of opinion polling. The sense of participation can be generated through protests, public demonstrations, attendance at rallies, or other events; through grassroots lobbying activities; or through invitations to help shape the campaign itself, as, for example, by developing one's own blog or creating and sharing campaign-related videos or other similar materials. Importantly, the sense of participation can be reinforced by providing the opportunity to contribute financially to the campaign, and thus, in a sense, to become a part-owner. Finally, a sense of representation can be created through such devices as campaign rhetoric that gives voice to values and preferences held, or aspired to, by the public in question, by claiming and publicizing the fact of popular support *per se*, or by campaign actions such as petitioning or making demands in the name of a given public that are, in context, inherently representational in character.

Even in campaigns in which the role of public support is essential, the fact is that such support may or may not be forthcoming. Where it is present, campaign strategy can incorporate mechanisms to exploit it. This might include many of the motivational and representational activities described above, which can serve dual purposes—at once building support for the campaign and converting that support into influence on the target. Where real public support is lacking, however, but where the public is, or can be portrayed by the target or others as an important actor, the strategy must turn instead to creating the *appearance* that public support is present. A common pattern here is for the campaign to play a proportionately greater role in creating and generating expressions of public opinion, as, for example, in the form of newspaper op-eds or letters to government officials, or in the generation and publication of highly selective opinion polls. These techniques, often referred to as "Astroturf" campaigns—a name derived from the first artificial playing surface in an indoor sports stadium, Houston's Astrodome—amount to the public opinion equivalent of creating a campaign surrogate.

Media in the Campaign

Leaving aside paid advertising, which may be extensive in many electoral campaigns but is less common in other situations, to the extent that a campaign relies on the mass media to legitimize its objective (or even the protagonist itself), to carry its messages, to generate visibility, or for any other purpose, it must, in effect, recruit and mobilize journalists to serve this function. This is accomplished, not by soliciting the explicit support of reporters and editors, although having such support is a decided advantage to any campaign, but rather, by understanding and serving the cultural needs and wants of journalists as a group, and by facilitating the fulfillment of their professional obligations. In this, the strategist is able to take advantage of an exceptionally broad and deep body of scholarship on journalistic norms and behaviors, and on newsroom decision-making. We know for example, that journalists are storytellers, and the effective campaign will provide them with a good story to tell, complete with good guys (the protagonist), bad guys (the target, which can be another actor or simply a problem of some sort that needs solving), a socially beneficial objective, a responsible and public-regarding plan of action, and a morally imperative outcome. Such a story can be irresistible, even if it is woven nearly out of whole cloth, and can be rendered even more so if it can be aligned with the known values and predispositions of the journalists themselves. In addition, journalists pride themselves on their inherent skepticism and their widely self-proclaimed independence, both of which they project as a basis for deserving the respect of newsmakers, including the campaign protagonist or its agents, and the public alike. All of this provides the grounding for a measure of moral certitude on the part of many journalists that can border on hubris. Given this psycho-cultural posture, an effective campaign strategy that relies in any degree on managing media portrayals will incorporate mechanisms for explicitly valuing these same traits on the part of the journalists with which it deals even as it turns them to advantage in shaping, placing and gaining credibility for its story.

Box 2.3 The Strategist as Storyteller

Public relations specialist Michael Sitrick (1998: 42–43) pointed out that reporters, editors, and news producers share a common belief that a good story—in the full sense of the word—is what makes the news tick. Journalists need that story, and campaign strategists need to provide it, complete with dramatic personae, *Sturm und Drang*, a touch of novelty, and a satisfactory resolution. "For the would-be spinmeister," Sitrick observed, "the implications of this are clear. To get your message across, you must present it in the form of a story—that is, as a well-turned tale, complete with clearly drawn heroes and villains, exciting twists and turns, and all the other accoutrements of the storyteller's art. And the more taut and compelling your narrative, the better."

Once the psychic needs of journalists have been met, there remain their professional requirements. One of the most important of these is access to key campaign decision-makers and events. In some situations, campaign strategy will call for providing, and perhaps even maximizing, such access. In others, it may be that restricting or prohibiting access will better advance the cause. Which strategy to use may be determined by factors we will explore later in this book. At a more mundane level, journalists deal every day with the basic requirements of their jobs—obtaining information, finding sources that will express on the record the range of views or analyses they want to incorporate in a given news item, and completing daily assignments in a timely manner. In reality, most news is not so new. Rather, most news is predictable, schedulable, and formulaic. As a result, and notwithstanding the occasional unexpected newsworthy event, newsrooms operate in a highly routinized manner, and the routines and rhythms in question are widely known and understood both within and beyond the newsroom walls. The campaign that effectively anticipates these routines and rhythms as it services the media, and in the process facilitates the commission of journalism, will be rewarded.

When we think of the media, we often think in terms of journalists, news content, editorial content or the like, and to be sure, all of those are part of mass mediated communication. But journalists work for, and news is produced by, organizations that have their own issues and needs. Most of these organizations, at least in the United States, are private commercial enterprises, typically subsidiaries of corporations that may have news production and distribution as their primary function, or that may include a wide range of business lines of which the news business is but one. In either event, the commercial incentives are such that news organizations are revenue dependent for their well-being. That, in turn, means that they

Box 2.4 Reducing Access to Information to Improve News Coverage

Back in the 1970s, the country that today we know as Zimbabwe was called Southern Rhodesia. Its white, Apartheid regime was confronted by a violent insurgency and, in December 1976, signed on with a US public relations firm to help manage its image in the US media, and especially to de-link the regime with news of political violence. Acting, presumably, on the advice of its consultants, the government established an information office in Washington, conducted a press tour of a village that had recently been attacked by the insurgents, told reporters of the kidnapping of black children by rebels based in neighboring Botswana, drew attention to raids on Catholic missions and to the establishment of protected villages for the black population, and circulated a rumor that white women throughout the country were contemplating suicide at the mere prospect of majority rule.

One of the government's particular concerns was the extent of news coverage of violence *per se*. At the time, the regime was in the habit of issuing weekly bulletins listing the number of casualties by race, gender, age and political affiliation, information that it controlled completely and for which no other source was available. One might read that 17 white women and children had died in a given week, along with 520 vicious rebels. These reports actually generated about twice their weight in news stories referencing the violence. Almost immediately after the public relations contract was signed, the government ceased issuing its casualty reports. The result? Straight news of violent events was unaffected, but editorial commentary as well as that by international figures pertaining to violence in the country was substantially reduced within one month of the signing of the contract. By cutting off access to the casualty figures, the government was able to improve its news image (Albritton and Manheim, 1983; Manheim and Albritton, 1987).

are dependent on generating and maintaining an audience whose subscription fees directly support the organization and whose exposure to the advertising content that accompanies the news does so indirectly and in far larger proportion. Since the advertising content is seldom sufficiently attractive in its own right to draw an audience, the organizational imperatives require that the news content be sufficiently appealing to do so. The story selection, style of presentation, and personalities of those who present the news can all be factors in generating that appeal, and, more to the point, they must be so.

This economic imperative is accompanied by a far more subtle, but no less important, political one. The fact is, the news media—and let's take again here as a point of reference, albeit a momentary one, the United States—occupy a highly privileged social position. They are granted access to influential persons and institutions that are, effectively, off limits to individual citizens. They are granted credence. They are granted monopoly, or near monopoly, access to such valuable public resources as the broadcast spectrum. They are granted protections in law—even in constitutional law—that assure their rights of expression, and even their right to withhold information or the names of sources from duly constituted authorities of the state. Like other corporations, their owners are granted limited liability for their actions. And like other commercial enterprises, they are subsidized through the creation of state or common carrier infrastructure that they use in creating and distributing their products. In sum, the media occupy a distinctly advantageous social location. It is reasonable to expect that they would act in ways that defend it, not least of which is to assert and maintain the myth structure that assigns sufficient value to the media as to render this special treatment not merely tolerable, but socially essential. Small wonder, then, that any perceived threats to media legitimacy are met with immediate and overwhelming responses.

Where the goal, or simply the positioning, of the campaign is likely to accord with the imperatives of media organizations, strategy will focus on maximizing the apparent connectedness of the two. That's the "easy" challenge. There are, however, protagonists who conduct campaigns for purposes contrary to the self-interest of the media, or whose campaigns do not excite, or may even directly antagonize, those interests. In these circumstances, the campaign strategist may be called upon to overcome institutionalized opposition from the media. A strategy of that type will simply turn the privileged positions of these organizations around, seeking to exploit public (or elite) jealousy over the privilege itself, or perhaps its apparent abuse. Except in the most unusual circumstances, this is not a strategy that a campaign would typically adopt at the outset. But where the media have inserted themselves in ways the protagonist deems disadvantageous, or where they can be expected to do so, it may provide a means of offsetting these negative influences.

Campaigning in Context

All these relationships, wants, needs, perceptions and actions, and the attendant positioning of the players, take place in a setting that can also impact significantly on any given campaign, and that cannot be taken for granted. At the very least, the campaign setting is not necessarily, nor even inherently, neutral. It can very easily favor one side or the other. Laws and systems of laws, customs and systems of customs, cultural factors, social patterns and expectations, and the tenor of the times are but a few of the factors that can facilitate or support certain actors or deeds, and impede or raise the degree of difficulty for others. Importantly in this context, campaigns can be greatly affected by what social scientists have termed "focusing events"—events that occur, often independently of the campaign, that become game changers. Examples might include scandals, international crises, major economic changes, political realignments, policy failures or any of a host of occurrences that alter the status quo ante or the perceptions thereof. Such events can create windows of opportunity that can be exploited by a campaign that is sufficiently nimble to take advantage of them, can generate momentum (or stop it cold), and can energize or re-energize a campaign that is appropriately positioned to benefit. Think corporate scandals and corporate reform, deaths from tainted foods and regulatory reform, mass shootings and gun control. Some campaigns are able to take advantage of these fleeting opportunities, others are not.

Campaigns Arise from Asymmetries of Power

Before going further, we would do well revisit the distinctions we introduced in Figure 2.1, and to clarify a boundary assumption that delimits the argument of this book. For there are, in fact, two distinct archetypical styles of information-based campaigns, as represented by the endpoints of the continuum in the figure, and the complexity and requisite level of sophistication of a given campaign increases as one moves from left to right.

The first style, comprising in its purest form so-called public information campaigns (PICs), employs information, rhetoric, communication and persuasion to frame or reframe issues and to shape public opinion, either globally or within national boundaries. The objective is usually to persuade the public to change its behavior in some desired way. Say no to drugs. Abstain, or practice only safe sex. Stop smoking. PICs generally take the form of public relations, advertising, or argumentation and debate. They are likely to be effective primarily where the campaigner is accepted as legitimate, where the principal target is public opinion or some segment thereof, and where the message initially lacks sufficient visibility, clarity or exposure to be persuasive. In other words, PICs are intended to solve a *communication* problem.

The second style, comprising the information and influence campaigns (IICs) of particular interest here, employs these same techniques, but as components of more sophisticated, and far more elaborate, strategies and tactics designed to generate pressure on the target of the campaign sufficient to cause that target to alter its policies or behaviors in some significant way. Public relations efforts and other persuasive communications often play a role in these campaigns, but that role may range from central to largely peripheral, and the campaigns themselves are far more complex and more intellectually refined than their PIC counterparts. They are employed in situations where the campaigner lacks the leverage on its own to bring about the desired change on the part of the target, which may be another actor or a policy, but is seldom the public *per se*. IICs, then, are intended to solve a *political* problem, one that usually arises from an imbalance of power. For our purposes, they include all of the elements of PICs, but generally exclude the actual end case of an information-only PIC.

In our conceptualization, then, information and influence campaigns are designed to address problems that are in some measure political, and to do so using strategies and tactics that are in some measure, and perhaps significantly, communication-based. Given the inherently political nature of such endeavors, it follows that their underlying strategies are always grounded in and reflective of one or more extant power relationships. Indeed, IICs are perhaps best understood in terms of these relationships.

At the most basic level, let's posit two actors, A and B, with competing objectives, and posit further that, in some given arena, Actor A is superior in power to Actor B. In this relationship, Actor A is relatively unlikely to employ an IIC to bring about a change in B's behavior for the simple reason that it is more likely to have the capability to impose its will through more direct means. Actor B, on the other hand, must find a way to persuade Actor A to change its behavior if B is to achieve its objectives. This may require that B enlist others who may be better situated to influence A in its behalf. The greater the discrepancy in power, the greater the likely differential reliance on an IIC, i.e., the less need A has to resort to indirect means and the fewer alternatives to such a campaign B has available. A and B could be governments, corporations, NGOs, terrorist networks, drug cartels, activist organizations, or individuals, to name but a few of the possibilities.

That said, even A is likely to depend for its superior power on its own relationships with some set of supportive stakeholders, and it is that set of dependencies that opens the path to IIC influence. If A is a government, for example, the critical stakeholders might include citizens and taxpayers, political parties, organized interests, bureaucracies, legislators, media, domestic elites, international allies, and the like. If B is an NGO, stakeholders might include, among others, members, allies, donors, media, or the public. Indeed, one way of conceptualizing any social or political actor is to say that it occupies a point in social (or political or economic) space at which is precisely balanced, at any given point in time, an array of overlapping and competing interests that interact with one another in greater or lesser breadth depending on the scope of the enterprise. In this scheme, the function of the actor is to generate and maintain a sufficient balancing of these diverse forces to sustain itself and advance its own interests. Corporations must be responsive to both shareholders and customers, though their respective interests are served by different outcomes (higher versus lower prices, for example). Governments must be responsive to the needs of citizens, e.g., for security, and to taxpayers (an overlapping but not contiguous stakeholder group), e.g., for minimal or reasonable taxes, *and* to constitutional principles, e.g., for civil liberties, though not all are equally well served by any given action. The capabilities of each actor are determined by an admixture of resources, real power, sources of influence and grants of legitimacy.

Now let's throw in a wrinkle. Suppose that A, the more powerful partner in this little dance, is being targeted, not by B alone, but by yet another actor, C, who would also like to influence its behavior, but in a direction opposite to, or at least different from, the direction in which B is pushing.

Box 2.5 Moving Up the Food Chain

UANI, or United Against Nuclear Iran, is an advocacy NGO that backs the imposition of strong sanctions against Iran in order to pressure that country to abandon its nuclear weapons development program. The group engages in lobbying on Capitol Hill and in the executive branch, and some of its founders and advisory board members have actually held positions of influence themselves. They include the likes of Dennis Ross, who has served in a number of high-level State Department posts related to Middle East policy, top-ranking American diplomat Richard Holbrooke, and former CIA Director James Woolsey. So UANI is by no means a marginal player in influencing US foreign policy. Still, the group does not have the ability to impose its will on Iran. Iran is "A", while UANI is definitely "B". What to do?

Taking a page from the disinvestment strategy that eventually pressured the Apartheid regimes in Southern Rhodesia (now Zimbabwe) and South Africa to yield to majority rule, UANI has focused much of its effort on companies that, directly or indirectly, have maintained some form of economic engagement with Iran. Using the dual threat of adverse publicity and prospective congressional sanctions, UANI has convinced such companies as General Electric, Siemens, Eni, Munich Re, Allianz, Ingersoll Rand, Caterpillar, KPMG, and Royal Dutch Shell that continuing to trade with Iran was not in their best interests. Other companies on the group's to-do list as of this writing: Total, Petrobras, Daimler, Honda, and HSBC. Clearly UANI hopes and expects that corporate disengagement on such a large scale will accomplish what the group alone is not able to on its own—a decision by Iran's political leadership that the benefits of nuclear weapons development are not worth the costs. The strategy may or may not work in the end, but one thing is clear—UANI has enough influence in its own right to provide a good test (Morris, 2010a, 2010b, 2010c, 2010d).

Think two competing interests, each dependent on policies of the same government agency, but each with a different benefit structure. Decisions that advantage B may actually disadvantage C, and vice versa. This may not be precisely a zero-sum game, in which gains for one side are precisely offset by losses to the other—there could be some shared interest between the two—but in general, these two lesser-powered actors want different outcomes from the same superior actor. Should both B and C decide to engage in an information and influence campaign—and if one does so, the other is highly likely to follow—the situation becomes more complex, as reflected in Figure 2.2.

In the figure we see three classes of campaigns. The first is the unidirectional campaign that we have discussed earlier—one protagonist, one target. This is the architecture of the most basic IIC, and, for that reason, it is the architecture that we will employ for the greater part of this book. The second is a competitive, or bidirectional, campaign in which there are two competing protagonists of roughly co-equal power. Each will seek advantage relative to the target in a competition in which resources are essentially balanced, while luck, skill, circumstances, and strategic know-how—all factors that can affect the outcome—may or may not be. The third is also a bidirectional campaign, but in this case between two competing protagonists that are not equally matched. To the extent that power and resources are determinative of outcomes, the advantage here

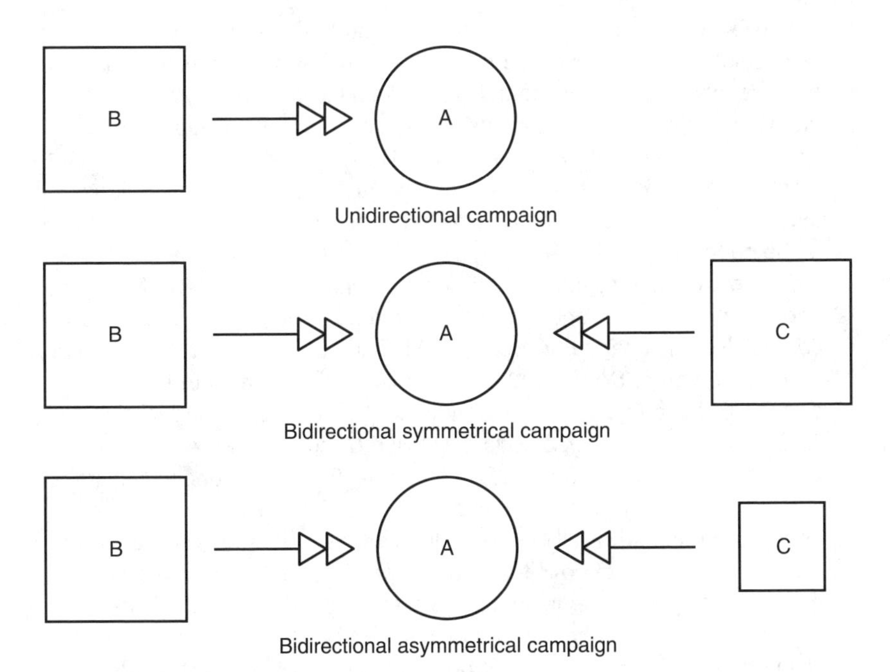

Figure 2.2 Directionality in Campaigns.

will clearly lie with the stronger of the two, but in the real world, other factors, including strategic skill, can sometimes overcome even significant imbalances of power. Clearly, the introduction of a countervailing campaign carries with it added degrees of difficulty for the strategist, who must incorporate additional oppositional messaging and alliance formation, some of which may actually be much more aggressive than that which would normally be deployed by the target itself. Even with that added contextual dimension, however, the underlying logic of each campaign is essentially the same as that of a simple, asymmetrical effort. For that reason, and to avoid further complicating our argument, we will keep our focus here on that basic commonality of form.

Box 2.6 A Battle of Co-Equals

For our purposes, power is best understood to be situational rather than absolute. Regardless of their absolute levels of power, all actors are likely to find themselves in specific situations in which others, including their targets or antagonists, have power greater than or equal to their own. As a result, those who might be targets in one setting may be campaigners in another. Consider, for example, the political competition between two more or less equally powerful package-delivery companies, FedEx and UPS.

FedEx began life as an air freight company, and for that reason, its labor relations were governed by the Railway Labor Act (RLA), which extends to airlines. UPS began life as a trucking company, as a consequence of which its labor relations were governed by the National Labor Relations Act (NLRA). In general, the RLA is regarded as the more employer-friendly of the two laws, and the NLRA as friendlier to unions. Much of that has to do with the rules set under each for workers to vote on being represented by a union.

By the early twenty-first century, both companies competed with one another for both air and ground shipments. But FedEx enjoyed a competitive advantage because of the less restricted labor rules under which it operated. So in 2009 UPS launched a campaign of lobbying, alliance building (including the Teamsters Union), advertising, and the like, to pressure the Democratic-controlled Congress into rewriting the labor laws to eliminate the FedEx advantage. FedEx responded with its own effort, ranging from a website criticizing UPS to a threat to postpone the purchase of billions of dollars worth of new Boeing aircraft (this was both an economic threat and a political one, since Boeing is a major employer in Washington State, generally regarded as a Democratic Party stronghold) if Congress did change the law. FedEx claimed that UPS was seeking a government "bailout"—a red flag term at the time because of extensive government efforts to rescue ailing financial services firms and automobile manufacturers—by using Congress to disadvantage a competitor.

The campaign took an odd turn when one group that had joined the UPS coalition, the American Conservative Union, was alleged by FedEx to have sold its services to the highest bidder. The evidence? FedEx produced a letter signed by the organization's executive vice president offering to produce *in behalf of FedEx* a series of op-eds and articles, contacts with more than 150,000 people in every state, and a radio advertising plan tailored to pressure individual key Senators—all for fees which were listed in the letter. UPS denied having paid for the group's support.

There are two points to make about this incident. First, for all practical purposes, FedEx and UPS are equal in power, and their dueling campaigns can be seen as an extension of their commercial competition, each targeting one another. But second, in this instance neither FedEx nor UPS had the power to achieve a resolution. That power rested with the Congress, and really with an elite group of leaders within the Congress. It was the members of this leadership elite and, perhaps, some number of their colleagues, who were the real targets of these campaigns (Roth, 2009).

In sum, then, IICs are driven by the need of one actor, the protagonist, to exercise influence over another actor, the target, where the protagonist does not have the ability to compel compliance with its wishes, and where both are dependent on the support of their own clients and constituents. It is in the context of this *external* imbalance between actors who are themselves engaged in the continual maintenance of *internal* balances that IICs are best understood. They represent efforts by a (co-equal or) relatively weaker party (the "protagonist") to impose change on a (peer or) relatively stronger party (the "target" of the campaign) through indirect action—by inducing imbalance in the internal stakeholder relationships of the stronger party, which has the effect of requiring the latter to respond to pressure from its stakeholder(s) by changing its behavior, *and* by channeling that behavior change in some direction that achieves, or at the least advances toward, the objectives of the campaign initiator. Relative strength or weakness is determined by the situation—A may have the advantage in one circumstance, B in another. So the strategy that serves B today may serve A tomorrow.

That being the case, there would seem to be less value in studying A and B—whoever or whatever they may be—than in studying the elements of the strategy itself—the type and range of decisions that can or must be made in the design and implementation of an information and influence campaign. We will turn to that task in Chapter 3.

3 Strategy and Tactics in Campaign Communication I: Winning the Argument

> Here comes the orator! with his flood of words and his drop of reason.
>
> Benjamin Franklin

> Reason may be the lever, but sentiment gives you the fulcrum and the place to stand on if you want to move the world.
>
> Oliver Wendell Holmes, Sr.

> . . . You do what you can with what you have and clothe it with moral garments.
>
> Saul Alinsky (1971: 36)

> . . . Action makes propaganda's effects irreversible. He who acts in obedience to propaganda can never go back. He is now obliged to *believe* in that propaganda because of his past action. He is obliged to receive from it his justification and authority, without which his action will seem to him absurd or unjust, which would be intolerable. He is obliged to continue in the direction indicated by the propaganda, for action demands more action. He is what one calls committed . . .
>
> Jacques Ellul (1965: 29)

When most of us think of campaign communication, we think in terms of argumentation. We think of the communication challenge in these situations as that posed by the need to generate sufficient power of reason, emotional appeal and evidentiary support so as to persuade the recipient, or collectively, the audience, to adopt a change of mind or behavior, or at the very least to move closer to the preferred views or behaviors of the campaign protagonist. As Aristotle put it in the second chapter of *The Rhetoric, Book I*,

> Of the modes of persuasion furnished by the spoken word there are three kinds. The first kind depends on the personal character of the speaker; the second on putting the audience into a certain frame of mind; the third on the proof, or apparent proof, provided by the words of the speech itself. Persuasion is achieved by the speaker's personal character

> when the speech is so spoken as to make us think him credible. We believe good men more fully and more readily than others: this is true generally whatever the question is, and absolutely true where exact certainty is impossible and opinions are divided. This kind of persuasion, like the others, should be achieved by what the speaker says, not by what people think of his character before he begins to speak. It is not true, as some writers assume in their treatises on rhetoric, that the personal goodness revealed by the speaker contributes nothing to his power of persuasion; on the contrary, his character may almost be called the most effective means of persuasion he possesses. Secondly, persuasion may come through the hearers, when the speech stirs their emotions. Our judgments when we are pleased and friendly are not the same as when we are pained and hostile. It is towards producing these effects, as we maintain, that present-day writers on rhetoric direct the whole of their efforts. This subject shall be treated in detail when we come to speak of the emotions. Thirdly, persuasion is effected through the speech itself when we have proved a truth or an apparent truth by means of the persuasive arguments suitable to the case in question.
>
> (Bekker Index 1356a)

That definitively traditional view not only grounds the very art of rhetoric, but in contemporary society it also echoes the widely espoused values of democratic systems, which are grounded in informed public consent. For this reason alone, most campaigns will make some show of providing a reasoned and appealing basis for supporting their objectives.

But in fact, such "pure" argumentation, as a central component of strategy, occurs in a relative few classes of campaign settings and primarily in certain types of campaigns—generally those that we described earlier as Public Information Campaigns, or PICs. Speaking very broadly, that is the case in no small measure because actual position-altering persuasion of the classical type is very difficult to achieve among "persuadees" who have already-established perceptions and preferences on the issue in question. Depending on such factors as their self-perceived self interest, the level and content of prior information they have in hand, their degree of personal identification with the existing issue position and with the issue itself, their autonomous interpretation of the "real" motives of the messenger, and the nature or relative attractiveness of the persuasive messages, many of those targeted by campaign communication will demonstrate considerable resistance to persuasion. This means that change-inducing persuasive effects will be greatest among, and may actually be restricted to, those who are least interested, least informed, and least engaged with the issue. Unfortunately for the would-be persuader, this same most susceptible cohort will be relatively unmotivated to engage in the dialogue that might produce the desired persuasive outcome, as evidenced by its initial availability as a message target, and, based on its demonstrated inertia, least likely as well to act on any change that persuasive communications might induce.

Persuasion in PICs

It does not follow that such issue-neutral, minimal-acting, persuasion-capable audiences cannot be engaged constructively in a campaign setting. To the contrary, these "swing" cohorts can sometimes be mobilized (or immobilized) to great advantage and in ways that materially advance the objectives of the campaign. But it does follow that this is far more likely to be true in some types of campaigns than in others. In particular, classical, change-inducing persuasion will be most effective in campaigns where the issue in question is new or non-controversial, where opinions are not well formed or deeply held, and where the purpose of the persuasive message, if not the overall objective of the campaign, is easily achieved. These conditions are found most commonly in PICs.

Most public information campaigns are inherently educational in nature. They seek to call attention to, and to redress or advance, some aspect of social behavior—the dangers of smoking, the threat posed by a communicable disease, the value of staying in school, the benefits of seatbelt use, the opportunity to support a worthy cause, the virtues of tolerance or purity of behavior, the importance of electoral participation. The objectives of such campaigns are often behavioral—stop smoking or don't start, stay in school, strap in, contribute time or effort, be open-minded, be a good person (however defined), vote—and they are typically portrayed as individual in nature and yet collectively pro-social in impact. Indeed, most of the action objectives of such campaigns are so closely associated with widely held, or at least widely espoused, societal values that there is little opposition to them and little likelihood that anyone would choose to launch a counter-campaign taking opposing views. Go ahead. Smoke yourself to death, but first drop out of school, choose a dead-end job, be selfish, never wear a seatbelt, demonstrate prejudice, and while you are at it, by no means vote? It seems unlikely, perhaps so much so that the argument appears trivial. But the point here is decidedly nontrivial: It is the very sociability of these situations that creates the conditions, and perhaps the only conditions, in which a campaign driven primarily by argumentation can achieve a substantial effect.

The strategies and tactics appropriate to these campaigns are by now fairly well known and understood. In a more contemporary form (the late 1980s), they were expressed quite succinctly by William J. McGuire, a leading student of persuasion and its converse, resistance to persuasion, in the form of a "communication/persuasion matrix," each of the elements of which plays a role in shaping campaign effects. In this scheme, the drivers of persuasion include the source of the campaign communication, the message, the channel, and the receiver. Responses to the campaign, which include both stages of persuasion and more advanced outcomes, include

Box 3.1 Appealing to Pro-Social Values in PICs

It is common for American First Ladies to adopt a cause to serve as the centerpiece of their time in the White House. These causes become foci for public information campaigns that receive substantial publicity. In the 1980s, Nancy Reagan adopted drug abuse as her cause, around which was built a campaign asking teenagers to "Just Say No." The following excerpt from Mrs. Reagan's September 14, 1986, remarks in a joint national address with the President provides a sample of the campaign rhetoric typical of these efforts.

> For 5 years I've been traveling across the country—learning and listening. And one of the most hopeful signs I've seen is the building of an essential, new awareness of how terrible and threatening drug abuse is to our society. This was one of the main purposes when I started, so of course it makes me happy that that's been accomplished. But each time I meet with someone new or receive another letter from a troubled person on drugs, I yearn to find a way to help share the message that cries out from them . . . .
>
> Drugs steal away so much. They take and take, until finally every time a drug goes into a child, something else is forced out—like love and hope and trust and confidence. Drugs take away the dream from every child's heart and replace it with a nightmare, and it's time we in America stand up and replace those dreams. Each of us has to put our principles and consciences on the line, whether in social settings or in the workplace, to set forth solid standards and stick to them. There's no moral middle ground. Indifference is not an option. We want you to help us create an outspoken intolerance for drug use. For the sake of our children, I implore each of you to be unyielding and inflexible in your opposition to drugs . . . .
>
> So, to my young friends out there: Life can be great, but not when you can't see it. So, open your eyes to life: to see it in the vivid colors that God gave us as a precious gift to His children, to enjoy life to the fullest, and to make it count. Say yes to your life. And when it comes to drugs and alcohol just say no.

(Found online at http://www.cnn.com/SPECIALS/2004/reagan/stories/speech.archive/just.say.no.html)

Communications Element → Effects Sequence ↓	Source	Message	Channel	Receiver
Exposure to Communication				
Attention to Communication				
Interest in Communication				
Understanding of Communication				
Attitude Change				
Placing Content & Concurrence in Memory				
Drawing on Content & Concurrence				
Behaving Responsively When Cued				
Consolidation of Position				

Figure 3.1 Framework for Identifying Components of Persuasive Communications.

exposure to the campaign's communications, paying attention to these messages, feeling an affinity and becoming interested in the campaign, understanding the campaign messages, acquiring the skills to respond to those messages, changing one's attitudes, filing away in memory the content of the campaign messages and the fact of one's concurrence, retrieving this information at an appropriate time, acting on the information in a way that accords with the campaign objective, and through such behavioral expression consolidating one's new position (McGuire, 1989: 44ff). A modified version of this matrix appears in Figure 3.1.

Sources of Campaign Communication

The column headers in Figure 3.1 point to more or less controllable elements of a given communication campaign that can be expected to contribute to its effectiveness. The source from which campaign communication emanates might be the campaign protagonist, but might be some alternative actor who is perceived to have an advantage in bringing about the desired outcome. That decision will be based on an assay of the attributes of the protagonist or others as a communications source. This assay might take into account such potentially effects-relevant source characteristics as personal or organizational traits, experience, known policy positions or associations, known objectives, established or prospective constituencies, known or suspected allies and enemies, and the status and origins of the would-be source's legitimacy and credibility. In each instance, the questions are whether, how, and within what constraints a given attribute of the source is likely to advance or retard effective persuasion. The list, then, is in effect an operational statement in a more complex environment of the notion of character employed by Aristotle. But other factors are likely to come into play as well. Are the appearance and mannerisms of the source likely to instill confidence and induce persuasion? Does the language employed by the source—visual as well as verbal—resonate with the target audience? That is, does the source's lexicon empower or impede change-inducing persuasion? And how good are the source's communication skills themselves? Can the source effectively connect with the audience, either individually or en masse? Finally, there are the questions of numbers: How many sources should there be? How uniform or diverse should they be—demographically, organizationally, and so forth? And to what extent should they agree with and reinforce one another, so as to sharpen the message or condense its appeal, and to what extent should they differ from one another, so as to broaden the message or its appeal? Either individually or in combination, these and similar decisions can affect the impact of campaign rhetoric.

Campaigns Messages and the Control of Language

Message effects can similarly be driven and conditioned by strategic decisions regarding content and form. The most effective campaigns are generally built around a relatively unified core message that literally *defines* the terms of debate. That core message can then be subdivided and differentiated to match the wants and needs of separate audiences or separate subsets of the same audience, so long as the partial-core messages remain consonant with one another so that differential messaging that overlaps into adjacent audience spaces does not create the impression that the campaign is inconsistent, saying one thing here, another over there.

The core message should identify the campaign protagonist and, in the same motion, identify that protagonist *with* the audience whose beliefs, preferences or behaviors the campaign seeks to put into play. Who is the protagonist? Who is the constituency the protagonist serves or represents, where that constituency is inclusive of, or in some other way, clearly and significantly connected to the audience in question? Why are the protagonist and the members of the audience natural, *de facto* allies? What are the issues in the campaign, and on what basis should they be debated? Why is this basis for debate—presumably the most advantageous for the protagonist or least advantageous for the ultimate target of the campaign–legitimate and preferable, while the alternatives are illegitimate or inferior? What is the moral high ground in this situation? Why does it belong, self-evidently, solely and irreversibly, to the protagonist?

Box 3.2 Effective Core Messages Connect the Protagonist with the Audience

As a component of its strategy to withdraw from military involvement in Iraq, in 2007 the United States began a hearts-and-minds campaign among the Iraqi public. The objective was to position both the engagement and the withdrawal in a context of Arab values, and in the process to raise broader questions about Arab World support for terrorism.

One aspect of this strategy was managed by a "Digital Outreach Team" of Arab-language bloggers in the State Department's Counterterrorism Communication Center. Members routinely participated in about a dozen mainstream chat rooms run by the likes of the BBC, Al Jazeera, other Arab news sites, and charismatic Muslim leaders. A key approach was to raise questions about events within a context of Arab values. Example: Why do many in the Arab World quickly condemn the deaths of Palestinian civilians, yet remain silent on the frequent killings of women and children in Iraq? That one generated four days of exchanges, most of it thoughtful civil discourse.

A State Department official summarized the underlying strategy: "We try to put ourselves in the mindset of someone receiving the message. Freedom for an Arab doesn't necessarily have the same meaning it does for an American. Honor does. So we might say terrorism is dishonorable, which resonates more."

In addition to actual content, the campaign itself may communicate a vital message—in this instance, said some at the State Department, that might include a recognition that the United States is not too arrogant to listen to Arab grievances (MacFarquhar, 2007).

These decisions regarding the substantive content of campaign messages will be complemented by a range of stylistic determinations. For example, campaigns may vary in the type of language they employ. In the abstract, and from the social psychological perspective, clarity and simplicity are desirable attributes in campaign rhetoric because they are likely to facilitate persuasion. But from a more political perspective, there are other circumstances in which complexity or deliberate ambiguity could actually be preferable. Political scientist Murray Edelman (1964) once set out a typology of power relationships that were established and maintained through linguistic structures. He suggested, for instance, that lawyers, courts, regulators and administrators maintain their positions of authority vis-à-vis the public by creating the *appearance* of clarity, rationality, dispassion, and equality in the form of openly published laws, forms and regulations, while simultaneously employing deliberate ambiguity, in the form of precedent, procedure, interpretation, and implementation, to retain privileged social positions, i.e., political power, for themselves. Politicians or leaders of social movements also rely for their power, in Edelman's view, on appeals that are openly ambiguous, albeit more emotional in nature than those employed in law or administration. It follows, then, that the setting and objectives of a given campaign may force difficult choices between the political objectives of the protagonist and the likely persuasive effectiveness of the language it employs. Other potentially important stylistic elements of campaign communication include such items as the selection of verbal and visual imagery—resonant phrases or evocative images, for example—and the demonstration of the protagonist's intelligence, compassion, and command of the situation.

An example of the dynamics of language as power that is a commonplace in a number of campaigns is the debate over so-called "codes of conduct." These codes are statements of the internal value structure of an organization—which could be, for example, a non-governmental organization, a religious institution, or a corporation. These codes function rather like a constitution does for a government—as a framework for converting shared values into styles of behavior, or conduct. But like a constitution, they can be far more ambiguous than they may appear at first glance. There can easily be, in other words, a disconnect between values and behaviors. And yet, the values are there as clear statements of commitment. And therein lies the potential for leverage in a campaign. Does the target have a code of conduct? If not, does it have an obligation to adopt one? If a code exists, is it fully legitimized? Was it, for example, developed in consultation with other affected parties? And just what does the code say? What *are* the values of the target? Are they the "correct" values? Are they simply abstract statements, or do they have the real and the "correct" meaning? And then, is the code being properly implemented? Who makes that determination? Are they to be trusted? In these exchanges, the campaigners will seek to employ the often-deliberate and unavoidable ambiguity of such codes—their style of language—as a key pressure point, a vulnerability that is greatly enhanced by the simple fact that the target has itself set the standard. (Manheim, 2000)

Messages have other types of stylistic attributes as well. They may be more, or less, informative. They may be well, or less well, organized. They may be explicit or implicit in their statement of the argument or point. They may be more, or less, repetitive. They may incorporate a variety of cues regarding such factors as the salience of the information they convey to members of the intended audience, or the implications or practical utility of their content. They may, as Aristotle correctly noted, appeal to reason and judgment, or to the emotions, or to some combination of the two. To the extent that the campaign can either control campaign-related communications directly, or hope to influence them indirectly, these and related decisions will be made with likely messaging effects in mind.

Box 3.3 Defining the Moral High Ground

The late community activist Saul Alinsky once advised: "Make the enemy live up to their own book of rules. You can kill them with this, for they can no more obey their own rules than the Christian church can live up to Christianity" (Alinsky, 1971: 128). A union organizing campaign among workers at a Catholic healthcare system took this quite literally.

In 1996 the Service Employees International Union (SEIU) embarked on a nearly decade-long campaign to organize workers at Catholic Healthcare West (CHW), a major West Coast hospital chain owned by several communities of women religious (nuns). In 1998, speakers from the union and one of its allies, the National Interfaith Committee for Worker Justice as it was known at the time, participated in a panel discussion on defining the "just" workplace under Catholic doctrine. In very simple terms, Catholic religious doctrine requires that employers provide a just workplace. The nuns who owned CHW believed that they fulfilled this obligation by giving workers the freedom to select union membership if they so chose. The union took the position that no workplace can be just if it is not unionized.

SEIU advanced its view through newspaper advertising asking how the Church could support unionization for farm workers, but not its own healthcare workers. It published a white paper, *A Time to Break the Silence*, arguing that CHW was out of step with Catholic teachings on the right to organize, and took the issue to local congregations nationwide on a National Day of Prayer and Reconciliation. It mailed videos to the various religious orders and purchased advertising on cable television systems in several markets, and bought a full-page advertisement in the influential *National Catholic Reporter*, all advancing its argument. It conducted prayer vigils and candlelight rallies at CHW facilities.

In the end, the union persuaded the National Council of Bishops that SEIU, and not the nuns of CHW, had the proper interpretation of Catholic teachings, thus setting one part of the Church against the other. The Bishops trumped the nuns, and pressured the company to facilitate organizing by the union (Manheim, 2001).

Campaign messages trace to a number of points of origin. In the case of PICs and other argumentation-style campaigns, these would primarily center on the protagonist's agenda or objectives. In other types of campaigns with more complex strategies, they would expand to include the relative priorities of various interim and end-case objectives and of specific elements of the protagonist's agenda, the availability and suitability of potentially unifying themes, the availability and suitability of potentially unifying images, and the probable appeal of message elements to the audience. In the most complex campaigns, in which, as we shall see in a later chapter, the strategy requires mobilizing several types of intermediary actors (third parties) to interrelate with one another in ways that advance the campaign, the strategist would also take into consideration potential interactive effects between message elements, on the one hand, and the relevant third party and/or channel effects, on the other.

Channeling the Campaign

The latter of these, channel effects, arise from, or are associated with, attributes of the specific means of communication employed by a campaign—interpersonal communication, various of the mass media, so-called "new" or Internet-based media, and so forth—and the ways in which those attributes interact with or otherwise influence audiences. (In a later chapter, we will introduce an additional notion of channeling, through networks of intermediary actors, but those types of channels are not generally treated as communication effects *per se*. So in the interests of parsimony, we will not include them in the present discussion.) Channel attributes and channel effects, then, are basically two sides of the same strategic coin, and in some ways difficult to separate for purposes of discussion. In the present instance, though, and recognizing that the distinction is somewhat artificial, let us at least try to distinguish between two different sets of criteria upon which the strategist can base channel-choice decisions: desired attributes, and desired effects.

Channels can vary from one another in many ways. In strategic terms, one of the most crucial is probably the degree to which they engage the audience member in the actual processing of the information they transmit. As early landmark research by Herbert Krugman (much of it compiled in an anthology by his son, Edward P. Krugman, 2008) demonstrated, some channels permit, or even require, the active psychological involvement of the audience member in the communication process, while others rely on audience passivity. Krugman was a researcher with General Electric who had an interest in advertising. In a series of experiments in the 1960s and 1970s, he measured human responses to communication using such indicators as brain wave activity and galvanic skin response (changes in the level of electrical resistance of the skin), interpreting greater volatility in each instance as indicative of a higher order of psychological involvement in the processing of incoming information. The 1960s being the age of Marshall McLuhan, who argued that media varied in their "temperature"—with so-called "hot" media being more intensely interactive than so-called "cool" media—Krugman set about the systematic comparison of television viewing and reading. He found consistently that television viewing, then emerging as the dominant form of political information gathering, was a relatively passive activity, demonstrating low volatility on his indicators, while reading was inherently psychologically involving.

For the strategist, this is a highly significant result. For it follows from this that certain types of messages—those that are intended to engage the audience in the making of rational choices, for example, as anticipated in the traditional, argumentation-based notions of persuasion, or those that seek to convey relatively complex information—will best be communicated by means of highly involving channels, such as print. But other types of messages, those that are intended to influence purchasing or other behaviors without activating the defensive mechanisms (see below) available to the audience, for example, or those that seek to convey very simple, and often primarily symbolic, information will best be communicated by low involvement channels like television. Of course, these distinctions are not always clear-cut. Today's computer-based "digital" media, for instance, comprise an ever-evolving category that includes such applications as print and video services provided by both traditional and non-traditional media organizations, delineated organization-based segments of cyberspace (web pages), more personalized web logs ("blogs") that often encourage audience members to post their own views on a given topic, user-driven libraries of amateur and professional videos, social networking, global and targeted advertising, specialized-interest online communities, simulation spaces and pseudo-societies like Second Life, and much more. Many of these new media are designed to maximize interactivity, either through personal engagement with the individual user, online communal activity such as the viral distribution of videos, or the facilitation of real-world communal interactions, for example, swarming. This makes these media highly involving, perhaps more so even than the printed word. But at the same time, cyberspace is replete with reading material and television-like video content that differ from their counterparts in Mr. Krugman's era primarily in that they are consumed via computer rather than television sets, books or newspapers. Even that distinction is blurring, of course, as computer and television technologies converge and book-like electronic devices begin to proliferate.

Variations in channels and channel characteristics, and the ability to select among them for message placement, provide the strategist with many other potential tactical choices as well. Information channels can be differentiated, for instance, by their relative credibility or legitimacy, either in general or with specific audiences, which characteristic can become bound to a given message. Some channels, too, are more easily or directly controlled than others. In fact, this is arguably an inverse relationship, in which the limits on controllability, in and of themselves, are the primary contributors to the credibility of a channel—the more independent the channel, the greater its credibility. It has long been a rule of thumb in electoral campaigns, for instance, that messages conveyed through news

Box 3.4 Uses of Digital Media in Campaigns

The evolution of digital technologies is revolutionizing, well, revolution, as well as many lesser forms of political activism. Two cases in point:

Following the 2009 election in Iran, a widespread suspicion that the winner, incumbent President Mahmoud Ahmadinejad, had employed electoral fraud to defeat his nearest competitor, reform candidate Mir Hussein Moussavi, gave rise to a pressure campaign against the government, which responded with various forms of repression. Because the government controlled the traditional media and was able to monitor and manage web-based activism as well, the protestors moved to social networking media such as Twitter to share news, exhort one another, and organize protests—at one point at a rate of 30 new postings per minute. One of these so-called "tweets" captured the essence of this new forum: "We have no national press coverage in Iran, everyone should help spread Moussavi's message. One Person = One Broadcaster" (Stone and Cohen, 2009).

Two years earlier, in a somewhat more whimsical but equally indicative vein, Italian IBM workers launched, in the online world known as Second Life, the world's first virtual strike—establishing sign-carrying pickets—actually avatars ranging from bananas to T-shirted young women and even what appeared to be an Elvis impersonator—demanding improved working conditions. The workers set up a virtual strike task force, prepared informative materials in three languages, and held more than 20 online strategy meetings. Though this might seem to have been a trivial effort at first glance, recall that the target audience included current and potential IBM employees, a tech-savvy group with a more than usual interest in cyberspace. It was, in fact, an interesting and sophisticated selection of a campaign channel. *And* the "strike" was successful. It led to renewed negotiations with the company and an eventual agreement, not to mention the resignation, about three weeks later, of the CEO of IBM in Italy (Au, 2007; Smith, Costello, and Brecher, 2009).

organizations are far more believable, and hence potentially influential, than those conveyed by candidate advertising precisely because they are filtered by journalists and given enhanced importance by virtue of their having been selected, and hence defined, as newsworthy. Electoral campaigners refer to such channels (and content) as "earned" media, and a great deal of effort has traditionally gone into influencing their content, which is to say, into approximating control as nearly as possible in the hope of determining which messages are gifted with this added, news-based credibility. We will address some of these efforts in a later discussion of information intermediaries.

Because news management of this type is never fully effective, and can be only minimally so, electoral campaigns also deploy direct communications. During the television era, roughly 1960 to the present day, the bulk of these efforts have taken the form of campaign advertising delivered through the purchase of time on broadcast and, more recently, cable television. Such purchases can be controlled in a number of ways—channel selection, timing, frequency, duration, precise content, surrounding content, audience demographics, audience size—that are beyond the capability of even the most effective news management. This advertising can be effective in some important ways, most notably reinforcing and mobilizing the campaign's supporters. But, because it is so easily identified with the self-interest of the source campaign, it is usually of only limited value in inducing the desired behavior change among undecided or opposing voters. Most recently, these direct communications have begun to assume new forms, primarily through a dramatically increasing reliance on digital media, where the proliferation of available "news" channels, the enhanced interactivity of many formats, the power of self-selection into the audience and the related ability to zero in on individuals and on like-minded clusters of individuals, and the emergence of user-generated or user-enhanced viral media, may be fundamentally altering the control-credibility equation.

In addition, when some campaigns have found themselves unable for some reason effectively to manage news content, they have adopted a strategy of undermining the presumed objectivity of the news media, either in general or selectively. Here the objective is to limit the influence of those channels that cannot be successfully controlled at the required level by depriving them of their inherent credibility. In the U.S. for example, conservatives often complain of the liberal bias of the East Coast elite media, while liberals rail against the conservative bias of talk radio. The reverse of this strategy, or perhaps more correctly, its natural companion, is to promote the virtues of those "independent" channels that comfort a given campaign while attacking those that afflict it.

Channels and channeling strategies can also differ in terms of their:

- vividness, or the extent to which a given channel conveys rich imagery;
- intrusiveness, or the degree to which members of the intended audience can escape exposure;
- immediacy, or their time*li*ness, the extent to which they are "of the moment";

- permanence, or their time*less*ness, the extent to which they are likely to endure;
- informativeness, or the density of their substantive content;
- prestige, or the extent to which they convey a feeling among the audience of participating in an elite experience;
- and their entertainment value, or the degree of enjoyment, fantasy, or release associated with their use,

to name but a few. Marketing strategists have, in fact, identified many other potentially decision-relevant channel characteristics, including such elements as total reach, selective reach (e.g., upscale adults), audience-size cost ratios, breadth of distribution, localization potential, frequency controllability, time-of-day and day-of-week control, seasonal audience stability or trends, the predictability of audience levels, and flexibility in the timing of placement decisions (i.e., the ability to make a decision at the last minute). Strategists often design campaign communications to maximize the match between the attributes of message content, on the one hand, and these diverse channel characteristics, on the other.

Added to this mix is a difference in the information available to the strategist about such factors as the level and timing of audience exposure to campaign communications and the specificity with which those communications can be directed at the desired audience. The reach of traditional broadcast media—radio and television—is determined through various ratings services, most notably the A.C. Neilsen Company and Arbitron. These companies conduct audience research by recruiting individuals or families to "participate" in surveys of their program preferences and listening/viewing habits. Members of these samples may be asked to maintain diaries of their media use, or their behavior may be monitored through the use of so-called "people meters" or other devices that capture their presence in a room where a particular program is being viewed. Newspaper and magazine readership is similarly measured through distribution counts by the Audit Bureau of Circulation. Book sales and motion picture box office receipts are also measures of exposure to traditional media. All of these measures, however, have significant methodological limitations, whether arising from small or biased samples, unrealistic expectations of respondents' willingness or ability to observe themselves, the inability to monitor secondary audiences (think bar patrons watching a television program or hand-me-down readers of a book or magazine), and none of these provide clear, real-time evidence of message exposure.

Contrast that with the online world, where data-mining technology like that pioneered by such companies as Google and Amazon has the capability to provide user-specific, real-time data about not only who is online and onsite at any given moment, but what information they are receiving and, in some instances, how they react to it. Moreover, because over time self-identified (logged-in) users, or at the very least, their uniquely identifiable (using Internet Protocol, or IP, addresses) personal computers, establish patterns of preference for and reaction to online information that can be captured, stored, and converted to decision-making algorithms, it is possible for the strategist to communicate online with unlimited numbers of individuals while employing highly personalized messages.

Audience Selection: The Whole versus the Sum of the Parts

The fourth element of campaign communications specified in Figure 3.1 is the receiver of all this communication or, in the aggregate, the audience. Of interest to the strategist in this regard are differences that occur—and the ability to reach and differentiate—both within and across audiences. This distinction will become especially important in a moment when we turn our attention to communication effects, but it is well worth keeping in mind here as well. For the key to both breadth and selectivity in defining the audience(s) for a campaign lies in segmentation, the ability to pick and choose among prospective receivers those who will actually be targeted by the campaign. Segmentation is the art and science of using the available information about the audience, which is to say the work product of all that rating and data-mining, to best advantage.

In very general terms, we can think of audiences as being structured in one of three ways, as illustrated in Figure 3.2. If (effectively) all of the members of the audience are alike with respect to some perception, preference, behavior, or attribute, we describe that audience, represented in Figure 3.2(a), as being homogeneous. Where the audience is divided into more or less tightly bounded and clearly differentiated subgroups, as in Figure 3.2(b), we characterize it as clustered. And where the audience is widely scattered and generally disorganized with respect to a given characteristic, as in Figure 3.2(c), we describe it as diffuse. In the first instance, since all members of the audience are essentially alike or like-minded, there is no reason to engage in audience segmentation. There is only one

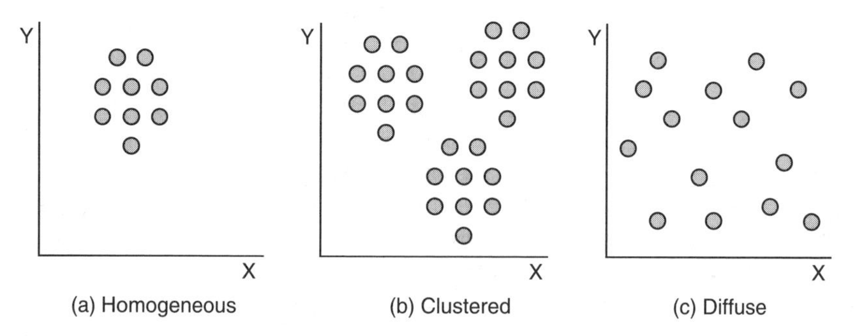

Figure 3.2 Segmentation and Market Structures.

segment. And in the third instance, where the audience is, for want of a better term, perfectly differentiated, there is no reason to engage in audience segmentation. There are *no* segments, only individuals. Only in the conditions specified in the second instance, that of clustering, does audience segmentation make real sense as a component of communication strategy.

In reality, of course, these three conditions represent the endpoints and midpoint of a continuum of audience structures, so the true decision criterion with respect to the value of segmentation is simply whether and to what extent functional segments can be (a) identified, (b) isolated, so that the members of each segment receive only, or almost only, the messaging intended especially for them, and (c) reached.

Thinking here primarily in terms of the general public—and recalling that not all IICs are designed to engage the general public—there are at least five basic forms of segmentation available to the campaign strategist, depending, of course, on access to the relevant audience research. The first, most basic, and perhaps most easily accomplished of these, at least for campaigns that rely on traditional media as primary channels, is geographic segmentation, targeting audience members on the basis of their locations—by country, region, state or province, county, city, or neighborhood, or, for some purposes, by population density (urban, suburban, rural) or other areal characteristics. There are ways of tuning national media and some digital media to limit the geographic distribution of information, but this is generally most easily accomplished through an emphasis on appropriately bounded local channels, such as newspapers, radio, cable systems, area-code limited telephone or automated telephone contacts, or delivery (ZIP) code-limited direct mail.

A second basic form of segmentation, and arguably the most commonly used, is demographic segmentation—reaching those individuals and groups among the potential audience who/that are of greatest interest to the campaign, whether the objective for each is to mobilize, persuade, or demobilize, so that the appropriate messages can be delivered with the greatest efficiency and with minimal spillover into other audience segments where they may have unintended or undesired effects. Key demographic categories employed in many campaigns include such groupings as age, gender, income, occupation or employment status, education, religion, and race/ethnicity/nationality. In some campaigns, other characteristics such as family size or life-cycle status (young single; young married, no children; and so forth) may also be employed. The idea of segmentation is to design messages in demographically appealing clusters, and then to deliver them efficiently to the targeted subgroups of the overall audience. In the case of mass media, particular outlets can be judged both by the extent that they reach the intended segments and by the extent to which that reach is segment-specific. This latter characteristic is often referred to as narrowcasting or, particularly for digital media, micro-targeting, and is typically used to distinguish, for example, specialized cable networks designed to appeal to, say, women or young adults, across their full spectrum of content, from over-the-air *broad*cast networks that are designed to reach the maximum possible undifferentiated audience, while providing a mix of content that will have somewhat specialized demographic appeal that varies from one program or content cluster to the next.

A third basic form of segmentation is a division of the potential audience based on a known distribution of psychological states. This is commonly termed attitudinal segmentation, though technically it incorporates more than attitudes *per se*. The core idea here is to identify those individuals who hold particular perceptions, preferences and/or loyalties that are of interest to the campaign, and to reach them with specialized messages that appeal to, leverage or simply address their existing states of mind. An additional layer of segmentation can be added here to the extent that the strategist can ascertain, or estimate, the susceptibility of individuals or sets of individuals to persuasion of one type or another. This might include the sort of argumentation strategy we have discussed above, but it is perhaps more likely to employ other approaches to inducing attitude change that we have yet to address. (We will remedy that in Chapter 4.) If one can know in advance with some degree of certitude which members of a given audience are, for example, favorably or unfavorably disposed toward the campaign or its objective, what campaign-relevant information or beliefs they hold, and what social or other identifications are important (or

Box 3.5 Strategic Audience Segmentation

Digital media are facilitating whole new dimensions of audience segmentation. Consider, for example, the following assessment by a group of labor activists.

> With a single keystroke, social movements can now push information out to millions of people and lift up marginalized voices into national, and even global, spheres. But scale increasingly does not just mean trying to reach the whole world, especially as it has become increasingly difficult to break through the online noise. Scale is also about surgically communicating with discrete sets of readers. At [Global Labor Strategies], for example, rather than targeting the global labor movement writ large, we have tried to target the narrow subset of the global labor movement that is grappling with long-term, strategic questions of worker and class representation in the global economy. Two decades ago we could never have precisely and cheaply carved out this audience. (Smith, Costello, and Brecher, 2009)

anathema) to them, and if one can identify and employ channels that reach these clusters of likeminded souls with substantial efficiency, it may be a rather straightforward matter to design messages that will incorporate the relevant appeal. The next step up the ladder of sophistication—designing messages that will, depending on the goals of the campaign, facilitate or impede actual attitude change—is more challenging, to be sure, but where the strategist has in hand the relevant estimates of susceptibility to persuasion and the ability to maintain contact with the target audience over the requisite time period, even segmentation by persuasive potential can be within reach.

A fourth basic form, termed psychographic segmentation, is similar to attitudinal segmentation, but is based instead on a mix of sociological and other factors, principal among them social class, life style and personality, as well as some elements of demographic analysis. Where attitudinal segmentation seeks leverage in clusters of differences in the internal building blocks of audience predispositions, psychographic segmentation is an effort to leverage differences among groups of audience members in the way that they relate to the larger society. Taking lifestyle segmentation as an example, if suburban soccer moms are more likely than successful small town residents to respond favorably to a given campaign or share its objectives, then the campaign will be wise to engage them through its communications.

The final basic form of segmentation, known as behavioral segmentation, is similar to attitudinal segmentation in that it relies on prior knowledge of audience attributes and an ability to reach relevant subgroups with differentiated messages. But in this case, as the name suggests, the attributes in question are behavioral. They include things like participation patterns, group memberships, benefits sought, or even just the inclination (or disinclination) to act in ways that interest the campaign. Individuals who in the past have routinely joined groups that reflect, represent, or advance their interests, for example, will be more likely to join such groups in the future than those who are not inclined to be "joiners". That knowledge, especially when combined with more detailed information regarding which specific groups, or types of groups, these individuals joined, can be put to good use in designing behaviorally segmented messaging. By extension, discoverable information capturing any other behavioral tendencies can also be employed to advantage, subject only to the strategist's ability to isolate and reach the audience segments in question.

In every one of these approaches to segmentation, the appeal and potential paradigm-changing impact of new media and their accompanying data-mining is evident. To be effective, traditional segmentation strategies require the making of informed judgments about audience clusters based on the shared characteristics of their members. These aggregate judgments invariably incorporate assumptions about the commonality of the members of a given segment that mask the nature and degree of differences across individuals, and that may well overstate the functional homogeneity of the segment. The more "mass" the medium, the more likely it is that such errors will creep into the strategy. Moreover, even in the best of circumstances, the delivery vehicle(s) or channels by which individual members of a segment can be reached are differentiable only as a matter of degree from general audience channels. They cannot for the most part be customized at the level of the individual. But in the world of cyber-channels, not only can the targeting of messages be based on individual-level data and uniquely addressable channels, but in many instances the individuals self-select into virtual communities operated or exploited by the campaign, and volunteer information regarding their beliefs, preferences, wants, needs and behaviors that usually remains well beyond the reach of traditional audience research.

Effects of Campaign Communication

Returning to the matrix summarized in Figure 3.1, we now turn our attention from the columns representing communication attributes to the rows representing communication effects. This is an area that has been of great interest to mass communication scholars for many years, as even the very selective summary of their efforts in the literature review in Appendix B will attest. These measures of impact are generally referred to in that literature as "media" effects, and although the approach we take here, focusing as well on channels that are not considered part of the traditional media, is somewhat more inclusive, we will adopt that language for the moment.

Maguire's conceptualization of effects, on which Figure 3.1 was based, focused primarily on micro-level, or individual-level, effects, and, because he wrote as a social psychologist with an interest in the mechanisms that change attitudes and behaviors *per se*, centered on the staging of those mechanisms. That receiver-derived view of communication effects is both a valid and a valuable perspective and one with which the strategist must be conversant. It is, however, a perspective that we will wait until the next chapter to examine. Here we will limit our consideration to the view from upstream, which is to say, to a protagonist-derived perspective on communication effects.

From that perspective, a given combination of messaging and channeling can have a variety of different types of effects, any one or more of which can be managed to serve the interests of the campaign. Among the possibilities:

- *Personal or social gratification.* Media may be used by some members of the audience, at some times, to satisfy a variety of needs—for information, for escape, for a sense of identity, for a measure of social interaction, or simply for entertainment. To the extent that such motives are in play in a given communication situation, messaging that is designed to provide such gratification can serve as a carrier for content that advances the interests of the campaign, much as oscillating radio frequencies carry the audible or visible content of broadcast media. They facilitate access to the audience by enhancing the likelihood of its members' exposure and attentiveness. An interesting variant on this theme is provided by the notion of vicarious, or parasocial, interaction—a feeling that is generated in audience members, by their media use, that they are actual participants in a reality that they experience only through the media. An example would be the sense that one is an actual character in a soap opera, interacting with other characters through the act of viewing. To the extent that such a sense of personal engagement can be generated through campaign communication, it can be used to heighten or reduce the prospects for persuasion in certain circumstances. (We'll say more about this in the next chapter.) Now consider the interactive nature of certain digital media applications, where the individual audience member is posting to blogs, submitting homemade videos to distribution sites, or exchanging messages with members of a virtual community. In many ways, such activity would seem to constitute real interaction with the technology, but vicarious interaction with society. It may well be this similarity that holds the key to the most effective strategic uses of digital media.

- *Emotional arousal*. One possible effect of campaign communication is to arouse emotional responses in members of the audience, or even mass arousal in the audience as a whole. This is typically accomplished by the effective use of powerful symbols—what Murray Edelman called condensation symbols—that connect the campaign messaging with strongly held personal or cultural values, which that messaging is designed to activate. Arousal strategies are commonplace in IICs, and are often deployed to motivate specialized publics, like the members of certain activist, ideological religious communities, or some self-perceived class of societal victims charged with populist anger against a more or less clearly delineated elite, to discharge what amounts to a duty to advance their common values and interests by acting in some way against a group of nonbelievers or oppressors, whom the campaign will conveniently define. In its simplest form, this is basically a friends and enemies strategy that builds on existing or manufactured affinities and enmities. Because arousal is a non-rational phenomenon, even though the decision to employ it is clearly a rational one, it can be both powerful and difficult to manage.
- *Knowledge gain*. To the extent that a campaign distributes substantive information, and to the extent to which members of a campaign audience are exposed to, attend, and internalize that information, the campaign contributes to the knowledge base associated with the

issue(s) it addresses. We know from the argumentation model of persuasion that this can be important in two ways. The first is knowledge creation, the distribution and processing of new information on a new topic that was not previously possessed by the audience. The second is knowledge modification, the distribution and processing of information that relates to, and reinforces or repositions, pre-existing knowledge on a pre-existing topic. As we will see in our later discussion of the dynamics of attitude change, this is a very important distinction. In the first instance, the persuader writes on a clean slate, and has the opportunity to define the issue in question for the audience. In the second instance, the persuader confronts a static body of existing information and must find a way to move it in the desired direction. For the moment, however, let us simply note the common element of both circumstances: that communication has the potential to affect the body of knowledge used by the audience to evaluate and respond to the campaign, and that the communication strategist must, and can, manage this process.

- *Agenda setting*. This is a fancy name for a simple idea: Members of the audience tend to think mainly about those topics or issues that are receiving media coverage at any given moment. The more, or the more prominent, the coverage of an issue in the media, the more people will have that issue in their top-of-mind thought space, the more aware of it they will be. Agenda setting, then, is, above all, a quantitative phenomenon—the more coverage an object receives, the more aware of it, or focused on it, the audience will be. To the extent that this effect is operative—and the evidence suggests that it is a commonplace of public affairs communication—the implications for strategy seem clear. Where one's interests are best served by increasing public attention to a given issue (or actor, or element of the campaign setting . . .), they will be best served by taking steps that maximize media coverage or other relevant information flows, i.e., tactics that facilitate such flows and draw attention to them. Issue white papers, hold news conferences, stage media events, flood the blogosphere, employ advertising. Conversely, where one's interests are best served by reducing public attention to an issue, they will best be served by taking steps that minimize media coverage or other flows, i.e., tactics that impede such flows and distract from the issue. Deny access to key individuals or information, redefine the issue, stage distractions, withhold information, preemptively shut down websites, threaten litigation against would-be critics.
- *Framing*. If agenda setting determines in some measure whether and to what extent members of an audience think about a given object, framing refers to the actual content of what they think. More specifically, it is built around the idea that the specific content of media (or other relevant) portrayals of issues or actors influences the choices that

Box 3.6 The Name of the Game is the Name

Fighting the nation's wars is an intensely physical undertaking—dangerous (to say the least), dirty, rough-and-tumble . . . in sum, the ultimate in reality. But the same cannot be said for the labeling of these events, which can sometimes seem to represent the ultimate in unreality. Mission Accomplished.

In point of fact, naming can be a very important aspect of any military undertaking, and the Pentagon, and sometimes the White House, devotes considerable thought to doing so. The name of a war, mission, initiative, or strategy needs to convey critical messages to critical audiences—inspiration to the troops, moral reassurance to the public, respect to allies, and fear to the enemy, among others. Shock and Awe. Once upon a time, the names of war-related events were chosen purely as labels, and the names selected over the years have included those of Athenian leaders, Civil War generals, snakes, comic book characters, sports, movies, and even rappers, among many others. Many have actually been more or less random, or at least seemed so. But no longer. Today, naming is framing, and that is simply too important to be left to whim or chance. It is a marketing exercise.

In the words of General Sean McFarland, "Who is your target audience? If it's just internal consumption, you want to give a name the soldiers and Marines will get pumped up about. But if it's more for [foreign] consumption, it has to translate well. And if it's going to be in newspaper headlines and be commented about on op-ed pages, then you have to give it a more politically correct name" (Davenport, 2010).

audience members make about what information to retain and associate with that object and the judgments or type and level of emotions they apply to it, which is to say, *how* they think about the items on their personal or collective agendas. So framing effects are fundamentally qualitative phenomena; they are a function of the nature of message content. Here, too, the strategist finds a panoply of opportunities for communication management—as many as there are choices among specific images, words, associations, or other cues. In effect, a frame conveys an explanatory and/or emotional context in which the audience is encouraged, intentionally or otherwise, to view or understand the issue in question. Where a given frame is reinforced through continuity of portrayal, through multiple channels, and over time, and especially where that frame accords with audience predispositions or preconceptions, it will color the interpretation of the issue. Thus it is clearly in the interests of a campaign to incorporate in its communications a consistent thematic frame that is designed with existing audience perspectives in mind.

Box 3.7 Managing Information Flows to Control Agendas and Frames

Consider two examples, decades and political poles apart, that reflect common understandings of the strategic utility of information control in managing agendas and framing.

Case 1. It is 1982, you are Ronald Reagan, and your objective is to reduce the scope of government. You have just passed an historic tax cut, and you want to back it up by reducing the demand for government services. What to do . . . One solution implemented by the Reagan Administration was to reduce sharply the role of the federal government in gathering, processing, and disseminating a wide variety of social, economic, and other data—using the just-implemented federal budget cuts as a justification for cutting the budgets of statistical agencies. These so-called CESTAs (centralized statistical agencies) included the Bureau of the Census, Bureau of Economic Analysis, Bureau of Justice Statistics, Bureau of Labor Statistics, Energy Information Administration, National Agricultural Statistics Service, National Center for Education Statistics, and National Center for Health Statistics. Smaller agencies, fewer data; fewer data, fewer demands; fewer demands, smaller government. *Voilà*!

In the words of one analyst (Morin, 1994: 436), "Budget changes can have the force of reordering agency preferences and performances. Such changes can reflect the programmatic preferences of the president" (Chelimsky, 1985; Gardner, 1983; Morin, 1994).

Case 2. It is the first decade of the twenty-first century, you are a climate scientist who believes in the threat of human-caused global warming, and your objective is to save the world. Literally. It is a high-stakes undertaking, because, based on your science, advocates are pressing world governments to commit immense resources to the fight. What to do . . . One advocacy organization, the Institute for Public Policy Research in the UK, commissioned a consultants' report in 2006 that analyzed this problem and offered the following recommendation:

> Much of the noise in the climate change discourse comes from argument and counter-argument, and it is our recommendation that, at least for popular communications, interested agencies now need to treat the argument as having been won. This means

> simply behaving as if climate change exists and is real, and that individual actions are effective. This must be done by stepping away from the "advocates' debate" described earlier, rather than by stating and re-stating these things as fact. The "facts" need to be treated as being so taken-for-granted that they need not be spoken.
>
> (Ereaut and Segnit, 2006: 25)

In other words, reframe the issue as one that has already been decided. And that, we know from some leaked or purloined email exchanges involving scientists at a major research center in the UK, is exactly what some of the most influential climate researchers did. They collaborated to keep evidence contrary to their findings and policy preferences out of the peer-reviewed literature, then claimed that all of the peer-reviewed literature backed their views. When scholarly journals appeared to be breaking this de facto censorship, they conspired to denigrate and marginalize these publications and their editors. When the data did not fit their preconceived notions of appropriate results, they cooked the data. When outsiders began using public access (freedom of information) laws to access their data, they conspired to hide or even delete them. And, when scholars sought out the raw data upon which the principal climate change models were constructed, it turned out that the data had been discarded. (An inventory of these emails and related documents was summarized by *Wall Street Journal* and was found online at http://online.wsj.com/article/SB10001424052748704779704574553652849094482.html.)

Two different eras, two different issues, two very different actors, one common strategy: Restrict the flow of information to control the policy agenda or the framing of the issue.

It should be clear that these various communication effects need not, and generally do not, operate independently of one another. More than that, they do not function in a binary world, one in which a switch is flipped and the effect in question is simply turned on or off. Activation (or deactivation) can occur in stages and by levels, and may be cumulative, cyclical or interactive. In developing a strategy for employing one or more of these tools, then, the campaigner needs to take into account the desirability of some of these attributes. Here let us consider three of these in particular: primacy, recency and duration. All three relate in some way to timing. Primacy is that condition in which the first messaging or framing is the most influential. The mechanism here is simple. The communication that literally defines the portrayal of an object in the process establishes the terms by which it will be understood and interpreted. Recency is an opposing condition in which the most recent messaging or framing is the most influential. Again the posited mechanism is simple. Individuals will best remember, and thus be most influenced by, those communications to which they have only just been exposed. The third condition, duration, refers to the speed with which, and the degree to which, a given communication-induced perception, interpretation, belief or preference decays over time. Some framing effects endure, while others erode rapidly.

This notion of duration, incidentally, was one of the first tested in the early days of scientific approaches to persuasion, and one of the earliest examples of the mutuality of interest between basic and applied research in this area. That point, as well as an important substantive finding, is nicely illustrated in Figure 3.3, which is based on a 1959 study of advertising recall conducted by Hubert Zielske. The graph on the left illustrates the differential impact of clustering thirteen message-delivery points either at one-week intervals or at equal intervals throughout a one-year period. The graph on the right illustrates the percentage of the audience recalling an advertising message after a single delivery and after thirteen deliveries at one-week intervals. (The use of thirteen delivery points here derived from the network television practice at the time of creating thirty-nine new episodes of prime-time series programming, i.e., three quarters of thirteen weeks each, which then became the basis for advertising sales.) As the figure makes clear, new persuasive messages have a very short half-life, regardless of their initial impact. But as it also makes clear, decisions regarding the timing and aggregation of messages in the form of *campaigns*

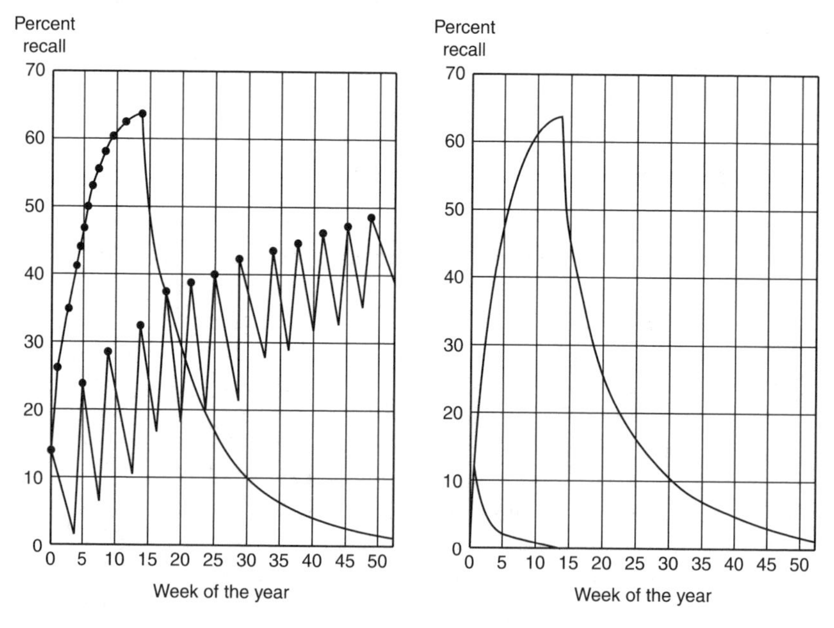

Figure 3.3 Temporal Sequencing of Advertising Recall.

can be used to amplify the effects of individual messages and, if it is an objective, to maximize these effects at a single point in time.

The operation and extent of primacy, recency and duration in any given campaign situation are empirical questions, the answers to which can be employed in shaping communication strategy. But in the context of IICs, they may be related to one another somewhat systematically. It may be that primacy establishes a set of initial perceptions, the durability and influence of which are a function of the extent to which they are internalized by members of the audience in ways that generate either personal interest or some sense of engagement with the issue. Depending on the strength of the resulting interest or engagement, and on the campaign's ability to reinforce, extend, and activate them through subsequent communications, the initial perceptions will demonstrate a variable half-life—longer where stronger, shorter where weaker. Where the personal connection between the individual/audience and the frame has decayed sufficiently, or where it was never really established in the first place, the lack of personal involvement with the issue in question opens the door to influence by alternative, more recent communications, which is to say, to recency effects.

All of the classes of effects we have addressed here can be seen to have one thing in common—they are means to an end. Gratification effects tie the members of an audience to media use *per se*, which is to say, render them relatively more available to the campaign for purposes of persuasion. Knowledge gain establishes or alters the base of information that audience members will bring to bear on a given issue. Agenda setting influences the rise and fall of specific issues or other objects of attention in the public mind. And framing effects help to shape the evaluations and preferences associated with those issues or objects that are prominently in mind at any given moment. Ultimately, of course, because we are interested not in abstract notions of how and why people can be influenced through communication, but rather in practical notions of how best to accomplish that to advance a specific campaign objective, we need to go a step further—from the means to the ends, where the ends are effective persuasion, either in the form of attitude change or, more likely, behavior change. We will turn to that task in the next chapter.

A Bit of Perspective

Let us make two last points before concluding. First, many of the concepts we have employed in this chapter, and much of the underlying scholarly research from which they are derived, focus on message content, delivery, and effects as if individual communications, or small clusters of communications, operating in isolation, are the primary instruments of persuasion. In the world of research in this area, much of which is experimental or quasi-experimental in character, that is often the case. In the world of real-world

IICs, it can almost never be so. Because IICs are, after all, *campaigns*. They are more or less long-running *aggregations* of messages and other products of campaign strategy, the purpose of which is to work collectively to attain the desired objective, and they occur in highly complex, multi-layered social and physical environments. For that reason, it is both unduly limiting and counter-productive to think exclusively in terms of more or less singular messages that are delivered under more or less isolated circumstances over a relatively short period of time. Rather, the strategist should think of the campaign as a long-, or at least longer-, running series of opportunities to employ combinations of message content, delivery and effects to generate the desired movement (or, in some cases, the desired inertia). In that context, it will be the combination of long-term planning, message *building*, audience *building*, and environmental sensing—*enlightened* by an understanding of the concepts developed in this and other chapters—that will maximize the prospects for strategic success.

Second, it is not clear just how many members of the general public, where engaged, are actually persuaded by a campaign, or for that matter, whether they need to be. Especially where the target of the campaign is relatively sensitive to its public image, it may be that all of the visibility and noise associated with would-be persuasion, more than any actual persuasion, is enough to cause the target to respond, and hence to get the job done. Did Phil Knight, to return to our Chapter 1 example, respond to the anti-sweatshop activists because the public was persuaded of their argument, or, perhaps, did he respond preemptively because he feared they might be? Campaign strategists must cope with such uncertainties, but at the same time, they often feel they cannot afford to take any chances.

4 Strategy and Tactics in Campaign Communication II: Shaping the Decision

> Information is a strategic resource—less understood but no less important to national security than political, military, and economic power. In the information age, influence and power go to those who can disseminate credible information in ways that will mobilize publics to support interests, goals, and objectives. What is required is a coherent approach as to how we think about managed information dissemination . . .
>
> Defense Science Board Task Force on Managed Information Dissemination (United States Department of Defense, 2001: 7)

> To assume a perfect correspondence between the nature and amount of material presented in an information campaign and its absorption by the public is to take a naïve view, for the very nature and degree of public exposure to the material is determined to a large extent by certain psychological characteristics of the people themselves.
>
> Herbert H. Hyman and Paul B. Sheatsley (1947: 413)

While rhetoricians, democratic theorists, philosophical purists and others may object to the characterization, for the strategist substantive argumentation is often tangential and actual content peripheral to the truly essential decisions regarding the persuasion of individuals. Far more important is an understanding of why and how such persons of interest to the campaign hold the attitudes, perceptions, preferences, beliefs, and expectations that they do, and by what mechanisms these diverse elements can be accessed and influenced. From a purely strategic standpoint, if one understands the psychological dynamics that generate and maintain these states and that govern their projection into the campaign setting, one can then shape the content of campaign communications to exploit these tendencies. Argumentation and content, then, are often best understood not as the essence of persuasion, but rather as the pre-screened and carefully structured packaging that draws targeted individuals to engage with the campaign so that more fundamental persuasive elements, intended to take advantage of underlying psychological structures and processes, can be conveyed effectively.

Psychological Structures and Processes

What might those elements be? And once identified, how can they be accessed and turned to advantage? To answer those questions we will draw primarily on knowledge developed over the last three quarters of a century or so in the field of social psychology, bringing in as well some ideas from advertising theory, political communication and other areas.

As a practical matter, in approaching a persuasive effort, the strategist must be concerned with four basic questions: What perceptions and preferences does an individual, or a likeminded group of individuals, hold that are of potential interest to the campaign? How are these perceptions and preferences organized and, in the case of groups, how are they distributed; how do they relate to one another? What purpose do they serve? How, and to what extent, is the individual aware of, or committed to, them? Let us begin with these basics, then move toward a more nuanced set of considerations.

One might think that the natural starting point for a characterization and analysis of the public mind is with a look at the results of public opinion polls, which purport to measure precisely such things. But in developing or understanding campaign strategy, it is often less the results of such inquiries that are of interest than the questions themselves. What is it that the strategist chooses to measure, and why? The answer to that question can be quite instructive, because opinion surveys and other campaign-related research should advance, and may well reveal, the strategist's approach to persuasion.

Over the years, researchers have developed many ways of thinking about the nature and dynamics of persuasion, which, from this more structural perspective, is best understood as either generating a change in a belief, a cognition or perception, a preference, an attitude, or an expectation, *or* generating enhanced resistance to such a change. The theories vary in the ways that they conceptualize and target individual psychological processes. To help put them in context, let us take a very brief tour of the real estate inside the human brain.

The brain is a mass of neurons, or nerve cells, that collect, process and store incoming information from and about the environment beyond the organism, which is to say, the world in which we all function. All of this collecting, processing and storing is, at the most basic level, an electrochemical process by which minute electrical charges are generated and passed through chains of cells, leaping from one to the next across gaps, known as synapses, which are themselves filled with chemicals known as neurotransmitters that serve to facilitate or impede the flow of current. Some of these chains ultimately produce memories, while others are linked to behavioral responses to the environment. Cognitive scientists, or those who study these phenomena, have been employing an array of new tools, such as magnetic resonance imaging, or MRI, to "observe" this activity, noting, for example, that particular kinds of external stimuli tend to generate patterns of enhanced activity in one or another part of the brain, which they can literally see heating up or cooling off differentially. This research is both fascinating and promising, and is a likely source of guidance for the communication strategist of the future. But it is only now beginning to be applied to the kinds of message and channel variables that form the basis for strategic decision-making, so for the moment we are forced to rely on more impressionistic renderings of the landscape in cognitive space.

To that end, think of a belief or a perception or a cognition as a point in space—a sort of minute free-floating mental object. One possibility is that this object—and let's use the term cognition as a shorthand—so, this cognition, is an isolated one, present but unconnected to any other elements. By its mere presence, our cognition is of potential interest to the would-be persuader as a building block of some strategy, but its lack of integration into any broader psychological structure might well minimize its utility. A second possibility is that our cognition forms the basis for a more complex structure, one that ties it to some preference or judgment by which the individual in whose head we are currently swimming about assigns to the cognition a value, positive or negative. One common term for such judgments in this context is affect. And this combination of a cognition with an affect is known as an attitude. Now you see where we are going. It is actually, of course, a little more complicated than this, because in one way or another, most notions about attitudes incorporate not merely internal structures, but ties to external objects. One general definition, for example, holds that an attitude is a predisposition to respond to a particular stimulus in a particular manner. That stimulus, or object, is known as the "attitude object"—the thing the attitude is about. But we are getting ahead of ourselves.

Stepping back, yet another possibility for our cognition is that it is connected in some way, either consciously or unconsciously, to one or more other cognitions held by the same individual. Think of this as a set of points in space that are in more or close proximity with one another, perhaps anchored together in some geometric relationship. When one of these several cognitions comes to mind, others are likely to join it because the individual in question thinks about (though that may be too purposive a term) these elements together, or at some level understands them to be a group. These combinations of interlinked cognitions are known as belief systems. Belief systems can be broad or narrow in scope, and can vary widely in the degree to which they are organized, which is to say, the extent to which they function as integrated entities. The more attention an individual pays to a given object and the more orderly the way s/he thinks about it, the more organized the belief system applied to that object will be. And carrying that argument one step further, belief systems themselves may be shaped and connected through broader, overarching systems of personal values, judgments about the kinds of things one wishes to believe or prefer.

In much the same way, attitudes—those more complex combinations of cognition and affect—can be organized into hierarchical structures known as attitude clusters. Perceptions and judgments about the *attributes* of a given object, for example, can be aggregated into an attitude cluster that produces a net perception and judgment about the object itself, and perceptions about individual objects can be clustered to produce a net perception and judgment about groupings of such objects. So, for example, the judgments one makes about particular characteristics of a person or a company or a regime may well be set against one another as one forms a higher-order attitude about the person or the company or the regime as a whole. These may in turn be conflated to generate a still higher-order attitude about a group of people who have something in common, or about companies in a particular industry, or about regimes of a particular ideological stripe.

In a sense, perceptions and beliefs, either on their own or in more or less integrated systems, are static phenomena. To be sure, they can develop and change, but in and of themselves they are not self-actuating. But when linked to judgments or preferences to form attitudes or attitude clusters, they take on a sort of psychological momentum. These affective elements convert the static to the dynamic by adding two components of motion, direction and intensity, to the mix. Affects can be positive or negative, favorable or unfavorable, supportive or unsupportive, with respect to a particular object or observation, and whatever their direction, they can vary quite widely in their intensity, in the degree of psychological force they exert. They provide a normative, and potentially an emotional, basis for, in effect, putting one's cognitions to use. They cause the individual to lean one way or the other and determine just how far that lean extends. When we speak, then, of attitudes as predispositions to respond to new experiences or information, it is this leaning that we have in mind.

In this more structural context, we can think of efforts at persuasion as having a range of objectives, some of them far more easily achieved than others. Arrayed from what may be the most easily achieved to the most challenging, some of these would include:

- reinforcing an existing, deeply held, perception, preference, or attitude, or one firmly integrated into a belief system or attitude cluster;
- reinforcing an existing, lightly held, perception, preference, or attitude, or one that remains isolated or only loosely integrated into a belief system or attitude cluster;
- attaching a new preference to an existing perception, or linking an existing perception to an existing belief system;
- implanting a new perception where none existed previously;
- introducing a belief system to integrate existing perceptions, or an attitude cluster to integrate existing lower-order attitudes;

- stimulating action based on an existing attitude or preference, or on an existing attitude cluster or belief system;
- stimulating action based on an existing perception that is not linked to a conscious preference;
- stimulating action that occurs without reference to perceptions, preferences, or attitudes;
- changing an existing, lightly held, perception, preference, or attitude, or one that remains isolated or only loosely integrated into a belief system or attitude cluster;
- changing an existing, deeply held, perception, preference, or attitude, or one firmly integrated into a belief system or attitude cluster.

In the context of a particular information and influence campaign, any one or more of these objectives may come into play, and the objectives of campaign persuasion will almost certainly vary across audiences and evolve over time. The challenge to the strategist is to construct that mix of communications and other actions that best advances the campaign.

Theories of Persuasion

This is where the various theories of persuasion and resistance to persuasion come into play. Over the years, social psychologists have developed quite a number of these, each emphasizing some alternative understanding of the dynamics of persuasion or the relative import of various change agents or points of access to the process. In truth, none of these theories is truly global in either its emphasis or its explanatory power. As a result, the strategist must become adept at drawing more or less extensively from some combination of theories to produce an informed, integrated, and sophisticated plan of attack. Realizing that we cannot do these relatively complex theories credit here, where our interest is primarily instrumental, let us touch briefly on a few of the more interesting frameworks to suggest the kinds of assumptions that a strategist might make about the dynamics of persuasion, and the kinds of strategic and tactical implications that might flow from each. (In organizing this discussion, we are guided in part by the excellent summary of this general topic provided by Daniel J. O'Keefe (2002).)

Belief-Based Approach. Perhaps the most basic approach to attitude change corresponds closely with our basic definition of an attitude. As developed in the 1960s by Martin Fishbein, it focuses on the individual's salient beliefs about a given attitude object. Individuals may have a large number of beliefs about an object, but at any given time some of these will be more salient than others. More specifically—and here is where the parallels to the earlier argument come clear—this approach defines one's attitude as the sum of these beliefs and their associated evaluations, a notion very similar to what we earlier characterized as an attitude "cluster." The theory actually offers an equation, in the form $A_o = \Sigma b_i e_i$, which in translation means that the attitude toward a given object is the sum of the associated beliefs weighted to account for their respective evaluations. For this reason, it is often termed the "summative" model.

Box 4.1 Listen Up!

The discussion of the dynamics of attitudes and perceptions in these pages may seem abstract, but it is often the key to designing and getting the most benefit from campaign-related research. Good research lies in knowing what questions to ask and how to ask them. *Benefiting* from good research means being a good listener—listening to what the data have to say.

Historian Nicholas Cull (2009: 28–31) offers a case in point. In the mid- to late-1990s, the country of Switzerland was experiencing criticism as the world focused on the fact that Swiss banks had been the depositories of, and had retained, a large horde of Nazi gold from the years before and during World War II, much of it from victims of the Holocaust. Whether in the form of class action litigation and legislative inquiries in the United States, an official report of the British Foreign and Commonwealth Office setting the amount in the stockpile at half a billion dollars, or other actions and allegations directed at both the country and its banking system—central to the Swiss economy—the attacks continued to mount, and Switzerland, an intensely independent country that had remained outside the European Union, found itself increasingly isolated in world opinion. The response? A strategic communication campaign.

But the Swiss did not make the mistake that so many countries and other actors do in such circumstances, one perhaps best described as "Ready, Fire, Aim!" In this instance, the government established a new unit within the Federal Department of Foreign Affairs, which it called Presence Switzerland (PRS), headed by a diplomat of ambassadorial rank and staffed with professionals in media analysis, public relations, and branding. This team, in turn, started where all good campaigns should start, with research. PRS designated seven countries as primary targets for influence—its four cross-border neighbors, Germany, Austria, France and Italy, and the three principal world powers, China, Russia and the United States. Within each of these countries, PRS then launched an ongoing, iterative image survey, using both public and elite opinion polling and media analysis, the results of which were used to develop strategy and tactics, both overall and for each target country.

The primary result of this research initially showed that the commitment of the Swiss to their existing core values of direct democracy, modernity, and humanitarianism, while it accorded with the preferences of external audiences, was not widely known or, where known, fully appreciated. Using this information, PRS was able to design maximally advantageous image-management initiatives and, over time, to assess their effectiveness. The agency was also able to identify and respond to country- and time-specific challenges, as, for example, when its surveys identified a spike of anti-Swiss feeling in Great Britain that turned out to have resulted from the perception that Switzerland favored the Conservative Party over Labour at a time when the electorate had ousted the conservatives. This was traced to the fact that the Swiss Embassy had continued to sponsor activities tied to the Conservative Party after the election. The remedy: switch such sponsorship to Labour activities.

Some obvious and fairly straightforward strategies of persuasion follow from this conceptual scheme, all of them focused on the individual's beliefs. These might include efforts to generate a new and salient belief that is added to the right side of the equation, altering the outcome on the left side; altering the strength of a particular belief ("*b*" in the equation) to enhance or lessen its impact on the overall attitude; changing the evaluation of a particular belief ("*e*" in the equation), making it more or less favorable depending on one's persuasive objective; or altering the mix of beliefs judged by the individual to be salient, in effect substituting other existing beliefs for some previously included in forming the attitude, and in the process changing the terms of the equation. Survey and other data developed through campaign research can be used to identify those attitude-critical beliefs that are in play with respect to a given object, as well as other associated beliefs that might be exploited. Campaign communications can then be designed to enhance, minimize or move one or more of these beliefs as needed.

Cognitive dissonance. Developed in the 1950s and most closely associated with the work of Leon Festinger (for example, 1957), this is among the best known theories of persuasion. Cognitive dissonance theory is one member of a family of ideas known as balance theories, so named because they posit that individuals are psychologically most at ease when their beliefs, attitudes and other cognitive elements are consistent, or in balance, with one another, and that they are motivated to restore that consistency should anything occur that disturbs the balance. Dissonance, then, is a condition in which two or more of these cognitive elements are out of balance, and it is, according to the theory, necessarily a temporary condition demanding remedial action by the individual. Nor is this a simple binary condition. Dissonance can vary in magnitude from minimal to extreme, and the greater the dissonance, the greater will be the psychological pressure on the individual to reduce or eliminate it. Dissonance is likely to be greater where the number of dissonant cognitive elements is greater, or where the dissonant elements are particularly salient (important) to the individual. Finally, individuals will opt for the least costly path toward dissonance reduction, which is to say, they will do whatever is easiest to ease their minds. If that means rejecting new information, that is what they will do; if the new information is, for some reason, difficult to reject, their inclination to restore the balance will be channeled in some other direction.

In the world of cognitive dissonance, then, the key to changing an existing cognition, preference, attitude, or even behavior is, first, to induce dissonance, which has the effect of rendering the individual more susceptible to persuasion, then second, providing mechanisms to reduce the newly-induced dissonance in ways that advance the interests of the campaign. The first of these can be accomplished in some circumstances simply by pointing out to people the (nearly inevitable) inconsistencies that already exist among their various beliefs, attitudes, or behaviors. In other circumstances, the persuader might introduce new information in the form of new facts, altered settings, alternative interpretations, withdrawal of apparent social support for the existing cognitions, or revaluation of the importance of the issue or the cognitive elements—all designed to create a measure of dissonance. This is followed up by presenting an opportunity to restore the balance by moving away from the original psychological positioning to a new, somewhat different point that accommodates the new data. That opportunity might take the form of enhanced social support for the new position, personally valued and/or highly credible sourcing for the new information or interpretation, alternative but attractive value or preference structures, and the like. And, because the individuals being subjected to persuasion will generally seek out the path of least resistance that leads toward dissonance reduction, the persuader will want insofar as possible to foreclose all options that lead to dissonance reduction except the one (attitude change, behavior change, etc.) that serves the needs of the campaign. This can be accomplished by making the alternatives relatively more "expensive," as, for example, by denigrating the original sources of information or support.

Of course, not all campaign persuasion is intended to bring about change. Some, and arguably half in an evenly matched two-sided competitive situation, may be designed to *prevent* such change, or stated differently, to generate *resistance* to persuasion. On this side of the battle, the implications of cognitive dissonance theory are equally clear. The persuader must identify, advance, support, and reinforce information and actions that either minimize or prevent the generation of dissonance by the opposing forces, or that lead to a restoration of the *original* cognitive balance once dissonance has occurred. Though the direction of their use is the reverse, the mechanisms by which that can be accomplished are the same as those that might be employed to generate dissonance and channel its reduction to produce change.

Box 4.2 Dissonance Reduction Or Else!

When he was developing the theory of cognitive dissonance in the 1950s, Festinger came across news of a cult in Chicago organized around a woman who claimed to be receiving messages from another planet, Clarion, predicting that, on a particular date, most of North America would be inundated by a great flood. Fortunately, those who joined the woman's sect would be spared—by flying saucers that would pick them up and transport them to safety.

Festinger and his team infiltrated the sect and, for three months, acted as believers. They watched as fellow believers prepared for their fate by quitting their jobs and disposing of their possessions. On the day before the flood, they were told to be at the woman's house at midnight to be rescued, but no flying saucer appeared, and then, of course, no flood ensued.

Fortunately, the group received a message from God at 4:45 the next morning indicating that he had held off the flood because of their strength. That is when dissonance theory kicked in. Rather than avoiding publicity out of embarrassment, as one might expect, members of the sect became publicity seekers and zealous proselytizers, desperate to attract additional believers. Festinger's explanation: If they could find new converts, the dissonance created by the failure of events to match their expectations could be reduced (Crossen, 2006).

In campaigns, unlike controlled psychological experiments, of course, communication settings are relatively complex, and there are many sources and messages competing for the attention of each individual, few of whom are likely, in any event, to be focused on the issues at stake in the campaign or on campaign-initiated communications. This can be a source of opportunity for the strategist, because, as we argued above, inattention and low salience can facilitate persuasion. But it can also be a source of challenge, if only because penetrating the mass of extant communications competing to reach the individual can require great creativity or the expenditure of substantial resources. It is important to realize as well that theories like that of cognitive dissonance are designed to explain or predict the effects of persuasion at the individual level, and presume knowledge of the specific psychological elements at work in the head of a given individual. Depending on its research capabilities, however, a subject we will address later but whose outlines we anticipated earlier, a campaign may very well have data that are far less specific—describing classes or clusters within a prospective communication audience, not the attributes of specific audience members. As a result, the strategist is generally forced to interpolate within these classes or clusters, formulating and placing messages based on assumptions about how individuals in each grouping are most likely to respond.

Social Judgment/Involvement. This approach to persuasion was initially developed in the 1960s and 1970s, and is most closely associated with the work of Carolyn and Muzafer Sherif (see, for instance, 1967). To characterize it, let us return to our geography lesson on cognitive space. This time, picture a point in space representing any given attitude held by an individual. Now, picture surrounding that point a hollow sphere of variable circumference. The sphere is called the "threshold of rejection." [Actually the theory specifies more than one such boundary, but the distinctions are not critical in the present context, so we'll keep it simple.] The theory posits that discrepant information—which means newly arriving affective information that differs from that incorporated in the preexisting attitude—will generate attitude change if, but only if, it is sufficiently similar to the existing affect as to be non-threatening, represented by the distance between the extant attitude and the new information. The threshold of rejection marks the boundary beyond which discrepant information loses its persuasive power. Inside the sphere, the greater the difference between existing and new information, the greater the degree of attitude change that may result. Outside the sphere, the degree of discrepancy is irrelevant; any new information will be rejected because it is too different to merit consideration, and no change will occur. Finally, it is well to keep in mind that any shift in the position of the point of origin will bring an accompanying movement in the surrounding sphere within which persuasion is possible.

Clearly, then, if a would-be persuader seeks to employ this dynamic for change, she must have a good general idea of just how far from the point of origin for a given attitude and individual the threshold of rejection lies. And that gets us to the central concept underlying this approach. The theory holds that the threshold of rejection will move closer to, or further from, the point of origin depending on the degree to which the individual identifies with, or feels a sense of personal commitment to, the attitude in question. The greater the level of personal involvement, the closer in the sphere will be drawn, and the less susceptible the individual will be to persuasion. Conversely, the lower the level of involvement, the further out the sphere will extend, allowing much more room for persuasion-induced attitude change.

If we think about it, this makes perfect sense. On the issues that people care the most about, they will be relatively difficult to persuade. On those they care little about, they will be easier to persuade. What it suggests to the strategist—and again, we leave the controlled setting of the social psychologist's laboratory and return to the real world of field research and estimates, but also the one-off experiment for the longer-term campaign—is that one key to developing an effective strategy is gauging the degree of personal salience that members of a target audience attach to an issue. Where salience is high, one of two general strategies is available: move the point of origin, or move the threshold of rejection. Taking the first approach, because the persuasive impact of any given message is likely to be limited in this circumstance, substantial change will only be achieved, if at all, through a multi-stage effort to generate numerous small incremental movements. Baby steps. Over time, such modest incremental changes can accumulate into something more substantial, but it is a long and slow process. Given that expectation, the second approach may be more attractive. Here, rather than addressing one's persuasive effort at the attitude in question, the strategist focuses on the nature and origins of the underlying personal attachment to it. In some circumstances, it may be possible to erode that attachment without directly addressing the attitude, or in effect, to move the threshold of rejection further away, expanding the sphere of potentially acceptable discrepant information and, thus, facilitating persuasion. Where salience is low, the same strategies can be applied, but they will be easier to implement and proportionately more likely to succeed.

Elaboration Likelihood Model. The ELM, as it is generally known, is of more recent origin than the previous approaches, having been developed in the 1980s, principally by Richard Petty and John Cacioppo (1986). It focuses on the processing of potentially persuasive information, which it sees as occurring along one of two possible tracks that differ with respect to whether or not the individual to be persuaded actively thinks about the issue in question. The first track, or condition, termed "high elaboration," characterizes a process in which the individual engages with the issue through such mechanisms as attending closely to related communications, actively comparing this new messaging with previously stored information, and thinking through the arguments being proffered. It is very much akin to the process assumed to occur in the argumentation-based approach to persuasion we discussed in the preceding chapter. The second, termed "low elaboration," refers to situations in which the individual looks for cognitive shortcuts—cues or connections that allow processing of incoming information without much conscious effort. Here we can see parallels to Herbert Krugman's notion of low-involvement learning, which we also described in Chapter 3. Within each level of elaboration, the ELM allows for variations in the nature or degree of active engagement in information processing. One might thus argue that there is a continuum of sorts ranging from the most highly engaged persuasion to that which is the least engaged.

Paralleling the two general conditions, and also paralleling the *de facto* continuum between the extremes of each, the ELM suggests that there are two different paths to persuasion. One, termed the "central route," is built around more or less intense engagement and argumentation. It achieves persuasion by facilitating the individual's thinking thoroughly through the issue and the alternatives and coming to appreciate the persuader's position. The second, termed the "peripheral route," relies not on reason *per se*, but on packaging—attractiveness of the message or the medium, use of evocative symbols, use of an attractive or credible source, and so forth. The challenge to the strategist in this view, then, is to determine the degree of elaboration being employed by those he would persuade, then devising the most effective mixture of substantive arguments and peripheral cues. These could be enhanced or facilitated through the selection of channels, taking into account the differential degree of engagement experienced by users of different channels, per our discussion in Chapter 3.

Functional Approach. Finally, we should consider a somewhat different question: What is it that a given attitude actually does for the individual who holds it? Here we are guided by a so-called functional theory of attitudes and persuasion developed by Daniel Katz (1960). This approach focuses, not on cognitive structures, as was the case in each of the earlier formulations, but rather on the role attitudes play in establishing and maintaining the psychological well-being of the individual. In his initial formulation, Katz identified four basic functions performed by attitudes, which he labeled utilitarian, ego-defensive, value-expressive and knowledge. Utilitarian attitudes are those the holding of which maximizes one's sense of being rewarded and minimizes one's sense of being punished. If an individual finds her interactions with a given object pleasant, she will develop a positive attitude toward that object, the *function* of which is to *re*flect, and thus enhance, the interactive experience. Conversely, where her interactions are unpleasant, she will develop a negative attitude that *de*flects, and thus reduces, the unpleasantness. Ego-defensive attitudes are those that one holds in order to protect his self-image. These attitudes are often about other people or groups—colleagues, friends, competitors, those who differ from the individual in terms of demographics or ideology, and so forth—though they can also apply to governmental or other institutions, or to issue positions, that one perceives as threatening. The basic idea is that, by holding relatively negative attitudes about objects that are somehow threatening, the individual reinforces his own sense of self-worth. Value-expressive attitudes are those that are used by the individual to project her underlying values on objects in the outside world. That is to say, being the type of person that she perceives herself to be, it seems only natural that she would have a particular attitude toward a given issue, actor, or some other object. So she does. Finally, in fulfilling the knowledge function, attitudes can help the individual to organize his understanding of complex events or situations. If, for example, one holds judgments about various of the participants in a policy debate—some favorable, some unfavorable—and the debate itself is highly abstract or complex, his attitudes toward the participants can be used as a shorthand way of interpreting and evaluating the array of policy options based on the positions assumed by his perceived friends and enemies.

Once we adopt a functionalist perspective, it is not difficult to think of additional roles that attitudes might play beyond those posited by Katz, and, in fact, as this approach has experienced a bit of a revival in recent years, other scholars have suggested some alternatives (see, for example, Maio and Olson, 2000a). For the moment, however, let us consider more generally the implications of this general approach for the development of a communication strategy. The necessary first step toward accomplishing such a strategy is to determine what the campaign-relevant attitudes held by an individual are, and what function(s) they serve, or put another way, why the individual holds them. From that point, divergent strategies may be available depending on the persuasion objectives of the campaign. One alternative, designed to maintain the existing attitude, may be to reinforce a functional connection with messages that explicitly validate it. Or one may seek to change the attitude by challenging the functional connection in the hope of invalidating it. A third alternative is to exploit a given function by attaching the campaign or its objective to an existing attitude, in effect broadening the application of the attitude in question in ways that serve the campaign. Or, conversely, one can seek to establish a border between the attitude and the campaign or its objective, the persuasive message being that the individual may have a valid attitude toward some set of objects, but those objects are not relevant to the campaign.

Box 4.3 Elements of Information Operations

In recent years, the US Department of Defense, among other government agencies, has paid increasing attention to psychological operations (PSYOP) and information operations (IO) as components of its operations. The following excerpt from DOD's IO doctrine suggests the elements of this effort as they apply to persuasive communications.

> (2) The focus of IO is on the decision maker and the information environment in order to affect decision making and thinking processes, knowledge, and understanding of the situation. **IO can affect data, information, and knowledge in three basic ways**:
>
> (a) By taking specific psychological, electronic, or physical actions that add, modify, or remove information from the environment of various individuals or groups of decision makers.
> (b) By taking actions to affect the infrastructure that collects, communicates, processes, and/or stores information in support of targeted decision makers.
> (c) By influencing the way people receive, process, interpret, and use data, information, and knowledge. (United States Joint Staff, 2006: I-9)

So How Does A Persuade B?

While these five approaches represent the leading schools of thought with respect to persuasion, they by no means exhaust the possibilities. But even limiting ourselves to five approaches, and even ignoring, as we have, subtle variants of and within each, it is clear that there exists no simple answer to the question, How does A best go about persuading B? The answer in any given circumstance surely entails an element of science, but it entails as well an element of creative insight. One or more of these approaches may be of value, and once identified can point toward specific strategies and tactics, but knowing which one to use in a given situation is an art form, and the skilled strategist an artist. For our purposes, it may be most productive, then, to focus less on answers than on questions. To what questions should a strategist seek answers in formulating a persuasive strategy? Here are some possibilities.

- *Questions about the target's existing cognitive state.* What is the nature and distribution of existing attitudes, predispositions, preferences, perceptions, beliefs, needs, and expectations? How much has the target of persuasion thought about the attitude in question; how personally engaged is she with that attitude? How salient is the campaign or its objectives? How open is the target to persuasion? To what degree are the target's emotions in play? What are the cultural or linguistic hurdles in play in the situation? How great is the discrepancy between the target's existing beliefs and the new information? What motivates the target? Will the persuasion be beneficial to the target—or readily capable of being portrayed as such?
- *Questions about the target's general availability for persuasion.* Is the target actively seeking change? Direction or guidance? Has the target been previously persuaded by a similar persuader or information? Is the target aware of the persuasion attempt? What does the target think of the persuader?
- *Questions about the target's access to channels.* What channels does the target use in information seeking? What channels are available to the persuader? To what extent can the campaign control the channels it employs for persuasion? What are the target's social/demographic characteristics?
- *Questions about the setting in which persuasion will be attempted.* How many opportunities will likely be available to engage in persuasion? Is there a counter-persuasion effort in play? What are the target's expectations, if any, regarding the persuasive situation? To what extent can the campaign control the persuasion setting?
- *Questions about the source of any persuasive messages.* Which sources are judged as authoritative or credible (or likeable)? What attributes or behaviors might enhance the legitimacy of the persuader? What affinity, or points of similarity of self or circumstance, can the persuader establish with the target?

- *Questions about message content and objectives.* Is the campaign seeking immediate change? Slow change? Temporary change? Lasting change? Is the persuader willing to settle for partial persuasion? How complex is the information? How easily understood? Is the information accurate, credible? What cues should be embedded in the message? Should the message be explicit or implicit? Should the message be primarily logical or primarily emotional?

These questions, and others like them, suggest the range of determinations and decisions that can be incorporated into an effective strategy of campaign-related communication. It is most unlikely that any single campaign would have the answers to, or would be positioned to employ to advantage, the full compendium of potentially useful information. But if we set that as a standard, it is surely the case that the strategist is best advantaged by gathering and applying the most comprehensive information available.

The next logical question, of course, is what to do with it. One set of answers is found in Chapter 3, in our discussion of channel selection and control, agenda setting, framing, and related processes. When viewed in this new context, many of these techniques can be employed to shape and place messages for maximum persuasive effect. A second set of answers can be found in discussions of alternative persuasive tactics relating to such factors as:

- the specificity of recommended actions (there is some evidence that greater specificity is more persuasive),
- the inclusion or omission of the conclusion to an argument (inclusion—effectively doing the "work" for the audience of figuring out the point of a message—appears to be the more effective strategy),
- the use of one-sided versus two-sided messages (presenting "both sides" of an issue but refuting one appears to be more effective than providing both sides without refutation, with the effectiveness of one-sided messages falling between the two),
- the use of examples (less complete, but more effective) versus statistical arguments (more complete, but less effective),
- making incremental small requests that are likely of acceptance versus making a large opening demand whose rejection creates opportunities for lesser persuasion (moderate discrepancy seems to be the most effective in general, but this would seem to depend greatly on such factors as issue salience or personal involvement),
- fear appeals (the stronger the appeal and the greater the fear it generates, the more persuasion seems to occur),

and others that have been examined by scholars, but on which we will not focus further attention here. (O'Keefe, 2002) What both approaches have in common is the light they cast on how the content and presentation of persuasive messages can be managed so as best to achieve the persuasion objectives of the campaign in its dealing with individuals, either alone or in collectivities.

The Interaction of Agendas

A third, and rather more structural, way of thinking about this same relationship between information content and potential persuasive effects comes from a theoretical construct developed by the author some years ago (Manheim, 1987), termed agenda dynamics. The basic idea of agenda dynamics as it applies here is that the information that is directed at a target during a would-be persuasive episode has a certain dimensionality to it. That is to say, we can conceive of a space—rather akin to the notion of cognitive space—that represents the content of information being transferred directly, through the mass media, through internet communications, or by any other means to the target. The dimensioning of this space would be along axes that represent characteristics of that content. For example, based on our discussions to this point, it is reasonable to expect that the sheer volume (visibility) of the communication would be important, as would the degree to which it is favorable or unfavorable (valence) toward a given object. Similarly, the communication might include a great many cues that suggest that the information in question is important, or salient, to the target, very few such cues or none at all. Such a space is represented in Figure 4.1(a). The content of a

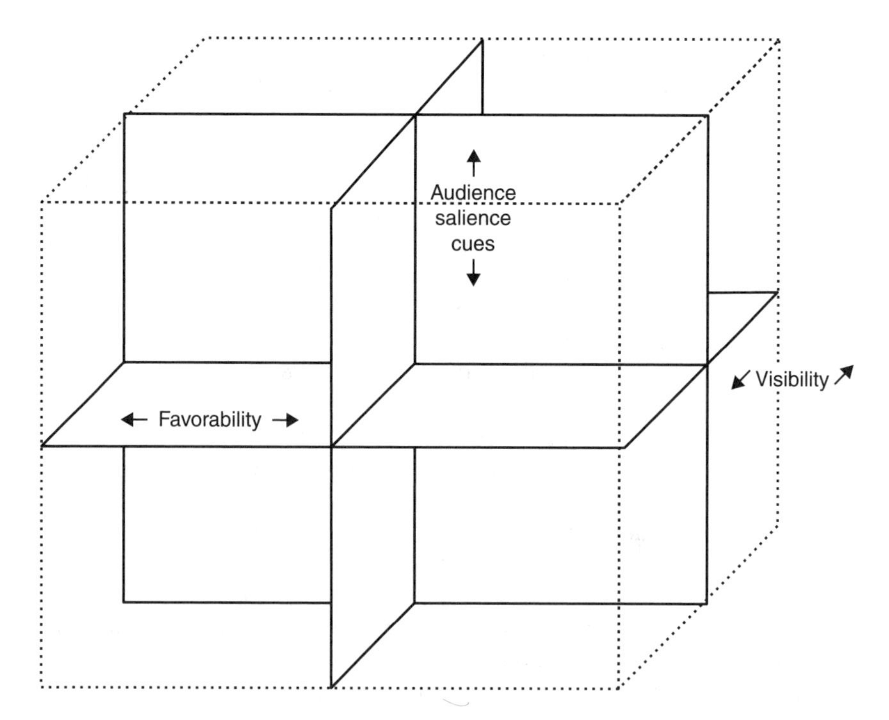

Figure 4.1(a) Dimensions of Information Space.

given message or cluster of messages might be high or low on each dimension, with the combination of the three resulting in the "placement" of that communication in a particular location within the space. This placement, and movement of the message(s) within the space over time, can potentially be managed by the strategist.

Similarly—and this draws even more directly on the idea of cognitive space—we can think of certain important characteristics of the target's preexisting mental state vis-à-vis the object about which we are communicating (a policy or policy outcome, an individual, a company, a country, a political movement, etc.). For example, she may be more or less aware of the object in question, and more or less favorably inclined toward it, at the outset of the persuasive attempt. Similarly, she may see this object as more or less central to her own interests or well-being, which is to say, as more or less personally salient. These dimensions are represented in Figure 4.1(b). Again, a given object will score high or low on each individual dimension, thereby generating a position within the indicated three-dimensional space.

Agenda dynamics suggests that the combination of attributes—visibility, valence and salience—incorporated in a given series of persuasive messages through framing and other mechanisms will interact with the psychological attributes that characterize the prior positioning of the

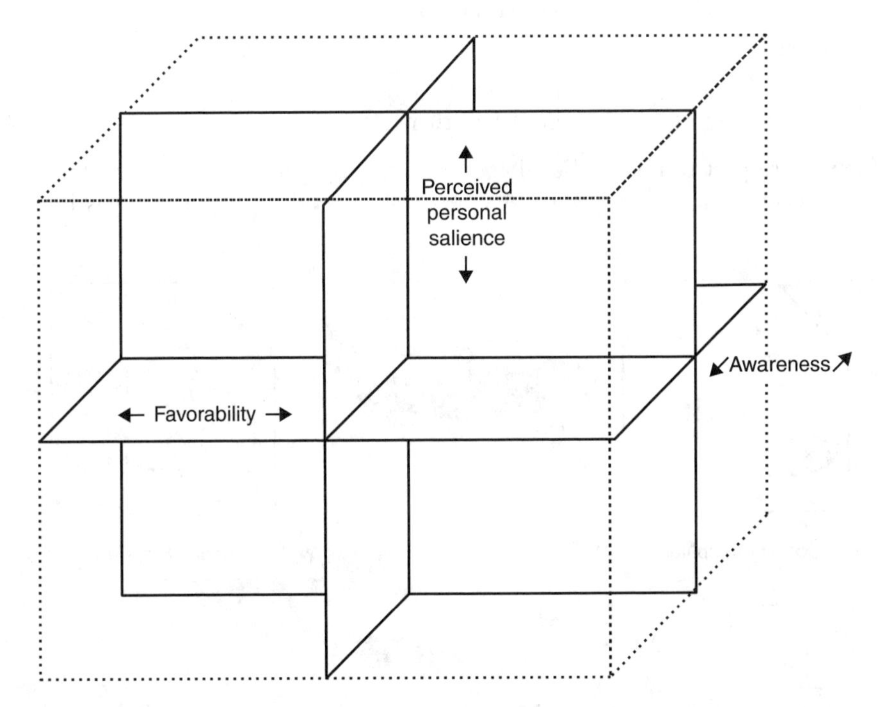

Figure 4.1(b) Dimensions of Cognitive Space.

targeted individual in ways that are likely to affect the outcome of the persuasive effort. That is to say, messages of greater number, frequency, or length can be expected to raise awareness (akin to agenda setting); those that consistently support a particular viewpoint or valence may guide or reinforce similar judgments by the individual; and those that indicate the salience (or the irrelevance, in alternative persuasive circumstances) of a given issue or other object may be associated with a greater internalization of this salience by the individual. None of these is seen as deterministic—producing lockstep movements—and all are subject to other factors, such as source credibility, effective channeling and the like. Nevertheless, to the extent that such structural interactions do occur, the strategist will find evident benefit in moving to influence systematically the "location" of any persuasive messages in information space and, depending on the approach(es) to attitude change being employed in the campaign, may also want to manage the "movement" of this placement through time, thereby creating a structurally dynamic change strategy. Such a strategy might be employed, for example, if one were using the social-judgment/involvement model, in which perceived salience can be equated with the distance between the extant attitude and the threshold of rejection, and where incremental change is the objective. This duality of movement, within each space and between them, is represented in Figure 4.2. The return, or feedback, exchange in the figure represents the role that research or other information about the target plays in influencing the shaping of persuasive messages.

Campaigns as Sociological Phenomena

With respect to informational content, campaigns represent either efforts to generate support for new ideas or efforts to modify support for existing

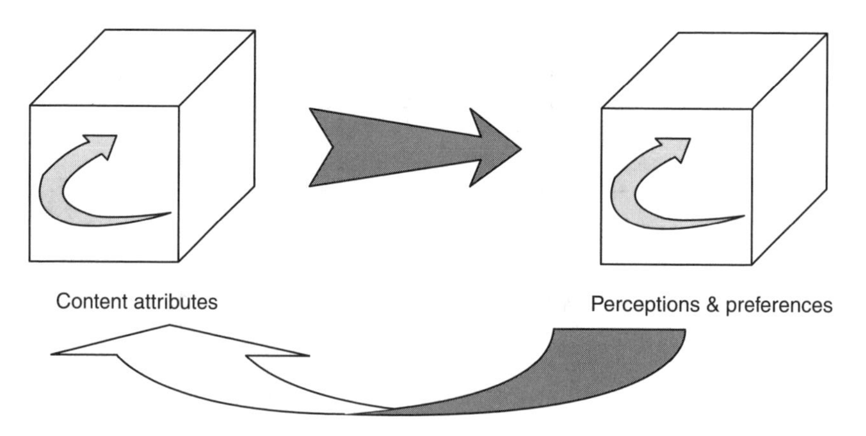

Figure 4.2 Content–Cognitive Interactions.

ideas, usually with an eye toward converting the result into behavioral change of some sort. In our discussion to this point, we have tended to view this as an individual-centered phenomenon. But in fact, to the extent they focus on or employ individuals as elements of strategy, campaigns are frequently more concerned with aggregate-level effects—with influencing, mobilizing or otherwise affecting large numbers of individuals who share a social or political space and interact with one another. It follows that the sociology that operates in that space can be every bit as important as the psychology, and sometimes more so.

Back in the 1960s, sociologist Everett Rogers (1962) pointed out that some people are more open to innovative ideas than others. Some are real risk-takers when it comes to acting on new information; some, though more small-c conservative in such matters, are nevertheless relatively open to changing their ways once the benefits of doing so have been demonstrated; and still others are more resistant to change, or even all but immovable. The distribution of such attributes, he found, more or less closely resembled a normal curve. Now, when we layer upon this foundation the complex variations across individuals that we have just described in terms of the nature and strength of their existing perceptions and preferences, their exposure to discrepant or conforming information, the campaign setting, the available channels of communication, and the like, the challenge to the campaign strategist—to bring about a desired change—is self-evidently complex.

And yet, just as certain components of this socio-political fabric would seem to constitute natural impediments to change, others can be seen as natural facilitators. People, after all, do not generally function in isolation. Rather, they function among networks of friends and acquaintances and within the context of social, economic and political groups and institutions that bring them into contact with one another. The more interconnected they are, it would seem, the more opportunities will exist for naturally occurring exchanges of information, preferences, and models of behavior among them—or for a campaign to stimulate such exchanges artificially. In other words, the natural tendency of its members toward interpersonal connection and exchange is an inherent facilitator of potential campaign diffusion through a given population. The more open each member of such a population is to influence, and the more aligned or common the other influences to which each is exposed, the more efficient this mechanism can be as a transmission line for the campaign. Campaign-generated change can literally cascade through social space.

In truth, things are not quite that simple. Social network theorists tell us, for example, that the density of a given network—essentially the extent of interconnection among the members—has a complex effect on the spread of innovation. At one extreme, where density is very low—where each member is connected, for instance, with only one other member—change can be introduced into the network, but the momentum behind it will soon be lost for lack of reinforcement. And at the other extreme, where density is very high—where each member is connected to, and tries to anticipate the preferences of many other members in forming its own—the reinforcement of multiple interconnectivity actually tends to preserve the status quo. But in the middle ranges of network density, there exists the potential for a more or less rapid adoption and development of social support for new views or behaviors advanced by the campaign. The nature and degree of social interconnectedness in the targeted population or subgroups, then, can be an important strategic factor in campaign development.

Though we have devoted two full chapters to strategic considerations in influencing individuals, their attitudes, preferences and behaviors, in many IICs individuals play a limited role, if any. Rather, the emphasis is on generating movement, change, action, or inaction on the part of organized groups, formal organizations, institutions, or even governments. In Chapter 5, we will turn our attention to information and influence at these higher levels of aggregation.

5 Networks and Netwaves: Organizing for Influence

> But even if it is true that everyone can be connected to everyone in only six degrees of separation, so what? How far is six degrees anyway? . . . As far as extracting resources is concerned, or exerting influence, anything more than two degrees might as well be a thousand.
>
> Duncan J. Watts (2003: 299–300)

> The most successful movements simultaneously seek information about their [potential supporters] while managing facts about themselves. On the one hand, if a movement understands a potential supporter's key interests and concerns, its proficiency at tapping and persuading the target will grow. On the other hand, if a movement limits undesired news about itself—from opponents, the media, or even loose-lipped members—while producing positive and credible data, it will enjoy greater appeal.
>
> Clifford Bob (2005: 52)

> . . . The term *netwar* refers to an emerging mode of conflict (and crime) at societal levels, involving measures short of traditional war, in which the protagonists use network forms of organization and related doctrines, strategies, and technologies attuned to the information age. These protagonists are likely to consist of dispersed small groups who communicate, coordinate, and conduct their campaigns in an internetted manner, without a precise central command.
>
> David Ronfeldt et al. (1998: 9)

In Chapters 3 and 4, we focused on strategic approaches to persuading individuals to change their minds, to act on their preferences, or to change their behaviors. In electoral campaigns, whether for candidates or ballot issues, this may well be the single greatest success-critical aspect of a campaign. For in electoral campaigns, organizations and institutions—interest groups, political parties, media organizations—generally act upon individuals, and it is, collectively, individual behavior that determines the effectiveness of the campaign and, in some measure, the outcome of the election. Similarly, in some campaigns directed against corporations, the effective manipulation of consumer purchasing behavior, as through a boycott, may have a direct impact. But in many other types of information and influence campaigns, the dynamic is actually the reverse. To the extent that they are brought into the campaign at all—and that is not a given—individuals may, to a greater or lesser extent, act upon organizations, and it is the behavior of those organizations that is potentially determinative. Consumers who may be induced to boycott a merchant, for example, where that merchant is not the actual target of the campaign but is intended to become a pressure point against another company that is one of its suppliers or clients, have at best an indirect effect on the ultimate target. Indeed, they may be entirely unaware of the objectives being served by the pressures they generate. In this chapter, we will turn our attention to the organizational and institutional actors that play more central roles in this broader class of campaigns, and to the strategies that can employ them to advantage.

In an election campaign, the objective of the winner is usually to gain control of some agency of power—a government, a corporate board of directors, a membership organization—and to *become* the decision-maker. But in many other campaigns, the objective is, rather, to *influence* the extant decision-maker(s) without taking control of them, and without taking actual responsibility for their policies and actions. This is at once a narrower objective and a broader one. It is narrower in the sense that the goal is to affect only a small number of specific decisions, and perhaps only one. It is broader in the sense that, to accomplish this, the campaigner may find advantage in, or may be forced into, generating pressure from a wide variety of internal and external sources. Together these observations provide our starting point for the present discussion.

Dynamics of the Target's Decision-Making

Leaving aside all the particulars of a given campaign, what is usually at stake in these broad-spectrum IICs is a set of outcomes determined by actions of the decision-makers atop a given targeted social structure. The structure could be a government, a corporation, an advocacy organization, a religious hierarchy, or any other similar organization. The outcomes in question may take the form of public policy, organizational policy, or any of a wide range of organizational or institutional behaviors. That being the case, it is constructive to begin from some understanding of how such decisions are made. To an author who values parsimony, that is a dangerous statement, for it is an open invitation to explore the many dark corners of organization theory, management theory, and public administration. Let us resist the temptation. Since our real objective here is to understand how campaigns can impact these processes, let us instead employ a single, and admittedly narrow, conceptualization of target decision-making—one that opens directly upon the kinds of pressures that campaigns are capable of generating.

Building on the approach that we employed in Chapter 4, let us imagine a three-dimensional space that characterizes the positioning of target decision-makers at any given point in time. This is accomplished in Figure 5.1.

The figure specifies three dimensions of the target's decision-making: preferences, likelihood of action, and freedom of action. Preferences represent the substantive content of the policy or action in question, or in the context of the campaign, its consistency of direction with, and degree of closeness to, the outcome preferred by the protagonist. Likelihood of action is, not surprisingly, an indication of the extent to which the target is inclined to act on its underlying preferences, possibly influenced by constraints or incentives. Freedom of action refers to the range of motion, or the degrees of freedom, available to the target should it choose to act. This dimension, too, is subject to influence by constraints or incentives that might expand or contract that range. The assertion here is that we can locate any given policy or behavior within this space at a point in time, which is to say, we can specify its content relative to the protagonist's preferences, the likelihood it will be implemented or converted into actions, and the extent of any constraints operating on the decision-makers in choosing among various alternative actions. And, having done that, we can construct a strategy for moving it within this space to a point that is likely

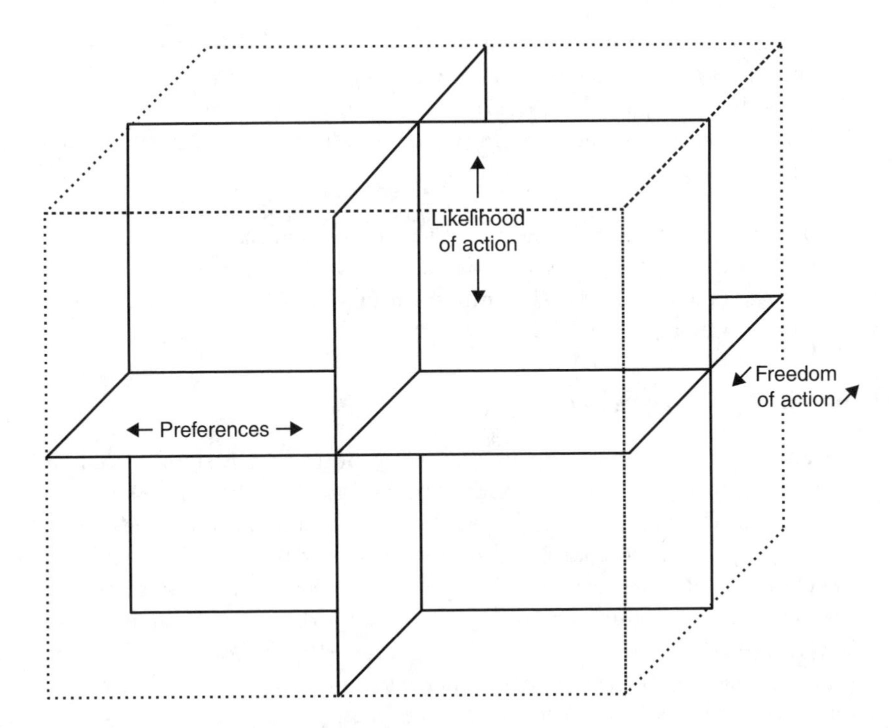

Figure 5.1 Dimensions of Target Decision-Making Space.

to produce a more desirable outcome for the campaign, i.e., for generating a *change* in the policy or behavior of the target. We can accomplish this by altering the preferences of the decision-makers, by adding incentives that encourage them to act or disincentives that discourage action (depending on the objectives of the campaign), and by so structuring the campaign setting that they are either more, or less, constrained to act. The first of these can be accomplished by processes akin to persuasion; the second by adding, modifying, or eliminating points of pressure, including the generation or defusing of a "crisis"; and the third by imposing or reducing transparency in the decision-making process, increasing or limiting attention to the issue, and the like. Such efforts might, for example, produce an outcome that is more favorable, more likely, and more focused on the objectives of the campaign than would otherwise be the case.

In general, then, conceptualizing the target in this way suggests that an effective campaign will be one that is designed less to persuade any actor of the desirability of the outcome sought than it is to move the issue to the optimal location in this (or some analogous) decision-making space, which is to say, to so manage the political process that the desired outcome becomes more or less unavoidable. It also suggests the full range of prospective objectives of a campaign with respect to the target. These might include:

1 initiating a behavior;
2 modifying or reinforcing a behavioral dynamic (an ongoing behavior);
3 modifying or reinforcing a static position or condition of the target;
4 ceasing an ongoing behavior or withdrawing a position; or
5 not initiating a behavior in which the target has yet to engage (reinforcing *in*action),

—each in some manner that advances the interests of the protagonist. The question before us is that of how and through what mechanisms—including, but not limited to communications—such objectives can best be accomplished.

Power Structure Analysis

To answer that question, let us pick up a notion we first presented in Chapter 2, that of stakeholder relationships. In that earlier discussion, we argued that IICs were a manifestation of an imbalance of power between a given campaign protagonist and its target—a set of actions designed to generate and exercise leverage through intermediaries that was somehow greater than that which could be exercised by the protagonist directly. Specifically, the strategic objective is to bring to the support of the protagonist the energies and resources of other actors on whose support the target depends in some measure, and to convert these third parties into *de facto* agents of the campaign or, if you will, force multipliers.

Those who engage in IICs often refer to the identification of these key stakeholders as "power structure analysis." Power structure analysis includes as well an assessment of the nature of each such relationship, the self-interests of each stakeholder that it sees as being advanced by its association with the target, and the strengths and weaknesses of each relationship. The results of this analysis, when arrayed against the capabilities and resources of the protagonist and its assessment of the opportunities extant in the campaign environment, constitute the basis for formulating an order of attack against the target. The campaign itself then takes the form of systematic efforts to "manage" these relationships to the advantage of the protagonist. Figure 5.2 illustrates the elements of power structure analysis.

Figures 5.3(a) through 5.3(c) suggest just three of the potential applications of this general strategic view. In each instance—where the target is a government regulatory agency, a corporation, and an advocacy group, respectively—the central idea remains the same even as the actors assume different roles.

Per Figure 5.3(a), the regulatory agency, as is typical of governmental organizations, depends on policy proposals from advocacy groups, on support from the public, and on a willingness by affected companies to comply with regulations it may issue—just a very few of the stakeholder relationships it must balance.

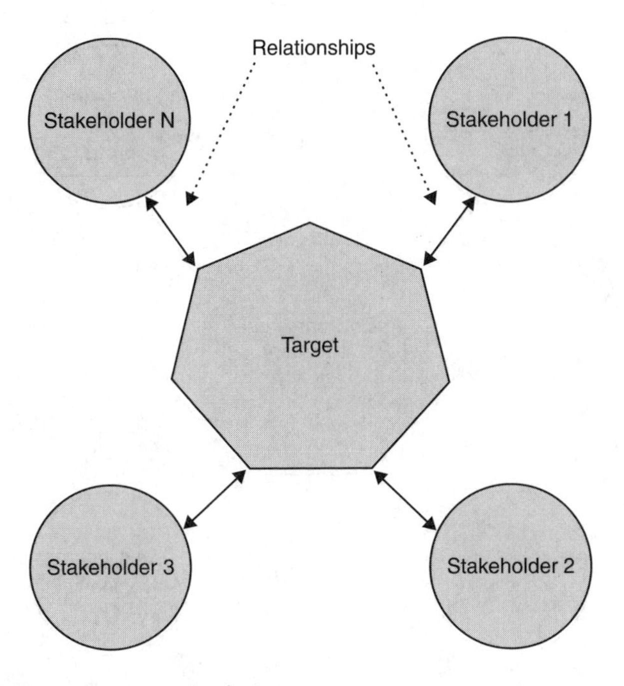

Figure 5.2 Power Structure Analysis.

Box 5.1 Google This!

In January 2010, Google announced that it had been the target of hackers—presumed to be agents of the Chinese government—who were trying to access the company's proprietary software codes and to harass pro-democracy activists in China and their supporters abroad. Other companies reported similar experiences in the same time period. The mechanism was an email with a click-through link that was aimed at individuals in each target firm who had access to the information of interest. When clicked, the link embedded a program used by the hackers.

What made these emails particularly interesting in the present context is that they were not sent directly to the individuals targeted within each firm. Rather, they were sent to "friends" of the actual targets who, prior reconnaissance had shown, were linked to them in social networks. The idea was that the targeted individuals would be more likely to click on links in emails they received from their friends than from unknown sources. In effect, the hackers were using the networked relationships of the targets to lower their resistance. They identified a relationship-based vulnerability, and they exploited it. It worked (Menn 2010a, 2010b).

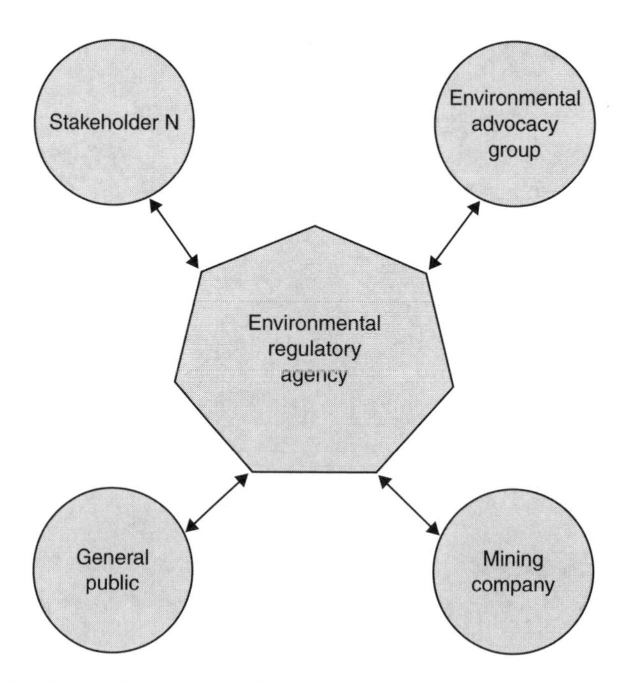

Figure 5.3(a) Power Structure Analysis: Environmental Regulatory Agency.

Similarly, as per Figure 5.3(b), a company must manage demands from advocacy groups, must comply with government regulations (or accept the costs associated with non-compliance), and must maintain the support of its shareholders—again among many other complementary and competing relationships. Interestingly, about a decade after the development of power structure analysis by activists, R. Edward Freeman (1984) wrote an exceptionally influential book in which he employed a precisely parallel analysis of stakeholder relationships as the basis for what was then a new approach to management decision-making in corporations. The difference was one of emphasis—Freeman's argument centered on ways to establish and use these relationships, not to pressure a firm, but to strengthen it and assure its success in the marketplace. That use of alternative lenses notwithstanding, however, for our purposes we can be confident that, at least in one subset of IIC activity, those on both sides understand the game in similar ways.

Finally, per Figure 5.3(c), even an advocacy group can be characterized as the nexus of diverse stakeholder interests, in this case, its members, others who may provide it with financial support, and government agencies or other actors with which it seeks to maintain a position of influence in return for which it must provide information, ideas, or other forms of support.

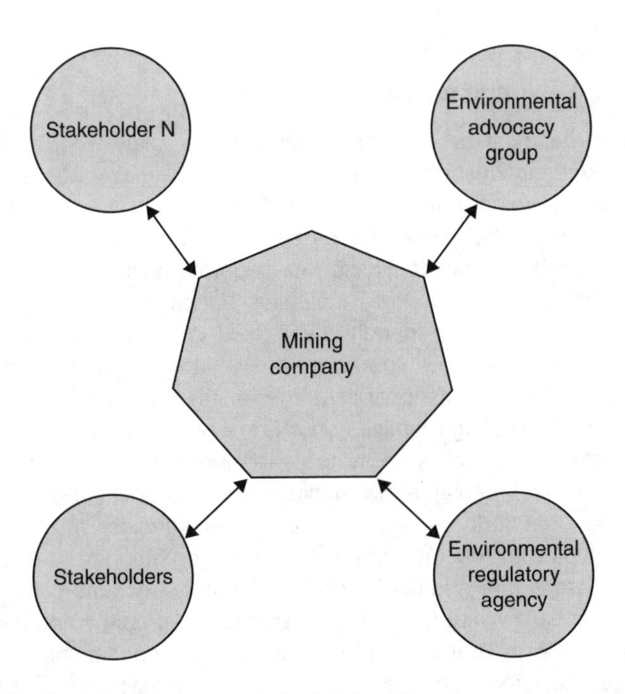

Figure 5.3(b) Power Structure Analysis: Mining Company.

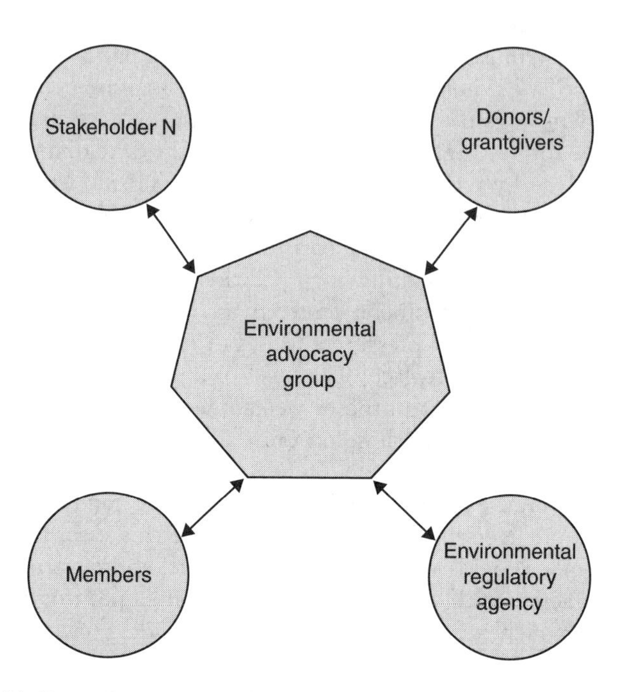

Figure 5.3(c) Power Structure Analysis: Environmental Advocacy Group.

Box 5.2 Leverage for the Environment

Perhaps the most detailed and sophisticated analysis of a target's stakeholder relationships and points of vulnerability ever published is a spiral-bound volume from the World Resources Institute (Ganzi, Seymour, and Buffet, 1998) that parsed the financial services industry. The authors began by identifying four separate types of leverage that environmentalists might use, including bottom-line leverage, or a demonstration that eco-friendly investment can improve profitability; policy leverage, or the vulnerability of the industry to tax and other policy pressures; reputational leverage, or the impact of pro- or anti-environment investing practices on a firm's public image; and values-based leverage, which exploits the willingness of some investors to promote environmental stewardship even if it costs them money. They then set forth an analysis linking stakeholder interests and relationships with resource flows, differentiating among the dynamics of eight separate segments of the industry—commercial banks, investment banks, mutual funds, pension funds, property and casualty insurance, life insurance, venture capital, and foundations. In each instance, the authors provide maps to guide efforts at influence in which they specify particular points of access, issue frame considerations, and the like. In a concluding section, they return to the theme of alternative forms of leverage, and use their analyses of each segment as a basis for weighing the relative utility of each. The volume concludes with a graphic comparison of the eight industry segments on four key attributes—availability of information, risk aversion, time horizon, and regulation. These graphic comparisons provide a quick visual indication of the vulnerabilities and strategies that might be most in play in campaigns directed at each part of the industry, respectively.

Power structure analysts examine each of these relationships, seeking ways to maximize the ability of the campaign protagonist to influence its target by mobilizing other, more influential actors. Writing in a different context, three management scientists, Ronald E. Mitchell, Bradley R. Agle, and Donna J. Wood (1997) have provided important insights into how a strategist might prioritize the stakeholders the campaign hopes to engage. They suggest that three stakeholder attributes in particular—power, legitimacy, and urgency—hold the key. Every stakeholder can be characterized as possessing one or more of these attributes in varying—and variable—degrees. As the attributes increase in degree, and as they overlap and reinforce one another, the stakeholder in question increases in its salience to the target.

As illustrated in Figure 5.4, Mitchell and his colleagues identified eight classes of stakeholders derived from this analysis. They include:

- the dormant stakeholder, who holds but does not exercise power with respect to the target;
- the demanding stakeholder, driven by urgency, but lacking a basis for influence;
- the discretionary stakeholder, who has an accepted voice and likely access, but is not necessarily motivated to put them to use;
- the dominant stakeholder, powerful and legitimate, but acting in an unharried manner in the full measure of time;
- the dangerous stakeholder, powerful and driven, but lacking in legitimacy;
- the dependent stakeholder, legitimized and in need, but lacking in power;
- the definitive stakeholder, in whom reside power, legitimacy, and motivation; and
- the non-stakeholder, or outsider, in effect the null case, lacking in any meaningful access to the target.

Armed with this type of information, the strategist can make a rational and highly sophisticated judgment as to which stakeholder(s) to attempt

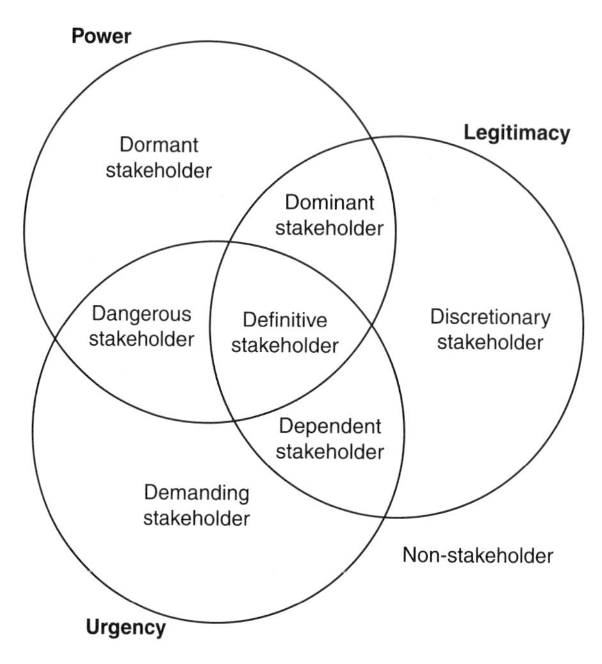

Figure 5.4 Classes of Stakeholders, by Key Attributes.

to mobilize, using what general types of appeal, and to what optimal ends, all based on an extant set of attributes and relationships. For example, one might encourage engagement on the part of a dangerous stakeholder, or pressure a dominant shareholder to disengage. More than that, the strategist might seek to impart a sense of urgency to those lacking it or reduce it for those least likely to advance the interests of the campaign; to enhance the legitimacy of those for whom it is low or, in the alternative, challenge the legitimacy of those for whom it is high, again depending on the interests of the campaign; to empower a dependent stakeholder; and more generally to introduce a dynamic element into the distribution and exploitation of stakeholder attributes.

Whether explicitly or implicitly, virtually all IICs employ this general strategy of power structure analysis. Indeed, one might well argue that this strategic approach is their defining characteristic. And it has two seemingly contradictory implications. One: Every IIC is identical. Two: Every IIC is unique. Because every (or virtually every) IIC employs the same overall strategy, these campaigns are readily characterized, compared, and predictable. But this common strategy produces differing specifics in every campaign that arise from inevitable idiosyncrasies of the protagonist, the target, and the campaign environment.

Taking the first of these two points, it is the common origin in power structure analysis that generates the underlying regularities of the campaigns. These include the reliance on motivating and mobilizing third parties with direct influence on the target, the generation and channeling of messages designed to achieve this motivation and mobilization in terms of stakeholder self interest (as distinct from messages designed to persuade stakeholders to adopt the interests of the protagonist *per se*), the framing of campaign objectives (where public) so as to define the moral high-ground position and assign it to the protagonist, the building of the alliances required to enhance the protagonist's power and legitimize its actions in the eyes of key target stakeholders and to extend its reach, the pursuit of information and research to support all of the aforementioned functions, and the marshalling of the organizational and financial resources (including training and fund-raising) required to facilitate the campaign.

Campaigns as Relationship Management

The dynamic of the campaign, then, is one in which the protagonist develops or employs a series of relationships of its own through which it acts upon key stakeholders of the target, with the objective of pressuring or encouraging them to act, selectively, in their own self-interest in ways that advance the objectives of the protagonist by causing behavioral change in the target.

Box 5.3 Personalization, Pejoratives, Power

In 2009 and 2010, a coalition of progressive political groups including, among others, America's Voice and Media Matters, wanted to influence the debate over reforming immigration policy, but were disadvantaged because they were relatively small, lightly resourced, and not especially influential on Capitol Hill. So they hired Chong + Koster, a communications firm specializing in digital media, to increase their leverage.

The firm adopted a strategy with three key components. First, it determined that by latching onto a prominent celebrity associated with the issue—in this case CNN's Lou Dobbs, a leader of the *opposing* side—the coalition could focus its energies in such a way as to gain visibility and the clout that would accompany it. The consultants felt there was an opportunity to exploit a potential disconnect between Mr. Dobbs' interests and those of the network. To accomplish this, it developed an advertisement that it knew would be too controversial to be accepted for airing on CNN, then used the rejection of the advertisement to drive donations to the cause and to build pressure on Mr. Dobbs.

Second, in an effort to keep the news coverage generated by this manufactured controversy alive long enough to have an impact, the consultants placed dozens of different paid online advertisements, which they targeted at media employees, especially those of CNN/ Time Warner, using the nano-targeting capability of a Facebook feature, workplace targeting. Part of the strategy here was to call out individual CNN personalities by name in the advertisements, especially Latinos, asking them to pressure Mr. Dobbs as well. This added what amounted to a second level of celebrity-centered messaging. For an advertising buy of less than $2000, within four days the coalition had reached some 900 employees of the mainstream media, including about 200 at CNN. This effort was supplemented with banner ads directed at a more general, progressive and Latino audience through relevant blogs.

Finally, the consultants leaked the story of their strategy to ClickZ, a digital advertising publication, which posted the story. This led to an explosion of visibility as the story became the top return on Google searches (web, news and blogs) for the term "Lou Dobbs." At that point, MSNBC, a rival cable network with a progressive political slant, aired the original television advertisement, even as the story itself went national.

Mr. Dobbs resigned his position at CNN, and the coalition raised a large sum of money online to use in influencing the immigration policy debate (Koster and Davis, 2010).

This strategic dependence on intermediaries to fulfill a variety of campaign functions generates what we can think of as a campaign architecture—an interlocked network of individuals and organizations that interact with one another under the guidance, stimulus, or sheer opportunistic actions of the campaign protagonist in ways that advance the objectives of the campaign. Where the protagonist lacks credibility or legitimacy, it will recruit allies or surrogates to speak in its behalf, thereby lending to the effort their own, presumably higher, standing. Where the protagonist lacks access to the public or some other more specialized audience, it will recruit or find ways to "manage" mediating agents such as prominent politicians, celebrities, or prominent intellectuals (e.g., Nobel laureates), or various news or other media, to deliver its messages. Where the protagonist lacks access to, or influence with, the target—as is the case in most IICs—it will recruit or find ways to mobilize stakeholders of the target as more direct points of pressure. This role specialization and sequencing of effort is illustrated in Figure 5.5, which uses the example of a campaign directed by an advocacy group against a corporation. When viewed from the perspective of the protagonist (lower left), the campaign can be seen as a series of concentric rings reaching out toward the target (upper right).

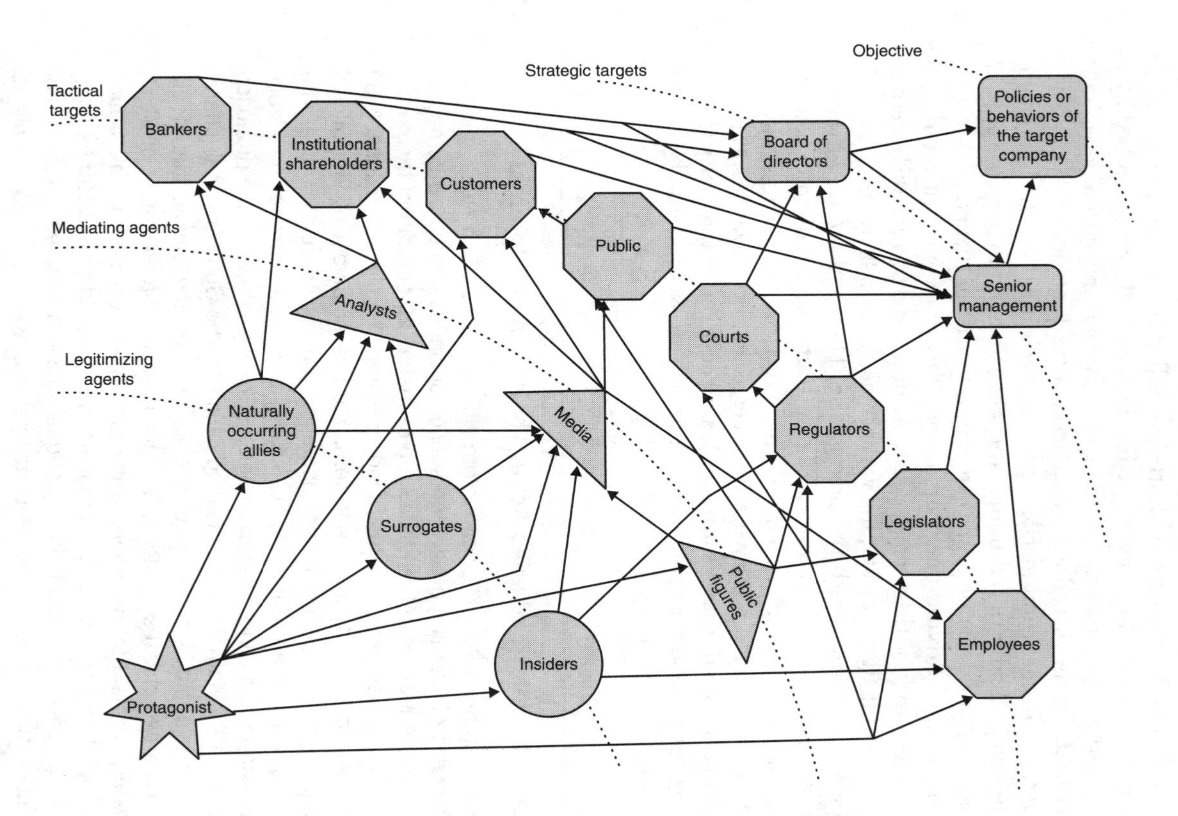

Figure 5.5 Role Specialization within Campaigns.

In some ways Figure 5.5, and the process it captures, is suggestive of some of the drawings by M.C. Escher in which objects that are clearly of one type at one extreme of the drawing are transformed seamlessly into objects of an altogether different type at the other extreme. In the figure, the lower left-hand corner is clearly controlled by and associated with the protagonist, while the upper right-hand corner is clearly controlled by and associated with the target. The space in between is transformational, in this instance from the direction and interests of the protagonist to those of the target, with the combination and assigned roles of the stakeholders blending gradually to accomplish the whole. That, albeit with variations, is precisely the dynamic of the campaign, at least in theory.

The critical driving force throughout this process is self-interest, but not merely that of the protagonist. For some, or many, of the intermediaries the campaign may employ will not necessarily share its objectives or value an association with the protagonist. They will *all* act in their *own* self-interest. The key to a successful campaign, then, is often to determine what the self-interest of each intermediary is in its dealings with other actors in the campaign and with the target, then to find avenues of approach, or forms of appeal, that resonate with a given actor in ways that stimulate it to select out and act upon a *subset* of its self-interest that can be turned to advantage by the campaign.

Box 5.4 Intermediaries Act in Their Own Self-Interest

In March 1998, Marriott International Corporation was in the process of spinning off its food service business into a new company, Sodexho Marriott. At the time, approximately 20 percent of the parent company was owned by the founding Marriott family, approximately 30 percent by individual shareholders, and the remainder by institutional shareholders—mutual funds, insurance companies, and the like. The company was also interested in issuing millions of shares of new stock to use in acquiring other companies or new properties, and proposed that, at the same special meeting called for the Sodexho deal, shareholders approve a new structure, favored by the family, that would create two classes of stock. So-called "super shares", most of which would be held by members of the family, would carry 10 votes each rather than just one. Only the regular shares would be used for transactions. Critics objected that this dual class structure, which is not uncommon at family-founded companies, was intended simply to assure that the family retained control of the company.

At that time, the hotel workers' union was engaged in a bitter organizing dispute at Marriott's hotel in downtown San Francisco. Sensing an opportunity to pressure the company, the union launched a campaign to line up votes against the proposal. It established a campaign website, and launched a counter-solicitation asking shareholders to oppose the new stock structure. The change was approved at the special meeting, but the company immediately came under so much pressure that it agreed to resubmit the issue to shareholders at the regular annual meeting in May.

Enter Institutional Shareholder Services (ISS), a company that was in the business of advising institutional shareholders on how to vote their proxies at the annual meetings of the thousands of companies in which they might hold stock, and a very influential voice in this area. ISS became a de facto ally of the union, and led a campaign among its clients to defeat the proposal—not because of the union's desire to pressure the company, but because its own self-interest and that of its clients pointed in that direction. As a result, the institutional shareholders, who had no common cause with the union, became its agents in pressuring Marriott over organizing workers in San Francisco, the restructuring of the stock was stopped, and Marriott got the message. As summarized afterward by the union's research director, "We demonstrated an ability to identify with our fellow shareholders in Marriott and to build an alliance with shareholders that many people didn't think was possible." (Manheim, 2001: 220–221)

Taking this from an alternative starting point, look back at Figures 5.3(a)–(c). Even from these simplified examples, it is clear that any given actor will have its own sphere of interests, and will have, as well, different roles to play in its dealings with various other actors. A member of the public, for example, may also be a member of an advocacy organization *and* a shareholder in a corporation. A group advocating public policy may also be a membership organization and a grant-seeker. And so forth. These different roles, at different times, in different settings, and in interaction with different other actors, may lead to distinctly different behaviors. The strategic challenge to the campaign is to anticipate what those behaviors might be, and to isolate and stimulate selectively those that might serve its purposes.

Stakeholders and Campaign Tactics

Over the years, campaign strategists have developed an extensive collection of tools that can be turned to this end, with the particular mix adopted in a given campaign to be determined by such considerations as the identity of the stakeholders to be "featured" and the nature of their relationships with the target and with other actors; the opportunities and constraints inherent in the campaign setting; the "facts on the ground" and the range of available, potentially credible, messaging and positioning; the attributes of the protagonist, the target, and any intermediaries; the nature of the issues to be developed; the resources available to the protagonist; and the nature of the policy or behavior change that is the campaign's objective. It is not feasible here to provide a comprehensive list of the full range of possibilities. What we can do, however, is to bring together in summary form some of the more commonplace strategies and tactics that have been deployed in IICs of various types, as well as a few that have been especially innovative. This is accomplished in Table 5.1.

With the exception of the initial category, which incorporates overarching strategies and tactics, Table 5.1 is arranged by the type of stakeholder at which a given communication or action is directed. Organizing the table in this manner, rather than by a classification of strategies and tactics *per se*, is intended to emphasize an important point in this discussion—that the selection of strategy and tactics is not an abstract exercise, but one that must be made in a particular context and with a particular purpose in mind. The stakeholders included in the table do not by any means exhaust the variety of individuals, groups, or organizations that can be employed for leverage on a campaign target, but they are among the most common types of stakeholders that tend to be drawn into these efforts. Some of the entries in Table 5.1 reflect arguments we have made in the discussion to this point, while others will be supported by subsequent analysis. Still others have been extensively developed elsewhere. (Manheim, 2000) Because the circumstances of any given campaign will dictate the relative utility of any strategy or tactic, I have made no effort to prioritize the items in Table 5.1 except in the most general of ways.

Table 5.1 Strategies and Tactics Directed at Selected Stakeholders

1.0 General thematic strategies and tactics directed at the target

- Define and claim the moral high ground
- Develop frames that accentuate this moral superiority
- Demonize the target
- Disseminate the message through one or more networks of seemingly neutral third parties with greater legitimacy or credibility than the protagonist or, in the absence of such allies, through surrogates with public-regarding names and images
- Deconstruct and disrupt the target's support network by assessing its key stakeholder relationships and exploiting any vulnerabilities that correspond to potential protagonist strengths (including messaging/ positioning availabilities)
- Polarize the target and its stakeholders
- Select and attack the most responsive, as opposed to the least responsive, target in a given set of prospective targets, using the disposition toward responsiveness per se as leverage to maximize behavior change

- Direct attacks outside the routine experience or expectations of the target
- Distract and occupy the attention of leaders
- Build and maintain pressure over time
- Maximize attention to the campaign where the cause or protagonist is popular; minimize attention where the cause or protagonist is unpopular
- Personalize the campaign
  - Bad actors (target)
    - Attack the qualities of the target
      - Stewardship
      - Accountability
      - Social responsibility
      - Public regardingness
    - Attack the reputation and character of its leader(s)
      - Character
      - Values
      - Actions
    - Pressure interlocks
      - Claim conflicts for leaders serving on other corporate or organization boards (including among others universities, religious institutions, charities, nonprofits)
      - Pressure other companies, universities, civic associations where directors interlock
    - Stigmatize target's friends and allies
    - Threaten and intimidate leaders, directors, others they engage with
  - Their victims
  - The cavalry (the protagonist)
- Deprive the target of resources (e.g., by pressuring a company's customers to go elsewhere or its principal shareholders to sell their holdings, cutting off government funding of the target or one of its activities, removing a program or agency from a government's annual budget)
- In general, restructure the target's options and decision-making calculus by changing its perceptions of the cost of continuing its current behavior
- Systematic integration and sequencing of campaign activities and resultant pressures

2.0 Themes and actions directed at individuals, the public, or segments thereof in such diverse roles as consumers, voters, constituents, members of secondary associations, or citizens

- Fear appeals based on nature of the target
  - Personal or public safety
  - National security
  - Product safety
  - Product quality
  - Damage to environment
- Appeals based on human rights or humane values
- Appeals based on civil rights
  - Race
  - Ethnicity
  - Gender
  - Sexual preference
- Appeals based on the expressed values and rules of the target itself (laws, customs, codes of conduct)

(Continued Overleaf)

Table 5.1 Continued

- Question the values and rules
- Question the target's commitment to the values and rules
- Question the target's achievement of the values, adherence to the rules
- Question the independence of those who judge the target as acting on its values, within its rules
- Encourage third-party (protagonist-allied) evaluations of the target's values and behaviors

• Solicit and use endorsements of individuals, celebrities, affinity groups

Box 5.5 The Perils of Leveraging Celebrity

Corporations, cause groups, and even government agencies often rely on endorsements by celebrities to add luster to their names or draw attention to their issues. Case in point: Kathie Lee Gifford and Wal-Mart.

Kathie Lee Gifford is an Emmy-winning American television personality who was perhaps best known for her fifteen years (1985–2000) as co-host of *Live with Regis and Kathie Lee*, a nationally-broadcast talk show. In 1995, she developed her own clothing label, selling products through Wal-Mart and becoming closely identified with that company.

In 1996, Charles Kernaghan, head of the National Labor Committee and dedicated campaigner against child labor and sweatshops, revealed during Congressional testimony and in a corresponding white-paper report that Gifford's clothing line was being manufactured by child labor in Honduras. Kathie Lee cried, promised an investigation, and terminated the agreement with the offending factory. But matters only got worse. At a press conference a few weeks later, one of the workers described the working conditions:

> The treatment at Global Fashion is very bad. The supervisors insult us and yell at us to work faster. Sometimes they throw the garment in your face, or grab and shove you. They make you work very fast, and if you make the production quota one day then they just increase it the next day . . .
>
> Even the pregnant women they abuse. They send them to the pressing department where they have to work on their feet 12 or 13 hours a day in tremendous heat ironing . . .
>
> I'm an orphan. I live in a one room home with 11 people. I have to work to help three small brothers . . .

Turned out she wanted the jobs returned to the factory. "If I could talk with Kathie Lee I would ask her to help us" (Duke, 2005; and National Labor Committee, found online at http://www.nlcnet.org/articlephp?id=436#diaz).

Kathie Lee may have cried, but Wal-Mart, the real target of the NLC campaign, suffered a huge black eye, the more so because of her celebrity status. And in the process, Mr. Kernaghan, known ever after as the Man Who Made Kathie Lee Cry, demonstrated not only the power of celebrity and the risks that it entails, but also the use of personalization as a campaign tactic. Small wonder, then, that when class-of-his-own golfer Tiger Woods crashed and burned—well, crashed—in 2009 when his marital infidelities came to light, companies like AT&T and Accenture that had ridden his celebrity coat tails quickly left the scene of the accident.

One of the most interesting challenges associated with the role of celebrity has to do, however, not with tears or Tigers, but with Norma McCorvey. You will know her as Jane Roe, as in *Roe v. Wade*. Through that litigation and years of subsequent campaigning on the abortion issue, Ms. McCorvey has become literally the poster child of freedom-of-choice advocates. But in July 2009, she was arrested for disrupting the Senate confirmation hearings of Supreme Court Justice Sonia Sotomayor as part of an anti-abortion demonstration, and later in the year she began appearing in television commercials expressing her regret over having had an abortion. "I realized," she says in the advertisement, "that my case, which legalized abortion on demand, was the biggest mistake of my life" (Kane, 2009; the advertisement was found online at http://www.virtuemedia.org/norma.htm).

This would seem to have left the pro-choice side with a bit of a dilemma.

- Encourage public expressions of concern or dissatisfaction
- Develop themes portraying protagonist as ally of public
- Advertising
  - Billboards
  - Print
  - Broadcast
  - Online
  - Direct mail
  - Telemarketing
  - Viral
- Internet initiatives
  - Blast emails
  - Blogs
  - Attack/watch websites
  - You Tube videos
  - Twitter, Facebook groups, and other social networks
  - Online petitions and letters
  - Swarming
- Strikes
- Boycotts
- Picketing and demonstrations
- Sit-ins
- Public disruptions
- Unbounded acts of violence and intimidation
- Bounded acts of violence and intimidation
- Mobilizing or demobilizing public opinion at specific levels
  - International
  - National
  - Regional
  - Local
  - Sub-local

Box 5.6 The Compleat Sit-In

Sit-ins are a well-established tactic of civil rights, labor, student, and other activists. Like other civil disobedience actions, these events may look spontaneous, but the most effective ones are guided by a plan.

(Continued Overleaf)

An example is provided by a 21-day sit-in at the university administration building undertaken by the Harvard Living Wage Campaign in 2001 to call attention to low wages on campus. The group organized itself into two teams, one to operate inside the building and the other on the outside.

The inside team had a six-point plan that included splitting into groups to seize different areas of the building, distributing letters to workers disavowing any interest in disrupting their work or threatening them, and posting notices for the police that they were committed to nonviolence, had no drugs, and would not destroy property. They were also careful not to touch any administrator, lest they be charged with assault and battery.

The outside team worked from a 10-point plan that included facilitating community support through regular major events, producing news releases and contacting reporters daily, designating police liaisons, maintaining a 24-hour-a-day picket line in front of the building, and constructing a tent city outside the building.

Using lawyers from the AFL-CIO as intermediaries, the students eventually vacated the building in return for an agreement to form a committee to recommend new workplace policies (Offner, 2010).

Table 5.1 Continued

3.0 Themes and actions directed at the media
- Thematic campaigns linking numerous more localized actions
- Themes that question true motives of the target
- Associate the target with conflict, risk, uncertainty, unreliability
- Timing to match news cycles
- News releases
- Video news releases
- News conferences
- Staged events
- Special reports, white papers, backgrounders
- Informal media contacts, editorial board visits
- Control/facilitate access to key protagonist actors, allies
- Development/placement of TV news magazine-format features
- Supply finished content to media
- Demand complete transparency on the part of the target
- Coalition building and naming to mask protagonist and/or its interest
- Channel media initiatives and access to cause-friendly reporters
- Take advantage of reporter inexperience with issues
- Use celebrity actions or endorsements to increase attention
- Build extensive Nexis/Google database to pre-frame subsequent news coverage
- Develop independent media production and distribution capabilities
- Purchase/placement of attack advertising

4.0 Themes and actions directed at legislators and the legislative process
- Encourage hearings called by protagonist-friendly legislators on issues of critical interest to the target
- Instigate legislative investigations
- Encourage introduction of legislation affecting the target or its interests
- Solicit "Dear Colleague" letters from legislative allies
- Solicit public intervention by legislators on an issue or in a dispute

- Leverage legislative activity as a marker of credibility for other aspects of the campaign, notably those directed at the media
- Pressure government leaders to increase public funding or support that benefits the protagonist, perhaps at the expense of the target
- Pressure government leaders to cut off funding for programs or initiatives that benefit the target
- Raise and direct campaign contributions
- Provide campaign volunteers, advice
- Grassroots, grass-tops and Astroturf organizing
- Action at all legislative levels
  - o International
  - o Regional/Supranational
  - o National
  - o State/Provincial
  - o Local

5.0 Themes and actions directed at regulators and the regulatory process

- In general, offset costs of the campaign by using regulatory authorities as de facto partners
- Freedom of Information Act (FOIA) or similar requests for documents relating to the target that may include statements of violations and/or penalties or mandatory remedial actions, information about internal operations
- Generate pressure from key legislators on regulators to investigate or address issues or target
- Orchestrate waves of complaints (environmental, product safety, human rights, etc.) that, by substance or sheer volume, necessitate inspections, regulatory action
- Challenge the target in routine proceedings
  - o Licensing
  - o Zoning
  - o Mergers/acquisitions
  - o Issuance of tax-exempt or taxpayer subsidized debt
  - o Policy conferences
  - o Trade negotiations
- Use target's own major initiatives and needs as focal point for regulatory efforts
- Reveal and challenge target's political activity
- Leverage regulatory activity as a marker of credibility for other aspects of the campaign
- Leverage regulatory activity to facilitate the motivation and mobilization of other stakeholders in pressuring the target
- Redefine regulatory standards
- Leverage global compacts
- Leverage regulatory rivalries
- Leverage international alliances
- Action at all regulatory levels
  - o International
  - o Regional/Supranational
  - o National
  - o State/Provincial
  - o Local

(Continued Overleaf)

Table 5.1 Continued

6.0 Themes and actions directed at the legal system
- File private litigation to which the protagonist is a party
- File private litigation through surrogates
- Support private litigation that is ostensibly independent
- Initiate/participate in/encourage class action litigation
- Set traps for the target through potential counter-litigation
  - Use extensive discovery to obtain otherwise unavailable information about the target
- Redefine legal standards
- Venue shopping
  - Domestic
    - Federal
    - States
  - International
    - ATCA (Alien Torts Claims Act)
    - World Court
    - Non-US jurisdictions
- Use litigation as a basis for publicizing and legitimizing claims made elsewhere in the campaign

7.0 Themes and actions directed at advocacy groups, NGOs, religious groups, civic groups, community activists
- Identify and mobilize allies; establish formal alliances
- Create issue-centered coalitions
- Link domestic initiatives to existing transnational advocacy networks
- Formation of surrogates and umbrella organizations
- Training, education, development of knowledge base
- Morality and other value-based appeals
- Self-interest and issue-interest appeals
- Appeals from religious and/or community leaders
- Mobilization of specialized publics (taxpayers, patriots, clergy, students, or victims (real or claimed) of the targeted actor, policy, or behavior, are among the possibilities)
- Localization of claims, disputes, themes as affecting "community"
- Local, national, or international community "hearings" or "white papers" on campaign-related or other useful issues
- International exchanges of expertise, concern

8.0 Themes and actions directed at bankers, investment bankers, insurers, principal lenders and creditors, international financial institutions
- Issuance of special reports or "audits" alleging improper reporting, financial irregularities
- Claims of malfeasance by target or its principal officers
- Demands for transparency, as in the criteria for granting credit or the terms of loans to the target
- General efforts to raise the level of uncertainty or risk associated with the target, possibly including publicizing of the campaign itself
- Initiatives to restrict or channel the actions of public pension fund authorities in ways detrimental to the target
- Intervene in bankruptcy or other proceedings to obtain confidential records
- Currency-related initiatives

9.0 Themes and actions directed at industry analysts, financial analysts, ratings firms, institutional shareholders
- Produce and distribute special reports critical of the target
- Establish specialized newsletters and websites
- Monitor and respond to target's financial reports and conference calls
- Attend and disrupt shareholder meetings
- Meet individually with analysts to discuss target's prospects and practices
- Flood target-related Internet chat rooms with attacks on the target and other disparaging information and opinion
- Direct pension-fund investment in ways that reward or threaten target
- Initiate shareholder resolutions directed at management practices, corporate governance, or corporate policy, and organize proxy support for them
- Develop domestic networks of investment-action allies
- Participate in international networks of investment-action allies
- Gain influence or control over proxy advisory firms that advise or vote shares of institutional shareholders
- Pressure financial services firms to reveal proxy votes as a source of public pressure to support protagonist initiatives
- Redefine fiduciary responsibility
- Employ specialized themes
    - Social Responsibility
    - Transparency

Extra-Systemic Intermediation: Thinking Outside the Box

Campaign networks can sometimes be developed using non-obvious or even extra-systemic pressure points. In IICs that are inherently global in character, or that can be strategically globalized by the protagonist, for example, additional and potentially powerful intermediaries can be brought into play. This dynamic is exemplified in Figure 5.6, which is based on the so-called "boomerang model" developed by political scientists Margaret Keck and Kathryn Sikkink (1998). The action here is initiated (lower left) by one or more domestic NGOs or other actors within a given political system seeking to bring about a change of policy or action, but these protagonists lack the wherewithal to accomplish their objectives. So they reach out to prospective partners—allies or other like-minded interests in the international system who may have greater access or influence within their own respective domestic systems. The pressure for change thus moves across boundaries from one political system to another (for example, from the United States to the European Union), and percolates upward within the second system. There, the objective may be to recruit governments or their agencies, international organizations such the United Nations or the Organization for Economic Cooperation and Development, or even corporate competitors, to adopt the protagonists' preferred policy position and to try to impose it on the original government, corporation, or other actor through treaty negotiations, trade agreements, regulatory schemes,

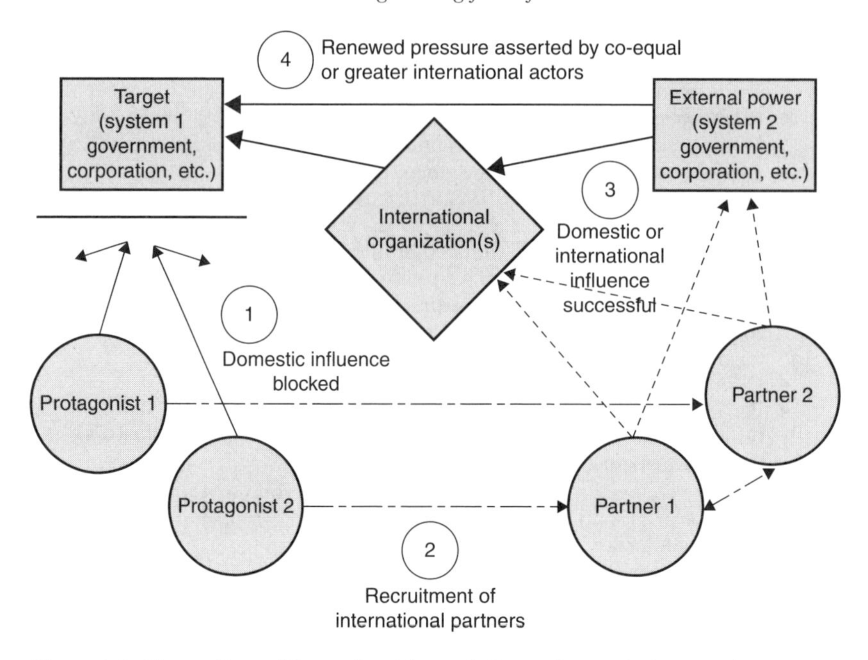

Figure 5.6 Channeling of Campaign Through Extra-Systemic Intermediaries.

publicity and moral suasion, product development, marketplace pressures, or some other device. By this mechanism, the agenda of a weak domestic actor may be multiplied many times over as it is grafted onto, or even transformed into, the agenda of an external government or quasi-governmental entity. This can be accomplished, at least theoretically, where the issue in question is not particularly salient to the new power player (e.g., government) but where the domestic pressures on that player are sufficient to cause it to act. But it is most readily achievable where the demands arising from below accord closely with established self-interests of the second power and thus provide it with opportunities to advance its own interests. Consider for example, the multi-dimensional rivalry between the United States and the EU in the early twenty-first century, and the channeling of domestic U.S. demands for climate-change policy or antitrust actions against major U.S. companies through the political, diplomatic, and regulatory structures of the UN or the EU to enhance the pressure on the U.S. targets, whether corporate or governmental.

The Campaign as a Social Network

While there can certainly be isolated actors and actions within the context of a given campaign, the essential structural form and dynamic of these

Box 5.7 Throwing a Boomerang

For many years, environmental, human rights, and labor activists in the United States were frustrated in their efforts to reform both public policy and corporate behaviors to accord with their interests. Then, in the late 1990s, they hit upon the idea of implementing a comprehensive *global* code of conduct, legitimized and backed by international organizations, that would increase the pressure on their domestic targets for voluntary compliance with what the activists regarded as appropriate policy standards.

In 1998, the Council on Economic Priorities (CEP)—a modest US-based activist group that traced its roots to the anti-Vietnam War movement—took the first step in this direction, promulgating SA8000 (SA for Social Accountability), a set of labor, human rights and environmental principles. The following year, CEP morphed into a new organization, Social Accountability International (SAI), and moved to establish itself as a global arbiter of corporate social responsibility. Also, and significantly, in 1999, Kofi Annan, Secretary General of the United Nations, delivered a speech at the World Economic Forum in Davos, Switzerland, calling for a UN-based, worldwide corporate responsibility initiative. The stars aligned. SAI and other US-based activist groups joined with their counterparts in Europe and elsewhere to endorse and help to shape the UN effort.

The result was a document known as the *United Nations Global Compact* (UNGC). The UNGC sets forth ten basic principles that signatory companies pledge to adopt, and that ratifying nations pledge to enforce. In keeping with the customary ambiguity of such documents, the UNGC principles are stated in very general terms, and room is provided for cross-national variation in the interpretation. But the language does vary in emphasis from some established US policy, enshrining the so-called "precautionary principle" in environmental policy, for example, to a level beyond its general acceptance in the US, and advancing a more union-friendly interpretation of the principle of workplace representation than is common in US law, and the UNGC implementation *process* seems intended to press toward compliance with common interpretations. EU governments, seeing an opportunity to press US-based companies to adopt practices that are commonplace among their European competitors, are generally strong advocates of the compact.

We can see here the operation of the boomerang model at a fairly high level, bringing international pressure through established global-governance organizations, most notably the UN, for policy change on a number of US actors and across a range of issues, all at the same time.

enterprises is the social network—a collection of inter-connected and/or interacting participants through which, in this instance, the protagonist seeks to exercise influence upon the target. The participants might include any third parties that have relationships with the protagonist, the target, or one another and that can serve as pathways of influence. These might take the form of government agencies or legislative bodies (or legislators or staffs), quasi-governmental international organizations, advocacy NGOs, denominational religious organizations, national or international media, political parties, or public opinion, to name but a few—or subsets thereof that could be defined geographically, demographically, or in some other manner. These actors can be linked to one another, to the protagonist or to the target by such factors as interlocking leadership or directorates, shared staff, flows of funds, programmatic interlocks, formal partnerships, common memberships, more or less frequent coalition behaviors, or a host of other means. It is this potentially great diversity of essential network nodes and links, some pre-existing and some needing to be forged, that constitutes the strategic challenge in planning an effective IIC, but that renders the IIC such a robust form of action when it is put to work effectively.

If a protagonist is successfully to initiate and manage a campaign that is dependent on such intermediaries, then that protagonist must accomplish certain tasks relative to its network. These strategic requirements include (doubtless among others):

- *Identification.* The protagonist must either possess prior knowledge of, or conduct research to determine, which intermediaries might be available for its purposes, how and with what other entities they interact, what interests they might hold in common with the protagonist (if any), whether they have any standing or influence vis-à-vis the target, and how they might be motivated. This includes the identification of pre-existing networks that link these intermediaries to one another.
- *Network formation.* Where an existing network does not exist, the protagonist must form it, or help or encourage others to do so.
- *Recruiting.* The protagonist will need to recruit individual intermediaries or aggregates of such actors to advance its campaign objectives, or more correctly, to advance their own objectives in ways that serve to advance those of the campaign.
- *Relationship Maintenance.* The protagonist will need to assess its existing relationships with prospective intermediaries to assure that its recruitment strategy does not risk alienating such actors simply because it chooses to bypass them in a campaign that touches on one of their interest domains.
- *Activation.* Whether a given network is pre-existing or a creation of the campaign, it must be activated.

- *Expansion.* Networks of either class can be extended to include new members or by forging new links between existing members. Similarly, the interests or objectives of a network can be expanded, which is to say, a protagonist may find a network of intermediaries that can be encouraged to broaden its purpose or focus in ways that bring the interests of the protagonist within its sphere of activity or common purpose where they had previously been beyond it.
- *Focusing attention.* It is not enough that a network of intermediaries exist or be created, and that it be activated. The protagonist must also focus the action. This requires a framing of positions, a call to action, a staging of events, or some other activity that sparks intermediary involvement in the campaign *per se.*
- *Channeling.* In any network of reasonable complexity, some participants will be disproportionately more active or influential, and certain channels will be busier or more accessible, than others. The protagonist must find a maximally efficient pathway through the network, and one that is at the same time maximally effective in pressuring the target to change its behaviors. In some instances, the shortest, most direct path may be the best choice, but in others, where, for example, certain (potential) network participants may carry negative baggage of their own, a more circuitous path may be preferable.
- *Motivation.* The protagonist must motivate intermediaries to advance its interests. Where the intermediaries are knowing partners and natural allies, this can be a relatively straightforward process in which the protagonist simply makes its needs or wishes known. Where the intermediaries are unknowing or disinterested participants, however, as is likely the case for those that are target-proximate, the challenge is to motivate them selectively to act in their own interests rather than in those of the protagonist, but to do so in ways that nevertheless advance the objectives of the campaign.
- *Direction or control.* Networks are characterized by internal dynamics that will lie more or less beyond the direction or control of the protagonist. At the most passive extreme, the interests of the protagonist are advanced simply by being placed into the network setting, with no further effort at management, in the hope that they might emerge at the other end in the optimal form and with the optimal effect. Most protagonists, however, will be unwilling, or perhaps unable, to stand back and let things take their course—and often for good reason. As a result, a protagonist is likely to pursue one or both of two strategies—carefully shaping the activation of the network (through selection and recruitment processes, message framing and delivery, point of entry, and the like) so as to maximize its chances of success, or intervening in the network from time to time and place to place (for example, through communication, funding, surrogate formation, or perhaps even threats) to keep things moving in the desired direction and at the desired pace.

Box 5.8 Network-Building in Mexico

Mexico is a country with a long history of revolution and agrarian discontent, but what happened in the southern state of Chiapas in 1994–1996 marked a new form of rebellion, not only for Mexico, but for the world. Analysts have termed it "social netwar."

The Zapatista National Liberation Army (EZLN), or the Zapatistas for short, launched an insurrection on New Year's Day 1994, when they occupied a handful of towns, declared war on the central government, undertook an international media campaign to gain sympathy for their cause, and invited foreign observers to come to Chiapas. That outreach, coupled with a heavy-handed response by the Mexican government, attracted the attention of numerous human rights, indigenous rights, and other activist NGOs, which proceeded to swarm around the Zapatistas—both physically and electronically. Drawn from the US, Canada, and Europe, these groups linked up with Mexican NGOs and began to pressure the government—for a ceasefire, for withdrawal of the troops it had dispatched to the area, for negotiations, for access, for democratic reforms. In the process, they legitimized the movement, globalized the conflict, and converted an obscure movement headed by a ski-masked leader, known as Subcomandante Marcos, into a worldwide sensation. Had they not succeeded in building this support network, the Zapatistas would have been, well, zapped.

The network was grounded in several US and Canadian NGOs that had earlier come together to oppose the North American Free Trade Agreement (NAFTA) and US policy in Central America, and, as Marcos continued to urge NGOs to come to Mexico, the coalition expanded to include at least nine human rights NGOs (e.g., Amnesty International), a half dozen ecumenical NGOs, a like number of indigenous-rights advocates, and a handful of trade and development groups, as well as at least nine NGOs that specialize in infrastructure-building and network facilitation (e.g., the Association for Progressive Communications and Global Exchange), which played a crucial role in facilitating interaction among the various organizations and their collective efforts to build awareness and support in the world community. The presence of these NGOs and the attention they brought helped to keep a lid on the governmental response to the rebellion, while their commitment to nonviolence both restrained and protected the Zapatistas themselves. As a result, much of the rebellion was played out through media and communication strategies (Ronfeldt, Arquilla, Fuller, and Fuller, 1998: 5, 45–69; Cleaver, 1998; Schulz, 1998).

Not only was the network-building strategy in this instance explicit. It was generally regarded as essential to the success of the movement, which endures to this day and which has been developing a set of independent local political and social service structures paralleling those of the Mexican government.

- *Endorsement*. Where a protagonist has certain marketable strengths that may complement a network through which it is operating, it might choose to express public approval of certain actions or actors, even as it preserves its own anonymity as the initiator of the action. In a campaign where the protagonist possesses such attributes as high legitimacy and affinity, for instance, an endorsement of the network can facilitate its operation, and even lend it a faux veneer of independence.
- *Funding*. As suggested above, a protagonist can provide either open or latent financial support to a network or to selected participants therein. In the alternative, the protagonist might recruit other, expressly financial intermediaries, such as individual high-worth donors or activist foundations, to provide support for the network. A more subtle variant of this that may be peculiar to U.S. domestic foundation activism is so-called fiscal sponsorship, which is designed to circumvent legal restrictions on political activity by tax-exempt organizations by, in effect, allowing foundations to underwrite the infrastructure costs of selected activist NGOs or other organizations without participating directly in their activism.
- *Communication*. Though campaigns have many dimensions and employ diverse resources, information, whether for purposes of education or persuasion, is an essential currency, and in most instances probably the primary currency, of exchange. Protagonists must communicate effectively if they are to initiate, manage and optimize the actions of intermediaries working, knowingly or otherwise, in their behalf.

As noted earlier, these various actions are directed at intermediaries, each of which has its own attributes and inclinations. Some entities, such as some civil society NGOs, are relatively transparent, while others are less so. Some are broadly legitimized, others more narrowly so. Some are highly visible, others less so. And so forth. All will have defined spheres of interest that both contribute to and limit their reach and legitimacy. The challenge to the campaign is to marshal these forces in a more or less organized manner, point them in the desired direction, and push.

Mapping the Campaign

Social network theorists in sociology, political science and other fields have developed techniques for mapping and analyzing these structures. The principal elements of these networks are *nodes*—the individuals, groups, organizations or institutions that are members of a given network—and *links*—the exchanges of money, personnel, programs, and other resources or activities that flow between or among the nodes. The nodes may be more or less central to the operation and maintenance of the network, depending in part on their assigned role and in part on the number and manner of their connections with other nodes. The links connecting them, where present, may be more or less intensive, and may be either uni- or bidirectional. Figure 5.7 illustrates a hypothetical network of this type. In the figure, the target might be a corporation, a policy-making governmental entity, or the like. The campaign, in this hypothetical instance, is waged by a collection of advocacy NGOs with financial support from activist foundations. Acting directly in some instances (NGO E with Stakeholder D) and indirectly, as through Coalition A, in others, they appeal to, collaborate with, or bring pressure on key stakeholders of the target.

Some relationships or exchanges in our hypothetical network are unidirectional (for example, Foundation D to NGO E) and others bidirectional (as between Foundations A and B or NGO E and Stakeholder D), and some are more important than others (for example, the paths between Foundation A, NGOs A and B, and Coalition A), indicated here by heavier connecting links. Not all network members are engaged equally, or for that matter, actively, in the campaign (Coalition B), and not all of the target's stakeholders are engaged (Stakeholder C). The point here is not the identities of the actors in this particular example. Funding of campaigns can also come from governmental or international organizations, corporations, individuals, or a host of other sources. Similarly, campaigns themselves can be waged by entities as diverse as governments and terrorist groups. The stakeholders attaching to any given target can range more widely still, including shareholders, regulators, legislators, treaty partners, the public, the media, religious or community groups, financiers, taxpayers, voters, and on and on. Rather, the point to be taken here is that, whatever their composition, the relationships and exchanges that characterize any given campaign can be represented in this general manner.

While they can be quite extensive and complex, as Figure 5.7 only begins to suggest, networks tend to resolve themselves into one basic architectural form or another. As illustrated in Figure 5.8, some of these basic forms include chains, circles, stars, and all-channel, or fully interactive, networks. These (and other) forms have attributes that may render them either advantageous or disadvantageous in the context of a given campaign. For example, chain networks, particularly if they are unidirectional, can provide security to those initiating action by masking their identity at more than one step of remove; but they are also easily disrupted by the simple expedient of breaking the chain. Star networks are inherently hierarchical, can facilitate centralized direction and continuity of action,

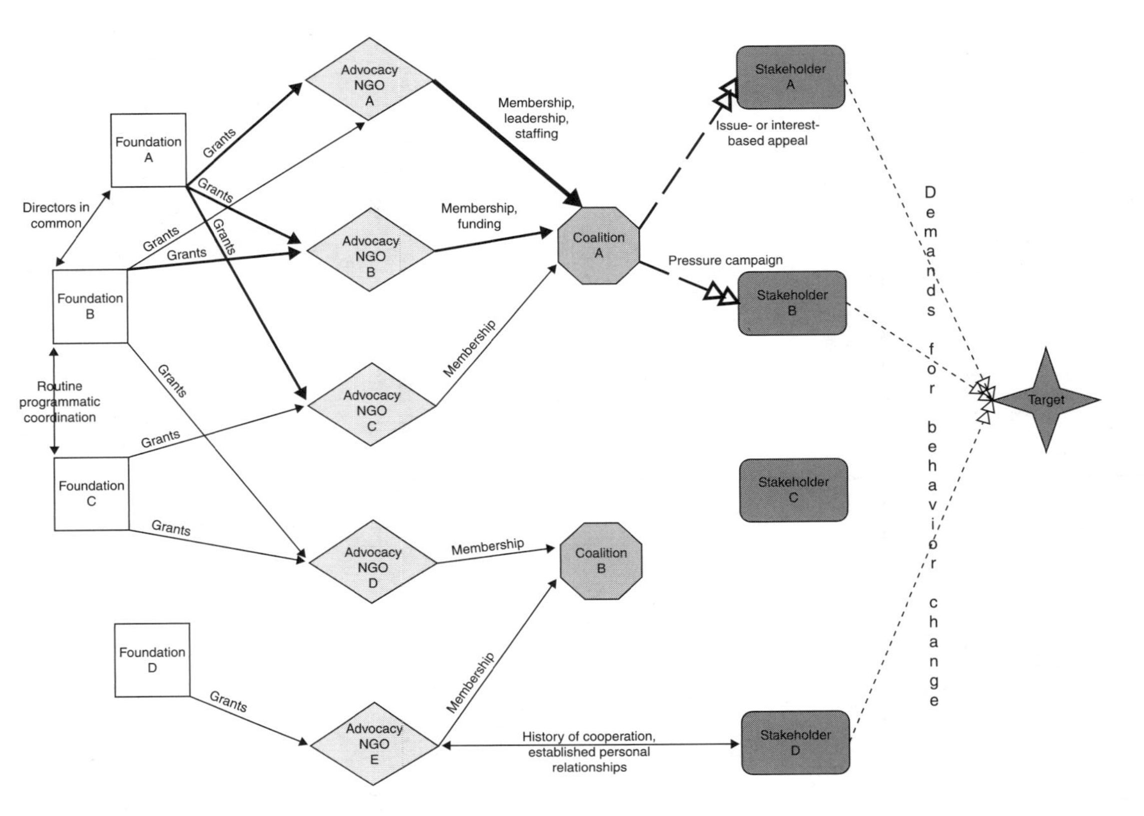

Figure 5.7 Map of Hypothetical Campaign Network.

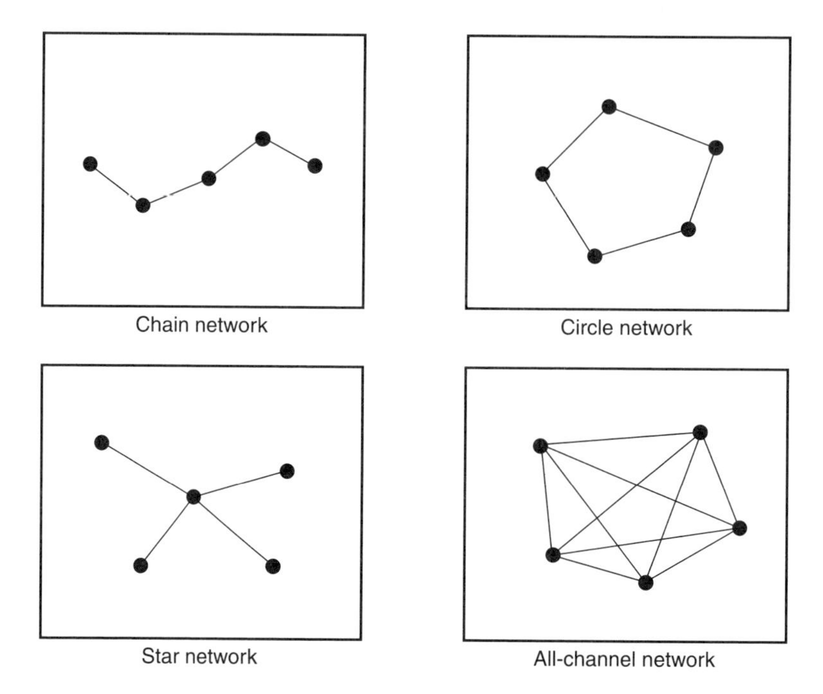

Figure 5.8 Basic Forms of Network Architecture.

and can easily withstand defections at the periphery, but they are fatally impaired by decapitation, the discrediting or elimination of the central actor, since no other actor has knowledge of the network's components. And an all-channel network is fully redundant, a strength with respect to continuity and the flow of resources, but a potential weakness with respect to effective command and control.

Campaign Sequencing Within Networks

Analyses of this sort can be quite revealing, especially when applied to the network(s) associated with specific campaigns, and as a planning tool can be of great benefit in identifying, evaluating, and assigning roles to prospective allies in such a campaign. But for our present purposes, a more general way of characterizing the use of networking in IICs may be of equal or greater value. Though in the end it gets us to the same place, rather than focusing on the identities and specific contributions of participants and on their interconnectivity *per se*, as in Figure 5.7, this approach begins with an emphasis on the sequencing of the campaign and the ways it might employ those nodes and links. We can begin to understand that process using the illustration in Figure 5.9.

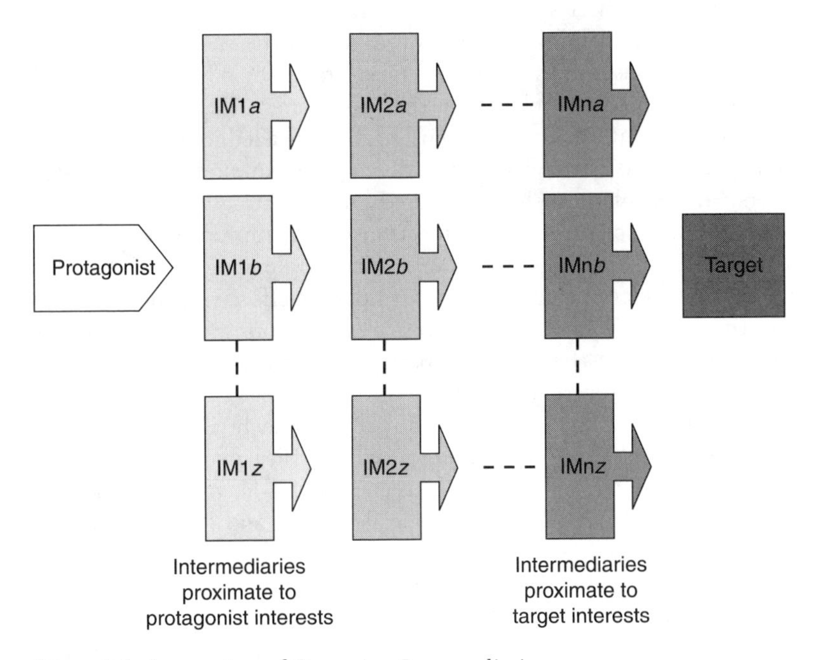

Figure 5.9 Sequencing of Campaign Intermediaries.

In the figure, potential intermediaries that might be recruited into, or otherwise deployed in, the campaign (designated "IM") are arrayed in columns, or waves, based on their affinity with or proximity to the campaign protagonist, at the left, or the campaign target, at the right. Put another way, to the left of the figure are those entities that have the most in common with, are natural allies of, or routinely cooperate with the protagonist. Those at the right are those that are closest to and may have some measure of influence on the target. The ranks between the extremes are entities that, because of their own established relationships and proclivities, have the potential to connect relatively more protagonist-proximate intermediaries with those that are relatively more target-proximate. These waves are numbered from 1 to n, with the lowest numbers being protagonist-proximate and the highest target-proximate. Each rank, or wave, comprises some variable number of separate entities, which are designated here as *a* through *z*, where the designation serves only to differentiate one from another. Thus IM1*a* and IM1*z* are both equally closely associated with the protagonist, while IM1*a* is closer to the protagonist than IMn*a*. The ellipses in the figure merely indicate the presence of unrepresented waves, and unrepresented entities within each.

The effect of this alternative approach to network analysis is to focus the attention of the strategist on certain structural attributes of a range of prospective intermediaries, some of which may not be "the usual suspects," and on the ways each might be employed within the campaign strategy. The organizing concept is simply this: understand the positioning of each prospective intermediary relative to the protagonist, the target, and the other prospective intermediaries, then use this knowledge to plot a course through these successive waves of (knowing or unknowing) campaign "partners," assigning to each a role based on its particular attributes and relationships, and shaping campaign actions and communications so as to facilitate the resulting sequential development. By managing these multi-layered series of relationships among third parties effectively, one can thus convert the strengths of the protagonist's associations and messages into pressure generated on the target by parties who may be unaware of, and unmoved by, these front-end assets.

A simplified version of this strategic approach is illustrated in Figure 5.10. In the figure, the protagonist identifies a subset of its most proximate intermediaries—think friends and allies—for the initial stage of the campaign. In this hypothetical example, IM1*a* and IM1*z* are judged potentially to add value to the campaign based on their relationships with, or influence over, other prospective intermediaries in subsequent waves. IM1*b* has no such identifiable connections, and would add no value to the campaign; hence it is excluded. Through invitation, negotiation, communication or other means, IM1*a* and IM1*z* are then recruited to the campaign, and provided with support and encouragement in contacting their counterparts in the next wave. The process continues seriatim until it reaches the final wave, which comprises the direct stakeholders of

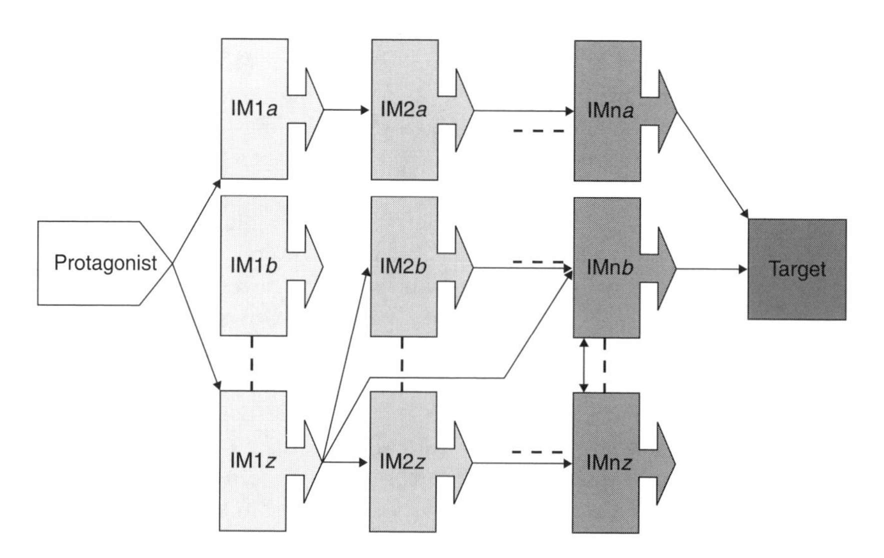

Figure 5.10 Network Structure Arising from Sequencing of Intermediaries.

the target. Along the way, the messages and other means used to stimulate successive waves of intermediaries are determined, not by the core messaging and objectives of the protagonist, but by messaging and motives particular to the entities that are directly involved in each exchange, so that ultimately the stakeholders are moved to action based, as earlier, on their own needs and interests.

While sequencing of the campaign based on the respective proximity rankings of the participants is central to this approach, the actual patterns of contact and influence will occur based in large part on pre-existing relationships among the various intermediaries. Since these parties exist and have interests outside of the campaign itself, these patterns may or may not follow precisely the sequences designated in campaign strategy. In the figure, for example, in addition to its relationships with entities in the designated second wave of the campaign (IM2*b* and IM2*z*), IM1*z* has a relationship with IMn*b*, which the campaign identifies as even more proximate to the target. This channel, if recognized and exploited, might provide the campaign with a shortcut to a later wave, with a means of anticipating or reinforcing communications that will reach the same target-proximate entity from another source, or with some other strategic advantage. So it is the organizing concept of sequencing, and not any particular fixed and inflexible sequence, that underlies this strategic approach.

That point is reinforced with a look back at the example presented in Figure 5.5, which can now be seen as an application of this proximity-based sequencing. In that instance—and this is not unusual—a primary criterion for sequencing is the role assigned to each actor—legitimization, outreach, and so forth. That helps to make explicit a key point related to this approach: While the sequencing of a campaign's rollout should be "strategic," it need not be conceptualized only in temporal terms. To the extent such a plan is linear—or really, multi-linear—its linearity can be based on criteria other than time. The campaign represented in Figure 5.5, for example, employs a sequencing strategy based on function in which temporal considerations are secondary.

Finally with respect to Figure 5.10, to which we now return, note two aspects of the positioning of IMn*z*. First, although this intermediary is a direct stakeholder, it is not assigned a role in the campaign involving direct contact with the target. There are any number of reasons why this might occur—lack of sufficient leverage on the part of the campaign, the absence of a sufficiently important self-interest on the part of the intermediary, a shortage of campaign resources, or simply the assignment of a lower priority in the campaign, among many others. Though not specifically illustrated in the figure, some stakeholders are simply beyond the reach of a particular campaign. Second, note that IMn*z* maintains a reciprocal relationship *within its wave* with IMn*b*. Most immediately, this represents the likelihood that different stakeholders may share interests and may communicate with one another. More generally, it is the case that many of the intermediaries within a given wave are likely to have such networked relationships with one another, so there are likely to be naturally occurring exchanges of information and other resources within waves that are largely, or wholly, independent of the protagonist or the campaign. On the one hand, this integration of participants can greatly strengthen and reinforce the campaign structure. At the same time, it can impose substantial challenges to message discipline in campaign communications, the consistency and continuity of which can be tested through these independent exchanges.

Optimal Pathways to Influence

The objective in all of this networking is to find, or create, a pathway of influence leading from the protagonist to the target. Once a network and one or more potential pathways are identified or established, the strategist has many choices as to how best to activate and exploit it. These may well resolve themselves into five basic approaches, which can, of course, be used in combination as circumstances dictate. They include:

- *Path of least distance.* More often than not, though not always, simplicity is the strategist's best friend. Here that mantra translates into selecting the pathway that employs the fewest intermediaries, and the fewest links, possible to achieve the desired objective. Other things being equal, simple networks are more easily managed and controlled than more complex ones. And at least one student of such social networks, Duncan Watts (2003: 300), suggests that any pathway longer than two steps may actually be too long. Yet in reality, it may be difficult to anticipate or control the number of intermediaries that become engaged in a given campaign (including some who may act on their own initiative, independently of the protagonist or its agents), and, as we noted earlier, those who do will bring their own strengths and weaknesses to the effort. But at the very least, the efficiencies inherent in a shortest-distance line of attack point to a guiding strategic principle—a "rule of parsimony," if you will—that can be applied even imperfectly to streamline both thinking and implementation.
- *Path of least resistance.* This is an alternative application of the rule of parsimony, one that substitutes for the straightest-line geometry of the road-builder an appreciation that, even in rivers that bend in upon themselves, one does not need a pump to keep the water flowing downhill. Almost by definition, this strategy conserves the resources of the protagonist, and may be the only option available to those with very limited resources. It is facilitated by the availability of naturally occurring allies, by an especially weak target, or by the relatively high vulnerability to influence of target-proximate (stakeholder) intermediaries.

As such a strategy is rolled out, it may also provide the fewest challenges to the protagonist seeking to maintain low visibility or low transparency, or to one lacking in legitimacy. Least-resistance pathways have the virtue of simplicity, which may appeal to protagonists, including individuals, who may lack an internal infrastructure capable of sustaining a campaign. They tend to be highly efficient. These advantages may be offset, however, to the extent that bias toward efficiency or parsimony results in only minimal impact on the target.

- *Path of greatest and most sustained pressure.* This strategy tends to be more public, more confrontational, long(er) lasting, and more expensive. It may be required for targets that are powerful, well positioned, and well defended. But it raises the risk of discovery or explicit association with the campaign for a protagonist that is disadvantaged by that, and may impose associational, financial, political or other burdens on key intermediaries. All of that said, where the target has demonstrated a high degree of resistance, where the issue in question is highly visible and hotly contested, or where the stakes are sufficiently high—and where the protagonist has the resources and the standing to sustain it—this can be an effective strategy.
- *All paths, all channels.* Here the idea is simply to overwhelm the target with multiple points of pressure of varying character and influence. This approach may find utility where there is no single channel of sufficient influence to induce the desired change in the target's behavior, but where it is not necessary to resort to the least-resistance approach. One might expect to find this style employed where a central issue or demand of the campaign is broadly popular, and/or the target is broadly unpopular. A particular advantage of this multi-path strategy is that it generates pressure across many different dimensions of the target, and in the process can illuminate and exploit weaknesses in the internal organization of its decision-making. Target organizations that are known to have internal communication issues, top-down management styles, patterns of jealousy or jurisdictional disputes among senior decision-makers, and the like would be candidates for such a strategy. At the same time, precisely because they can become highly complex, using many channels and multiple messages, all-channel campaigns can be difficult to control. That, in turn, can leave the protagonist vulnerable to risks associated with the actions or reputation of intermediaries that may join the campaign of their own volition or may, at the very least, be unresponsive to central guidance.
- *Netwaves against the wall.* Think big splash. Taking advantage of focusing events, such as periods of crisis, policy failures that can be tied to the target, or failed performance by the target itself, or of pseudo-events, such as campaign-generated research reports and policy papers, the idea here is to overwhelm the target with a multi-channel, intense, but short-lived attack designed to weaken it going forward,

and perhaps, to weaken it sufficiently to induce the desired behavior change. This strategy is highly opportunistic, and more episodic in character than some of the alternatives, and is especially dependent on the protagonist's ability to communicate quickly and effectively through mass media, viral media, and the like, with diverse parties—its own proximate intermediaries, target-proximate intermediaries, and perhaps the target itself. It can be used to effect where the time available for a given campaign is limited, especially where the waves themselves can be temporally controlled with precision, or where a longer-running campaign appears to have reached an impasse and needs fresh momentum. But its success depends on factors whose nature and timing may lie well beyond the control of the protagonist.

The strategist is, of course, free to mix and match among these alternatives as the resources and requisites of the situation require, and is by no means limited to just these approaches. But taken together, these five different ways of implementing a campaign should suggest the richness of network-based efforts at influence. In Chapter 6, we will explore these implications in much greater detail in the course of a far more systematic examination of the criteria for campaign decision-making and their relationship with campaign objectives.

Before we do that, however, let us pause to consider a point we have made in passing once or twice already. Campaigns are messy things, and seldom follow to the letter a closely written script. That is surely, and perhaps especially, true of efforts to manage complex relationships in the dynamic environment of an IIC. Accordingly, one must view strategic analysis like that we are offering here as a sort of rational frame, rather like the frame of an automobile. The frame sets the general limits for design of the body, but it does not describe the specific appearance of the auto itself, nor does it prevent a few bumps here and there. In the same way, networking strategy imparts some form and direction to the campaign, but it does not carry a guarantee that each will work out exactly as planned. That is where the skill of the strategist and the uncertainties of the real world bump up against one another.

6 Riding the Waves: Strategy and Tactics in Network Activation

. . . [I]t's the network, stupid.

Duncan J. Watts (2003: 311)

In Chapter 5, we set out the underlying strategic logic of information and influence campaigns, which is based on the development and exploitation of networks to leverage and advance the interests of the campaign protagonist. Here, we will look more closely at the components of those networks to develop a generalized understanding of how this might best be accomplished. At this point, the challenge to the strategist is straightforward: how best to meet the needs, and how best to exploit the capabilities, of prospective campaign intermediaries so as most effectively to convey the protagonist's needs to the target and achieve the campaign objectives. But if the challenge is straightforward, meeting it successfully is anything but.

The Differentiability of Protagonist Attributes

The place to begin is with self-analysis, i.e., with a set of strategic observations about the protagonist itself. What are its needs? Capabilities? Assets? Liabilities? Strengths? Weaknesses? The better the protagonist understands itself, the better positioned it is to develop an effective campaign strategy. And, since our interest here is specifically in the design of IICs, the criteria used in this assessment should be those deemed most germane to effectiveness in that arena. Consider, for example, the profiles of various classes of campaign protagonists summarized in Table 6.1. The rows in the table suggest principal attributes that might (a) attach to a given type of protagonist, and (b) affect the ability of such a protagonist to wage an effective campaign and the strategic style it might be required to adopt to do so. These include (among many possibilities):

- Legitimacy—the extent to which the protagonist and its actions are accepted as appropriate by the target or various intermediaries.

- Transparency—the extent to which the actions, the financing, the membership and leadership, the structure, and the decision-making processes of the protagonist are open to public view.
- Visibility—the extent to which the protagonist and its activities are present in the public mind.
- Resources—the availability of money, information, skilled personnel, and other forms of support available to the protagonist.
- Infrastructure—the extent to which the protagonist maintains, or can assemble and maintain, an internal organization that can be employed to develop and support the campaign.
- Identity of Interest with the Target—the closeness—whether real, perceived, or merely subject to effective portrayal—between the interests of the protagonist and those of the target.

The columns in Table 6.1 identify a range of prospective IIC protagonists that is offered not to be comprehensive, but simply to indicate the range of potential differences in pre-campaign positioning. Included are international governmental organizations (IGOs) such as the United Nations or its agencies, the World Bank, NATO or the Organization of American States; a national government acting beyond its geographic boundaries; a corporation; a non-governmental organization (NGO) operating in a civil society framework; a mass movement organization; a terrorist or insurgent group; or even a drug cartel attempting to broaden or protect its interests. The cells in the table have been filled with arbitrarily assigned values that are, again, simply intended to suggest the potential for differentiation among classes of protagonists. These values range from Very Low (VL) through Medium (M) to Very High (VH), which represent estimates of the level of each attribute that attaches to a given class of protagonist.

Table 6.1 Classification of Protagonists by Attributes

	International Governmental Organization (IGO)	*Foreign Government*	*Corporation*	*Civil Society-Type NGO*	*Mass Movement Organization*	*Terrorist/Insurgent Organization*	*Drug Cartel*
Legitimacy	L-H	L-H	M-H	H-VH	H	VL/H	VL
Transparency	H	M	H-VH	H	L-H	VL	VL
Visibility	H	H	M-H	L-M	H	VL-VH	VL
Resources	L-M	VH	VH	L	L-H	L-H	H
Infrastructure	H	L-VH	H-VH	L-VH	L	VL-H	VL
Identity of Interest with Target	M	L-M	L-H	L-H	VL-L	VL	VL

The table suggests, for example, that protagonists such as drug cartels, insurgencies, or terrorist organizations will be characterized by very low legitimacy, while the legitimacy of civil society organizations or mass movements, as a counterpoint, can be quite high. Similarly, insurgents and mass movement organizations are less likely to share interests with the targets of their campaigns than are civil society groups or corporations, and so forth. Of course, all of these judgments depend on the particulars of the protagonist in question and on the identity and nature of the target. An insurgent organization operating a campaign—and remember, we are talking here not about violence, but about the projection of soft power that might precede, accompany, or follow it—against a regime that itself lacks legitimacy will be positioned differently from a similar organization acting against a popular government. Consider, for example, the 1990s example of the Zapatista rebellion in Mexico, which was granted considerable support and legitimacy in some corners of the international system (Ronfeldt, Arquilla, Fuller, and Fuller, 1998). And staying in country, consider the alternative example of a Mexican drug cartel seeking to establish a political base to complement its illegal activities. While such a group might bear more than a superficial resemblance to a terrorist organization or insurgency, in the present context it would likely demonstrate at least two points of difference—far greater resources (the gains of its illegal trade) and neither the expectation nor the likelihood of achieving legitimacy.

Box 6.1 Different Strokes for Different Folks

One of the more unusual campaigns of recent years is that launched by the Taliban in Afghanistan in the spring of 2009. The Taliban, you may recall, ruled the country from 1996 to 2001, when they were ousted by Americans chasing Osama bin Laden through the Afghan mountains after the 9/11 attack. During that period, the Taliban was noteworthy for what Westerners would characterize as its intolerance and authoritarianism. Afghan men were required to wear beards and long hair, and barbers were attacked to enforce the requirement. Girls older than 8 were denied education, public flogging was commonplace, and the regime even destroyed the Buddhas of Bamyan, two sixth-century statues carved into a cliff, a designated World Culture site.

Fast forward to 2009. Tanned, rested, and ready, the Taliban was attempting a comeback. But they knew they had a bit of an image problem. What to do? Mullah Muhammad Omar, the Taliban leader, had the answer. He initiated an information and influence campaign aimed at the hearts and minds of the Afghan people. And the centerpiece? A code of conduct for the Taliban itself. No longer were members to engage in such actions as suicide bombings against civilians, burning down schools, or cutting off ears, lips, and tongues. Though compliance was, as of 2010, reportedly spotty, the objective was clear: to convert the Taliban from an unpopular insurgent movement to a local liberation movement with broad public acceptance (Rubin, 2010).

It is worth noting here that, in IICs, the nature and degree of the protagonist's infrastructure can represent either an asset or a liability. To the extent that infrastructure provides authoritative decision-making, adequate staffing including skilled professionals, routine and established access to key actors (including the media), organizational stability, and the ability to outsource tasks as required, it facilitates campaign activity. On the other hand, because campaigns are inherently iterative and depend on their ability to sense and respond to changes in the campaign environment or to the actions of competing interests, where infrastructure slows decision-making, impedes flexibility, and imposes bureaucratic rules and structures, it is detrimental to a campaign. Infrastructure that renders a campaign sustainable through time is a plus, while that which renders it less nimble is a minus. So in essence, the question is whether the protagonist is strengthened by its infrastructure, or simply rendered muscle-bound.

Whatever the particulars of a given protagonist, the systematic analysis of its campaign-relevant attributes is important because those attributes play a central role in generating the boundaries of any campaign and in pointing toward both likely strategies and essential intermediate, or process-oriented, campaign objectives. Some protagonists will be easily able to engage in actions, or to pursue objectives, that are more difficult for others, or simply unavailable to them. Because of the freedom of action and underlying degree of acceptance afforded to civil society-type groups, for example, they are both better able and more inclined to conduct certain kinds of campaigns than would be a cartel or terrorist group, a corporation, a foreign government (as through its propaganda and public diplomacy), or even an IGO. Similarly, certain classes of protagonist will be able freely and openly to engage with a variety of prospective campaign intermediaries that lie beyond the reach of others. Corporations, for example, can employ legal or public affairs strategies that are unavailable to some other protagonists, either because they are very expensive or because they are precluded by statute from doing so. In manifold ways, then, the attributes of the protagonist set the direction and outer limits of campaign strategy.

Protagonist Profiles Drive Campaign Styles

Differentiation along these dimensions of protagonist attributes has the added effect of helping to establish the objectives of the campaign. Recall that IICs are employed primarily by the weaker party in an asymmetric power relationship, and are designed to mitigate that relative weakness insofar as possible. What we are doing here, in effect, is defining the nature of the protagonist's weakness. It should be no surprise, then, that the specific liabilities of the protagonist vis-à-vis the target will necessarily guide the development of campaign strategy. But it is also the case that the protagonist's profile—the compilation of its attributes—may be issue- or campaign-specific. A protagonist that lacks legitimacy in one situation or vis-à-vis one target, for instance, may have substantial legitimacy in another, and allies that are available in one campaign may be unavailable, or of lesser utility, in another. Protagonist attributes, then, are best understood as situational in character. The same is true of the campaign-relevant attributes of targets and intermediaries—a point worth bearing in mind through the subsequent discussion.

Table 6.2 suggests some of the ways that such protagonist characteristics might translate into campaign styles. In the table, we have taken the "row variables" from Table 6.1, which is to say, the array of relevant protagonist attributes, modified them to identify two contrasting values on each (low and high), and converted them to column headers. So in Table 6.2, the columns represent the possible attributes of any given protagonist. The rows in the figure represent various dimensions of the general style that might be adopted in a given campaign. As before, the selection here is intended to be suggestive of such dimensionality, not a comprehensive list of campaign styles. These elements include:

Table 6.2 Classification of Campaign Styles Associated with Protagonist Attributes

	Low Legitimacy	*High Legitimacy*	*Low Transparency*	*High Transparency*	*Low Resources*	*High Resources*	*Low Visibility*	*High Visibility*	*Low Identity of Interest*	*High Identity of Interest*
Transparency	L	H	L	H	?	?	L	H	L	H
Breadth	L	L-H	L-H	L-H	L	H	L	L-H	L	H
Intensity	L	L-H	L-H	L	L	H	L-H	L	L	H
Duration	L	L-H	L-H	L-H	L	L-H	?	?	L	L-H
Directness	L	H	L-H	L-H	L	H	L	H	L	H
Specificity	L	H	?	?	?	?	L	H	L	H
Scale	L	H	H	L	L	H	H	L	L	H
Redundancy	L	H	L	H	L	H	L	H	L	H
Policy Focused	L	H	?	?	?	?	?	?	L	H
Process Focused	L	H	L	H	?	?	L	H	L	H
Self Focused	L	H	L	H	?	?	L	H	L	H

- Transparency—the extent to which the existence and nature of the campaign itself is public, and is acknowledged by the protagonist.
- Breadth—the diversity of tactics employed in the campaign, including not just campaign communications, but the full range of campaign-driven activity.
- Intensity—the force, passion, and concentration of effort with which the campaign is being pursued.
- Duration—the time frame of the campaign, whether short-term, intermediate, or long-lasting (often a function of the campaign objectives).
- Directness—the degree to which the campaign confronts the target frontally and in the name of the protagonist.
- Specificity—the extent to which the campaign identifies and advances a clearly delineated objective, as opposed, for example, to some more ambiguously stated notion of "progress".
- Scale—the sheer size of the campaign effort, as measured, for example, by expenditure of resources or the number of participating intermediaries.
- Redundancy—the extent to which the campaign pursues its objectives through multiple and generally parallel paths, as opposed to a single path; the extent to which it is multi-linear rather than linear.
- Policy Focus—the extent to which campaign objectives are defined in terms of behavioral outcomes such as policy change.
- Process Focus—the extent to which campaign objectives are defined in terms of behaviors such as process change.
- Self Focus—the extent to which the campaign identifies and emphasizes the interests of the protagonist, *per se*, as opposed to some broader set of third-party interests, e.g., the so-called "public interest."

All are reflective of choices made by, or imposed upon, the campaign strategist.

The cells in each set of paired columns (e.g., low and high legitimacy) in Table 6.2 represent possible implications of the differing protagonist attributes for the selection of stylistic elements of the campaign. For instance, it is posited in the table that campaigns conducted by low-legitimacy protagonists will tend toward low transparency, while those conducted by protagonists that are accorded greater public acceptance will be more transparent. The rationale is simply that more legitimate protagonists have less to hide, and/or less reason to do so. To be sure, that is not a hard-and-fast rule, as the legitimacy of a protagonist might itself be based on perceptions that could be altered by the release of previously unknown facts, the shining of a spotlight on known but unappreciated facts, or the reinterpretation of seemingly unfavorable facts. But as a tendency of campaign style in the general case, it is a reasonable expectation. Similarly, albeit selectively, the table also suggests (other things being equal) that:

- High-transparency protagonists will be more likely than their low-transparency counterparts to conduct campaigns that are also relatively transparent. In part, this would be the product of the natural style of such a protagonist, but it could also be a reflection of the need to maintain continuity of messages and images. Consider, for example, the deleterious effects on the reputation of a seemingly transparent NGO that was discovered to have engaged in a "secret" campaign to achieve some objective. The incentive to avoid such a possibility would be considerable.
- Similarly, while a protagonist whose interests are very similar to those of its target might be expected to run a campaign that is relatively transparent, one run by a protagonist with vastly discrepant interests from those of the target might profit from a more opaque effort. If, for example, one assumes that the target's stakeholders interact with the target based on their own self-interest, it follows that there is sufficient continuity of interest between those stakeholders and the target to merit such interaction. A transparent attack on the interests of the target might thus be interpreted by some of the stakeholders as an attack on their own interests as well, and might produce an affirmative disinclination to pressure the target. In such circumstances, the campaign protagonist that is dependent on the actions of these stakeholders for its own success may better be served by masking its efforts.
- Well-resourced protagonists are more likely than poorly-resourced protagonists to conduct campaigns that are higher in their breadth, intensity, duration, scale and redundancy, for the obvious reason that they are better able to do so. But this overlooks one of the important components of some information and influence campaigns—fund-raising—which can consume a consider amount of (primarily) early-stage effort. If there are compelling strategic reasons why an otherwise under-resourced entity should conduct a campaign that is generally beyond its customary means, part of the campaign itself may be devoted to addressing this need by seeking foundation grants, governmental or quasi-governmental grants or aid (such as EU grants to support environmental campaigns), funding from better-heeled allies, or other sources.

Other cell pairings could be subjected to similar analysis, and none of these tendencies is argued to be determinative. And, as indicated by the question marks in certain cells, the implications of particular protagonist attributes as determinants of alternative campaign styles may, in some cases, be unknown, uncertain, or even irrelevant. For example, it is difficult to see why, in any systematic way, the levels of protagonist transparency, visibility or available resources would make the campaign more likely than not to take on a policy focus. Finally, there is a potential transformative aspect to this entire line of argument. If the circumstances call for a campaign of a given style, but such a campaign is inconsistent with the attributes of the protagonist, it might, in some instances, be possible to reconstruct the protagonist (or perceptions of the protagonist) before launching the campaign. The fund-raising example above represents one such transformation; it is possible to imagine others. The reinforcement or strengthening, the re-framing, or even the reconstitution of the protagonist in advance of the launching of a campaign is often a strategic option, and can be an important one.

Box 6.2 Packaging the Protagonist to Fund and Legitimize the Campaign

Clifford Bob (2005: 54–116) tells the fascinating story of how a Nigerian insurgent group, the Movement for the Survival of the Ogoni People (MOSOP), emerged onto the world stage in the 1990s under the leadership of Ken Saro-Wiwa, who himself emerged as an iconic opponent of Shell Oil, which was active in the region. The key was the development of a marketing plan for MOSOP itself—a plan that converted the group from one of many obscure ethnic movements into a leading voice for environmentalism in the Niger Delta, and in the process attracted the financial and other support of major transnational NGOs.

While the details of the campaign are many and quite interesting, it is this act of conversion that merits our attention in the present context. Knowing it was under-resourced and needed visibility and legitimacy, MOSOP set out in the early 1990s to gain the support of outside NGOs, but it failed, partly because its case was not well framed, but largely because its cause did not resonate with the agendas of these established international actors. But beginning in 1993, when MOSOP reframed its case in environmental terms—in effect claiming that Shell and other oil giants were plundering the Delta, and, with the complicity of the Nigerian government, suppressing the rights of the Ogoni to do it—the movement flourished. This environmental frame accorded with the interests, and attracted the support, of such groups as Greenpeace and Friends of the Earth, Human Rights Watch, Amnesty International, and others. The demonization of Shell both energized and gave focus to the campaign, but it was the underlying dynamic of matching the agenda of the would-be protagonist with the agendas of its potential supporters and intermediaries, that literally made the campaign possible.

Things did not end well, by the way, for any of the interested parties. Saro-Wiwa and several others were tried by the Nigerian government for incitement to murder some rival leaders, found guilty, and hanged in

1995. Shell was blamed by activists around the globe for these deaths, and was even charged in the United States under the Alien Torts Claims Act and brought to trial in 2008. That case was settled out of court in 2009 when Shell agreed to a payment of about $15 million. (Goldhaber, 2009) And as for MOSOP? Events have passed it by. Today military attacks by insurgents against oil company facilities are commonplace, not just in the Niger Delta itself, but even against oil rigs 75 miles offshore (Polgreen, 2008).

This brings us to the critical point of the argument in this chapter, which is this: The strategic needs of the campaign protagonist will lead it toward a style of campaigning that maximizes the prospects for a successful outcome. The requirements of that style, together with any deficiencies the protagonist may display in its ability to adopt it, will guide the selection of third parties in the campaign and the uses to which they are put.

Stylistic Requirements Guide Use of Intermediaries

That is to say, the requisite campaign characteristics, in whatever combination, point toward the most likely configurations of message content, message sourcing, alliance formation and the like that are likely to delineate any given campaign. Campaigns that are conducted by protagonists lacking in legitimacy, transparency and identity of interest, such as an unpopular insurgent movement, will probably look very different from those conducted by civil society-type groups that leverage their names and name recognition, their access to decision makers, and their willingness to garner public attention. But it is the constellation of associated traits, and not necessarily the protagonist *per se*, that leads to this determination. Thus, other things being equal, a foreign government that is lacking in perceived legitimacy in a second, target country will wage a different style of campaign—different channels, actors, language choice, media and message strategy and the like—than one that benefits from strong public acceptance. And a protagonist that maintains low transparency and low visibility will probably conduct a campaign designed to exploit and maintain those attributes, while a transparent and highly visible protagonist will follow a different path.

Box 6.3 Who Really Hates Wal-Mart?

Among the longest-running and most visible campaigns of recent years has been the one targeted at Wal-Mart. There are many dimensions to this campaign—labor unions that see the company and its policies as a threat to their ability to organize workers, small town merchants who feel threatened by the unrivaled pricing power of this giant corporation, land-use activists, historical preservationists, environmentalists, local politicians . . . the list sometimes seems endless. The campaign often plays out in local battles over zoning and licensing prefatory to the building of new Wal-Mart stores, especially where the company has not previously been present in the local market. But in some cases, it seems, some of the opposition to the company is not altogether as localized, self-generated, and independent as it appears.

It turns out that at least one consulting firm, Saint Consulting Group, has been behind much of the strategy and tactics of anti-Wal-Mart activism in recent years. Here is how one account describes the firm's activities:

> For the typical Wal-Mart assignment, a Saint manager will drop into town using an assumed name to create or take control of local opposition . . . They flood local politicians with calls, using multiple phones to make it appear that the calls are coming from different people . . .
>
> They hire lawyers and traffic experts to help derail the project or stall it as long as possible . . .
>
> (Zimmerman, 2010)

Members of the local surrogates recruited by these professionals often believe they are actually aligning themselves with labor unions, and sometimes those unions are, in fact, Saint's clients. But more often, it turns out, the firm's client is actually one or another supermarket chain that is trying to preserve its local or regional (or national) market share against competition from Wal-Mart. Among them, according to the *Wall Street Journal*, have been Supervalu, Giant Foods, and Safeway. Were these protagonists to be known publicly, one must assume, their self-interest would be clear and their chances of success lessened.

More generally, over the years the firm has conducted about 1500 campaigns in 44 states. Of these, acknowledges founder P. Michael Saint, some 500 have focused on blocking a development—of oil refineries, shopping centers, quarries, landfills, as well as Wal-Mart stores—and of those, the majority have been clandestine, which is to say, conducted through unknowing surrogates. (Zimmerman, 2010)

But, as Saint Consulting and its clients found out in this instance, strategies employing surrogates are inherently risky, especially where the objective is to mask the protagonist. A few short days after the *Wall Street Journal* revealed the facts of the anti-Wal-Mart efforts on its front page, the firm reportedly had lost one existing client and one prospective client (Bustillo, 2010).

One of the key differences here is the extent to which third parties are employed as intermediary actors or communicators. Table 6.3, which employs the same protagonist attributes as Table 6.2, sets forth some of the possibilities. Campaigns can vary as to the number of third parties that are incorporated, the degree to which their roles are central or peripheral, the availability of natural allies or insiders or, failing that, the likelihood they will be replaced by unknowing allies or by surrogates created expressly for the campaign or for related purposes, and the likely diversity of third-party actors.

So, for example, a protagonist characterized by low legitimacy and low transparency will be relatively likely to filter, or perhaps "launder," its message through other, better positioned, voices or in other ways operate through third parties in order to mask or offset its lack of public acceptance and maintain its anonymity, and may well be forced to employ surrogates since some prospective allies might prefer to avoid any appearance of associating with it. In contrast, a highly legitimate protagonist will seek to exploit its legitimacy through open invitations to likeminded intermediaries to join in expressing their common values or preferences. And a protagonist with high identity of interest with the target might opt for the same reliance on third parties, not to mask a weakness, but to exploit a strength.

In the logic of the campaign, this is the point of origin for the development of networks and related strategies. The attributes of the protagonist

Table 6.3 Likely Use of Third Parties Associated with Protagonist Attributes

	Low Legitimacy	*High Legitimacy*	*Low Transparency*	*High Transparency*	*Low Resources*	*High Resources*	*Low Visibility*	*High Visibility*	*Low Identity of Interest*	*High Identity of Interest*
Number	H	L	H	L-H	L-H	L-H	L-M	M-H	L	H
Centrality	H	L	H	L-H	H	L-M	L	H	H	L
Availability of Natural or Knowing Allies	L	H	L-M	L-H	L-H	L-H	L	H	L	H
Availability of Unknowing Allies/Self-Interested Foils	L-H	L-H	L-H	L	L-H	M-H	L-H	L	L	H
Availability of Insiders	L	H	L	H	?	?	L	L-H	L	H
Surrogacy	H	L	H	L	L	H	H	L	H	L
Diversity	L	H	L	H	L	H	L	H	L	H

determine the extent to which it must, or can, be dependent on a structure of intermediaries, and even the types of intermediaries that are most likely to prove advantageous. If, as we argued at the outset, it is a power deficit relative to the target—whether absolute or situational—that gives rise to the need for an information and influence campaign, it is these attributes that create the template for developing the architecture of the campaign itself.

Form and "Feel" of the Campaign

Figures 6.1 through 6.3 are meant to illustrate how these layers of attributes—of protagonists, campaign styles, and third-party requirements—combine to generate the form and, for want of a better word, the "feel" of a given campaign. In Figure 6.1 we see the range of protagonists identified in Table 6.1, which are differentiated by the degree to which each, respectively, displays the attributes that will give direction and set the boundaries of campaign possibilities. In effect, these attributes serve as filters that will allow certain campaign attributes to come into play depending on the profile of the particular class of protagonist. In simpler language, what we have here is a picture of the argument that who the protagonist is will go a long way to determining what kind(s) of campaign it needs, or is able, to conduct if it is to maximize the chances of achieving its objectives.

Figures 6.2 and 6.3 illustrate the next steps in strategic development, the translation of optimized stylistic attributes, termed here the "campaign profile", as suggested in Table 6.2, *and* the translation of the requisite reliance on third parties, or intermediaries, as suggested in Table 6.3, into tactical decision-making. The first of these, Figure 6.2, shows that the peculiarities of each different campaign profile (on the left)—and the list here is not intended to be comprehensive—interacting with the optimal combination of intermediaries (on the right), will point toward the differential selection of tactics, based *here* not on the characteristics of the target or the campaign setting, but on the needs and capabilities of the protagonist. We will argue in a later chapter that target attributes and contextual elements *also* contribute to the selection of tactics, but for the moment, our purpose is to illustrate the central role in this decision-making that is played by front-end, as opposed to back-end, considerations.

Those front-end considerations can lead to a kind of internal campaign logic that can be applied in developing specific tactics or tactical approaches. For example:

- A protagonist with low transparency may be more likely to use certain low-visibility kinds of exchanges, such as money transfers, to recruit and support intermediaries because it is relatively less likely than others to be found out. The same consideration may lead to a lesser reliance on alliances with existing organizations, and a greater reliance

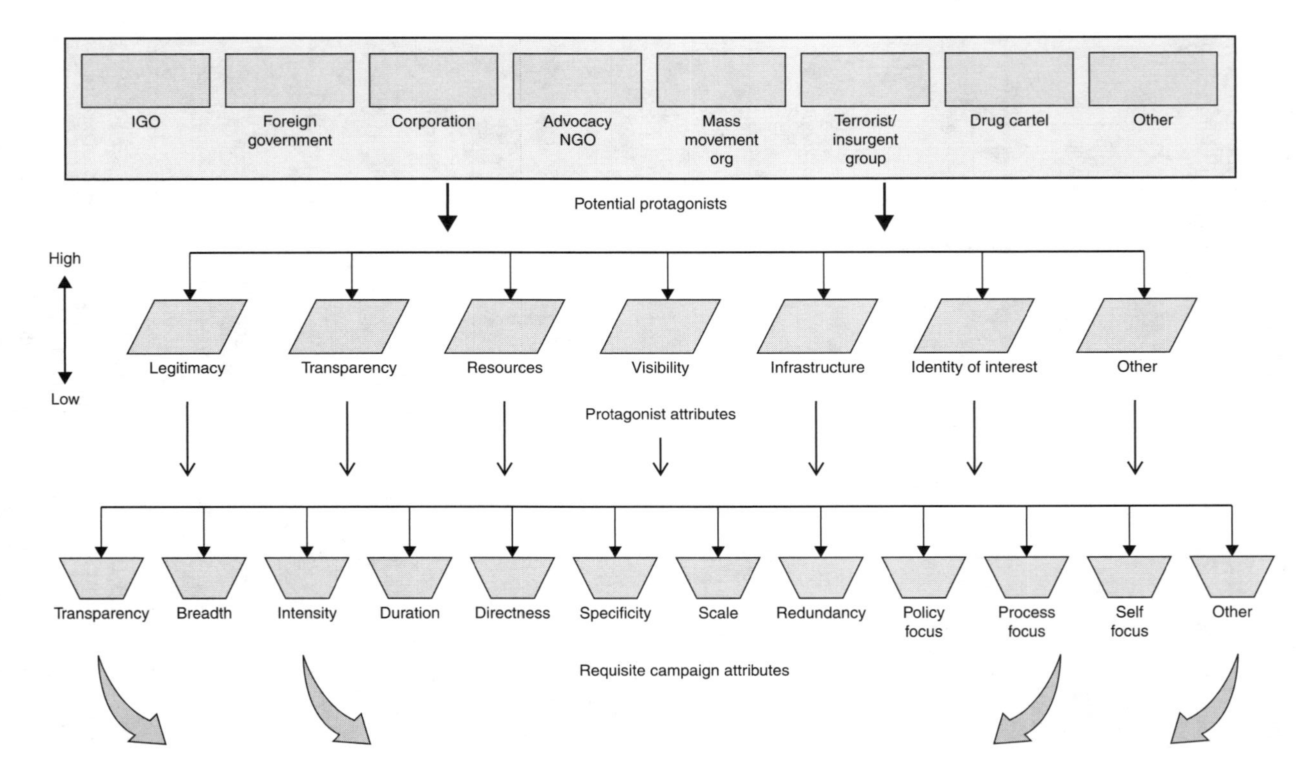

Figure 6.1 Dynamics and Flow of Influence in Information and Influence Campaigns.

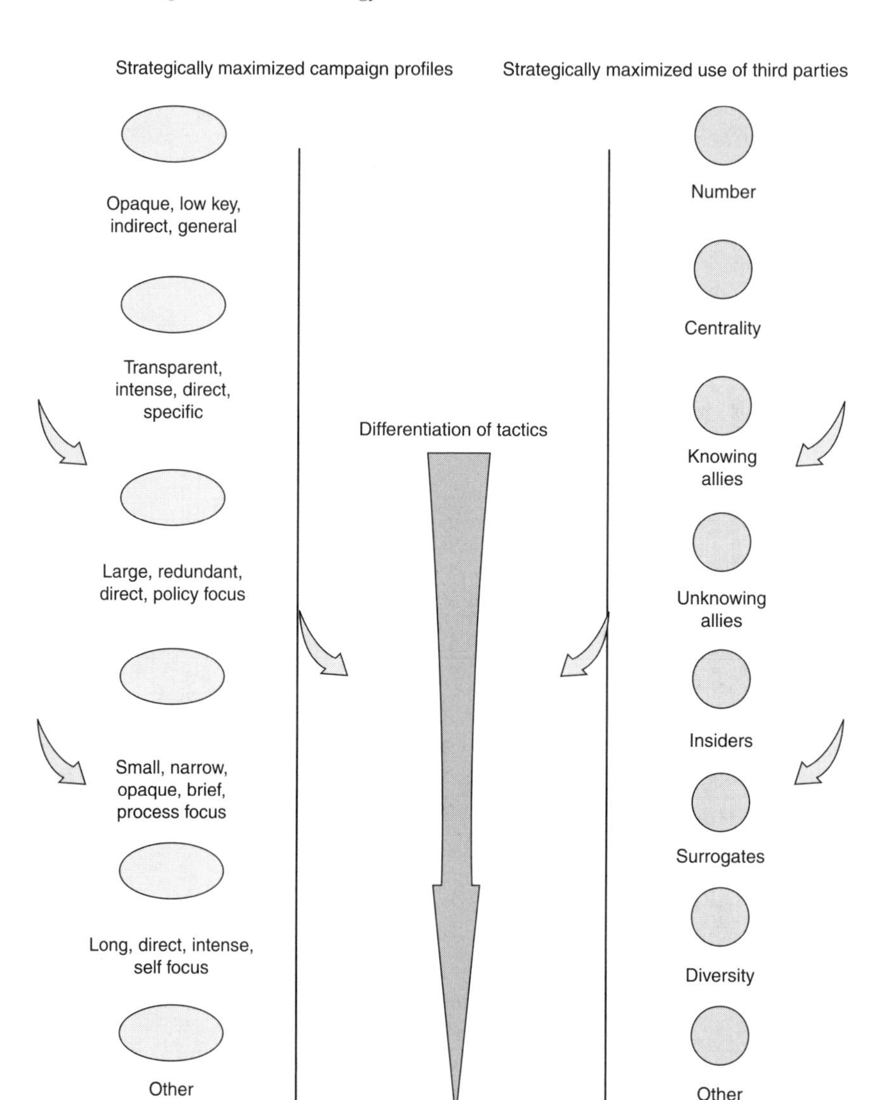

Figure 6.2 Attributes, Strategic Requirements, and Campaign Tactics.

on the creation of surrogates and virtual organizations. It may also require that such intermediaries have a short half-life to reduce the potential for discovery. In contrast, a highly transparent protagonist is less likely to rely on exchanges of questionable or hidden resources, and more likely to rely on openly developed alliances with similarly transparent intermediaries, such as many civil society-type organizations. Since these intermediaries most likely exist independently of the campaign, they will also be likely to have greater longevity than surrogates or virtual organizations.

- Visibility, as distinct from transparency, points toward strategies that are rather more nuanced. In normal public discourse, visibility is an asset to a protagonist that is favorably perceived by key audiences, and a significant detriment to one that is viewed unfavorably. So a protagonist with favorable standing would be inclined toward strategies designed to maintain or boost visibility as a way of reinforcing its position, while one with unfavorable standing would opt for strategies that are likely to reduce its visibility.
- In its strategic preferences and selection of tactics, a protagonist with low target affinity would be confronted with needs similar to, but not isomorphic with, those of one lacking in legitimacy. The similarity would be greater at those stages of the campaign closest to the target, where the absence of affinity would be most telling, but would be of lesser import in dealing with more protagonist-proximate intermediaries with which the level of affinity might be quite high. This points to a strategy in which intermediaries proximate to the protagonist are selected primarily for their access to, and credibility with, key intermediaries that are closer to the target. In effect, the first group vouches with the second for the validity of the protagonist's agenda. Whether that validation extends to the protagonist itself might be determined by the situation. In contrast, a protagonist with high target affinity might have no strategic need whatsoever for its own most proximate intermediaries, opting instead to work directly through those with most direct access to or influence on the target.

Figure 6.3 illustrates the projection of these tactics into the campaign proper. Effective campaigning requires the successful management of the protagonist's communications and actions, of its relationships with third parties, and in some measure, potentially, of the separate and independent relationships among those third parties themselves. Our emphasis in the present volume has been primarily on communication strategies, and that emphasis continues in the figure. It is important to bear in mind, however, that in a campaign, all actions communicate, and all communications impact on the relationships that constitute the underlying structure of the campaign.

Here the connections between the earlier discussions of argumentation and persuasion, on the one hand, and networks and relationship management, on the other, are crystallized. The voices, channels, messages and audiences illustrated in the figure correspond with those we examined in Chapters 3 and 4, while the relationships referenced in the figure are those we began mapping in Chapter 5. And as we also suggested in Chapter 5, and especially through the inventory of campaign tactics in Table 5.1, whether or not they literally "speak louder than words," the actions that

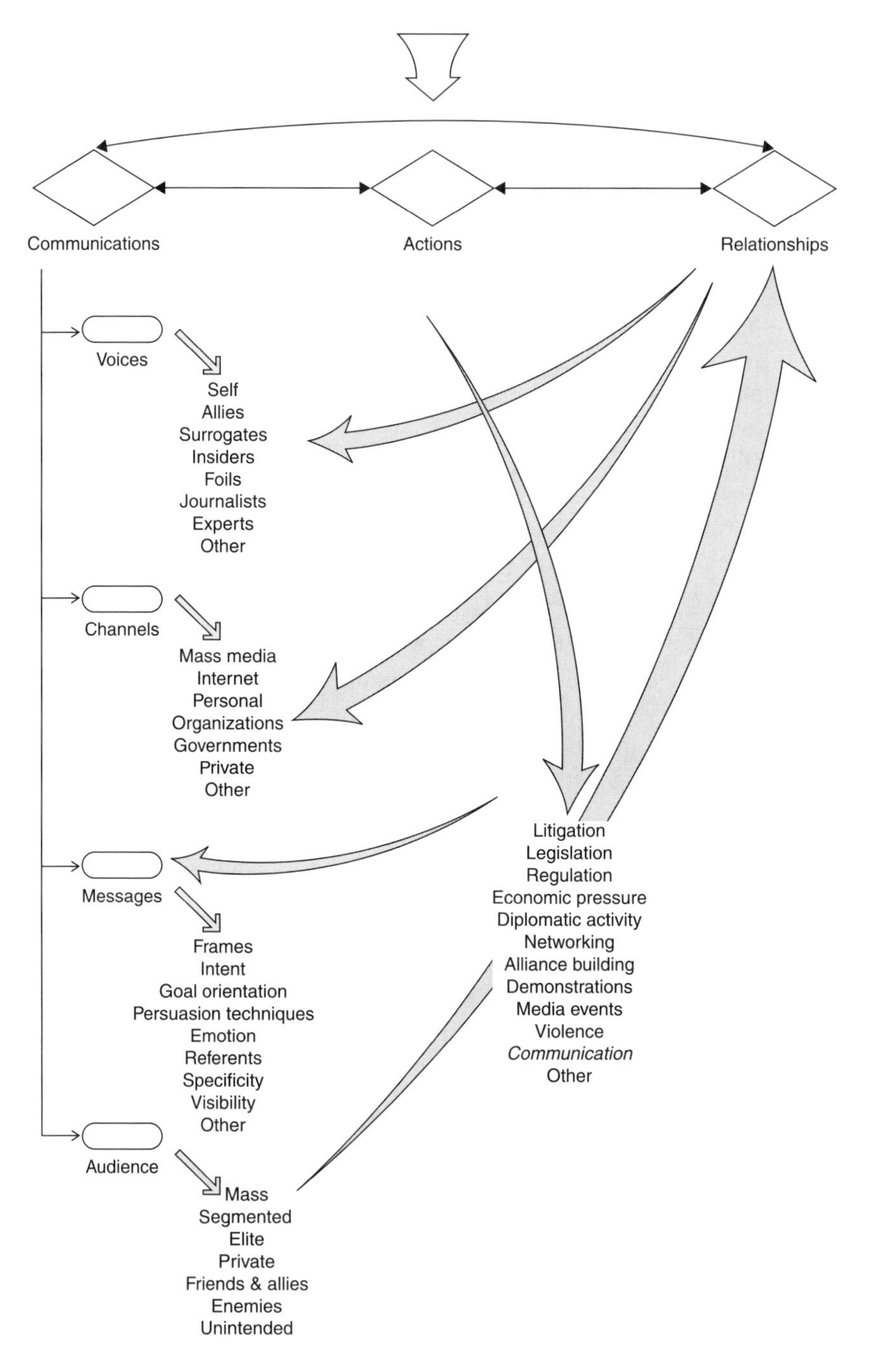

Figure 6.3 The Interaction of Communications, Actions, and Relationships in the Campaign.

accompany campaign rhetoric certainly do communicate. They stimulate and guide the participation of intermediaries, and they certainly get the attention of the target. Now the larger point should be clear: The tactics employed in an information and influence campaign will derive in significant degree, not only from the attributes of the protagonist, but from the strategic requirements that arise from managing the campaign *per se*. The fact that the campaign exists and takes a certain form, in and of itself, creates a set of strategic and tactical requirements that must be addressed in addition to, and in interaction with, the strategic and tactical requirements imposed by the objective of the campaign—to affect the target.

In an earlier discussion, we argued that, with respect to the target, a campaign was likely to have one of five objectives: initiating or reinforcing a behavior, modifying or reinforcing a behavioral dynamic (an ongoing behavior), modifying a static position or condition of the target, ceasing an ongoing behavior or withdrawing a position, or not initiating a behavior in which the target has yet to engage. If we think of these as the range of *macro*-strategic objectives of the campaign, we can see now that there are as well a series of *micro*-strategic objectives that relate to motivating intermediaries to act and channeling their actions in desired ways. Here, the idea is to use campaign communications and other means to move the various intermediaries around the board. A protagonist's profile vis-à-vis its target with respect to attributes like legitimacy or affinity may be different from its profile vis-à-vis certain intermediaries, particularly those to which it is proximate. It follows that the form or content of tactical exchanges between the protagonist and these friendly proximate intermediaries may well be different from the form or content of the overall campaign precisely because they are intended to serve as translators or interpreters, conflating the profile of the protagonist with their own profiles to advance the campaign, or simply as veneers to mask it.

In this multi-communicator, multi-audience, and multi-dimensional world, then, the overall communication objective of a campaign at every stage is not persuasion, in the classical sense, but influence in the broadest sense. It is to determine what positioning of each downstream actor optimizes the chances of the protagonist for a successful campaign, what change in extant positioning is required to move that actor to the desired location, and what communication strategies, frames and messages are best suited to accomplishing that. Persuasive communication as typically conceived can be central in facilitating movement on one dimension—preferences—but a more comprehensive understanding of potential, salutary communication effects is required if one is to fully appreciate and capture their role in a campaign.

Implicit in much of the discussion to this point has been the assumption of an underlying temporal linearity to the campaign. Because there is, in fact, a natural flow to certain stages of a campaign—identify the target, research the target and its stakeholders, plan the campaign, identify and recruit prospective intermediaries, identify and obtain the requisite resources, develop and optimize the message frames and communication channels, roll out the campaign—this underlying assumption has considerable validity. At the same time, however, campaigns are seldom smooth-running, tightly controlled exercises. Serendipity plays a role—things just happen. Windows of opportunity open and close. Some tactics work, others do not. Changes occur in the campaign environment. Unanticipated intermediaries insert themselves into the campaign on their own initiative and for their own purposes, perhaps consequentially. The target takes steps to defend itself. The campaign succeeds in some measure, and moves the target to a new place. These factors—and there are many more like them—can easily disrupt the linearity of the effort. Or more to the point, they *should* do so. For when material changes occur that logically would seem to require a reassessment, and possibly a redirection of effort, the campaign that fails to adjust simply fails. So while there is a natural linearity to campaign logic, there is an essential iterative element to any campaign. The strategist runs through the logical sequence once, then senses the environment, makes any necessary changes, and runs through the logical sequence once again. And once again. And once again. In a campaign of long duration—and some of them run for many years—numerous iterations will be required.

7 Feeling the Pressure: The Dimensionality of Targets

> I have with me two gods, Persuasion and Compulsion.
>
> Themistocles

> In the field of politics, force and consent are correlative terms, and one does not exist without the other . . . Every consent is more or less forced . . .
>
> Benedetto Croce

At the outset, I suggested that information and influence campaigns can be conducted at different levels of complexity and sophistication. We are now at a point where we can elaborate a bit more on that argument.

Levels of Campaign Complexity and Sophistication

At the most basic level—and let's call this Level I—campaigns may be comprised of strategically planned, crafted and delivered bundles of messages designed directly to persuade a target to alter its behavior in ways that serve the interests of the campaign protagonist. In a Level I campaign, by definition then, the protagonist is but one step removed from the target, and has the capability, independently, to deliver its persuasive communications. Those communications might take the form of more or less straightforward argumentation, as we emphasized in Chapter 3, or they may be developed with an eye toward one or more of the structurally-derived persuasive strategies we explored in Chapter 4. But in either event, there are no intermediaries required in the transmission from source to receiver, except, perhaps, for channels that are purchased, or otherwise fully controlled, by the protagonist. Level I campaigns are thus centered entirely, or nearly so, in communications *per se*. A public information campaign in which a protagonist uses such means as paid media, direct mail, and a website to "educate" the public (or a subset of the public) to perceive differently its own self-interest and to change its behavior accordingly—an anti-smoking campaign (or a sexual abstinence campaign) being the classic example(s)—would fit this profile.

If we return as well to our more basic premise, that IICs are employed where there exists an asymmetrical power relationship between the protagonist and the target, we can see that a Level I campaign is most likely to be employed where the power differential is minimal and may be situational in character, where the protagonist determines that new information or enhanced attention, in and of itself, are likely sufficient to bring about the desired change, and where the means are available to deliver that information to the target. But many power disparities are greater in degree and more complex in form than those characterized by this simple model. At the next level, for example, which we will perhaps not surprisingly term Level II, the protagonist may not have meaningful direct access to the target, but it may have means of communicating directly with, and/or otherwise influencing, other actors who are themselves influential with the target. We have termed these influentials the target's stakeholders, and the process of identifying them and evaluating their potential utility in a campaign we have labeled power structure analysis. Here, at two steps removed from the target, the strategic goal is to achieve the desired outcome through a more elaborate set of actions and communications that mobilize one or more of the stakeholders to communicate with, or to act upon, the target in ways that advance the protagonist's interests. It may, and very likely will, be necessary for campaign communications to frame and rationalize the issues in ways that appeal to the target, but the essence of campaign strategy at Level II is to influence the stakeholders. So the communications and actions at Level II are far more likely to focus, *selectively* as we have argued, on the values and interests, not of the target, but of those other actors on whose good will, support, and other exchanges it depends. Level II campaigns, then, are much more highly leveraged than those at Level I.

At the next step of remove—the Level III campaign—the leverage may come to resemble less that attendant to a fulcrum point than that of a clockworks in which the force exerted at point A is transmitted to point N through a series of interlocking gears. Where the protagonist lacks influence either with the target or with its key stakeholders, which is to say, where the asymmetry of power between protagonist and target is the greatest, the campaign necessarily becomes more elaborate, and perhaps more convoluted. This is the point at which we typically see the emergence of "netwaves," successive layers of intermediaries that function to bridge the gap between the protagonist and the target. Typically, the design of strategy at this level begins with a basic power structure analysis of the target and its stakeholders, but then adds as many successive layers as necessary of additional power structure analyses, this time applied to each of the stakeholders and other intermediaries as well. At each stage, the operational question centers on what degree and manner of leverage the protagonist might exercise on a given intermediary or group of intermediaries. If leverage is available, and if it is deemed potentially sufficient, the campaign structure is set. If still greater leverage is needed, the structure must be expanded by at least one more wave before it can be considered set. It follows that, at Level III, campaign strategy must be designed to mobilize in the desired direction whatever complex set of relationships among protagonist, intermediaries, stakeholders, and target are required to effectuate the effort.

Figure 7.1 summarizes the decision-making dynamic for a Level III campaign. As suggested in the Figure, campaign strategy operates through tactics that address three sets of operational objectives—those pertaining to the communications, actions and relationships, respectively, through which the campaign will be advanced—each of which must be managed systematically, consistently, and in constant interaction with one another. These three decision-making channels must be coordinated effectively if the objectives of the campaign are to be accomplished. And only if the objectives of the campaign are accomplished will the protagonist's desired outcomes—the reason for the campaign—be achieved. We will return to this point later in this chapter.

First, however, let us consider another implication of the figure. Note that Figure 7.1 makes a distinction between the "effectiveness" of a given campaign and its "success." This suggests that a campaign could be successful without achieving the desired outcomes, something we have not previously considered. And that, in turn, suggests that there are actually two different sets of criteria we might employ for judging campaign strategy. Did the strategy produce a campaign that functioned as intended—managing communications, actions and relationships to generate pressure on the target in a desired direction? And separately, was the pressure sufficient to cause the desired behavior change? The first of these is, in a sense, an assessment of campaign technique, and the second of the fundamental vulnerability of the target to influence in the first place. Not all campaigns—and not all well-crafted, technically sound campaigns—succeed. In fact, many do not. Information and influence campaigns, you will recall, are designed to generate leverage to offset inequalities in the distribution of power. But in the real world, those inequalities may be so great that even the best campaign cannot overcome them.

That suggests that target *selection* is an important first step in developing a campaign strategy. To this point, we have said a great deal about protagonists, intermediaries, and stakeholders, but relatively little about the targets of IICs. The time has come to remedy that.

Vulnerabilities Assessment and Target Selection

As we have regularly observed in these pages, the potential targets of information and influence campaigns are many and varied, as is the range of campaign objectives. But if the campaign is designed to counter, or counterbalance, the power of the target, just what is it that makes a target

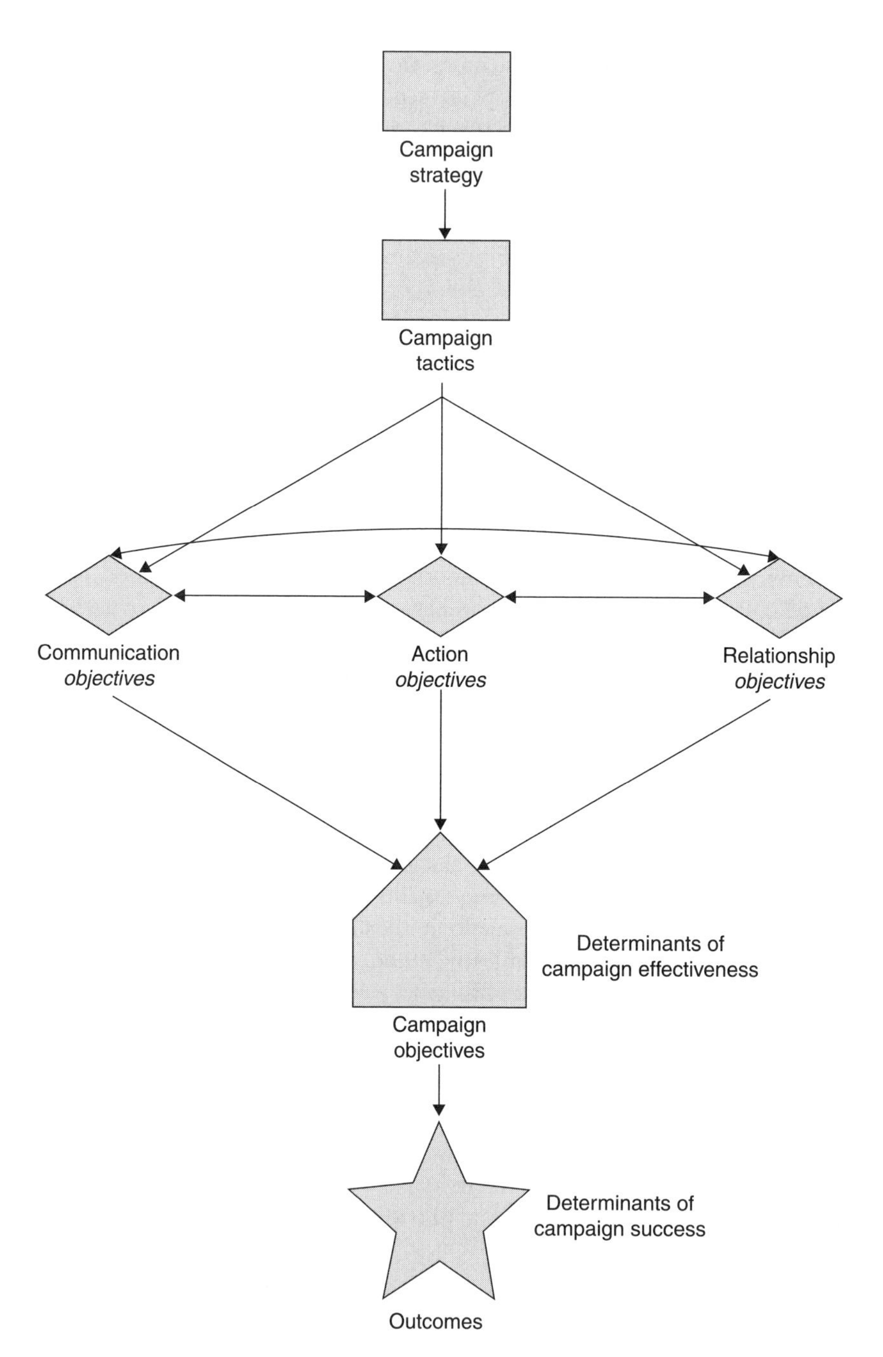

Figure 7.1 Strategy, Tactics, Objectives, and Outcomes.

powerful? In the context of the campaign, what are the dimensions of strength and weakness that define the vulnerability to influence? Or, put another way, what attributes of a prospective target can be put to best advantage in determining (a) the degree of its susceptibility to influence through an IIC, and (b) what form and content such a campaign might adopt to achieve maximal impact? Rather than focusing on the idiosyncrasies of targets, are there general tendencies that a strategist might seek out to determine the likelihood that an IIC can achieve the desired outcomes?

Drawing in part on our analysis from Chapters 3 through 6, and especially on our discussion of campaign protagonists and intermediaries, we can identify several generic attributes that increase the potential vulnerability of a given target and thus its attractiveness to the strategist. These include:

- *Low legitimacy*. Just as is true of a campaign protagonist, prospective targets vary in their inherent or perceived legitimacy. Targets of limited legitimacy, or, importantly, those that can be readily positioned as such, among key intermediaries, might include a head of state (Hugo Chavez of Venezuela to American conservatives) or a regime (the Saudi monarchy to guest workers from Pakistan), an industry (extraction industries such as mining or petroleum to environmentalists) or a company (such as one that contracts out work to sweatshop-style producers, to the general public), a policy (limits on immigration, responses to climate change, and the like), a relationship (Russia and Ukraine, Hamas and the Palestinian Authority), an individual actor (name your least favorite politician) or a class of actors (bureaucrats, conservatives, Social Democrats, environmentalists, entertainers playing at politics, greedy corporate executives), and so forth—in short, anything or anyone who can be portrayed believably to a key audience as lacking in legitimate authority. Of course, these characterizations are determined based not on the perceptions of the protagonist, but rather on those of key stakeholders and other intermediary audiences, or on those perceptions that can be generated among them. A real or perceived paucity of legitimacy creates an image vacuum that can be filled with adverse portrayals, as well as a broader strategic vulnerability that is somewhat akin to a medieval city without a protective wall. Low legitimacy both invites and facilitates campaign attacks.

Box 7.1 Exploiting the Perceived Illegitimacy of the Target

The conflict between the governments of Iran and the United States dates back to the overthrow of the Shah and the occupation of the US Embassy in Tehran in 1979, though the roots of suspicion lie deeper still. At the core of the conflict is the rejection by each side of the fundamental legitimacy of the other, and the exploitation of that rejection in campaigns for the hearts and minds of global and regional publics. The US, for example, was characterized in the early days of the Iranian revolution as "the Great Satan," while Iran was one of three countries designated by President George W. Bush in 2001 as members of the so-called Axis of Evil. The objective of each of these arguments, and of the underlying campaigns, is two-fold—to position the competing antagonists at the forefront of their respective constituencies, and to appeal to those constituencies for support of efforts to limit the ability of each side to impose its will on the other through global economic and political institutions.

Given the intransigence of the two sides, it is not surprising that the rhetoric has changed little over the years. In the words of Iranian President Mahmoud Ahmadinejad in 2008, for example:

> Today, the time for the fall of the satanic power of the United States has come and the countdown to the annihilation of the emperor of power and wealth has started.
>
> (Quoted by Agence France-Presse, June 2)

- *Widespread negative perceptions*. Though similar, a generally negative image is in a sense a less demanding standard than low legitimacy, one that allows for acceptance of the target as valid or rightful, but at the same time positions it as acting badly, espousing unpopular values, or the like. Extant negatives have the effect of attracting attention even as they deprive the target of the ability to defend itself affirmatively or proactively. More than that, if the target is generally accepted as legitimate but its actions are judged negatively, the target's underlying legitimacy can be used to generate internal leverage on values or behaviors that can be portrayed as inconsistent with that higher standing. When, for example, in one of the earliest anti-corporate applications of these campaigns activist Saul Alinsky sought to change the minority hiring practices of the Eastman Kodak Company in Rochester, New York, his leverage derived from contrasting the implicitly anti-social character of the targeted policy with Kodak's status as a pillar of the local business community and the centrality of that status to the company's internal culture and collective sense of self-worth.
- *High visibility*. Targets that are highly visible may be especially vulnerable to IICs in part because that visibility itself deprives the target of certain defenses against a campaign, such as the ability to hide from view (perhaps even in plain sight), while at the same time assuring that any campaign successes are likely to be widely noted. Such credit

claiming can then be employed by the protagonist in subsequent stages of the campaign, both to enhance its credibility and apparent potency and as a form of psychic reward to its allies and personnel. Where high visibility co-occurs with a highly negative target image or with minimal target legitimacy, the combination serves further to accentuate any negative perceptions and to render them even more difficult to counter or reverse. An end case on the spectrum of visibility is that of a cultural, economic or political icon such as Coca Cola or the U.S. dollar, the status of which enhances the attractiveness of the target as well as the impact of any campaign success.

- *High transparency*. Targets that are relatively transparent are inherently vulnerable to attack simply because it is easy to learn a great deal about them. Examples would be publicly held corporations, to the extent that they are required by law to reveal detailed financial and other information about themselves; membership organizations, which must report on their activities and operations in order to recruit, serve, and maintain their members; and government agencies that are subject to open access, freedom-of-information, or other legal requirements. As these examples suggest, the *degree* of transparency and, importantly, the *expectation* of transparency, can be vital factors in such assessments.
- *Low transparency*. At the same time, the absence of transparency can also be an important determinant of vulnerability. In the most obvious sense, it can represent a negative attribute of the target, since a no-comment culture generates doubt and distrust among outside audiences at the same time that it leaves the field open for others to describe and define the target and its actions. But there is a second, and perhaps less obvious, way in which low transparency might factor into a vulnerabilities assessment. Targets such as complex public policies or issue publics may be more susceptible to a campaign because the subtle changes that can produce desired campaign outcomes can occur outside of public view and may not be well understood even by those most directly affected. Modest changes in legislative language that may have broad but latent consequences that serve the interests of the protagonist would be an example. Our brief transit of the attitude-change landscape in Chapter 4 suggests that such subtle, low-engagement changes may be among the lowest hanging fruit in the campaign orchard.

Box 7.2 Buried Treasure

The debate over reform of healthcare policy in the US that dominated the news in 2009 and early 2010 centered around negotiations, deadlines, secret drafting sessions and, in the end, voluminous legislation, all reflective of the interplay among numerous competing campaigns waged by such diverse forces as pharmaceutical companies, insurance companies, large employers, small business, labor unions, and progressive and conservative cause groups. Each protagonist had its interests, and the floating alliances these produced added a patina of political confusion atop a protrusion of legislative language. In the end, there were winners and losers, but they were, arguably, determined not by the overall thrust of the resultant legislation so much as by the subtle twists and turns of hidden subparagraphs. That, even in this instance where the public gaze was fixed on the issue for months, it took journalists and politicians literally weeks to decipher some of this language and to figure out just what had been passed by Congress, and that the public had by then altogether lost interest in any devilry that might be uncovered, only reinforced the value of burying the treasure.

- *Responsiveness, or sensitivity*. Targets that have demonstrated a history of adjusting their behaviors in response to earlier campaigns may offer advantages to the strategist in a subsequent campaign because they have demonstrated a risk–reward ratio that is favorable to the protagonist. Put another way, such targets are already conditioned to behavior change, so the campaign can focus on specifically desired behavior changes rather than on "teaching" the target to change in some more abstract sense. A corollary is that targets that have demonstrated a concern for their public image and standing, for maintaining a good reputation, are proportionately more susceptible to campaign activity, as in the Eastman Kodak example noted above.
- *Association with risk*. Those targets that are, or can be, associated with definable external risks—nuclear accidents or war, unsafe products or services, threats to public safety or security, economic or political instability, terrorism, dangerous ideas—will be more susceptible to campaign activity than those that pose no such risk. The likelihood of attack increases to the extent that any such risk can be personalized for key intermediaries such as public opinion or the members of a particular group.
- *Risk aversion*. That said, it is also the case that targets that have displayed a particularly strong *aversion* to risk, which is to say a consistent pattern of behavior seeking to minimize or avoid risk or any association with it, ironically, have an increased vulnerability to campaign pressure for one very straightforward reason: Their behavioral preference vis-à-vis risk increases their susceptibility to threats and fear appeals and, potentially, expedites and multiplies their effects when employed by a protagonist.
- *Physical weakness*. Targets that are physically unable to defend themselves against attack are, as a result, more likely to be attacked. Physical weakness might be military in character, but in the present context it is

more likely to take other forms, such as financial weakness, inability to communicate effectively, weak infrastructure, weak intelligence capabilities (to detect and appraise the attack), weak leadership, and so forth.

- *Limited resources*. Although it is, by our definition, almost always the case that the target of an IIC is superior in power to the protagonist, it does not follow that the target has at its disposal limitless resources. To the contrary, even governments and large institutional targets operate within financial, personnel, temporal and other constraints, and the campaign setting and/or timing can, by accident or by design, exacerbate these limitations even more. Companies that are experiencing downward pressures on cash flow or profits, or government policy-makers who are operating in a period of high deficits, would be examples. In fact, from a purely strategic perspective, the absolute level of the target's resources may be less important in determining its potential vulnerability to a campaign than the level of its resources relative to its extant commitments.
- *Inherent structural vulnerabilities*. Targets are often complex entities, and some of their component elements—demographic groupings, cultural norms, religious values, political interests, economic interests—may be disproportionately susceptible to IIC influence. Examples might include European Muslims confronting a collective identity crisis that opens them to certain types of appeals, policies that appeal to significant subsets of a population, companies that are dependent on certain strategically important markets (IBM in the EU, Lenovo in the United States), and so forth. The more central these elements are to the core needs of the target, and the more of them the strategist can identify, the greater the leverage they afford.
- *Instability*. Targets that do not have long established and constant relationships with their key stakeholders, that are inconsistent in their policies and behaviors, that are governed or administered by shifting alliances or processes, and that do not invest in maintaining a stable operating environment, offer to the protagonist a virtual panoply of opportunities for leverage and pressure. On the other hand, targets that do maintain stable relationships, policies or behaviors, leadership and infrastructures, and that invest resources in stability *per se*, are by nature less vulnerable. An exception, or rather, a modification, to this argument may occur in those instances where the protagonist is successful in undermining one or another aspect of the target's stability. In that instance, it may be that the target is sufficiently inexperienced in dealing with the resultant instability that it actually enhances it through its own misguided responses.
- *A reputation for faulty, inefficient, or impeded decision-making*. A government, corporation, NGO, or other organization that is known to delay or defer decisions, or to make bad ones, may be disproportionately vulnerable to a campaign.

- *Self-generated leverage.* One common campaign strategy today is to use what might be termed a "big want" on the part of the target as a force multiplier for the campaign. When a target publicly commits itself to a major new undertaking—a company building a giant new facility or entering a major new market, a union publicly committing itself to organizing workers at a company, an advocacy group or a government committing vast resources to a specific policy outcome, a government granting public license to an insurgent group in a neighboring country to use it's territory as a base of operations in hopes it will overthrow the sitting government, a government seeking to stabilize another government by locating military bases on its territory—it effectively stakes some portion of its reputation on its ability successfully to navigate whatever set of processes and challenges stand between the target and achievement of this new goal. Achieving the goal may require various physical, financial, legal, legislative, regulatory, diplomatic, communicative, persuasive or other accomplishments, each of which puts the target at potential risk in a given sub-arena. That enhanced risk, combined with the raising of the stakes, can be turned to strategic advantage in a campaign, often in a highly cost-effective manner. In effect, the target grants to the protagonist control over some of its own resources to use as leverage against it; it subsidizes, or at the very least facilitates, the campaign.

Campaigns Are Complex, Communication Is the Key

The attack on the target or its interests that is embodied in an information and influence campaign is often dominated by campaign communications—framing, messaging, distribution, channel effects, and the like. But as we have seen, these efforts are broadly interdisciplinary in character, ranging well beyond polemics to generate pressure for change—an observation that increases in validity the further one moves along the continuum of objectives from information toward influence. They incorporate psychology—in forms ranging from activating various mechanisms of attitude change to generating pressure on key actors through personalization, fear and the like. They incorporate economics—as in efforts to leverage the economic relationships between the target and its stakeholders (a company and its lenders, customers, or shareholders; a government and its trading partners), or to effect a redistribution of resources from or by the target. They incorporate politics—as in seeking to create and/or exploit weaknesses in the relationship between a target and its governmental overseers or negotiating partners, or in using extant issues and public perceptions to define or isolate the target or its policies or behaviors. They incorporate sociology—as in efforts to align the target with a social class or grouping, or to demonstrate the absence of such alignment; in the emphasis on pro-social values and internal institutional cultural norms; and most certainly in the development and exploitation of social network structures among campaign intermediaries. And they incorporate legal, regulatory, diplomatic, and even, in some circumstances, military pressures as well. A truly comprehensive campaign is a veritable cornucopia of confrontation.

And yet, campaigns *are*, fundamentally, communication phenomena. For all of these actions—diverse as they may be—are, in the end, designed to communicate a single message from the protagonist to the target: You must change your ways. Actions may or may not speak louder than words, but the point here is that they do speak. The pressure on the target may be political or economic or legal or diplomatic in form, but in the effective campaign, it will always be linked, directly or indirectly, to the objective. That linkage is not always achieved publicly, and in fact, there are often reasons in a campaign to avoid making the linkage transparent. Where the campaign is largely hidden from view, or the protagonist controversial, or certain key intermediaries are likely to withdraw should their role become public or should they come to realize that they are actually playing such a role, for example, a transparent linkage does not serve the strategic interests of the campaign. But in some way the protagonist must—literally must—communicate the linkage to the target. Otherwise, any pressure that may be generated will be interpreted as arising from some source other than the campaign, and the effort required to generate or direct that pressure will have been wasted. Credit must be claimed.

From this and earlier discussion, and from Figure 7.1, it should now be apparent that the selection of the communications and actions to be deployed in a comprehensive, sophisticated information and influence campaign is not best accomplished by taking a random walk through the possibilities. While there is often, to be sure, a significant degree of opportunism in the choice of tactics, at a higher level that selection is guided by such factors as the extant audience perceptions of the actors and issues; the available messaging and positioning; the nature of the relationships among the protagonist, the intermediaries, including but not limited to the stakeholders, and the target; the attributes of the target and the intermediaries; and the campaign setting. Each of these elements has the capability of opening, requiring, facilitating, impeding, or foreclosing entire clusters of tactics, and each must be taken fully into account by the strategist.

All of that weighing and considering, of course, can add layers of complexity to the campaign, and to campaign planning and decision-making. And there is a level at which such complexity is inevitable. There is, however, as we observed in a more limited context in Chapter 6, a countervailing principle that any strategist would do well to bear in mind. It is the principle of parsimony, perhaps stated most succinctly by Leonardo DaVinci when he observed that "Simplicity is the ultimate sophistication." The point is not that requisite complexity should be discarded in the interests of pure parsimony, but rather that complexity should not be valued for its own sake. Contemporary information and influence campaigns are, by their very nature, multifaceted undertakings, and they are not simple in any sense of the word. But, perhaps for that very reason, it is quite tempting indeed for the strategist to make them even more complicated than they need to be in order to achieve the desired objective. It is that mad rush to complication that is to be avoided. To borrow from the French writer of the early twentieth century, Antoine de Saint-Exupéry, the campaign strategist achieves perfection "not when there is nothing left to add, but when there is nothing left to take away."

8 Guarding the Castle: Deterring, Deflecting, Minimizing or Defeating Information and Influence Campaigns

> Achieving victory in every battle is not absolute perfection: neutralizing an adversary's forces without battle is absolute perfection.
>
> Sun Tzu (Huang 48)

> It is quite natural that we should adopt a defensive and negative attitude towards every new opinion concerning something on which we have already an opinion of our own. For it forces its way as an enemy into the previously closed system of our own convictions, shatters the calm of mind we have attained through this system, demands renewed efforts of us and declares our former efforts to have been in vain.
>
> Arthur Schopenhauer (1970: 124)

> Publicity is justly commended as a remedy for social and industrial diseases. Sunlight is said to be the best of disinfectants; electric light the most efficient policeman.
>
> Louis Brandeis (1914: 92)

> The trick, as in jujitsu, is to find a way to turn a rival's apparent advantage into a drawback.
>
> Edward Dolnick (2008: 227)

In medieval days, the seat of power was the castle, which provided protection against marauding knights, rampaging barbarians, rebellious serfs, and all manner of challengers. The castle may not always have occupied the moral high ground that is at issue in the contemporary information and influence campaign, but it nearly always occupied the actual high ground.

As a defensive system, the castle evolved over time in response to changes in the strategies, tactics and implements of war available to those who would besiege it. Ramparts evolved from earthen mounds to rock walls, and rock walls from simple geometries to complex battlements with overlapping lines of sight to permit the control of all of the potential avenues of attack. Altitude relative to the surrounding territory was its own form of intelligence gathering, as the view from genuinely high and unobstructed ground is wide and clear, so castles tended to be built, where possible, on hillocks or mountain tops with commanding views of their approaches. But not all fiefdoms are mountainous, and circumstances dictated that many castles needed to find other devices to bolster their defenses. Among these were dry moats, flooded moats, flooded moats (rumored to be) filled with frightful beasts—all channeling access to a few, relatively easily controlled, gated points of entry. Castles were built over springs or around streams to assure access to a water supply, and provided storage space for grains and foodstuffs, fodder and shelter for diverse livestock, barracks and arms for defenders, refuge for supporters fleeing from invading hordes, and ample supplies of firewood, large pots, and oil for boiling and dispensing among the enemy—over the counter, as it were. The walls were high, steep, and as smooth as the local materials and masonry permitted, and laced with small holes or crowned with architectural dentistry to facilitate defensive archery and to protect those who were thus deployed. The territory surrounding the castle was given over, where feasible, to the production of food and other critical materials, and was populated with loyal subjects of the castle's owner. Among them, and especially in more distant lands, spies were embedded among the locals to provide early warning of any impending threat. Particularly in the later years, it truly was systemic defense in depth.

Sometimes it worked. Sometimes it didn't. It was an iterative process of sorts. Defenses would be erected against all, or most, known threats. Then some brilliant strategist or inventor would come along with a new kind of threat. Laying siege. Establish protected water supplies and store food. Battering rams to penetrate gates. Reinforce the gates and set them at heights or angles that limited their vulnerability. Mound-building to scale earthworks. Build higher walls, of wood. Fire to burn down wooden walls. Build rock walls. Portable ladders to scale rock walls. Boil oil, collect urine and excrement. Tunneling to undermine the walls, divert water supplies, or simply provide an unannounced arrival in the defenders' midst. Build and flood a moat, and possibly a series of defensive tunnels. Archers to span the distance across a moat or a no-man's land, first with longbows, then with crossbows. Develop protective architecture (slit windows, dental work) in and on the walls. Catapults, and then trebuchets, to knock down all but the stoutest of walls. Cannons to do the same. Give up on castles and find some alternative system of defense.

This iterative character of castellar defense revealed itself only slowly over many years, over decades, even over centuries. The pace of travel, of communication, of innovation, of construction, of testing—in short, the pace of history itself—was deliberate, the rate of acceleration minimal. The iterative character of attack and defense in contemporary information and influence campaigns, on the other hand, has been greatly compressed in time, as befits an age of instantaneous communication. It is—actually quite literally—as the flicker of a light to the wielding of the quarryman's chisel. Information, not rocks or arrows; perceptions, not parapets;

relationships, not breastworks. The alternating stages of challenge and defense, the duel of competing messages and frames, may last little more than a single news cycle, and sometimes less. But in both cases, the shaping and evolution of defenses occurs in anticipation of and response to the shifting form of the attack.

The Logic of Defense: Reverse Engineering

In the case of the castle, the key to intelligent and maximally successful defense against each succeeding generation of offensive capability lay in assessing the territories and battlements to be defended as the would-be attacker might assess them, noting both apparent and latent strengths and weaknesses; identifying those lines and means of attack most likely to be deployed by the attacker, and determining the relative likelihood, form and potential of each; evaluating the resources, capabilities, and limitations of the attacker itself, both generally and as they were likely to impact on the expected confrontation; and then designing and devising defense in depth that would, if it worked, absorb the attack and consume the attacker's resources until they were exhausted—or better still, so demonstrate the capacity to do so that the attacker would direct its energies elsewhere. In other words, the best defense in such a complex situation was to reverse engineer the expected attack, then fortify one's defenses at the most critical points, sometimes visibly for the deterrent effect, sometimes invisibly for the benefit of surprise, but always for advantage (Sun Tzu 101).

In the case of the contemporary information and influence campaign, the key to intelligent and maximally successful defense is very much the same. It is built around solid intelligence, insightful analysis, an understanding of the dynamics of the attack or expected attack, and defense in depth or, at least, at strategically selected junctures. Like castellar defense, it begins with reverse engineering of the campaign itself, either as deployed by the protagonist or as it is expected to be deployed.

The starting point for devising a sound defense must be the identification of an operational theory of the campaign—a conceptual framework that will consistently explain and predict its development. In the present context, this is actually easier than it sounds. The dominant operational theory of IICs is power structure analysis, which provides the basis for strategic decision-making by the protagonist. It follows, then, that effective reverse engineering begins with the application of this same conceptual scheme to shape the target's defensive strategy. Recall that the protagonist uses power structure analysis to identify, assess, and assign roles to the key stakeholder relationships on which the target depends for its routine functioning. These various stakeholders are examined with an opportunistic eye, not necessarily as objects to be persuaded of the merits of the protagonist's preferences, but rather as objects to be persuaded to act, selectively, in their own self-interest in ways that advance the objectives of the campaign. In devising its defenses against that campaign, then, the target must undertake a similar analysis *from the perspective of the protagonist*. This amounts to gaming the range of likely attacks, employing the perspective, objectives and underlying strategy of the protagonist to anticipate the most likely lines of attack. In this process, the target identifies its own critical stakeholders, examines the interests of each, both generally and as they relate to the target, and identifies and assesses the strengths and vulnerabilities extant in each of these relationships. Each of these factors is evaluated for its centrality to the well-being or continued success of the target and the likelihood that it can be activated by or in behalf of the protagonist, and the results are prioritized to generate foci of reinforcement or improvement. In essence, at this level the objective of defensive strategy is to harden the target—to reduce its susceptibility to pressure generated through its stakeholder relationships. That may be attempted across the board, or it may be approached selectively, where the goal is less to prevent or deflect an attack than to channel it to the relationships that are least salient to the target or most easily defended—basically inducing the protagonist to squander its efforts and resources in the areas where they matter least and are least likely of success.

Box 8.1 Reverse Engineering the Corporation

At least one commonly targeted set of institutions, corporations, should be well positioned to implement a defensive strategy based on reverse engineering of the IIC. In his 1984 book, *Strategic Management: A Stakeholder Approach*, management scholar R. Edward Freeman set forth a theory of management that called for an emphasis on identifying, assessing, maintaining, and strengthening the critical relationships upon which every company depends—with its shareholders, customers, financial backers, employees, regulators, political and community groups, and the like. He identified three levels at which this process must operate—understanding who the stakeholders are and just what their stake in the company is, understanding how the company manages its relationships with these stakeholders, and understanding the transactions and bargaining that occur between and among the company and its stakeholders.

If that sounds familiar, it should. For it is the very same concept that activists had begun to apply in the 1970s as a basis for designing strategies to disrupt and redirect the policies of those same corporations—power structure analysis. In fact, if one were to set the power structure maps devised by activists side by side with the stakeholder maps proposed by Freeman, it would be difficult to tell one from the other. And in later years, as the emphasis in strategic management has come to focus squarely on advancing corporate social responsibility, these stakeholder relationships have remained at the center of the action, providing, conceptually, both the rationale for policy change and the mechanisms by which to achieve it. In effect, then, management and anti-management are using the same playbook.

Well, not quite. For although both sets of actors have adopted the same analytical tool, they employ it to diametrically opposite ends. Management uses stakeholder analysis to facilitate the company's movement toward its objectives, while the activists use it to impede or redirect that same movement. And that gets us to our point. To defend itself against IIC-driven pressure from its stakeholders, a company need only use the tools already in hand in a new way—by understanding and anticipating how they might become cudgels rather than comforts.

In some instances, especially where the designated target is but one member of a *class* of more or less equivalent targets (for example, companies in the same industry, countries in the same region or alliance, unions subject to the same labor laws), and where the protagonist has exercised some discretion in initially selecting a particular target, this strategy has the potential to reduce the vulnerability of that initial target, and/or to raise the cost or complexity of the requisite attack, to the point where the protagonist decides to direct its efforts toward some other member of the class—perhaps even a competitor. Ironically, then, the mounting of an early and effective deterrent to an expected campaign sufficient to redirect the efforts of the protagonist might actually end up strengthening the competitive position of the initial would-be target, something the protagonist would hardly have set out to do.

The same strategy of reverse engineering can then be extended outward to deactivate likely campaign intermediaries. In gaming inbound attacks, the target strategist must ask not only which stakeholders are most likely to be engaged as points of pressure, but how a given protagonist might expect to achieve that. One set of answers to that question will point to the particular intermediaries—or at least to the classes of intermediaries—that are most likely to have a role. Employing the same logic as the protagonist, for example, the defensive strategist can determine a set of needs that the protagonist will have to address through its intermediaries. These might include, for example, acquiring legitimacy, visibility, or resources, or mitigating any other weaknesses attendant to its basic profile. What intermediary, or class of intermediaries, might help a similarly situated protagonist address a given problem? Chances are the answer would be reflected in the campaign. Intelligence gathering at this stage, centered on the protagonist and on past campaigns in which it has engaged, will also help to identify its tendencies in alliance formation and networking, fundraising, campaign behaviors and the like. What specific intermediaries are routinely associated with *this* protagonist or have been employed by *this* protagonist in past campaigns? These past proclivities can be good indicators of future actions, and they are often easily determined for all but the least transparent protagonists by such straightforward means as reviewing news accounts, Internet postings and public records.

We can illustrate this process of reverse engineering of relationships with reference to Figure 5.8, which is reproduced here as Figure 8.1. Recall that this figure illustrates the selection and activation of networked pathways through which the protagonist might project its campaign upon the target. The final rank of intermediaries, designated IMn, of course, represents the target's key stakeholders.

Now consider the variation on this process introduced in Figure 8.2. Here, the dotted lines and open-style arrows represent actions of the target as it anticipates and responds to the pressure gradients of the inbound campaign. Four such actions are represented, each reflective of a strategic alternative that may be available to the target. The first and most straightforward of these shows the target operating on the middle stakeholder, IMn*b*. In the original schematic of the campaign, IMn*b* has been assigned by the protagonist as the primary point of pressure on the target, as indicated by the number of earlier-stage intermediaries that converge upon and act through it. Assuming that this stakeholder has been selected because of its real importance to the target—a point on which, in the illustration, the target concurs—the defensive strategist will act to shore up this relationship by reinforcing affirmative elements of the association and mitigating

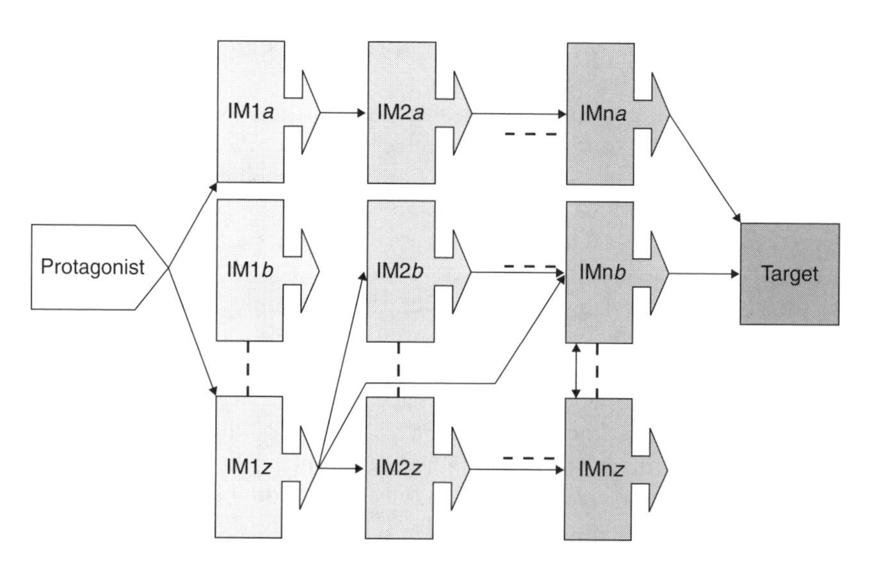

Figure 8.1 Network Structure Arising from Sequencing of Intermediaries.

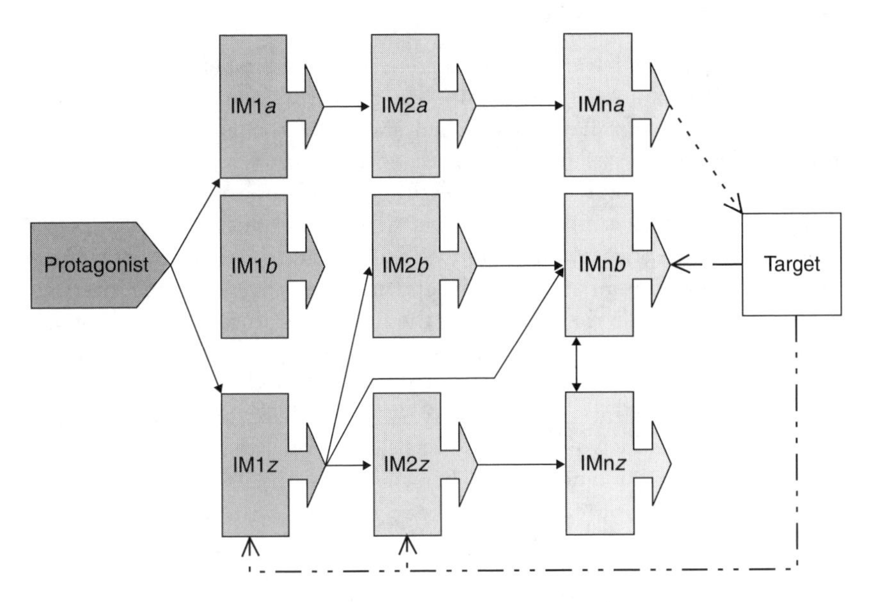

Figure 8.2 Reverse Engineering of the Campaign Network Structure.

any negative elements. That action is represented by the connecting arrow in Figure 8.2. As we noted above, however, not all stakeholder relationships are equally critical to the target, and there may be circumstances in which it is expedient to channel a campaign challenge through pathways of minimal importance. That strategy is illustrated in the figure in the relationship between the target and stakeholder IMn*a*. Note that the target has not sought to preclude pressure arriving through this channel, but has merely discounted it. This is represented by the dotted line (maintaining the channeling of pressure) but open-style arrow (indicating a decision of the target).

Next, consider the remaining target actions, as represented in the initiatives directed at IM1*z* and IM2*z*. These intermediaries might represent advocacy NGOs, governmental agencies, other governments, the media, or any other kind of actor. In both cases, the target is acting directly on such intermediaries in an effort to discourage or minimize the chances of their participation in the campaign, to take them out of play or to deflect them if they are already engaged. The identification, selection, and influencing of these entities can be among the greatest challenges to the defensive strategist. But, because they have the potential in some cases to pull the ground out from under a campaign without ever having to engage either the protagonist or its issues and preferences, meeting those challenges successfully can be especially rewarding. We have already spoken briefly of the identification of success-critical intermediaries. So let us now turn to the matters of selection and influence.

Power Structure Analysis Redux

Recall that intermediaries, like protagonists and targets, have certain attributes that can be used to determine their prospective contributions to a campaign. They *also* have established stakeholder relationships of their own—allies, sources of funding, other entities that they serve and upon which they are in some way and measure dependent. Some or all of these independent, preexisting relationships will be of value in the campaign (and constitute a primary reason for their selection as intermediaries), while others may not. But all of them exist and are of importance to the intermediary in question. To the extent that the target's strategist can employ his or her own small-scale form of power structure analysis, and can find points of access that can be stimulated to discourage or redirect actions by the intermediary, that intermediary may be neutralized and taken off the board. The means by which this might be accomplished are precisely those we have explored at length in earlier chapters. And as in the campaign itself, the target's approach in attempting to neutralize real or potential intermediaries need not engage them in allying with, or even addressing the needs of, the target. Rather, and just like that of the inbound IIC, it can (and often must) address elements of their own self-interest. If, for example, the target has friends among the foundations that support an advocacy group or allies in international organizations that can affect its interests, it may be able to work through those third parties to restructure the decision matrix of a given intermediary actor. The deactivation of an intermediary is generally best accomplished quietly, subtly, and out of view of the public and the media, partly because it might come to be portrayed or viewed as somehow an improper exercise of power on the part of the target, but more fundamentally because it preserves the dignity and freedom of action of the intermediary itself.

This is where basic network architecture can come into play. Returning to Figure 8.2, compare, for example, the campaign connections operating through IM1*z* and IM2*z*. Within the context of this hypothetical campaign, IM2*z* is a node in a linear network. If IM2*z* can be neutralized or deactivated, one pathway through the network is broken. Pressure generated on and through stakeholder IMn*b* will be reduced proportionately. But this portion of the network is redundant, and other channels are available to reach this key stakeholder. On the other hand, if the defensive strategist were able to neutralize IM1*z*—which in its outward-bound activity more closely resembles the star form of network architecture, *all* of the sources of pressure on stakeholder IMn*b* would be eliminated, and in the limited example, the campaign itself would have been largely neutralized. Finally, note that the target has initiated no action to neutralize any of the intermediaries in the "*a*" (top-most) rank. This channel, directed at generating pressure through IMn*a*, is linear with no redundancy, and could be disrupted if any single intermediary were successfully taken out of play. Recall, however, that the target made a strategic determination that IMn*a* did not represent a viable source of pressure. From this it follows that there is no need to disrupt this channel of attack. Indeed, there may be reasons to preserve it, either to burn through the protagonist's resources, as we suggested earlier, to allow the protagonist an operating campaign channel as a face-saving maneuver, or even to observe and model the protagonist's campaign techniques for future reference.

The obvious extension of this defensive strategy is to the protagonist itself. This might be as simple, and even transparent, as direct outreach—seeking a mutually satisfactory negotiated outcome. It might require nothing more sinister than a sunshine strategy, publicizing the fact and dimensions of the campaign itself, which might in some circumstances embarrass the protagonist—especially one lacking in legitimacy—into submission. It might more closely resemble efforts to neutralize intermediaries, which is to say, analyzing the dependency (stakeholder) relationships of the protagonist, then working systematically to remove its supports, offering to substitute for and enhance them (that is, to buy off the protagonist), or in some other way pressuring it to end the campaign. Or the target

Box 8.2 Co-opting the Protagonist

One recent trend in the ongoing dance between corporations and their environmentalist critics has been the hiring by the former of key leaders of the latter. A case in point occurred in 2002, when Burson Marsteller, a global public relations firm with a number of clients—Monsanto, Union Carbide, the Three Mile Island nuclear plant, etc.—that had experienced eco-wrath, hired Lord Melchett, formerly head of Greenpeace UK and at the time still a member of the board of Greenpeace International, to provide them with advice. Needless to say, this caused quite a stir among activists, though Greenpeace tried for a time to remain sanguine, suggesting that his appointment might open a new channel of communication between offending companies and their critics. That view, however, was not universally shared. One activist asked, "How can you have a man who is on the board of Greenpeace International and a policy advisor to [a conservation group] taking money from the [genetically modified foods] industry and companies with some of the worst records imaginable?" (Vidal, 2002). In the face of intense media coverage (like that we have just cited), however, Greenpeace changed its mind and asked Lord Melchett for his resignation, not from Burson Marsteller, where he continued to use his knowledge of the organization and the broader environmental movement to advise clients, but from the Greenpeace International board (Beder, 2002).

might try to disrupt the protagonist's command and control mechanisms, as, for example, by depriving it of access to certain channels of communication, or by some non-literal analogue to the military strategy of decapitation of an enemy's organizational units. This could be accomplished, for example, by isolating, compromising, subverting, hiring or appointing, or in some other way co-opting one or more key leaders or strategists.

The end state of such a strategy would be to wage a counter-campaign against the protagonist, either by the target or by allies or surrogates that it recruits for that purpose. From the target's perspective, that is a very dangerous strategy that can easily backfire, especially where the target acts directly in ways that are discoverable, or where the third-party veil masking its role is pierced. There is, for one thing, a hackneyed old aphorism that is directly on point: "Don't wrestle with pigs. The pigs love it, and you'll only get dirty." Recall that IICs generally occur where there is an asymmetry of power. The more powerful actor—typically a government, a corporation, or some other well-established entity—generally benefits from being viewed as steady and secure, but suffers when viewed as unstable or risky. In contrast the less powerful actor—typically an advocacy group, a social movement, a labor union or the like—benefits when it demonstrates an ability to generate risk and uncertainty, enhances its own status among its supporters to the extent it is able to "call out" a more powerful adversary, and enhances its public stature to the extent it is treated as an apparent equal by such an adversary. The target, then, has much to lose and little to gain from such an exchange, and more generally must guard against over-reacting to the pressures generated by the campaign. Indeed, spurring such over-reaction is often a key objective in the protagonist's selection of tactics. Precisely because the target is the superior power, actions that it might take vis-à-vis the protagonist—even if they precisely mirror those taken by the protagonist against the target—can easily be portrayed and seen as a form of bullying and can detract from the target's legitimacy. The underlying asymmetry of power generates differential expectations.

For these and other reasons, such counter-campaigns are extremely rare. But even with respect to far less aggressive defensive efforts, expectations and the associated "optics" of the campaign are critically important. And that means that the successful management of perceptions and preferences—among the general public and its relevant subsets, among key elites, among the various news and other media, among other intermediaries and stakeholders—is critical to mounting an effective campaign defense. The strategic defender must be every bit as proficient as the protagonist, for example, in understanding and taking advantage of the dynamics of attitude change that we outlined briefly in Chapter 4, and must also have the capability to recognize and respond to efforts by the protagonist to employ these dynamics. When employed by the defense, there are at least two sets of challenges. First, how can the target persuade a given individual or group of individuals (or audience), and most

Box 8.3 Outsourcing the Counterattack

The many companies that have been targeted by labor unions for organizing-related IICs are typically in precisely the situation we describe here—under attack on many fronts, but constrained in their ability to respond. Some number of them—no one is sure just which ones or how many, and that is the point—have come together to create a surrogate organization, the Center for Union Facts (CUF), to carry the battle to the unions. CUF maintains a website (Unionfacts.com), conducts and publicizes research that embarrasses union leaders, designs and purchases large volumes of print and television advertising, advises disgruntled union members, and in general adopts a highly confrontational stance vis-à-vis organized labor. Presumably, the member companies love it. It may be vicarious, but it satisfies their urge to strike back—and in ways they would not dare do themselves. It is as close to a counter-campaign as most will, and perhaps should, ever get.

especially its stakeholders, that their interests remain tied to and consistent with its own? Here, the challenge is very similar to that confronting the protagonist, and can be advanced by the careful selection of frames and arguments, and the reliance on the most relevant theories of attitude change. But at the same time, there is a complication: the campaign. The target's strategist must therefore *also* take into account, and seek to counter, inbound persuasive efforts initiated by the protagonist. The challenge in this second instance is not so much to persuade as to induce *resistance* to persuasion.

Inducing Resistance to Persuasion

Needless to say, just as social psychologists have developed numerous theories about how to achieve persuasion, they have as well developed approaches to resisting it. The classic example is the inoculation theory developed by William McGuire in the 1960s. The idea here is that an individual can be inoculated against persuasion in much the way that one is inoculated against a disease—by exposing him or her to the negative argument in a way that is easily resisted, then relying on this resistance to protect against more virulent forms of attack. McGuire actually identified four basic approaches to inducing resistance to persuasion. One involves inducing the subject to take some public stand—a statement, an action—that identifies him or her with the position that is to be defended—to act out the existing perception or preference, thereby raising the psychological cost of later changing positions. A second approach is to draw explicit linkages between the belief in question and the individual's personal values, reference groups, or other beliefs. This provides a cognitive anchorage that may keep the individual from drifting to a new position. Third, a strategist might limit the likelihood of persuasion by creating or enhancing mental states in the subject(s) that represent barriers to persuasion—things like inducing anxiety about the issue, raising self-esteem, encouraging aggressiveness, or employing ideological preconditioning. Inoculation represents a fourth approach, one in which the individual is presented with an easily refuted attack on his or her existing beliefs, motivated to defend the status quo, and provided with the information and arguments that can be used in constructing a defense [McGuire, 1961; Kiesler, Collins, and Miller, 1969: 133–135]. A variant on this is forewarning: "You may hear someone say that . . ." More contemporary analyses have extended and complemented these approaches. Some, for example, treat resistance not as an outcome—the failure to be moved by pressure to change one's beliefs—but as a condition or motivational state—the desire to resist or counter efforts to induce change. Others see resistance as an attitude in its own right—comprising affect, cognition and behavioral intent. But as a practical matter, McGuire's four categories will suffice to suggest the nature of this added dimension of psychological warfare that may be available to the defensive strategist and some of the ways it might be brought to bear.

As with affirmative persuasion, once an approach has been adopted, its implementation on the scale required to mitigate the adverse effects of a campaign is generally accomplished through message structures, frames and the like—all closely paralleling the mechanisms we described in Chapters 3 and 4 but for the directional purpose and content of the information. Just as there are in any campaign certain themes, frames, facts, messages and other forms of information that advance the interests of the protagonist—whether to persuade individuals, to manage media portrayals, to motivate intermediaries, to claim and define positions of moral superiority while depriving the target of same, or for some other purpose—there are similar structures available to the target to enhance its standing and protect its prerogatives. To the extent that these information structures are already widely distributed and generally accepted among a given audience—to the extent that the target has a good reputation among that audience, for example—the target may actually begin from a position of advantage. But where it is confronted with novel frames and claims, and where the attack is waged beyond the boundaries of existing images and perceptions, the target is often at a significant disadvantage. The stakes in the race to determine the terms of debate that shape a given campaign, then, are substantial. Because of the underlying power asymmetry, the target may, in some cases, have an advantage in the level of resources it can bring to this struggle for communication preeminence, but as we will see in a moment, it may also be subject to certain structural disadvantages that can be difficult to overcome.

Box 8.4 Anticipating and Resisting Demands for Information

The tactic of stonewalling requests for inside information is not unusual among government agencies (consider the vast amount of classified information) or corporations, but neither is it limited to them. Consider the following excerpt from one of the purloined University of East Anglia climate change emails we referenced earlier. Phil Jones (one of the two most prominent climate researchers) to Michael Mann (the other one), February 2, 2005:

> The two [climate-change skeptics] have been after the CRU station data for years. If they ever hear there is a Freedom of Information Act now in the UK, I think I'll delete the file rather than send to anyone. Does your similar act in the US force you to respond to enquiries within 20 days?—our does! The UK works on precedents, so the first request will test it. We also have a data protection act, which I will hide behind. [Another researcher] has sent me a worried email when he heard about it—thought people could ask him for his model code. He has retired officially from UEA so he can hide behind that. (From the selection of emails published online by *Wall Street Journal*, November 24, 2009; found online at http://online.wsj.com/article/SB10001424052748704779704574553652849094482.html)

Either way, an effective defense must involve not only capable, strategically guided outbound communication, but also the careful and competent management of the target's proprietary, or at least its non-public, information. Because IICs are sophisticated, research driven enterprises, they depend, sometimes extensively, on access to information about the target, which they require in order to make good strategic and tactical decisions. Some of this information will come from public sources, but in some instances, it can also be gleaned or extracted from the target. A government agency that is targeted in a campaign, for example, may be presented with numerous and extensive freedom of information requests (or the system-defined equivalent). Or a corporation may find itself engaged in campaign-related (or even seemingly unrelated) litigation in which unusually wide-ranging discovery requests are issued. In such situations, compliance with the requests will be governed by relevant legal requirements, but there is often some measure of discretion as to what items to include, and what material to redact. Except where there is an advantage in claiming and demonstrating openness, the incentives here will generally favor limiting to the fullest extent possible the disclosure of any information that might be employed to the advantage of the protagonist in the campaign.

Strategic Goals May Vary

All of this, of course, is based on the presumption that the target wants to resist the pressure campaign, needs to mount a defense, and has the resources to do so. That is not always the case. Sometimes protagonists get lucky, and sometimes they make their own luck. Recall that the objective of IICs is to change the policies, behaviors, or status of the target, and that they are waged by weaker actors against stronger ones. The campaign succeeds if it accomplishes such change. From the target's perspective, it may be that the policy or behavior in question is not seen as particularly salient, that it is far down on the target's own set of priorities. Or it may be that the arguments or frames set out by the protagonist are actually persuasive. Or it may be that the target sees the making of concessions on a given issue as preferable to the risk that the campaign may broaden to more important areas. Or times may have changed. Or there may have been a leadership transition, or regime change, in the target. Or the campaign may have actually found and successfully exploited a significant vulnerability, leading to a recalculation of the costs and benefits of the target's original position. Or, as in the case of campaigns targeting legislators or legislative bodies on matters of public policy, the very objective of the target may be some form of responsiveness. Any of these or other circumstances may lead to a change in the target's policies or behaviors in ways consistent with the objectives of the campaign. (We will assume here that one other type of possible campaign objective, a change in the target's status—that is, a voluntary surrender of its relative power, as by a government to an insurgency—would be of sufficient import virtually to *require* the mounting of a defense.)

In these circumstances, the target's strategic goals are a bit different. If there is a full acceptance of the protagonist's objectives, the target will need to frame this affirmatively and seek out ways to benefit from it. If there is a partial acceptance of the protagonist's objectives, the target will need to frame its acceptance as broadly as possible, while preserving insofar as it can its apparent authority and independence of action. Depending on the situation, it may also be advantageous to construct an apparent partnership, either with the protagonist or with selected intermediaries and/or stakeholders, built on some assertion of common values and designed to limit future attacks. But whatever the circumstances, the strategist at this point will look for mechanisms to maintain both the real and the apparent control the target exercises over its own actions.

The target's strategic goals, or at the very least its actual strategy, may also vary when it is the object of competing campaigns seeking to move its policies or behaviors in competing or inconsistent directions. In these instances, there may well be opportunities to form fixed or floating alliances with one or the other protagonist, to use the messaging or alliance structures of the respective protagonists to advantage, or simply to step back and watch, permit, or even encourage the conflict between the protagonists as a means of gaining strategic intelligence regarding their interests and capabilities, maintaining the moral high ground, or simply allowing them to burn through their respective resources, which will then not be available for attacks directly on the target.

Information, Organization, and Effective Defense

Returning to our earlier analogy, the outermost perimeter of castellar defense took the form of observers and observation points dispersed far and wide away from the core—an early form of remote sensing or a tripwire. Dust in the distance might be enough to cause the sounding of the alarm, and those in the castle were probably quite happy tolerating some number of false positives lest they be caught by surprise when the real hordes arrived outside the main gate. Whether or not a given target is inclined to yield or to resist, it is similarly well-served by establishing an effective early warning system.

This is not quite as straightforward as it sounds. If there is no campaign underway, or if there is a campaign underway but the target remains unaware of it—which is quite possible in the earliest stages of campaign development—how does one know what to look for, where to look? Most powerful organizations routinely monitor the economic, political and other environments in which they operate—they clip news accounts, track legislation and regulatory activity, follow relevant litigation, measure their images among the public, observe Internet chatter and postings of interest, solicit consumer or citizen comments, and so forth, and may even engage in more direct forms of gathering intelligence on known critics or foes as well. So the "where" is easy. And by this point in our discussion, so is the "what," which follows directly from the theory and nature of the typical campaign. What classes of protagonists—and what specific actors—are most likely to engage in a campaign directed at the target? What classes of intermediaries—and what specific intermediaries—are likely to be recruited by these various protagonists? How are they interconnected with one another and with the protagonist(s)? With the target? Which of the target's stakeholders are most likely to be put into play by one or another of these networks, should it emerge? By what mechanisms? And what policies or behaviors of the target are the most likely to attract such attention and pressure? Of and by whom? The answers to these and similar questions can be used to generate specific expectations regarding who interacts with whom, what they say or what other forms their exchanges take, what forms of communication or content (as, for example, in news stories) are most likely to spawn campaign activity, and the like. These expectations are the "what." When they show up in the various channels that are being monitored, the target needs to take heed. Some, and perhaps many, false positives are inevitable. (This is especially the case in the mapping of protagonist-related networks, where the many non-instrumental, or even random, links among the nodes will almost surely and substantially outnumber, and may even mask, those of real significance.) The sensitivity of the tripwires can be adjusted if needed. But the development of a system of such sensors is an essential component of any defensive strategy. Recognition of a threat and the time to prepare for it are invaluable.

One final point is in order before we conclude our discussion of strategic defense against the information and influence campaign. As we have noted earlier in this volume, many established organizations that are likely targets of IICs tend to be highly compartmentalized. Governments and their component agencies, corporations, international organizations, and even the largest NGOs have evolved in this direction, whether to better serve their respective citizens or clienteles or simply to reflect the accumulation of competing internal power centers over time. One consistent result of this pattern is that problems or challenges that may arise within one or another of these localized fiefdoms tend to be closely held. Indeed, each component is often judged on its ability to keep such problems from rising to the point at which they become known to higher authorities within the organization. Cross-communication and cross-consultation within such an organization is effectively discouraged by these norms and practices, a fact that may be well known in the larger environment within which the organization functions. A campaign protagonist that studies its prospective target carefully is almost sure to become aware of this phenomenon, and a campaign strategist possessed of such intelligence is almost certain to design a campaign that seeks to take advantage of it. That might take a simple form, such as by administering a series of relatively discreet attacks, each against a different part of the system, in such a way that the outside world becomes aware of them at the same time as, or even before, the top leaders of the targeted organization. Or it may take the form of more complex efforts to further disaggregate the target—to set one component against another—so as to enhance its vulnerability to pressure.

For the defensive strategist, then, the prime directive must be to assure insofar as possible—and sometimes these organizations' cultures may prove remarkably resistant—that all campaign-related information gathering, all campaign-related decision-making, and all campaign-related actions are fully integrated and are empowered from the very top of the organization. This requires taking advantage of the norms of information sharing and collective decision-making where they exist, and establishing and reinforcing them where they do not. It requires maintaining control of the target's own actions and communications at all times, recognizing that literally everything said or done in its name, regardless of how seemingly remote from the campaign it may be by either content or intended audience, can be put into play by an able and motivated protagonist. It requires an appreciation that, when the game is on in an IIC, the game is omnipresent; there are no secrets, no coincidences, no hiding places. It requires educating all of the principal decision-makers in the organization regarding the nature of the campaign and of the strategy that is being implemented to defend against it. And it requires affirmative and informed buy-in by the highest levels of leadership all along the way. Absent those building blocks, an effective defense may be impossible, no matter how compelling the strategy.

9 Information, and Influence

> The social scientist today—and particularly the practitioner and investigator of behavioral change—finds himself in a situation that has many parallels to that of the nuclear physicist. The knowledge about the control and manipulation of human behavior that he is producing and applying is beset with enormous ethical ambiguities, and he must accept responsibility for its social consequences.
>
> Herbert C. Kelman (1969: 582)

> Power corrupts, but lack of power corrupts absolutely.
>
> Adlai Stevenson

> Strategic Communication is best viewed as an unpredictable and risky tool, and should be used accordingly.
>
> Steven R. Corman, Angela Threthewey, and Bud Goodall (2007: 11)

In our contemporary society, information and influence campaigns are ubiquitous. From psychological states to nation states, they touch every aspect of contemporary political life. Campaigns are employed by all manner of social, economic, and political actors—advocacy groups, corporations, governments, international organizations, and even insurgent and terrorist groups, among others—for a wide variety of purposes: to condition public opinion and generate support for particular public policies or behaviors; to expand or contract the freedom of action of policymakers, and to shape the menu of policy options among which they choose; to alter the decisions and behaviors of corporations on everything from environmental and employment practices to the design of product lines and determinations of which markets to enter or avoid; to generate legitimacy and acceptance for a wide variety of advocates, regimes, and even insurgencies; to impose the protagonist's political, social or religious values on other actors; to shape global perceptions of acts of violence (Do they constitute terrorism?); to mitigate perceptions of weakness following acts of concession; and many more. Though we seldom pause to recognize and observe these campaigns, or to credit them with influencing our own behaviors or those of our institutions, they nonetheless—or perhaps for that very reason—play a central role in what we take to be democratic life. They shape and channel debate on many of the most central issues of the day, and many others far more obscure.

Do Campaigns Matter?

But are information and influence campaigns genuinely democratic in character? Do they energize political debate, or strategically minimize political participation? Do they support democratic institutions and practices, or subvert them? Do they, in other words, serve the core interests of the polity, or do they operate in shades of gray, exploiting the trappings of democracy in pursuit of the narrow interests of their respective protagonists? Those (if there are any) who have read my earlier works on strategic political communication will know that I have struggled with these questions, in one form or another and in one context or another, for more than three decades. And now I have an answer: It really does not matter.

The ivory tower is a wonderful place. If tall enough, it offers an enlightened view of all that surrounds it. And from the ivory tower, over these years, it has been possible to identify and track many trends in political communication and related phenomena—the expanding body of knowledge about how humans and their institutions make decisions and the factors that influence them; the rising popular dependence on television over print, then on digital media over television; the growing numbers and sophistication of the class of political managers; the estrangement of advocates of all stripes from compromise and the growing personalization of political conflict; the temporal collapse of the news cycle, followed more recently by the literal collapse of the newsroom as an institution; the globalization of everything—business, activism, governance; the growing recognition, and technologically-driven growth, of social network structures; and yes, the incorporation of all of the above into yet another locus of growth, the information and influence campaign. It has been interesting, and frankly more than a little worrying, to watch all of this evolve. Look out below!

But as intelligence gathering goes, the ivory tower shares with its architectural cousin, the castle of old, a serious shortcoming. It tends to be rather remote from the everyday world. And in the everyday world, the growing use of campaigns to exercise influence, and yes, their growing sophistication and their inherently self-interested and manipulative character, are now fully integrated into the political mainstream. The reason this does not matter is not that these efforts should not be judged on their objectives and evaluated on their methods. It is that as empirical phenomena, their march is by now inexorable. They constitute the "new" normal. Because we—or rather, those possessing the requisite skills and knowledge—*can* conduct information and influence campaigns almost at will, and because the disparities in the distribution of political or economic or social power that drive them *will* be with us always, they simply "*are*." In that sense, it is probably less important to critique these campaigns from a normative perspective than simply to recognize and understand them as central elements of our lives.

Information and influence campaigns are real, and they look very much as we have described them in these pages. I readily confess that, as one who has observed IICs and related strategic exercises in politics for a long time, I have never seen any single campaign that employed every strategic trick in this book, or even approximated doing so. Even where the campaign strategists might possess every requisite skill for doing so, they *always* lack the time and the resources to put them all to use, and they are further constrained by the specific realities of any given campaign setting. It cannot happen. At the same time, this book is not a work of fiction. In one form or another, and to one degree or another, as the sidebar exemplars that have populated these pages only begin to demonstrate, I have seen virtually every one of these strategies implemented at least once. If you will pardon the vernacular, I ain't makin' this stuff up.

That said, this book—being a book, after all, with a table of contents and chapters and lots of drawings with circles and arrows—*is* artificial by nature. As anyone who has been within fifty feet of one will attest, information and influence campaigns are chaotic and serendipitous. They often lack, and cannot obtain, requisite intelligence. Their strategic decisions are not always rational, and even when rational, the implementation of those decisions seldom approximates perfection. Their resources are limited, and they may come with conditions that severely limit the strategist's freedom of action. They bring together skilled professional campaigners with highly motivated, but generally less skilled and often uncontrollable, volunteers. They lurch about, much like a standard-shift automobile in the hands of a student driver, generally moving in the desired direction, but not always smoothly or uniformly. They are buffeted by the actions of third parties, including their own allies or self-proclaimed allies, operating beyond their control and assuring that the campaign is not, in any sense, a closed system. They are at best stochastic exercises, sometimes purely random walks through networks of interconnected actors, and never fully, or nearly, deterministic. And in the end, they do confront forces that are, by definition, more powerful than they are themselves. In these pages, then, we have imposed a structure and an orderliness on the logic and practice of campaign strategy, but such tidiness will almost surely be denied to the real-world strategist in some significant degree. And that, too, may be a reason why it really does not matter.

Except, of course, it does. It does matter.

It does matter, when the political life of a community or a nation is taken hostage by an army of strategists intent on manipulating their way to some objective, where that manipulation is based, not on assessing the public will or public interest and serving it, but on exploiting it, or circumventing it, or ignoring it altogether. It does matter when a membership organization is pressured to act against the interests of its members, or a company against those of its shareholders, without regard to the larger consequences of such pressure. It does matter, when the key to political influence resides not in encouraging open debate, but in avoiding it, not in rationality, but in emotion. It does matter, when unknowing intermediaries are induced to act to the advantage of others whose interests they might not wish knowingly to serve.

Yet it also matters when inequalities in the distribution of power impinge on the rights or well-being of those in the weaker position. It matters when the boundaries between the powerful and the powerless are fixed and inviolable, when the disparities are great, and when there are no established, meaningful avenues for influence. And for the disadvantaged partner in such a dyad, in some circumstances, an information and influence campaign can be a great leveler, sometimes issue-specific, sometimes actor-specific, and sometimes more broadly.

Are There Limits?

The question is not whether these campaigns should exist—there is little reason why they should not—but within what bounds, if any, they should be conducted. IICs are, at their core, exercises in projecting the self-interest of a protagonist onto a target, though some protagonists, such as certain advocacy groups or some insurgents, will argue that their self-interest equates with a broader societal interest. But even where there is no such claim (other than a purely tactical one, perhaps), these efforts by protagonists to achieve some objective they define as advantageous are not inherently deleterious to the larger society. In fact, they often can be portrayed as exercises in public education, collective bargaining, or pluralist democracy, and they can sometimes represent an essential safety valve for releasing pressures that are naturally generated by disparities in power. They are, in sum and in general, legitimate exercises in self- and collective expression. And yet, we must ask: Should there be limits to such efforts? Must campaigns, for instance, always be truthful? If so, what is true, and what false? Must they be conducted according to some ethical guideline? What is that guideline? How, and by whom, is that guideline, once accepted, to be enforced? If information and influence campaigns are often about defining and claiming the moral high ground, is there a moral high ground to the campaigns themselves?

In effect, what we are asking is this: *Should there be a code of conduct for information and influence campaigns?*

At some level, all but the most cynical among us are likely to respond to that question in the affirmative. Of course there should be boundaries for such activities, just as there are for other forms of expression. But where do those boundaries fall? What range of action falls within them, and in what venues? And what approaches, strategies, tactics, words or actions are unacceptable? The problem is, in rendering such judgments we all bring to the table different values, different preferences, different standards of judgment, and even different perceptions of circumstances and events. At the very least, we can expect that those who see themselves as prospective protagonists, as a class, will almost inevitably opt for the broadest acceptable boundaries on campaigns, while those who see themselves as prospective targets, as a class, will opt for the narrowest. This division is not merely one of anticipated self-interest. It is also a reflection of the very sets of power imbalances that give rise to campaigns in the first place: the greater the limits set on campaigns, the greater the likelihood that such imbalances will be preserved. The question thus dissolves into a more fundamental battle of preferences, between those who prefer and/or expect to benefit from a system biased toward change, on the one hand, and those who prefer and/or expect to benefit from a system biased toward stability and the status quo, on the other. So even as we agree in principle on the need for limits, we are unlikely to agree on what those limits should be.

In thinking through these issues—and I have no illusion that they will be resolved here—it might be helpful to revisit the continuum of campaign styles we set out in Figure 2.1, which is reproduced here as Figure 9.1. As the figure suggests, some campaigns—those at or toward the left end of the range—are primarily information centered. They are designed to define the terms of debate, educate a public or some other audience, and, in more advanced forms, engage in persuasion. These are basically *communication* campaigns, and the value we generally assign to the free and unfettered flow of information—protected to the extent that it is by the First Amendment in the United States and by similar organic laws elsewhere, but at the same time constrained by laws governing libel, slander, truthfulness, commercial speech, the protection of official secrets, and the like—argues for granting them wide latitude. As we move from left to right, however, and especially toward the right end of the range of campaign

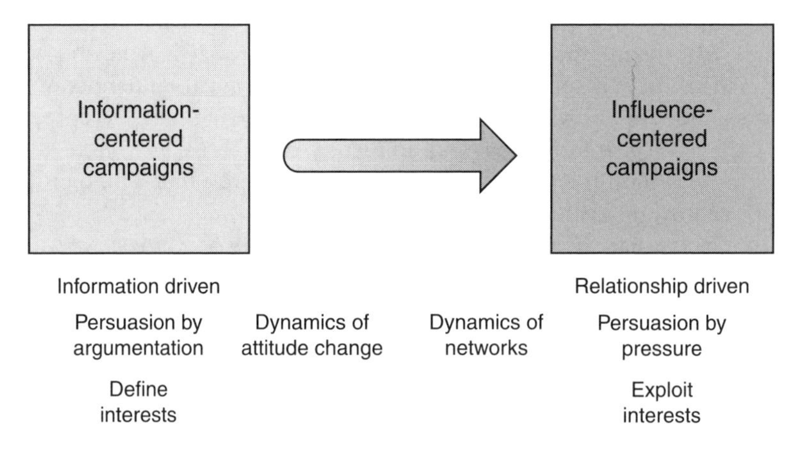

Figure 9.1 The IIC Continuum Revisited.

styles, we find campaigns that are built more and more on the strategic manipulation of interests, often through actions that generate pressure, not only on the target of the campaign, but on intermediaries—innocents, if you will—that are engaged only because of their relationships with the target and, possibly, still other intermediaries. These are basically *action* campaigns, where the action is designed to impose either symbolic or actual harm on one or more actors. If there is an area that deserves a more critical eye as we weight the social acceptability of these campaigns, perhaps it is to be found here. Might these campaigns be somehow less legitimate, or at least less self-evidently so, than their communication counterparts? Might they appropriately be held to a different standard?

Interestingly, this debate has already been joined in this general vicinity of the continuum, at least with respect to one set of actors—international NGOs. In 2001, Gary Johns, at the time a senior fellow at the Institute for Policy Analysis, a conservative Australian think tank, proposed a set of protocols for these groups—in effect, a code of conduct for their campaign and other activities. Centered around the principle of transparency, it called for openness in such matters as the group's governance structure and qualification for tax exemption (if any); its representativeness (for example, the number and type of its membership), ties to local communities, and international connections; the sources and applications of its funding; the nature and extent of its claims to expertise; and truthfulness in fundraising. (Johns, 2001) In effect, Johns was launching a campaign of sorts against advocacy NGOs, challenging them to adopt some of the same standards in their own activities that they demanded of the governments or corporations they sought to influence. The response came in 2005, when a group of NGOs, including, among others, Greenpeace and Oxfam, adopted what they termed the *International Non Governmental Organisations' Accountability Charter*, in which they accepted the call for transparency, and added commitments to freedom of speech, political independence, good governance, ethical fundraising, and professional management (International Advocacy Non-Governmental Organisations (IANGO) Workshop, 2006). We'll see your bet, and raise you.

Like all debates over codes of conduct, this one is far easier to resolve at the abstract level of shared norms than at the operational level, where actions speak louder than principles, and where differing perspectives are most likely to yield differing interpretations. But at least the discussion has been joined. For most classes of campaign protagonists and targets, even that measure of civil exchange remains elusive. And the campaigns continue largely unabated.

The First Rule of Ethics in Information and Influence Campaigns

It is also reasonable—*and important*—to ask whether campaign protagonists, their strategists, or for that matter their targets, are acting in an ethical manner. One way of understanding campaign ethics is suggested by the decision tree illustrated in Figure 9.2.

As the figure suggests, there are four critical decision points regarding any strategy or tactic under consideration for use in a campaign. First, does it need to be done? What is to be gained if a particular action is taken, or lost if it is not? If the action or decision need not be taken, the strategist is in Condition *B*, and questions of ethics never arise. Condition *A*, where a need seems apparent, leads to a second decision point: Can it be done? Is it

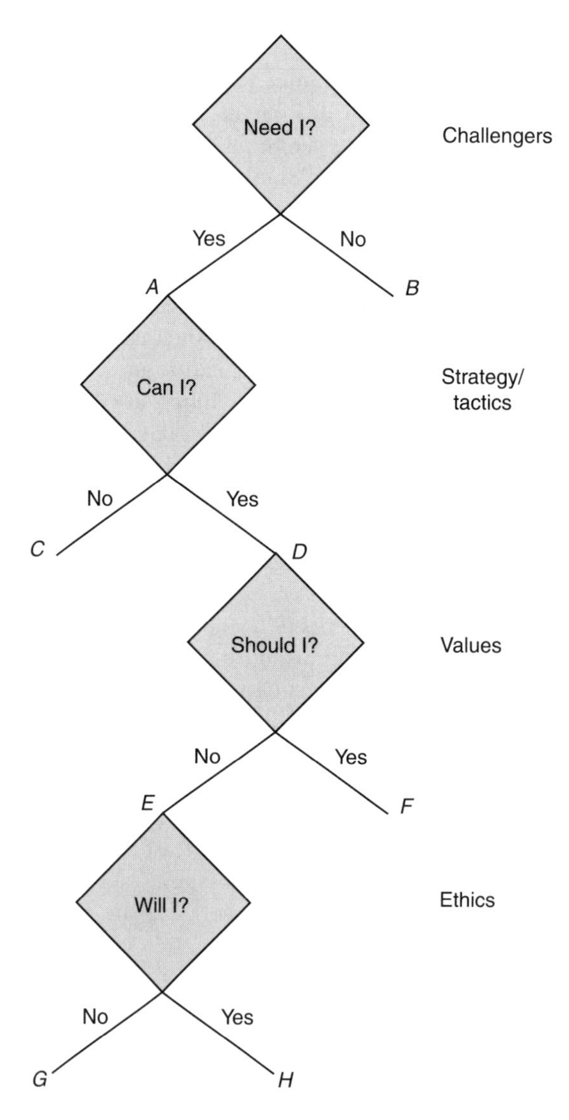

Figure 9.2 The Ethics Decision Tree.

feasible to employ a given strategy or tactic? If not, the strategist is in Condition *C*, and, again, questions of ethics never arise. Condition *D*, or that of feasible action, leads to yet another decision: Should it be done? It is at this point that the values of the strategist (or the protagonist) come to the fore. If the potential strategy/tactic is consistent with those values, there is no ethical issue in the mind of the decision-maker, producing Condition *F*, in which the strategy/tactic is likely to be implemented with a clear conscience. In the alternative, Condition *E*, the strategist recognizes that the proposed strategy/tactic is inconsistent with his or her values. It is at that point that we get to the ultimate decision point regarding ethics. If the strategist acts in a value-consistent manner, the result is Condition *G*, in which no action is taken—an ethical outcome. If, however, the strategist acts in a value-inconsistent manner, and implements the strategy/tactic regardless, Condition *H* results. The strategist has failed the test of ethics.

Though this seems like a straightforward basis for determining or judging ethical behavior, in point of fact, it is not. For, once we have crossed the threshold of feasibility, every subsequent decision hinges on the values of the strategist, which may differ from those of other actors in or aware of the campaign, or even from widely held social mores. Indeed, given the variety of vantage points, needs, behavioral opportunities, and values extant among the community of strategists, judgments regarding ethics constitute a veritable minefield of ambiguity. Consider the words of early campaign strategist Saul Alinsky (1971: 25), which go well beyond what we might think of as situational ethics, a term of art applied to an already limited measure of constraint:

> The men who pile up the heaps of discussion and literature on the ethics of means and ends—which with rare exception is conspicuous for its sterility—rarely write about their own experiences in the perpetual struggle of life and change. They are strangers, moreover, to the burdens and problems of operational responsibility and the unceasing pressure for immediate decisions. They are passionately committed to a mystical objectivity where passions are suspect. They assume a nonexistent situation where men dispassionately and with reason draw and devise means and ends as if studying a navigational chart on land . . . *The means-and-ends moralists or non-doers always wind up on their ends without any means*. [emphasis in original]

Alinsky's point, which he reinforces with a series of rules of "means and ends" that make clear his view that ethics are a political outcome, not a guide to action, is that philosophical discussions of ethical standards and behaviors are of no interest to the strategist except for what they reveal about power relationships. Ethics are determined, not by philosophers, but by winners. Alinsky may have been engaging here in hyperbole, and there are surely many campaign strategists who maintain a moral compass. But at the same time, many advocates, particularly those working in the context of social movements of the left or right, tend to look to what they see as higher-order moral imperatives. If it moves you closer to the desired end, it is justified.

There is a level at which ethical judgment may not even be a normative test at all. Arguably, it simply does not matter whether or not one agrees with Alinsky. The empirical reality—the principal fact on the ground—is that the world is filled with campaign strategists who share Alinsky's views in some measure, or who, though they may give lip service to disagreeing or may even do so as a matter of basic belief, find themselves captive to moments, circumstances, job expectations, personal pressures or any other forces that steer them in another direction. *That* may be the single fact that determines the nature and role of ethics in information and influence campaigns, and that sets the boundaries of campaign behavior. Ethical constraint, by whatever standard, must be explicitly in the self-interest of the strategist (and other actors), or it may be unlikely to prevail.

With that in mind, allow me to suggest the first, and the only, rule of ethics in these campaigns:

$$E = MC^2$$

Since we began this volume by quoting Professor Einstein, is it not fitting that we conclude with another nod to his insight? And it is but a nod, for the "equation" that constitutes this rule is intended to be less mathematical than conceptual, and more prescriptive than descriptive. In the equation, *E* represents ethics, or more correctly, the adoption of ethical standards of behavior within a given campaign. It is comprised of the interaction between two components: *M*, which represents the combined volume and valence of Media coverage of strategic decisions made in the campaign, which we can think of here as a proxy for the standards and expectations of the community in which the campaign occurs, and *C*, which represents the Conscience of the decision-maker. The superscript "C^2" can be read two ways. It can be read as a mathematical power function, "C-squared," suggesting that Conscience is the more important variable in the equation and merits disproportional weighting. Or it can be read, not as a mathematician might render the term, but as "C-*square*"—a reminder that the optimal turn of conscientious behavior in this context is that which is most small-c conservative, or, to be colloquial, the most "square". The equation thus advises that the strategist or other decision-maker should act conservatively and with an eye toward how his or her actions might be judged under the magnifying lens of public attention—sometimes called the "*Washington Post* Test," *and* in a manner guided by his or her conscience. In effect, the formulation $E=MC^2$ represents an incentive system in which self-interest becomes self-regulating, whether as a matter of personal values and preferences or, in the alternative, out of fear of discovery. Nor are the two mutually exclusive.

Box 9.1 The Ultimate "*Washington Post* Test"

Hurricane Katrina, which struck the Gulf Coast in 2005, was the costliest, and one of the five deadliest, storms ever to strike the US. There were many victims, perhaps not least among them the reputation of the Federal Emergency Management Agency (FEMA), which was responsible for managing the response to the storm and which, by every account, failed miserably to do so. So it is not difficult to understand why, two years later, the agency was still just a tad sensitive about its image. Alas, it was as adept at managing that as at managing the Katrina emergency.

On a Tuesday in October, 2007, FEMA held a news conference led by Vice Admiral Harvey E. Johnson, Jr., the agency's deputy administrator and second-ranking official. Well, perhaps. For at this event, FEMA employees *posed* as journalists and asked questions, while real reporters were restricted to listening in on a telephone conference line and were not permitted to ask questions. Perhaps FEMA thought no one would notice? They felt the need. They determined they could. They decided they would. They did. And they got caught . . . by the *real Washington Post*. Talk about failing the test!

For Admiral Johnson, it was an embarrassment. "We can and must do better, and apologize for this error in judgment," he stated afterward. But the real loser was obviously John P. Philbin, FEMA's director of external affairs (as in press conferences). By Thursday, he was no longer serving in his post at FEMA. Seems he had (earlier) been named as the head of public affairs at another agency . . . the Office of the Director of National Intelligence (Hsu, 2007).

There is, as well, another dimension of campaign ethics that merits our attention. For want of a better phrase, let us think of it as a fiduciary responsibility, not to the protagonist, but to the society at large. As I have argued earlier in this chapter, the growing share of daily political life that is given over to campaign-driven communication and behavior comes at a price. Protagonists may base their actions in claims to free speech and free expression, and their ability to engage in campaigns may be both facilitated and limited by a social and political version of the free market. But in the end, to the extent that they are built around strategies of persuasion, whether of individuals or organizations, campaigns trade in the management of free will. For the manifestation of strategy in the political arena is the generation, channeling, constraint, and guidance of free will as exercised by those who are subjected to its mandates. While it is true, then, that the strategist may owe a duty of loyalty to the protagonist, it is also true that he or she has as well as broader responsibility to be as sure as possible that the decisions made and implemented in the course of an IIC, whatever their intended objective, do not impose harm on the underlying social structure within which the campaign operates. Frankly, it is not clear to me, based on years of observation, whether or to what extent campaign strategists are cognizant of this responsibility, let alone factor it into their actions. Fortunately, however, the system itself is not without its defenses.

Systemic Constraints

Notwithstanding their ubiquity and their growing sophistication, and notwithstanding the willingness of some strategists to test the boundaries of civil behavior, information and influence campaigns do not operate without systemic constraints. To the contrary, they constantly bump up against their inherent limitations. These are of three basic types.

First, not all campaigns achieve, or even approximate, strategic perfection. The attributes of protagonists that we identified in Chapter 6, for example—such factors as their legitimacy, resources, and infrastructure—are, in fact, highly variable. Particular protagonists will have more or less of each one, and those distributions may even be situation-specific. There are, to be sure, some protagonists that are better or worse positioned to engage in a campaign than others, but *all* protagonists are at *all* times less than optimally positioned. Similarly, the settings in which campaigns occur vary in the degree to which they are conducive to information gathering, alliance formation, and all the other elements of the campaign. Windows of opportunity open and close, interests shift. Even with a perfect strategy—and that is another unreachable objective—the circumstances of the campaign will limit its effectiveness. Campaigns can be very well planned, very well managed, and very well implemented, but they are complex undertakings in a complex world, and they simply cannot be perfect.

Second, campaigns tend to generate resistance and counter-activity. To the extent that a target is well defended or is able to generate an effective counterstrategy—and that is not always the case—the protagonist's efforts will be limited to some degree in their impact. One side pushes, the other pushes back. And, as in military conflicts, the advantage often lies with the defender. These disadvantages and setbacks can be mitigated to an extent by the protagonist through iterative adjustments to the campaign strategy, but they are unlikely to be offset altogether.

Finally, there are finite limits on the core strategic capability itself. Even for a perfectly situated, highly skilled, and fully resourced protagonist, campaign strategy can never be perfect. That is because the knowledge structures on which the most sophisticated campaigns are based—knowledge about the nature and dynamics of attitudes, media tendencies, institutional behaviors, network structures, stakeholder interests, and all of the other factors that are in play in a campaign—all of these are probabilistic in nature, not determinative. Doing A (framing a message a particular way, employing a particular communication channel, etc.) may improve your chances of accomplishing B (changing the views of a targeted segment of the public, motivating particular allies, etc.), but it does not guarantee that B will occur, let alone that a chain or complex of such accomplishments will obtain the overall objective of the campaign.

Campaigns can be highly sophisticated, they can be effective, they can achieve their ends. But they are not perfect. They never will be. Thank goodness.

The Enduring Challenge of the Information and Influence Campaign

We are left, then, in the somewhat chaotic circumstance of the present, in which strategy, albeit within some limits, is king—in which the determination and effective implementation of that which will work not only guides the action in information and influence campaigns, but sets the limits to how they will be conducted. Theory, trial and error, and the evolution of strategic knowledge. If it works, do it. If it does not, look for something else that will. It is a fascinating dynamic to observe, but at some level a perilous one to encourage, especially as campaigns become ever more effective and still more ubiquitous. We are, after all, testing in these campaigns the capacity to generate pressure, and sometimes great pressure, in social, economic, and political systems that have not been fully engineered to contain it. When, in the most sophisticated of these efforts, clever management transforms itself into purposeful manipulation—of information, of issues, of people, of organizations, of economic and political institutions—and when such manipulation becomes commonplace, the ethical and other challenges posed by some individual campaigns pale beside the resultant heightening of systemic risk. Influence, after all, is an entirely legitimate part of democratic life. Manipulation is not.

How, then, to justify writing this book—a book that imposes order and structure on the helter-skelter world of campaign strategy and that would seem, in the process, to do nothing so much as codify and advance this style of political action. Is it not dangerous to write such a book? Yes. But let me ask you this. Given the rapid proliferation of ever more advanced information and influence campaigns in contemporary society, and the routine daily application of these very strategies across a wide spectrum of issues and actions, is it not more dangerous not to?

It is a magnificent feeling to recognize the unity of a complex of phenomena which appear to be things quite apart from the direct visible truth.

Albert Einstein

Appendix A Need to Know: Strategic Intelligence and Research in the Campaign

The single most important key to success in an information and influence campaign is good intelligence. That includes solid intellect and street smarts—both of which will be tested time and again in the typical campaign. But it also refers to knowledge and data, to what and how much the strategist knows—and *understands*—about the protagonist, the target, the prospective campaign intermediaries, the campaign setting, the issues, the range of potential outcomes and effects, and a host of equal and lesser elements. Successful campaigning requires a mastery of such information, a mastery that can only come from research.

Obviously, IICs are not exercises in basic scholarly research of the sort we will review in Appendix B of this volume. But that does not mean that they are not research driven, either by the theories and findings of scholars, some of which can be highly relevant to a campaign, or by their own, more narrowly designed efforts. Theory can be important in a campaign; solid applied research almost always is.

It follows that any well-crafted campaign will incorporate in its overall planning and implementation a significant strategic research component. The function of this component is to anticipate and answer questions that arise, and to provide information that is required, as the campaign strategy is developed and its implementation evaluated. It is not possible here, of course, to list every question that might come up in a given campaign. Based on the analysis presented in this volume, however, it is possible to extract classes and examples of questions that might arise at one or another point in the course of strategic decision-making in a campaign, and to suggest in general terms the methodologies that might best be applied to answering them. Table A.1 summarizes some possible results of this exercise.

Recall from our earlier discussion that some campaign protagonists have relatively well-developed organizational infrastructures. In general, these more institutionalized actors are not one-shot campaigners, but rather, regular, and perhaps even frequent, users of IIC techniques. In the present context, it is worth noting that one aspect of these infrastructures is often an institutionalized research function that generates information of value

Table A.1 Utility of Research in Information and Influence Campaigns, by Method and Research Question

Research Question	*Existing Polling*	*Survey Research*	*Ratings Analysis*	*Focus Groups*	*Elite Interviews*	*Archival Media Analysis*	*Real-Time Media Tracking*	*Online Search*	*Data Mining*	*Social Network Analysis*	*Financial/Industry Analysis*	*Institutional Analysis*	*Legal Discovery*	*Effects/Assessment Research*	*Documents/Public Records*
General campaign environment	X					X									
Existing perceptions of protagonist, target, third parties, issues	X	X		X	X										
Existing preference structures regarding protagonist, target, third parties, issues	X	X		X	X				X						
Operative decision dynamics for attitude change		X		X	X										
Exposure, attention, interest, understanding and internalizing of campaign communications		X		X					X						
Issue/audience segmentation	X	X	X						X						

Access to communication channels; related preferences, patterns	X	X	X	X	X				X						
Changes in perceptions and preferences during the campaign		X		X	X				X					X	
Existing media portrayals of protagonist, target, third parties, issues						X									
Changes in media portrayals of protagonist, target, third parties, issues during the campaign						X	X							X	
Information available in and about the campaign		X			X	X	X	X							X
Identification and evaluation of potential allies					X	X	X	X		X	X	X			
Attributes of protagonist, target and third parties	X	X		X	X	X		X	X	X	X	X			X
Relationships among intermediaries, stakeholders, target					X	X		X		X	X	X			X

(*Continued Overleaf*)

Table A.1 Continued.

Research Question	*Existing Polling*	*Survey Research*	*Ratings Analysis*	*Focus Groups*	*Elite Interviews*	*Archival Media Analysis*	*Real-Time Media Tracking*	*Online Search*	*Data Mining*	*Social Network Analysis*	*Financial/Industry Analysis*	*Institutional Analysis*	*Legal Discovery*	*Effects/Assessment Research*	*Documents/Public Records*
Vulnerabilities assessment of target, stakeholders, intermediaries, protagonist	X	X	X	X	X	X	X	X		X	X	X	X		X
Relative influence of stakeholders (power, legitimacy, urgency)					X	X		X			X	X			
Identification of issues with potential leverage	X	X		X	X			X	X		X	X	X		X
Message/frame effectiveness (expected, observed)		X		X	X									X	
Network architecture linking protagonist, intermediaries, stakeholders, target						X	X	X		X	X	X			X
Campaign effects, effectiveness		X		X	X		X	X						X	

to, across, and well beyond the particular informational needs of individual campaigns. For example, the World Wide Fund for Nature (WWF International), based in Gland, Switzerland, maintains a transnational research program, principally comprising focus group and survey research, to measure the following sets of campaign-relevant variables:

- the relative importance of the environment as an issue,
- the specific environmental issues that are perceived as important,
- how people behave relative to the environment, and whether they are concerned enough about it to change their behaviors,
- whether and in what ways environmental activism makes any difference in perceptions or behaviors,
- whether and to what extent people are aware of environmental groups, and
- the public's image of WWF and its degree of willingness to participate in activities linked to the organization. (Corrado, 2002: 126)

A similar concern with research—or more correctly with the absence of effective research—is evident in a recent examination of the strategic communication efforts of the U.S. government as components of the nation's military policy, public diplomacy efforts, and other concerns and initiatives. The value of such research, its outlines, and its context and contribution to the overall objectives of strategic communication were stated succinctly in a 2004 report prepared by the Defense Science Board, which is charged with advising the Pentagon on applications of gains in scientific knowledge. Here, at some length, is an excerpt from that report (United States Department of Defense, 2001: 53–59), which will serve to conclude our discussion.

The argument of this study is that the U.S. Government must take a dramatically more disciplined, methodical and strategic approach to global communication. This, we believe, means selectively borrowing private sector best practices and creating a range of insurgent U.S. strategic communication vehicles, programs and products as detailed below. They are based, for example, on the following approaches:

Analyze Perceptions: Utilizing cutting-edge research and political-strategic methodologies to better understand global perceptions toward the U.S., including American values and policies.

Formulate Key Objectives and Strategies: One reason the U.S. has had difficulty managing the post-war occupation of Iraq is a near total confusion over objectives and strategies. The definition of post-war success has never been enunciated clearly. Similarly, in terms of U.S. strategic communication, a critical step in planning will be to detail exactly the destination toward which we must head. Put simply, the new strategic communication planning function must define what success looks like. And it must formulate a comprehensive strategic framework to achieve it.

For example, as with the private sector, it is important for the U.S. Government's new strategic communication function to develop an understanding of the U.S. "brand" positioning and strategy. In this sense, the word "brand" simply means a conceptual system to guide and navigate our constituents to an understanding of the meaning and essence of the U.S., including its values, interests and policies.

More specifically, strategic communication planning should very selectively borrow private sector best practices and begin to maximize the U.S. "brand" positioning in its five key dimensions:

Presence: How will we develop awareness of the U.S. "brand" in terms of its constituents and audience?

Relevance: How will the U.S. define the role of its "brand" in terms of the needs and wants of key target audiences?

Differentiation: How will the U.S. distinguish its "brand?" While the U.S. Government clearly shares respect for human dignity and other values with many nations, there are attributes that set us apart and are especially admirable and inspirational to others.

Credibility: How will the U.S. ensure that its "brand" fulfills its promises and delivers on defined expectations?

Imagery: What images, icons and symbolic elements will help communicate and enrich this "brand" meaning?

Determine Targets: Identifying audience targets that are "winnable" in terms of increased U.S. support will be critical to successful strategic communication. For example, this means borrowing from campaign and private sector methodologies and conducting political-style attitudinal research: identifying, as the highest priority, "soft support" targets. [David Morey and Scott Miller, The Underdog Advantage: Using the Power of Insurgent Strategy to Put Your Business On Top, McGraw-Hill, 2004, pages 36–49.]

The best private sector marketing and political campaign management use the attitudinal continuum below to organize, maximize and focus communication resources. And this approach should be utilized to improve the effectiveness and efficiency of U.S. strategic communication:

HO = The Hard Opposition: In a political campaign, for example, these individuals will come out and vote against you in any circumstances. Of course, political campaigns do not want to waste a penny chasing their "un-gettable" votes, but they must also be ready to counter their negative effect on other voters. In elections, as in product marketing campaigns, these are the activists who form-up against you.

SO = The Soft Opposition: In a political campaign, these individuals support your opponent, or prefer in marketing a competitive brand, but they might not vote, for example, in bad weather. In an election campaign, you try not to raise issues that will enflame soft opposition to vote. And in product or service marketing, you realize these consumers can be moved . . . eventually. But you never target to their wants and needs directly; that will take the focus off much more productive targets.

The UNDECIDED: Typically, a political campaign will do virtually anything to move the undecided before Election Day; after all, it needs whatever it takes to get to 50.1%. The 2000 U.S. Presidential election proved this. After hundreds of millions were spend [sic] through primaries and the general election, more millions were poured into the legal arguments that would decide the election. Campaigns will buy any vote they can. They'll run negative advertising. They'll rent fleets of vans to drive hard supporters to the polls. The votes of the undecided can move at any time and change in a light breeze.

SOS = Soft Support: Constituents who are leaning your way and who, research tells us, are six times less expensive to move to hard support as undecided are to move to soft support. To win, you must engage and activate this segment to vote—or in consumer terms to come back and buy your product again. Identifying, targeting and moving soft support to hard support is the highest priority of any U.S. strategic communications effort.

HAS = Hard Support: Extremely loyal constituents who must not be taken for granted, but who ultimately are critical to success in political campaigns or marketing. This is your loyal support. And you must, in campaign terms, hold these constituents until Election Day and motivate them to help pull the soft support to hard support.

Develop Themes and Messages: Based on the research referenced above—and specifically focusing on moving soft support constituents to hard support. A strategically formulated, focused and consistent set of themes and messages is a prerequisite for the success of a transformed strategic communication effort. These key themes and messages should, for example, communicate:

Identify Key Products and Programs: Again utilizing research, the new U.S. strategic communication effort must reach audience targets through a customized and even personalized dialogue that is relevant and credible to those targets. This will involve an array of products and programs:

Conduct Audience Polling and Analysis: Including ethnographic, psychographic, demographic, behavioral and tracking research. As with a successful political or marketing campaign, the reality is you simply cannot know too much about your audience and their perceptions. For example, using hypothesis-testing methodologies in qualitative focus groups and quantitative benchmark research is a critical prerequisite for strategic communication success.

Undertake Cultural Analysis: Including cultural factors involving values, religion, entertainment and education. Strategic communication must adopt a wide and incisive analytical view of how its audiences are continually influenced.

Conduct Media Analysis: Identifying daily influences on audiences including content analysis, agenda and biases, relevance and credibility, structure and control.

Communicate to Target Audiences: Identifying and organizing key targets based on the above attitudinal continuum, demographics and other attributes. For example, this should include lists of influential "opinion leaders" country by country. And this should include a "friends and family" database of soft supporters and hard supporters who "self-select" themselves and are constantly engaged in a personal, relevant and credible dialogue.

. . . .

Use Feedback to Monitor Success: Critical to the success of a new strategic communication effort will be creating a culture of measurement that helps the U.S. make necessary adjustments and learn from both past and present efforts and initiatives. This feedback loop must continually foster accountability and measure success against selected objectives—looping up to the highest levels of the new strategic communication function.

Specifically, as in the private sector, this monitoring and feedback system must measure progress against the ten strategic communication objectives below. Cutting edge private sector measurement, models and management systems, both qualitative and quantitative, should be applied to calibrate progress against the following:

- WHAT do we want to communicate?
- WHY exactly do we want to communicate this?
- WHAT do we want this to actually do?
- WHO are we trying to reach?
- WHAT do we want them to remember?
- WHAT attitude or behavior do we expect?
- WHEN will this be done?
- HOW much will it cost?
- WHAT exact results do we anticipate?
- HOW will we measure success?

Appendix B The IIC Knowledge Base: A Selective Bibliographic Inventory

Social (and other) scientists make a distinction between *applied* research—that which is designed primarily to identify and evaluate solutions to real-world problems—and *basic* research—that which is designed primarily to extend our general understanding of how and why things work. Problem solving versus theory building.

As one might expect, we find ample traces of applied research in the strategy development underlying advances in information and influence campaigns, which are, as we have argued, among the most sophisticated of all persuasive efforts. Perhaps the best example is found in the path-breaking work of Herbert Krugman (1964, 1965, 1966, 1971, 1977; Krugman and Hartley 1970; and the collection edited by Edward P. Krugman 2008), at the time (1967–1983) manager of corporate public opinion research for General Electric (and thus a most appropriate heir to the Edison campaign legacy), whose careful psychological experiments helped to guide the advertising efforts of his employer even as they contributed vital new conceptual insights to the emergent science of persuasion and attitude change. Zielske's (1959; Zielske and Henry, 1980) studies of the half-life of advertising recall were similarly applied science at their heart, and yet basic science as well in their impact. Much of the marketing and social marketing literature (Andreason, 2006; Andreason and Kotler, 2003; Fox and Kotler, 1980; Kotler and Levy, 1969; Kotler, Roberto, and Lee, 2002; Schultz, Tannenbaum, and Lauterborn, 1993) is based on research of a very practical bent.

And then, of course, one finds many of the typically anecdotal case studies of campaigns by students of labor (Ashby and Hawking, 2009; Brisbin, 2002; Bronfenbrenner, 2007; Bullert, 1999; Clawson, 2003; Getman, 1998; Jarley and Maranto, 1990; Juravitch and Bronfenbrenner, 1999; Rosenblum, 1998) and other social movements (Bakir, 2005; Bandy and Smith, 2005a, Berg, 2003; Grant and Taylor, 2004), the lessons of which are later often reflected in a variety of operational manuals and how-to guides (AFL-CIO, 2000; Bobo, Kendall, and Max, 1996; Coalition for the International Criminal Court, 2003; Ganzi, Seymour, and Buffet, 1998; Greer and Singh, 1995; Gregory, Caldwell, Avni, and Harding,

2005; LaBotz, 1991; Moyer, 2001; North American Congress on Latin America, 1970; Oppenheimer and Lakey, 1964; Ryan, 1991; Salzman, 2003; Shaw, 1996) and counter-campaign or other generally defensive or preventive guides (Bonini, Court, and Marchi, 2009; Deegan, 2001; Dezenhall, 1999; Nichols, 2001; Peters, 1999; Sitrick, 1998). Finally, we should note the writing of political consultant Frank Luntz (2007), arguably the premier linguistic tactician of the last twenty years, who, with a doctoral degree in politics from Oxford University, operates at the very boundary between theory and application, as he converts fairly abstract theories of persuasion into very simple rules of engagement regarding the design of political language.

Suffice it to say that applied research is a commonplace in, and a vital underpinning of, the development of IIC strategy. We'll have more to say about some of these resources below.

And yet, in perhaps no other area of professional communication practice is so central a role reserved for the theories and data developed in cutting-edge basic research. In every area from belief systems and media effects to social network analysis and the latest developments in digital media, the latest relevant social scientific findings find their way into ever-evolving campaign strategies. This is due in no small measure to the inherent competitiveness of the campaign setting, where any advantage one can gain may turn out to have been decisive. But it is, as well, a natural outgrowth of the origins of contemporary information and influence campaigns in the propaganda studies of the World War II era and its aftermath (early works by Cantril, 1940; Ettinger, 1946; Hoffer, 1942; Hovland, Lumsdaine, and Sheffield, 1949; Hyman and Sheatsley, 1947; and Lee, 1944, 1945 are representative), as so ably chronicled by Glander (2000). Voltmer and Römmele (2002) argue that the growing centrality of campaigns in contemporary life virtually requires the continuing enrichment of practice by applying the latest theoretical advances and research results, and suggest the ways in which this has occurred.

I make no claim here that the "knowledge base" underlying strategic decision-making in information and influence campaigns is in any way systematic, nor that it constitutes what scholars would think of as a unified literature. To the contrary, campaign strategists have drawn on an extraordinarily diverse collection of sources, theories, and data. It is that very diversity, in all its depth and richness, that powers this activity. Accordingly, my objective here is not to weave an apparently seamless single tapestry from these manifold threads, but simply to set forth in an organized manner an inventory of what I judge to have been the seminal ideas, key developments, most critical tests, and most illustrative applications of the intellectual foundations on which campaign strategy has been built.

Literature on Power, Power Relationships, and Strategic Communication

Machiavelli's (1992) sixteenth-century volume, *The Prince*, is generally regarded as the touchstone work on strategic political communication, and is still well worth reading today. Chapters 15 through 21, in particular, which cover such issues as faith, fame, and fear, commend themselves in the present context. Though Machiavelli is generally cited as a proponent of political manipulation on the pro-elite side of systemic power asymmetry, McCormick (2001), citing *The Discourses* rather than the more widely read *The Prince*, has portrayed Machiavelli as a democrat, arguing that the Italian theorist/strategist/operative actually provided a roadmap to constraining elites through direct and robust public participation in the form of tribunes, public accusations, and popular appeals. Freedman and Freedman (1975) played off of Machiavelli, staging a dialogue with a hypothetical prince over the course of which they educated him in the art of social control based on applying social scientific concepts and knowledge.

Deutsch (1963), employing the perspective of cybernetics, which he characterized as "the science of communication and control," (76) argued that governments were best understood not as centers of power, but as centers of communication. Chapter 9 of this work, with its emphasis on information processing by governments, capacity, selectivity, channels, social cohesion, networks, symbols of legitimacy, leadership, morale, and decision-making, provides a good sense of the comprehensiveness and richness of this very early conceptualization.

Lipsky (1968) anticipated our argument here about the use of information and influence campaigns to address asymmetries in the distribution of power, proposing a model (1147), reproduced in modified form below, by which relatively powerless groups might gain leverage through the media and other intermediaries, which he termed "reference publics," to generate pressure on a target so as to achieve material rewards. Though somewhat time-bound and overly focused on the then-active American civil rights movement, Lipsky's analysis nevertheless identified a number of the key elements of protest strategy, not least the need for and challenge of recruiting third-party advocates, and was ahead of its time in the analytical framework it advanced.

Domhoff (1980) compiled a series of essays on power structure research that incorporated many of the assumptions underlying the power structure analysis that is the basis for much IIC strategy, albeit at a more systemic social and political level. This power structure research owed much to the work of C. Wright Mills (most notably 1956), which called attention to the structure and influence in the U.S. of a so-called "power elite" and gave rise, in turn, to a related literature (in their latest iterations, for example, Domhoff (2009) and Dye (2002)) that both filled in the blanks regarding elite membership, recruitment, action and dominance, and at the same

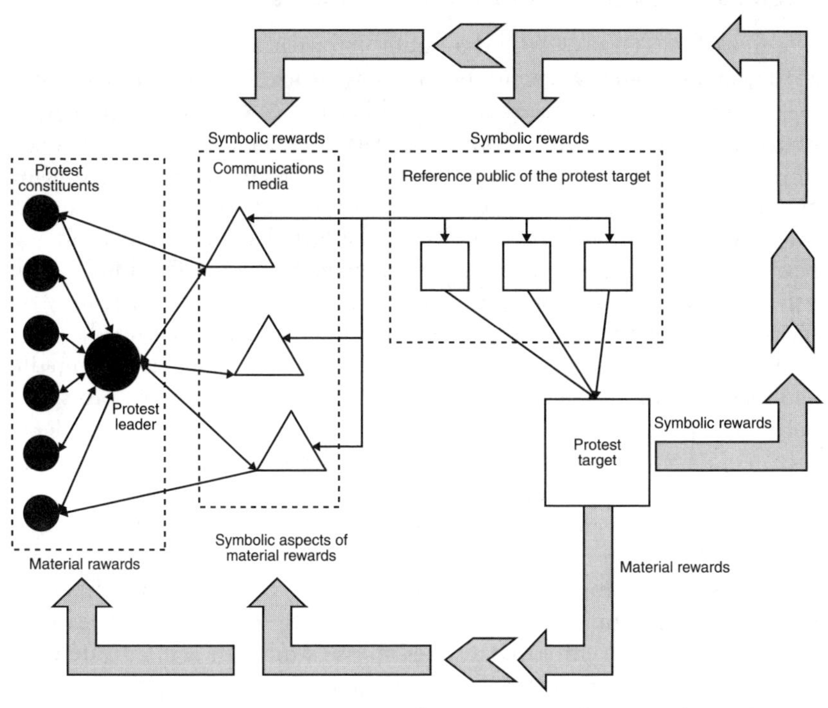

Figure B.1 Schematic Representation of the Process of Protest by Relatively Powerless Groups.

time opened a debate over whether this powerful leadership cadre was class- or position-based. Mills' work was juxtaposed with that of advocates of a pluralist theory of democracy (see, for example, Dahl, 1961, and, for a more contemporary analysis, Bennett and Manheim, 2001)), or one based on a competition of groups that were presumed to represent and articulate the full range of competing interests, and there ensued a long-running elitist pluralist debate, the details of which need not concern us here. Without entering either debate, Manheim (2004) argued that a progressive counter-elite grounded in Mills' teachings combined that perspective with the techniques of strategic campaigning to reassert its lost political influence. One of the most critical roles in the reverse engineering of the power elite is that played by activist foundations, which pool and direct millions of dollars to support their chosen causes. These foundations are constrained, however, by the need to retain their tax-exempt status, the terms of which require that they avoid explicitly political activity. Several foundations commissioned a report by a tax attorney, Colvin (1993), that set out six operating models by which they could both engage with the political system and retain their privileged tax status.

Literature on Public Information Campaigns

The most basic form of IIC, the public information campaign, has been an object of scholarly attention for many years. Hyman and Sheatsley (1947), for example, pointed out several barriers to successful information campaigns, including differential acquisition of information based on an individual's level of interest in a given topic, preferential seeking of facts aligned with and reinforcing existing attitudes, group differences in the way new information is processed, and the fact that providing/acquiring new information does not necessarily change attitudes. The implication was, and is, that those conducting such campaigns cannot rely simply on increasing the amount and distribution of information that is made available. Wiebe (1951–1952) proposed systemic requirements by which radio and television might be used to sell citizenship, which is to say, pro-social behaviors or values, much like soap. He saw the media as capable of producing the requisite high level of motivation, but argued that it was incumbent on the sponsor of the message to provide an effective social mechanism for converting that motivation to the desired outcome. In other words, the message effects alone will not suffice, no matter how strong. They must be accompanied by a recognizable, accessible, and compatible behavioral opportunity. In pointed contrast to Hyman and Sheatsley, Mendelsohn (1973) employed a series of case studies to demonstrate that, despite evidence that media alone were generally incapable of producing substantial attitude change, collaboration between social scientists and communication strategists, which is to say, the integration of social scientific knowledge regarding targets, themes, appeals, and media channels into campaign strategy, could produce successful outcomes.

One of the more interesting collections of essays on PICs is found in Salmon (1989a), which opened with the editor's (1989b) acknowledgement that the phenomena of social marketing and public information campaigns trace their origins to Weibe's (1951–1952) question: Why can't you sell brotherhood and rational thinking like you sell soap? One contributor, Pollay (1989), suggested that the packaging of the very notion of an information campaign is misleading. In his words, ". . . the bias and hope of information campaign planners to escape serious ethical reflections is manifest in the very language they commonly use, that is, substituting the term *information campaign* for *propaganda* or *persuasion*," and speaking of "managing social change" rather than "manipulating public opinion" (185, emphasis in original). Rakow (1989) made much the same point, albeit more broadly, in suggesting the outlines of a critical theory of campaigns. Taking a rather different tack, Devine and Hirst (1989) surveyed the range of social psychological theories available to guide persuasive strategy in a campaign. On their list: theories of message-based persuasion including the information-processing model, cognitive-response theory, the elaboration–likelihood model; and theories of behavioral-based persuasion including social-learning theory, heuristic effects, self-perception theory (on this see Bem, 1970), dissonance theory, and operant conditioning. Grunig (1989) provided a concise survey of approaches to market segmentation.

Rice and Atkin (1989) also brought together a series of essays on many aspects of public information campaigns. We have already made extensive use of William McGuire's (1989) chapter in delineating a basic communication model of these efforts. Other contributions included a variety of campaign case studies on such issues as crime prevention, forest fire prevention, family planning, rat control, smoking, and AIDS. Rice and Atkin (1994) summarized many of the key points of this volume in identifying the principles that lead to success in PICs.

Weiss and Tschirhart (1994) studied 100 public information campaigns undertaken by governments to advance policy objectives. They identified four core tasks to be achieved by a successful campaign, including capturing the attention of the correct audience, delivering a credible and understandable message, delivering a message that is influential, and creating a social context that facilitates the desired outcome, and delineated the issues and mechanisms associated with each. Of particular interest in the present context is the authors' discussion of the considerations associated with the engagement of mediating institutions, or in our terms, intermediaries, to carry a PIC to the desired audience—including the point that some potential intermediaries may resent being bypassed in a campaign that pertains to a domain of interest, and that a campaign that does so risks activating powerful, well-resourced, and newly motivated adversaries.

Klingemann and Römmele (2002) published a handbook emphasizing the linkage between public information campaigns and public opinion. In this volume, for example, Voltmer and Römmele (2002) identified two competing models that have been developed to explain the campaign process: a transmission model, that sees campaign communication as linear and directed, and an interaction model built on a presumed mutuality of knowledge and interpretations between the senders and receivers of messages. Rigg (2002) noted that PICs are designed to accomplish one or more of four general objectives: cognitive change, action change (a one-shot or short-term activity), behavioral change (a long-term activity pattern), or value change.

Elder et al (2004) reviewed eight studies of media campaigns designed to reduce drinking and driving, which were generally found to be both effective in reducing the undesirable behavior and cost effective relative to the resulting social benefits.

Literature on Communication and Media Effects

It is not our purpose here to review the extensive literature on communication and media effects. Clearly, however, these effects are essential building blocks of PICs, as well as more complex and sophisticated campaigns.

With that in mind, let us take a highly selective tour of the related scholarship.

A good place to begin developing an understanding of media effects is with one of the available introductory surveys. Shoemaker and Reese (1991), Bryant and Zillmann (1994), and Sparks (2002) are good examples of the genre.

Providing a sort of left-side bookend to this summary, Bauer (1964) pointed out that communication is a transactional process in which the audience plays an active role, and not an exercise in brainwashing—an argument he grounded in the social scientific analysis of the act.

In one early study, Hovland and Weiss (1951–1952) found evidence of a complex effect of source credibility. At the time of exposure to a persuasive communication, individuals discounted information that came from sources they regarded as untrustworthy. Over time, however, they tended to remember the information but forget their distrust of the source. Not only was the previously discredited information remembered, but, by the time a month had passed, lies actually seemed to be remembered better than the truth. Berlo, Lemert, and Mertz (1969–1970) employed semantic differential scales arrayed around the dimensions of safety, qualifications, and dynamism, to assess the criteria actually employed by message recipients to judge the credibility of message sources, arguing that it is these *perceived* attributes of sources, rather than any "objective" external criteria, that should be used to define credibility. Chaiken and Eagly (1983) found that the likeability of the communicator was a significant predictor of the persuasive effect of a message delivered via audio and video, but not for those in print. The authors attributed the differences in communicator salience to the more intensive processing of communicator cues by receivers in the electronic media forms.

Katz and Lazarsfeld (1955) provided the scholarly reference point for, if not the true origin of, the so-called "two step flow of communication" hypothesis, one by which messages are issued by the mass media to a seemingly homogeneous audience, then processed horizontally within the audience by peer-group interactions between influential individuals, termed opinion leaders, and their followers in a sociological exchange that assigned localized meaning to the messages. (Chaffee (1972), for example, incorporated the two-step flow into his somewhat more extensive examination of interpersonal processes in mass communication.) Though this framework is now regarded as overly simplified, it proved quite valuable in calling attention to the complexities associated with the processing of mediated information and the filters that serve to limit media effects, and remains influential. Bennett and Manheim (2006) suggested, however, that the two-step flow of communication hypothesis has been rendered obsolete by the development and systematic exploitation of new communication technologies, and by fundamental changes in the relationship between the individual and society. In their view, strategic advances in the design, placement, segmentation and targeting of persuasive communications have essentially supplanted the role of peer-group interaction in providing personalized interpretation of mediated messages. The two-step flow has, in effect, been reduced to a single step.

Katz (1961) compared two research traditions in the study of the diffusion of innovation—those based in rural sociology and in communication research. Of interest here: the media were found to make different contributions at different stages in the diffusion process, first to make potential adopters aware of the innovation in question, and later to legitimize the decision to adopt it. Then in 1962, Rogers produced the definitive treatment of diffusion in his aptly-named book, *Diffusion of Innovations*, which he then continued to develop through several subsequent editions. In the most recent of these (Rogers, 2003), he identified four aspects of the diffusion process, including the innovation itself, the channels through which it is communicated, time, and characteristics of the social system into which it is diffused. Rogers defined an innovation as a new idea, practice, or object. Innovations, he said, can vary in terms of their relative advantage compared to existing ideas or practices; their compatibility with the existing needs, values, and experiences of the potential adopters; their complexity or degree of accessibility; the extent to which they can be tested with minimal initial commitment; and the observability of their results. He saw adoption as a five-step process including knowledge acquisition, persuasion, the decision to adopt, implementation, and confirmation (observing a positive result), and, ever the taxonomist, specified five categories of adopters that he termed innovators, early adopters, early majority, late majority, and laggards. Adoption behavior, in his view, is a function of the social system, and can be illustrated over time in the form of an S-curve. The steeper the curve, the quicker the innovation is adopted. Rogers also identified a critical "take-off period" as a given innovation moves from narrow to broader adoption.

Krugman (1964, 1965, 1966, 1971, 1977; Krugman and Hartley 1970) conducted a series of experiments demonstrating that different media engage differentially with their audiences, with some requiring active participation in message processing and others effectively rewarding passivity. By comparing such biometrics as pupil dilation, galvanic skin response, and brainwave patterns, Krugman's work showed that different media were better suited than others to convey particular types of persuasive messages—for example, that print media were better suited than broadcast media for messages requiring intellectual engagement or internalization, while television was especially well-suited to messages designed to circumvent active information processing by the audience member, in effect, to exercise influence without engagement—and that persuasive strategies must be tuned to the dynamics of the media channels through which they are to be directed. The full body of Krugman's research, including many lesser-known works, has been collected into a *Festschrift*

(Krugman, 2008) by his son. As part of a more elaborate analysis of the hierarchy of effects, Ray (1973) tested Krugman's low-involvement approach against two alternative models employed in marketing—learning, where attitude change precedes behavior change, and dissonance-attribution, where behavior change can precede attitude change—finding the Krugman process to be the most commonplace. Manheim (1976) suggested that, because television use requires and rewards minimal engagement on the part of the viewer as demonstrated by Krugman, and because dependency on television for political information was high and increasing, citizens were losing their ability to process complex political information and their appreciation of the need to do so. Putnam (2000) argued more generally, twenty-five years later and in the context of a far broader social critique, that television viewing has become both addictive and pervasive, consuming people's time in an activity that encourages lethargy and passivity, even as the viewing itself is unsatisfying, and that heavy viewing tends to produce lower rates of participation in civic life.

In a review of literature focusing on the uses and gratifications approach to media effects, Katz, Blumler, and Gurevitch (1973) identified several assumptions inherent in this approach. These included (1) that the audience is seen as an active participant in mass communication, (2) that as a consequence, audience members take the initiative in linking their needs to media choices, (3) that the media are in competition with other mechanisms by which audience needs can be satisfied, and (4) that the audience is self-aware of its needs, and can report them to the media in the form of feedback or research responses, which allows the media to be responsive to them. Gratification, they argued, could derive not only from content, but from the form of a given medium and the setting in which exposure typically occurs. Rubin (1994) provided an updated survey of research within this framework.

Tichenor, Rodenkirchen, Olien, and Donohue (1973) tested a series of hypotheses that bear on the localization-of-conflict strategy that is widely used in IICs today. They held, for example, that increased levels of local media attention to a community issue are associated with higher levels of knowledge and a greater level of perceived conflict; and that higher levels of perceived conflict would generate more interpersonal communication about the issue in question and higher levels of knowledge, greater recall of media coverage of the issue, and higher levels of perceived conflict in media coverage of the issue.

Lanzetta, Sullivan, Masters, and McHugo (1985) studied cognitive and emotional responses to televised facial images of political leaders in the news, finding, among other things, that facial displays of such characteristics as reassurance, anger, threat, fear, and evasiveness are perceived differently and elicit different responses based on such factors as prior attitudes (especially partisanship), and that these effects are present even when the displays in question are embedded in the background of a newscast.

Graber (1984, 2001) employed schema theory—which refers to cognitive structures that organize knowledge about objects and situations based on past experience—to examine the ways that people process political information they receive from television news and the Internet, finding that people are better informed and more capable information processors than many might believe. DeFleur, Davenport, Cronin, and DeFleur (1992) compared factual recall from news stories presented through four media, finding that communication via print and computer screens produced higher levels of recall than that via television and radio. Zillman and Brosius (2000) argued, however, that heuristics—an alternative conceptualization based on cognitive mechanisms that simplify and expedite the reception and utilization of information in order to overcome the limited capacity of the brain—is a more promising approach to understanding learning from the media. In that context, they examined the influence of exemplification, or the inclusion of examples in the news, as one facilitating device, finding that exemplars have a significant and complex effect: they influence perceptions and enliven journalism, but at the same time they greatly enhance the media's potential to manipulate public perceptions. In a study of political discourse on television, Mutz and Reeves (2005) found that audiences have a tolerance for disagreement, but that increased levels of incivility in political discourse contribute to declining levels of trust in political institutions.

Margolis and Mauser (1989), writing even before the advent of the World Wide Web, concluded that, even though contemporary communications technologies enhance the already disproportionate influence of elites over media coverage of issues, they also afford citizens with increasing opportunities to develop independent sources and channels of their own, and that, in turn, provides the capacity, demonstrated only on occasion, to resist elite manipulation of public opinion. Boulianne (2009) found that, rather than contributing to reduced civic engagement, as Putnam (2000) and others had postulated, Internet use was associated with increased engagement, albeit on a very small scale.

Wolfsfeld (1997) noted that, just as there is an imbalance in the influence of competing antagonists on the news media, there is as well an imbalance in the reciprocal influence of the media on the antagonists. Among the factors determining this reciprocal influence are, on the one hand, the organization and resources of the antagonist, its place in the political environment, and the importance of the information it controls, and on the other, the size and status of a given medium and the political influence of its audience. Conflicts between political antagonists often play out through the dynamics of these imbalances.

Zaller (1996) provides the right-side bookend here, with his argument that, at least with respect to political communication, the effects of mass media, long presumed to be minimal, are in fact enormous. Media, he said, fundamentally shape the attitudes of citizens who are exposed to them.

Literature on Language, Symbols, Rhetoric, Drama, Culture, Pseudo-Events, and Knowledge Structures

Riker (1986) made clear the linkage between rhetoric and strategy, and made clear as well the place of rhetoric in the present analysis, when he coined the term "heresthetic" to capture the importance of structuring situations to assure, or at least facilitate, victory, even in the absence of persuasion. Here and in a later (Riker, 1996) volume, he provided several illustrative historical examples.

Much of the scholarly treatment of language and symbols in strategic political communication traces to the works of Kenneth Burke (see 1966 (originally 1935), 1984), a literary theorist and philosopher. Burke argued that human motives—and everything we think we understand about them—are really communication effects, and that this organic communication takes the form of symbols that are employed situationally. Edelman (1964, 1971, 1988) made Burke's and related ideas accessible to political scientists, and in the process planted the seeds from which grew the study of political communication and, as part of that process, the political side of information and influence campaigns. Edelman emphasized the role of symbols as the psychological organizing loci of politics, as, for example, in his (1964) delineation of four classes of political language—hortatory, legal, administrative, and bargaining—distinguished from one another in their respective uses of referential and affective symbols, and employed both to reflect and to preserve the power relationships (and, except in the last of these, the asymmetries) between the affected parties. Graber (1976) took a wide-ranging look at verbal behavior in politics, starting with such basic functions as the naming and classification of actors and events, and moving on to the media, public events, and elites, among other topics. Writing after Edelman (1964), she picked up on many of his core arguments, but developed them in new and original ways, particularly in a chapter devoted to condensation symbols. The book is also noteworthy for its extensive attention to the methods available for studying verbal phenomena and the challenges associated with the effort.

Anthropologist Edward T. Hall (1971) suggested that communication varies by the degree to which externalities—things outside the communication itself—contribute to its meaning. He identified two general classes, which he termed high-context and low-context communication. Factors contributing to high-context communication would include such things as a strong sense of personal and group identity and a clear sense of boundaries, a high degree of commitment to relationships, reliance on internalized understandings, temporal flexibility, and active engagement by the receiver in assigning meaning to the message. High-context communication derives much of its meaning, then, from the social setting in which it occurs, and less from the message content *per se*. Factors contributing to low-context communications would include a shifting outward (away from the receiver) of the locus of meaning, open and changing reference groups, low levels of commitment to relationships, more reliance on public or external knowledge, and temporal rigidity. Low-context communication gets its meaning mainly from the message. The distinction is meaningful in the present context because it points toward two different communication strategies, one that is exchange oriented in the first instance, and one that is delivery oriented in the second. With that in mind, as LeBaron (2003) points out, special attention must be paid when the communication occurs across cultural lines. Low-context communicators interacting with high-context communicators, for example, must recognize that nonverbal messages may convey more than they customarily would intend, including aspects of status and identity; indirectness and tact may be more important than directness and frankness; and it may be beneficial to focus on building relationships in the near term to facilitate communication effectiveness in the long term. Similarly, high-context communicators in such a cross-cultural dialogue would do well to note that messages might be more likely to be taken at face value and likely to be perceived as less nuanced than they are accustomed to; that roles and functions may be decoupled from identity and status; that directness in incoming messages is not generally meant to offend, and that directness in outbound messages may not be sufficient to get the receiver's attention.

Edelman (1993) examined the centrality of categorization schemes and metaphors employed by political and media elites to political maneuvering and persuasion, finding that many of these are driven less by facts and analysis than by the ideology and prejudices of those who adopt them. Notable among these schemes is the absence of explicit linkage between a given policy or problem and others with which it is, in fact, connected. The result, he argued, is that issues tend to be regarded as autonomous, and broader issue-clusters that may be far more significant tend to be ignored.

In the course of reviewing the literature on language and politics, Graber (1981) identified the major functions that language plays, among them the dissemination of explicit information, connotations, inferences, and symbolic meanings; interpretation and linkage, including reality creation, control over definitions, manipulation of expectations, and defining interpersonal relationships; and stimulation to action through direct appeals and mood creation. As she noted, words and messages can also substitute for action, even as symbols can also substitute for concrete rewards. Elder and Cobb (1983) updated and extended Edelman's early work, using symbols as a lens through which to view a range of fundamental political processes, including among others, identification, legitimacy, conflict definition, and mobilization. Even the most basic elements of language can have significance in the context of campaign strategy. Smith (1998), for example, identified a series of phonetic features in the names of political candidates, then tested their effect, finding that candidates who scored better than their opponents with respect to the sound of their names experienced greater electoral success.

Smith's analytical model incorporated three sets of variables—rhythm, vowel attributes, and consonant attributes—and specified a method of scoring that should be equally applicable to any other naming objects, including issues, organizations, coalitions, policies, and the like. Mueller (1973) linked political language and communication processes with legitimacy, arguing that political systems relying on the voluntary submission of their citizens for stability must maintain control of myth-sustaining information and communications. Holmström, Falkheimer, and Nielsen (2010) used the image of a Scandinavian dairy company to illustrate the culture-bound nature of legitimacy and the challenge it poses in an age of globalization.

As Edelman (1964) made clear, one important attribute of language is its degree of ambiguity. Eisenberg (1984) assessed ambiguity as a component of organizational communication strategy, finding that it served four distinct functions: balancing the competing needs for consensus and independence, preserving privileged positions, fostering deniability (by rendering it plausible), and facilitating organizational change. Allport and Postman (1946–1947), for example, posited a basic law of rumor: the amount of rumor in circulation will vary with the personal salience (to the initiator) of the subject multiplied by the ambiguity of available information. They posed *sixty* questions to be used in evaluating rumors, among them:

- Does the rumor offer an economical and simplified explanation of a confusing environmental or emotional situation?
- Does the rumor explain some inner tension? Is the tension anxiety, hostility, wish, guilt, curiosity, or some other state of mind?
- Does the rumor justify in the teller an otherwise unacceptable emotion? In telling the rumor, is the teller likely to gain prestige?
- What relationship, if any, does the rumor bear to the news or the media?
- Is the story labeled a rumor or a fact? Is it ascribed to an authoritative source?

Scott and Smith (1969) parsed the rhetoric of confrontation, which they found to contain several core elements. Among these are radical division, or the use of language to dramatize the depth of social or political divides; the rite of the kill, which essentially employs language to establish that a given conflict is a zero-sum game, in which there can be only one winning side; and totalism, an expression of complete unity and complete commitment, having nothing to lose and expecting to win. Bowers, Ochs, and Jensen (1993) looked more broadly at the rhetoric of social agitation and social control, proposing strategies for each. On the agitation side, they identified several stages of action including petitioning for change, promulgation (seeking social support through such devices as picketing, leafleting, posters, graffiti, staging pseudo-events, recruiting legitimizing voices within the media), solidification (reinforcing the cohesiveness of the group through developing expressive symbols and slogans, internal publications, songs and other arts), polarization (finding and attacking issues, individuals, groups, or organizations that represent the opposition in some highly visible or symbolic way), and nonviolent resistance. On the control side they noted four rhetorical strategies: avoidance (including counter-persuasion, evasion, postponement, secrecy with a rationale, denial of means), suppression (harassment of leading antagonists, denial of demands, banishment of antagonists, or purgation, i.e., the actual murder of antagonists), adjustment (changing the name of an entity, sacrificing personnel, providing a social space for dissent, incorporating some personnel from among the antagonists, incorporating portions of the antagonists' ideology or program), and capitulation.

Combs (1980) focused on the dramatic aspects of political communication, which are demonstrated in political rituals and symbolic acts, institutional dramas, leadership, movements, and campaigns. He identified the elements of these dramas as including rehearsal, scripted lines, gestures, props, and costume—all physical aspects of dramaturgy—but also forethought about the action to be taken, the focus on a perceived audience, a sense of the dramatic potential of a given situation, and the actual performance. Cohen (1987) showed these same elements at work in the diplomatic arena. Gray (2001), in the course of a review of books relating performance to social activism, noted that social protests tend to be rehearsed, dramatized and staged with an eye toward their setting, costuming and props. In his words, "Activists, as the term implies, are also actors" (64). Though based in an electoral paradigm, Martel's (1983) outline of key strategies and tactics of value in political debates reflects a focus on similar elements of drama.

Boorstin (1961) coined the term "pseudo-event" to describe events that are not spontaneous, that are staged primarily for the purpose of being reported, that bear an ambiguous relationship to the underlying reality of a given situation, and that are often intended to be self-fulfilling prophecies (11–12). He went on to argue that an increasing proportion of people's everyday experience of external realities is actually the product of these artificial constructions. Greenberg (1985) demonstrated the use of staged media events by Friends of the Earth in the UK to attract public attention and gain legitimacy. He concluded that the theatrical nature of the events blended with the group's serious research met a need on the part of the media to find a legitimate environmental voice for their stories.

Berger and Luckman (1966) argued that knowledge is a social construct, and that much, if not most, of our understanding of reality is subjective rather than objective. Boulding (1969) picked up on this theme, contending that all human behavior depends, not on knowledge, but on what he termed "the image." The word "knowledge" carries with it an implication of validity, of some underlying truth. But behavior is based on something more amorphous, on *subjective* knowledge, or what one believes to be true. "The true meaning of a message," he said, "is the change which it produces in the image" (7). Nimmo (1974) looked specifically at the manufacture, distribution, patterns and effects of such images in politics on levels ranging from the community to the regime. Funkhouser and Shaw (1990) pointed to the culpability of the media in creating what they termed "synthetic realities" to serve their own needs. DeLuca (2005) offered a rhetorical theory of social movements, with particular reference to the environmental movement, that incorporates an emphasis on imaging and ideation.

Bitzer (1999) suggested that pragmatic communication—often an objective in IICs—necessarily involves two rhetorical elements: exigency, or the presence of some social problem or defect, and remedy, or the availability of some means of redress. Those engaged in related exchanges, he said, will focus on such factors as the risk (in time, energy, prestige, danger, personal commitment, or money) associated with responding, the individual's sense of obligation or responsibility (or of other's expectations in that regard), familiarity and confidence based on having responded previously to similar situations, and immediacy, or perhaps more correctly, the belief that the situation will worsen significantly if not addressed right away.

Kelly (1963) examined the challenge confronting policy experts seeking to influence policy makers, which centers on the need for communication upward to the policy elites in a form that will be instrumental and utilitarian, and at the same time downward to the public in a form that will render the expertise understandable and policies that may be based on it seemingly reasonable and correct. Tichenor, Donohue, and Olien (1970) found that increasing the flow of news on a given topic produces knowledge gain about the topic on the part of highly educated individuals. The result is a knowledge gap between the higher and less educated segments of the audience that may be reduced through continued, intense media coverage, but that may endure in its absence. Eveland, Hayes, Shaw, and Kwak (2005) employed a panel design to test several models of unidirectional and reciprocal flows of communication (news) and political knowledge, finding support for the traditional assumption that communication produces knowledge gain. Gilens (2001) found that policy-specific raw facts have a substantial influence on the public's judgments about issues, and that, as a consequence, ignorance of such facts leads many people to adopt positions on policy issues that they would not hold were they fully informed. This effect is greatest for those with the highest levels of political knowledge.

Fast (2002) argued for the adoption by the U.S. military of a "knowledge strategy," one that integrates political, economic, military, and informational components to project national power through such mechanisms as information dominance and control over network nodes.

Literature on Attitudes, Beliefs, Cognitions, Persuasion, and Resistance

There are many good books available that provide general overviews of persuasion and attitude change and can serve as points of entry. Perhaps the best of the early entries in this category was Kiesler, Collins, and Miller (1969), which appeared at a time of rapid conceptual development. The book is especially notable for its treatment of two theories, cognitive dissonance and social judgment-involvement. The best contemporary example is O'Keefe (2002), which generally ignores social judgment-involvement theory, which received relatively little scholarly attention in the interim, but adds several more recent analytical frameworks. Perloff (2003) drew some nice connections between these theoretical approaches to persuasion and the way they are applied in campaign and other settings.

In his seminal work, Lewin (1936) created the foundations of topological psychology—a spatial approach (he spoke of the "life space") to characterizing psychological phenomena that found subsequent applications in, and fundamentally reformed, the analysis of attitudes. It is this concept that underlies the notion of cognitive space we have employed in the our own earlier discussion. Lewin's book was translated into English by Fritz Heider and his wife, Grace. So it should come as no surprise that Heider's own (1946) brief but equally seminal assertion that a balance among what he termed "cognitive configurations" was determinative, or at least co-determinative, of social perception and interpersonal behavior sparked the development of various schemes designed to characterize and explain the dynamics of attitudes and other cognitive structures, most notably the theory of cognitive dissonance. Cartwright and Harary (1956) formalized Heider's concept of balance as a series of graph-theoretic relationships, and generalized it to include asymmetric relationships, units comprised of more than three entities, negative relationships, relationships of different types, and such social systems as communication networks and patterns of power.

It was in this context that Festinger (1957, 1964) introduced, and through a later series of experiments added dimension to, dissonance theory, which we discussed at length above and which, arguably, remains one of the most vital, and most readily applied, theories of attitude structure and change. Arthur Cohen (1960) tested the dissonance-related effects of induced discrepancies between attitudes and behaviors, finding that those who had to work the hardest or overcome obstacles to understand a communication were likely to experience more dissonance, and hence would be more likely to change their attitudes than those for whom understanding came easily or, more to the point, was more greatly facilitated by the persuader (i.e., "spoon-feeding" the discrepant information). Cohen also found that those individuals who were most open to new information were those who were subjected to the least external pressure to accept it. Grupp

(1971) employed cognitive dissonance theory to explain reported changes between the motivations to join, on the one hand, and the satisfactions derived from, on the other, the John Birch Society. In particular, the failure of the organization to achieve its stated aims was mitigated by the satisfaction associated with participation in its activities and by the social support derived from sharing that activity with others. Though writing in a different context, Albrecht and Adelman (1987) offered useful insights on the processes and importance of social support, the assignment or withholding of which is one key mechanism in dissonance-based persuasion.

Osgood and Tannenbaum (1955), working within the general framework of balance theories and with an emphasis on semantics, provided an early attempt to quantify the direction and degree of attitude change based on what they regarded as the three critical variables: the existing attitude toward the *source* of new information, the existing attitude toward the concept referenced by the source, and the nature of the assertion linking the source with the content. They anticipated that, when presented with incongruities (inconsistencies across frames of reference, i.e., the three stated variables), individuals would adjust their attitudes. Their evidence supported this expectation, but introduced both an accelerating factor (polarization) and a retarding factor (resistance due to incredulity). Osgood (1960) asserted that the congruity approach was superior to other balance theories because it did a better job of both specifying cognitive interactions and quantifying the resolution of inconsistencies. Abelson (1959) argued that resolving structural inconsistencies among beliefs can take any of four forms: denial, bolstering, differentiation, or transcendence.

Rosenberg (1960) conducted a rather unusual test of the introduction of inconsistency between beliefs and preferences in which he placed subjects under hypnosis, introduced preference changes, then measured beliefs in posthypnotic testing at three time points. A week after the initial session, he "removed" the subjects' hypnotically induced amnesia and explained the experiment to them. Some, it seems, were beginning to suspect they might have been hypnotized. Before that, however, he did find evidence that the change in preferences he introduced had indeed carried over to the associated beliefs.

In a study of voters' attitudes in the 1980 and 1984 election cycles, Krosnick (1988) found that those attitudes that people consider to be personally important to them are more stable over time than those they regard as less personally important. He also found that variations over time in the less salient attitudes were the product of true attitude change. Linking his work to dissonance theory, he went on to speculate that, because of the bias toward consistency in personally important attitudes, any conflict induced by a persuasive communication between an important and an unimportant attitude is likely to be resolved by a change in the unimportant attitude, while inconsistency between two important attitudes is likely to be resolved by denial, bolstering, or some other mechanism.

Sherif and Sherif (1967) provided a comprehensive summary of the social judgment-involvement approach to attitude change, which, as noted, focuses on the success-critical placement of communications in cognitive space relative to the thresholds of rejection and acceptance, which are established based on the degree of involvement of the individual in the attitude in question. Boninger, Krosnick, and Berent (1995) found that attitude salience is a function of at least three factors—self-interest, social identification, and value relevance—and that self-interest, in particular, had a greater impact than previous studies had suggested. Holbrook et al (2005) found that a high degree of personal salience assigned to an attitude leads to the acquisition of attitude-relevant information and its storage in long-term memory, but that relatively extensive knowledge is not a driver of attitude salience. Personally more salient attitudes were also found to lead to higher levels of selective exposure to relevant information and to a greater degree of attitude elaboration, or thinking about the issue.

In both the cognitive dissonance and social judgment-involvement approaches to attitude change, an important factor in the persuasive impact of new information is its degree of discrepancy from the individual's existing beliefs. Kaplowitz and Fink (1997) examined a number of models for representing this degree of discrepancy mathematically. Importantly, the authors also measured the duration of changes induced by more and less discrepant information, finding, for example, that in some circumstances the more extreme initial effect of a highly discrepant message may decline over time to the point where it is less than that of a more moderate one.

Katz (1960) argued that attitudes and attitude change can best be understood in terms of the functions they perform for the individual, which is to say, the reasons why people hold or change their attitudes. He posited four such functions: instrumental or utilitarian, ego-defensive, value expressive, and knowledge—advancing one's interests, protecting one's sense of self, demonstrating one's values, and organizing one's world, respectively. Katz went on to elaborate strategies for arousing and changing attitudes serving each of these functions. Cook (1980) provided a clear link between the value-expressive function of attitudes and the use of standards, which he defined as "ostensibly self-transcendent bases of agreement for justification of preferences," as a basis for political appeals. This is precisely the formulation we see in information and influence campaigns that employ codes of conduct. Interest in this functional approach has experienced something of a resurgence in recent years. The contributors to Maio and Olson (2000a) ably summarized recent developments in the literature, in the course of which they provided an especially rich examination of the several different functions that attitudes might perform—for example, knowledge (Thompson, Kruglanski, and Spiegel, 2000), social identity (Shavitt and Nelson, 2000), and value expressive (Maio and Olson, 2000b)—and the connections between the functional approach and other perspectives on attitude change and persuasion—for example, elaboration likelihood (Petty,

Wheeler, and Bizer, 2000) and social judgment-involvement (Levin, Nichols, and Johnson, 2000).

Anderson and Fishbein (1965) found evidence that summation theory provides better predictions of attitude than congruence theory. Fishbein (1967a, 1967b) then set out the basic terms of the belief-based approach to attitude change we discussed earlier, including its basic algebraic expression in which the attitude toward a given object is the sum across all beliefs about that object of the strength of a given belief weighted by the associated evaluation. Beginning from Fishbein's characterization, Danes and Hunter (1980) examined three factors that might contribute to transforming belief change into intention change, which in the context of their writing (consumer behavior) is the functional equivalent of what we have treated here as behavior change; these included consistency, contingency, and discrepancy relevance. They then tested multi-message modeling employing these factors, finding the greatest change-inducing effects for discrepancy relevance. Ajzen and Fishbein (1980) also built on Fishbein's summative model of belief-based attitude change by elaborating what they termed the "theory of reasoned action" and applying it to the prediction, explanation, and influencing of behavior. Their basic idea was that people are generally rational, and make systematic use of whatever information they have at hand. In such a system, intentionality plays a central role. Ajzen and Fishbein characterized intentionality as a function of two forces, the preferences of the individual with respect to a given behavior and the social pressure he or she is under, either to engage in that behavior or to avoid it. Outcomes, they said, are determined by the degree of continuity or discrepancy between the two and, where discrepant, by the relative strengths of each vis-à-vis the other.

As described in detail in the main text, Petty and Cacioppo (1986) promulgated the elaboration likelihood model of persuasion, which assigns a central role to the complexity of the information being conveyed in determining the most appropriate path to successful persuasion—high elaboration for complex information requiring psychological engagement on the part of the targeted individual, or low elaboration for simpler and less demanding information.

Converse (1964) argued that politically significant beliefs ought to be viewed, not in isolation, but in the context of higher level clusters of "idea-elements," or belief *systems*, and that these systems would best be understood as constraints on variability. In a related empirical test, he found that the level of such constraint declines as one moves from more to less politically sophisticated individuals. Rokeach (1972), too, examined the workings of belief systems, arguing that beliefs, attitudes, and values are best understood as distinctive phenomena. And of the three, he argued, values and value systems are by far the most important. Values, he said, are the most dynamic of the three because they incorporate not only cognitive, affective, and behavioral components, but also motivation. Moreover, while both attitudes and values are assumed to be determinants of behavior, values are *also* determinants of attitudes. In addition, values are fewer in number than attitudes, and thus provide a more parsimonious explanation of behavior. All of this led Rokeach to call for a shift in scholarly emphasis away from theories of attitudes and toward theories of value organization and change.

Zielske (1959) and Zielske and Henry (1980) tested the duration and decay of message recall in advertising, finding that effects are cumulative so long as the messages are clustered relatively closely together in time. Taking a different tack on the question of duration, Petty and Priester (1994) considered the implications of the elaboration likelihood model for media-induced attitude change, concluding that efforts to produce lasting changes in attitudes with behavioral consequences are probably best accomplished through the central route to persuasion, while efforts to produce shorter term or less consequential changes in attitudes can employ the peripheral route. Echoing an argument we have made earlier, they noted that consequential or enduring attitude change requires that the individual be motivated to change, and that such motivation is best accomplished through strategies that increase the perceived personal salience of the new information in question.

Doob (1947) defined an attitude as "an implicit, drive-producing response considered socially significant in the individual's society," a construct that not only emphasized the cognitive–behavioral link, but also focused attention on the externalities of attitudes and hinted at the complexities of their connection to public opinion. Kelman (1958, 1961) identified three alternative mechanisms of attitude and behavior change arising from social influence: compliance, identification, and internalization. Compliance occurs when an individual is receptive to influence in order to gain the acceptance or approval (or avoid the disapproval) of a social group or another individual, possibly, but not necessarily, the change agent. Identification occurs when receptiveness arises because the individual wants to establish a relationship with a particular group or individual and sees adoption of the change as the means to this more general end. Internalization occurs when the content of the new attitude or behavior itself is judged to be intrinsically rewarding. Schein (1969) examined the changing of attitudes or behaviors as a phased process, including unfreezing (motivating to change, as by withdrawing support or confirmation, inducing guilt or anxiety, or reducing threats or eliminating barriers to change), changing (developing new responses based on new information), and refreezing (stabilizing and integrating the changes by tying them to personality or ongoing social relationships). McGuire (1976), writing in the context of consumer decision-making, provided a concise summary of the stages by which individuals process new, incoming, and potentially persuasive information. These include exposure, perception, comprehension, agreement, retention, retrieval, decision-making, and action.

Lewin's spatial approach has continued to influence the conceptualizing of cognitive processes and has made cognitive mapping a commonplace analytical tool. Smith (1968), for example, provided a broadly integrative schematic map of the relationships among personality, attitudes, and political behaviors. Key elements of the map included the historical, economic, political, and societal contexts that establish meanings and assign cultural norms; the social environment and experiences that shape the individual and the way s/he processes information; the structures and functions of attitudes; and the situational norms and constraints within which the individual behaves. Hamilton (1997) delineated what he termed the "omnistructure" by which persuasive messages are processed, which he saw as including five phases: message exposure, perception, orientation, goal-directed thought, and causal attribution. He provided detailed conceptual maps of each process, and of the interactions among them. One interesting aspect of Hamilton's approach in the present context is its emphasis on the stages of evaluation of new information, including both pre-message and post-message evaluations of the source (e.g., with respect to its dynamism, competence, and trustworthiness).

Zimbardo et al (1970) considered the circumstance in which a persuasive communication is issued in a setting that includes distracting activity. They found that attention cues play a critical role in such situations. If the audience is cued that the message is the signal and the distraction is noise, persuasion will occur. On the other hand, if the audience is cued to attend to the distraction, it will perceive the message as noise, and persuasion will fail. Sears and Freedman (1971) reviewed the literature pertaining to selective exposure and its role in minimizing attitude change. They found some evidence for the existence of *de facto* selective exposure in that most mass media audiences seem to contain over-representations of persons predisposed to agree with the views set forth, but more limited support for the affirmative role typically assigned to purposeful selective exposure in resisting persuasion. This latter finding, they suggested, pointed to a greater than expected role for higher-level information processing, which is to say, the evaluation of information, as a defensive mechanism. Observing that the mere-repeated-exposure paradigm of influence—in which a subject is repeatedly exposed to a particular stimulus, toward which he or she develops a preference—is "a robust phenomenon that . . . has been demonstrated across cultures, species, and diverse stimulus domains" (224), Zajonc (2001) argued that such exposure, *per se*, actually induces affect irrespective of subjective impression or familiarity, an effect that is enhanced when the exposure is subliminal.

Chaudhuri and Buck (1995) identified four broad advertising strategies—product information appeals, spokesperson appeals, mood arousal appeals, and status appeals—which they tested on 240 advertisements for products in 29 different categories. They found that product information appeals (for example, demonstration, comparison, problem solving, ingredients, price, value) tended to produce cognitive change in viewers/readers, and that mood arousal appeals (such as sexual cues, vignettes, patriotic appeals, nostalgia, fitness, enjoyment, or excitement) tended to produce affective change.

Kahneman (2003) reprised his work with Tversky (see below), comparing two systems of cognitive processing, intuition and reasoning, with respect to their effects on the accessibility of one's complex judgments and preferences. He characterized the intuitive system as fast, parallel in form (in the sense of computer circuitry), automatic, effortless, associative, relatively inflexible, and emotional; while the reasoning system is slow, serial in form, controlled, effortful, rule-governed, flexible, and emotionally neutral. The two systems relate to one another in that judgments and preferences are controlled by default through the intuitive cognitive system, but can be modified or deliberately overridden by reasoning (or, by extension, appeals to reason).

Starting from the assumption that explanations and predictors of attitude organization and change are more or less constant across cultures, Tanaka (1971) noted that cultural differences nevertheless matter because they can produce differing evaluative judgments. In a sense this is a hardware–software argument, with an underlying psychological process providing continuity of processing, and shared culture determining its applications. To facilitate effective cross-cultural persuasion, he called for a multi-channel, multi-stage strategy in which actions are used as the principal "language" of communication.

McGuire (1961) examined the development of resistance to persuasion through prior refutation of anticipated arguments, or what has since come to be known as the inoculation theory of resistance, an approach he positioned as a means of defending against persuasion based on selective exposure to information. In effect, inoculation takes the ability to control audience exposure out of the hands of a prospective persuader by pre-exposing that audience to the message, and in the process raising its awareness of any extant beliefs that might be challenged or circumvented by the persuader. His study found evidence that this approach does generate a significant degree of immunity to persuasion. In a related study, McGuire and Papageorgis (1962) found strong evidence that issuing a prior warning to individuals that their beliefs are about to be attacked enhances the effects of immunization against persuasion. Anderson and McGuire (1965)—in an early test of inoculation theory find that cultural truisms appear strong but are highly vulnerable to persuasion because of limited experience in defending them. To get subjects to develop defenses, it is necessary to threaten them; positive reinforcement does not work. Watson (1969) delineated several sources of resistance to persuasion, not only in the personality of the individual (homeostasis, habit, primacy, selective perception and retention, and dependency, among others), but also in social systems, where it arises from conformity to norms, cultural coherence, vested interests, views that are sacrosanct, and the rejection of outsiders. Pfau (1997) reviewed the research on inoculation to that date, finding the theory to be useful in those situations where there is an expectation that strongly-held attitudes are likely to be seriously challenged. He identified the key elements of effective inoculation as the introduction of a threat, which serves as a motivational catalyst, and refutational preemption, which provides the content with which individuals can defend their existing attitude against change. In one recent anthology, Knowles and Linn (2004a) provided a particularly good selection of writings on the nature of resistance to persuasion (see, for example, Briñol, Rucker, Tormala, and Petty 2004), strategies for creating attitudes that display resistance (Wegener, Petty, Smoak, and Fabrigar 2004), and strategies for overcoming resistance where it is encountered (as in Knowles and Linn 2004b). Fully half of the book is devoted to the last of these three foci.

Literature on Public Opinion

If one could read only three books on public opinion, one might do worse than to select Lippmann (1922), Lane and Sears (1964), and Zaller (1992). Walter Lippmann all but literally invented the study of public opinion, even coining the term "manufacture of consent" that would be prominently adopted by Herman and Chomsky (1988) more than six decades later. Writing in an era even before the general availability of radio, Lippmann wrote of the importance of images, or what he termed, the pictures in our heads, in shaping our views of political reality, of the significance of stereotypes, of the workings of the newsroom and the role of the publicist, and of the centrality of all of the above and a host of related phenomena to democratic practice. Robert Lane and David Sears, writing concisely and in the midst of the behavioral revolution in American political science, linked public opinion with the latest theories of the day in social psychology and attitude change, looking at such factors as cognitive structures, salience, primary-group influences, the relationship between information availability and opinion, and the respective roles of rationality, conformity, and intensity. Their discussion of the pressure toward primary-group conformity was particularly detailed, including a listing of group characteristics that might influence conformity, among them size of the group (the smaller the group, the more pressure toward conformity), frequency of contact, duration of the group's existence, degree of member participation in group decisions, cohesiveness, the salience of group membership, homogeneity, and feelings of acceptance, to name but a few (36). John Zaller's more recent effort benefited from an additional three decades of research, but also from the rigor of a razor-sharp analyst. Zaller examined the mechanisms by which news and other political information diffuse through a population, passing through the filters of extant values and predispositions, to produce electoral preferences and responses to public opinion surveys. In his phrase, the "moving part" in this argument is media coverage of public affairs information. It includes two types of political messages: persuasive messages, comprising arguments or images providing one or more reasons to assume a particular position, and cueing messages, which provide contextual information about the implications of the persuasive message. Zaller argued in part that, the greater a person's level of cognitive engagement with an issue, the greater is his/her likelihood of exposure to and comprehension of issue-related messages, and that people tend to resist arguments that are inconsistent with their predispositions, but only to the extent that they possess the contextual information to recognize the inconsistency.

Early on, Davison (1958) helped to clarify the boundary between personal attitudes and public opinion, characterizing public opinion as comprising a mix of psychological and sociological processes through which the behaviors of each member of the public relative to a given issue is a function, not only of the formation of individual attitudes and opinions, but also of group opinion processes, inter-group communication, and what he termed "personal sampling," by which he meant a process of informal, and inherently idiosyncratic, information seeking. Lemert (1981) argued that the notion of public opinion was itself a subjective one, a self-generated frame used by an individual to characterize citizen attitudes toward any given object of controversy.

Downs (1972) identified what he termed the "issue-attention cycle," a rhythm of sorts by which the public becomes aware of a given policy problem, clamors for a solution, discovers the complexities associated with the various options, and loses interest in the problem. For the strategist, this suggests both a dynamic that can be exploited to advantage and a naturally-occurring time constraint that may impinge on a campaign. Hilgartner and Bosk (1988) approached this problem by treating public attention as a scarce resource, and modeling the competition for, and selection of, issue attention in the media and other social venues. They found that issue growth is facilitated by interactions among various social arenas (media, foundations, legislative committees, NGOs, etc.), but limited by their individual and collective carrying capacities (time, space, staffing, financial resources, etc.). The resultant ebb and flow of issue attention produces waves of problem definition as cross-cutting networks of interested parties compete for access to the public agenda. Of particular interest in the present context was this latter finding—that problem-centered "communities" of "operatives" exist, and that they interconnect across seemingly unrelated arenas. These are, in effect, personal links between nodes in potential issue-specific networks. Henry and Gordon (2001) tested the notion of cyclic attention to issues on a recurrent issue (air quality) using a rolling-sample methodology derived from that used in political tracking polls, finding, among other things, confirmation that the public reacts less to issue-related messages during periods of declining interest due to boredom.

Noelle-Neumann (1974) found evidence of what she termed "the spiral of silence," a self-reinforcing tendency within a public to mask or suppress dissenting views, not as a collective action, but as the aggregate result of individual self-censorship. The basic argument here was that, for individuals, the fear of social isolation is more important than the risk of error, which leads them to join in opinions that receive substantial public support rather than to oppose them. Scheufele and Moy (2000) reflected on this conceptualization a quarter-century later, concluding that the core notion may be robust, but that research to that date had failed to account for cross-cultural differences that impact on the likelihood of expressing a minority view.

Davison (1983) posited a so-called "third person effect" in which persons exposed to a persuasive communication in the mass media believed themselves to be little influenced, but believed the communication would have a greater influence on others, who were presumed to be more impressionable. His analysis concluded with the question of whether individuals overestimate the effects of persuasion on others, or underestimate the effects on themselves. Chong (1996) examined the development of common frames of reference on political issues. He posited and tested a model with the following elements: (1) a given issue can be interpreted using any of a number of frames of reference; (2) differing frames of reference predispose the individual toward different positions on the issue; (3) an individual's preference regarding the issue is based on the frames of reference selected; and (4) frames of reference can be held in common if there is a particular interpretation of the issue that has been popularized through political discourse (200–201).

Mondak, Mutz, and Huckfeldt (1996) began from the common proposition that social context influences political attitudes, but found this problematic because people actually function within *several* social contexts—their families, neighborhoods, states, nations—more or less simultaneously. They set out to determine which of these is most important with respect to economic issues, finding that the accessibility of information is an important factor in this determination, and that people generally apply the most relevant contextual interpretation that is available to them, which may or may not be the one that is ideally most relevant.

Literature on Agenda Dynamics, Framing, and Priming

In their modest but exceptionally influential piece stating and testing the theory of agenda setting, McCombs and Shaw (1972) argued that media influence public opinion, not by the viewpoints they express, but by the issues to which they draw attention through the simple mechanism of affording coverage. They were drawing explicitly here on a statement by Bernard Cohen (1963: 120): "The press may not be successful much of the time in telling people what to think, but it is stunningly successful in telling its readers what to think about." But in naming this observed phenomenon, McCombs and Shaw placed themselves at the symbolic forefront of a significant body of conceptual development. Cook et al (1983) provided a uniquely well designed test of the impact of agenda-setting in a study that employed a field experiment with both the general public and governmental and interest group elites as subjects, taking advantage of pre-publication knowledge of a forthcoming television news magazine story and access to the journalists themselves. The authors concluded that the news story did influence the perceived importance of the issue among both general and elite audiences, but that collaboration between the journalists and government staffers, and not the change in public opinion, accounted for the subsequent policy action. Iyengar and Kinder (1987), employing experimental design in a laboratory setting in which they manipulated the order and emphasis of broadcast news stories, found significant evidence of agenda-setting and priming, a related form of media influence calling the attention of audience members to particular ways of filtering their opinions. Willnat (1997) also focused on the underlying cognitive processes by which media agendas might gain prominence in the public mind. His analysis, too, centered on priming, or the effects of prior context on the retrieval of information and its interpretation, which he viewed as expanding the notion of agenda-setting beyond the mere transfer of attitude objects to changes in audience attitudes and behaviors.

Dearing and Rogers (1996) provided a comprehensive summary of the historical development of the concept of agenda setting and of the body of related research to that point, identifying salience as the "mission critical" variable in agenda-setting effects. Issue salience, they noted, is determined by a process of social construction in which cues from the media and from the communication environment are determinative. Writing nearly a decade later, McCombs (2004) brought together much of the related research into an updated statement of the theory. Neuman, Just, and Crigler (1992) took a different view than much of this literature seems, at least implicitly, to suggest. They argued that audiences are not nearly as helpless nor as dependent on the media as some effects theories might contend, but rather are independent in their thinking and active in processing information from the news, drawing on a reservoir of common knowledge and interacting with the media to arrive at the meaning of the information they receive.

Manheim (1987) delineated the model of agenda dynamics employed here in Chapters 4 and 5, and specified a typology of hypotheses (510–513) illustrating its operations both within and across agendas. He identified four general classes of hypotheses, including those relating to the initial location of an item on the media, public, or policy agenda; to changes in the location of the item on one of these three agendas; to the movement of a given item from one agenda to another (e.g., movement from the media to the public agenda, better known as agenda setting); and to the development patterns of specific issues or images, or of general classes of issues or images, over time.

Bakir (2006) employed the Greenpeace–Shell–*Brent Spar* case to study use of the media by NGOs to impact the policy agenda. He found that the primary media effects were the shaping public perception of risk, rather than of policy preferences *per se*, and the shaping of policymaker perceptions of public opinion. Indeed, according to Salmon, Post, and Christensen (2003), the goal of so-called "public will" campaigns is to "alter the policy potential of a social problem in such a way that it moves from having a relatively low profile on the unstructured and somewhat amorphous public agenda to a much higher profile on the more structured and concrete policy agenda" (4). They went on to argue that it is the power, resources, and skill of those who seek to influence the public to support social change far more than the objective characteristics of the social problems being addressed that leads to success in mobilizing the public will.

Berger (2001) in a study of corporate agenda setting, in this case undertaken by the Business Roundtable, an organization of corporate CEOs, distinguishes between "public" and "private" agenda setting. The former has to do with influencing policies of broad or general interest, the latter with influencing those of narrower scope, lower salience, or more limited visibility. He identified a space in which private interests have proportionately greater influence, but also one in which their influence can be constrained by changing the conditions in which it is exercised, notably by raising (e.g., through the media) the visibility of the issue being contested.

One of the most heavily studied of political communication phenomena in recent years is framing. Tannenbaum (1955) laid the conceptual groundwork for the study of framing by pointing out the importance of studying messages, not as unified wholes, but as composites of multiple elements, any one or more of which might predispose recipients to a particular interpretation or meaning of the total message. He termed such an element an "index," and identified two classes of effects it might have: attracting attention to the message or influencing how it is decoded. These cueing mechanisms, Tannenbaum observed, could be verbal or nonverbal in character. In an essay arguing for the integration of similar conceptual frameworks across disciplines, Entman (1993) singled out framing as a potential case in point. In the process, he provided a unifying definition of the term: "To frame is to select some aspects of a perceived reality and make them more salient in a communicating text, in such a way as to promote a particular problem definition, causal interpretation, moral evaluation, and/or treatment recommendation for the item described" (52). Salience for Entman had a somewhat different meaning from that we have employed in the present instance. For Entman, salience referred to making a particular piece of information more noticeable, meaningful, or memorable to an audience, whereas we have defined salience in terms of linking information explicitly to the extant, self-defined self-interest of that audience, and might see parts of his definition as more tied to the visibility of the item in question. These are, however, subtle differences, and while they may be of interest to scholars, are unlikely to matter greatly to the strategist. McCombs (2004), on the other hand, argued that framing is essentially a subset of agenda-setting, which he termed "second-level agenda setting." In his view, framing amounts to the establishment in the public mind, not merely of the issue addressed in media content, but of attributes thereof, by transferring not merely awareness, but a sense of the issue's salience as well.

In a classic study of framing effects, Tversky and Kahneman (1981) found that seemingly inconsequential differences in the presentation of alternatives—mainly between specific numerical outcomes and probabilities that amounted to the same thing—produced large and systematic differences in preferences expressed by their experimental subjects. Lundy (2006) found that the differential framing of benefits in messages directed at internal audiences within an organization resulted in differentiated cognitive processing of the topic.

Many contemporary analyses of the media framing of issues trace their origin to Gamson and Modigliani's (1989) analysis of media coverage of, and public opinion regarding, the nuclear power industry. The authors noted that every issue is accompanied by a sort of culture, an ongoing discourse of "metaphors, catchphrases, visual images, moral appeals, and other symbolic devices" (2) that provide interpretations and meanings for related events as they occur. For many issues, they argued, there also exists a counter-culture of contrary content, with the result that policy-making is often a contest of competing symbols, and policy adoption represents the victory of one interpretation over another. This competition occurs at the societal level, but also at the individual level, where citizens must make sense of the alternative constructions of reality with which they are presented. In the case of nuclear power, the authors identified a series of "packages" of perspectives on both sides of the issue, thematic bundles that they on occasion, and we today with regularity, would term frames. They found tentative evidence that frame-change in media coverage of the issue contributed to frame-change in public perceptions.

Iyengar (1991) demonstrated that the predilection of television news to employ episodic framing (stories that emphasize specific events or cases, as opposed to thematic framing, where the emphasis is on underlying causes or processes), carries over to the public, resulting in an inability, or at least a reduced likelihood, to hold public officials accountable for broader problems and for their resolution. Payne (2001) began a consideration of the development of international labor standards from the premise that frames are constructed by what he termed "norm entrepreneurs" in order to maximize their resonance with audiences. This construction occurs, however, not in a vacuum, but in a competitive environment where the ultimate objective may be less to generate audience resonance than to produce desired policy outcomes. In that context, the objective of frame construction is to create a power resource—not new power, but a new or stronger connection with an existing power structure—that can be employed to construct new social norms. Entman (2003), in a study of frame competition following the September 11, 2001 attacks, and more expansively elsewhere (2004), proposed a "cascading activation model" in which foreign policy frames are seen as spreading downward from the top level of a multi-layered system including, in order, the administration, non-administration elites, news organizations, news texts, and the public. He concluded that such cascades help to explain the occurrence of elite discord, which in turn, creates a political space in which competing frames may develop. In a subsequent article (Entman, 2008), he extended this analysis to mediated public diplomacy, suggesting that the influence resident at the top of the cascade was far more limited in the international system, where it depended on such additional factors as cultural congruity or the willing acquiescence of foreign elites, than in domestic political communication.

In an extensive review of the literature, Hallahan (1999) identified seven different modes—he termed them models—of framing applicable to public relations, including the framing of situations (or more correctly, of the relationships among individuals in situations), attributes (characteristics of objects and people), choices (posing alternatives in negative or positive terms), actions (similar to choices), issues (selection of explanatory terms), responsibility (attribution of causality, which tends to focus on persons rather than abstract societal actions), and news reports (use of culturally resonant themes determined through a competition among sources), which tend to be employed in combination with one another.

Benford and Snow (2000) offered a richly taxonomic review of the literature on collective action frames and framing processes, which they saw as forging a shared understanding of a given social problem among movement adherents, attributing blame for the problem, articulating alternatives, and urging collective action for redress. They argued that action frames vary with respect to their degree of flexibility or rigidity, their inclusiveness or exclusiveness, their interpretive scope, and their resonance, among other factors. Frames are developed and deployed strategically to achieve such goals as recruitment, mobilization, and resource enhancement, as well as projecting values and beliefs. Ultimately, they suggested, a key objective is often to *re*-frame perceptions among extra-movement audiences so that extant conditions, actions, or events are viewed through a new lens.

Framing strategies can take advantage of research findings even where the findings themselves have no direct link to the concept. Brashers (2001), for example, explored the varied dimensions of "uncertainty management," or the steering of communication audiences through ambiguous, complex, and unpredictable situations in which information is unavailable or inconsistent and in which they feel insecure in the level of their own knowledge.

While he did not address framing *per se*, his observations may suggest to the strategist the value in treating with uncertainty, perhaps with an eye toward either reducing or even increasing it among a given audience, depending on the objectives at hand.

Pan and Kosicki (1993) argued that news frames are the product of an interactive "sociocognitive" process involving sources, journalists, and audience members, all linked together by a shared culture and each playing a well-defined social role. They saw these arguments as reflected in the syntactical, script (story), thematic, and rhetorical structures present in the news, and more to the point here, as products of implicit or explicit decision-making during the construction of the news.

Druckman (2001, 2004), in a noteworthy and potentially consequential critique, suggested that framing effects, which seem on their face to undermine the notion that people act rationally in rendering political judgments, may be artifacts of the experimental conditions under which they are established, most notably the forcing of decisions on their participants absent either context or external social contact, and that these effects can be largely mitigated when credible advice or assistance in decision-making, in the form of elite competition (counter-framing), deliberation, or outside expertise, is available. In a related study, Druckman and Nelson (2003) found that interpersonal conversations, a mainstay of real-world persuasive situations which, they argued, tended to be left out of most framing experiments, significantly limit the effects of framing outside the laboratory.

Chong and Druckman (2007a, 2007b) explored yet another determinant of framing effects, the presence of competing frames. Beginning (2007a) from a discussion grounded in a belief-based approach to attitude structure and change, they first developed a conceptual model, based on such factors as the presence and weighting of salience cues and the degree of conscious deliberation employed by individuals, to suggest which frame is likely to prevail given the differential information, motivation, and engagement of the audience. They then (2007b) applied this model more formally in a series of experiments designed to examine framing effects in differing competitive environments, finding that in general frame content proved more important than the frequency of exposure, that weak frames are generally ineffective and can be counterproductive, and that the effectiveness of strong frames, though altered, was able to survive competition.

Nelson, Oxley, and Clawson (1997) focused on whether and how the framing of news stories actually affects public opinion. They posited a model in which the influence of framing on opinion is fundamentally different from the process described in belief-based theories of persuasion. In belief-based schemes, persuasion occurs when a persuader successfully delivers new and discrepant information which is converted into attitude change. The source of influence is thus external to the person being persuaded. In contrast, Nelson and his colleagues argued, framing works not by delivering new information, but by activating existing information that is already stored in the recipient's long-term memory. They demonstrated the distinction with an experiment focused on welfare issues. McLeod and Detenber (1999) studied experimentally the effects of pro-status quo framing in television news of social protest—in this instance an anarchist demonstration—finding that increasing levels of this frame in news stories led viewers to be more critical of the demonstrators, less likely to support their right to free expression, less critical of the police, and less likely to judge the protest successful, or even newsworthy.

Hansen (1991) argued that "cultural resonance" and linkage to powerful underlying symbolic attachments were essential to understanding why some environmental issues register strongly among the public while others do not. In a later study, Hansen (2000) used the *Brent Spar* controversy to examine the framing of environmental disputes. He found that Greenpeace did demonstrate the ability to generate media coverage of its claims, but it was less successful in influencing the frames that would be employed in the resulting news coverage. Ihlen and Nitz (2008) examined the 2003 competition by opposing interests—environmentalists and the petroleum industry—to frame media portrayals of an oil exploration project in Norway. They determined that none of the contestants won the competition. Rather, the customary "horse-race" frame was adopted by the media. The authors concluded that interested parties will likely be more successful in establishing their frames if they rise above a single-issue emphasis and focus on over-arching master frames with broader cultural resonance. Reber and Berger (2005) examined framing by the Sierra Club of three core environmental issues—oil drilling in the Arctic, coal-fired electricity generation, and urban sprawl—in chapter newsletters as well as regional and national newspapers. Using the organization's national website to define baseline frames, they found, not surprisingly, that the newsletters tended to follow framing guidance more than the newspapers, though not as closely as one might expect, and all of these media provided competing frames. They concluded that the Sierra Club and its allies do enjoy a frame advantage in the news media, but that the dilution of centrally determined framing may weaken the organization.

In a study of media framing of the labor movement, Christopher R. Martin (2004) identified five dominant frames within which labor issues tended to be presented. They included the adoration of consumerism and abundance of choice, the absence of a public interest in production, the driving role of great business leaders and entrepreneurs in the economy, a vision of the workplace as a meritocracy, and a negative view of collective economic action. Not surprisingly, he finds these frames to undermine the claims and interests of labor.

Krosnick and Kinder (1990) used media coverage of the Iran-Contra controversy, in which the U.S. administration obtained funds from the secret sale of weapons to Iran and directed the proceeds, again secretly, to support militia activity in Central America, to advance the notion of "priming"—the idea that increased media attention to a particular aspect of some higher-order object will lead to increased weighting by the public of that aspect in its evaluation of the higher-order object. In this instance, for example, media attention to Iran-Contra led to a proportionately greater weighting of this controversy in the public's performance evaluations of then-President Ronald Reagan. Sherman, Mackie, and Driscoll (1990) found that, after priming subjects in an experiment through the assignment of preliminary tasks that were supposedly unrelated to the actual experiment, prime-relevant dimensions outweighed prime-irrelevant dimensions in their evaluations and preferences regarding foreign affairs and economic policy. They determined that accessibility, rather than importance or utility, was the operative factor; priming simply brought the judgments in question more readily to hand.

In an effort to interweave the elements we have been discussing here, Price and Tewksbury (1997) developed a complex model that integrated the functions of agenda setting, priming, and framing based on the psychology of knowledge activation and use. Principal elements of the model include the knowledge store, or an individual's existing information about social objects and their attributes, goals, values, motivations, and affective state; active thought, or the real-time processing of interactions with information and the social environment; and current stimuli, which is to say, the incoming information itself. Arguing that framing itself was fragmented and lacking in a common perspective, Scheufele (1999) posited a process model of framing comprising four stages: frame building, frame setting, individual-level processes of framing, and feedback from audiences to journalists. He developed a typology based on two dimensions, media versus individual frames, and framing as an independent versus a dependent variable. With this model as context, Scheufele and Tewksbury (2007) later reprised the origins and basic tenets of three leading and inter-related concepts in political communication research that are of interest to the strategist—agenda setting, framing, and priming—and identified a number of boundary issues of interest to researchers.

Snow, Rochford, Worden, and Benford (1986) provided a critical linkage between framing and participation in social movements through the mechanism of frame alignment processes. These include frame bridging, or the connection of two or more ideologically congruent frames through their application to a common issue; frame amplification, or the clarification and "invigoration" of a frame as it applies to a given issue; frame extension, or making explicit the relationship between the frame and important values and beliefs; and frame transformation, or redefining the objectives of a movement organization so that they are not undermined by established interpretive frames. Paul S. Martin (2008) argued that negative news coverage of social issues stimulates political participation by drawing public attention to the issues in question within a context that calls for policy-related action. Playing off the title of this article just a bit, one might suggest that bad news for campaign targets is good news for protagonists, who are thus encouraged to develop negative frames.

Literature on Selected Elements of Frames and Messages: Icons, Celebrities, Standards of Behavior, Branding, Enemy Construction, Critical Events, and Exemplars

Holsti (1967) applied the then-emerging literatures on belief systems and on attitude change to explore the construction of enemies in the international system, focusing in particular on the nature and source of discrepant information in efforts to define enemies. Edelman (1988) provided a systematic view of the rationale for enemy construction and the mechanisms through which it can be achieved. Enemies, he said, "are identifiable persons or stereotypes of persons to whom evil traits, intentions, or actions can be attributed. *It is not the harm that matters, but the attribution.*" (87, emphasis added) Bullert (1999) highlighted the importance of enemy construction—in this case Nike Corporation and CEO Phil Knight—in the success of the anti-sweatshop movement.

Meyer and Gamson (1995) found that celebrity involvement in social movements can be either constructive or deleterious. On the one hand, celebrities can bring hard-to-achieve attention, marquee value for fund-raising, and other resources to the cause. On the other hand, they can also be sources of distraction or moderation and, to the extent that they are independent actors with their own, sometimes broader, agendas, can even eclipse the issue frames around which localized movements are organized. Thrall et al (2008) studied the role in issue advocacy and news-making of more than 200 celebrities, finding that these prominent personalities make relatively little impact on the shaping of traditional news, but have a significantly greater, and growing, impact on impression formation through nontraditional media including entertainment, unmediated narrowcasting (such as web sites), and horizontal media (such as MySpace, chat rooms, and email-this-page utilities). One implication the authors noted is that celebrities can play an important role in movement building and mobilization, even if their impact on traditional news coverage is minimal; and as mass mediated news itself loses significance to newer and more personalized forms of communication where celebrities are vital resources, that role is likely to increase in importance.

Bennett and Lawrence (1995) suggested that certain objects in the news take on a life that far exceeds that of the event that gave rise to them. These "news icons" begin as memorable images or word pictures that crystallize a given originating event, and that are so compelling that they become vessels of meaning that move across other, topically related stories and provide symbolic cues and cultural linkages suggestive of over-arching stories or news frames.

Critical events, sometimes referred to as focusing events, include time-limited or time-specific and generally dramatic interruptions in the normal flow of events. Examples would include major economic dislocations, environmental disasters, intense confrontations (large-scale rioting, terrorist attacks), fundamental changes in public policy, and the like. Critical events tend to draw extensive media attention, and to focus public attention; they redefine the social or political context in some basic way. This creates opportunities for strategists to exploit the potential for game-changing shifts in perception. Kraus, Davis, Lang, and Lang (1975) offered a research strategy for evaluating critical events, which can be important factors in determining social change and other outcomes. Some of the event attributes they saw as important included the degree to which the event is spectacular, the level of anticipation built up by the media in advance of a scheduled event, the availability of independent (unmediated) information about the event, and the degree of elaboration in subsequent media accounts of the event. Pride (1995), in a study of conservative activism surrounding a local school-tax referendum that he treated as a critical event, found, for example, that the activists were able to use the vote as a fulcrum, and to reduce post-referendum public evaluations of school performance despite data to the contrary. Giffard and Rivenburgh (2000) examined the hosting of global media events—in this instance six United nations summit meetings—as a means of enhancing the image of the host country. They found that hosting did raise the news visibility of each country, but that only the Western hosts, and not those from the developing world, received more positive coverage than before. Manheim (1990) illustrated the significant risks of such hosting with respect to the Olympic Games, finding that nations that sought explicitly to use the Games to improve their international images, such as Mexico and South Korea, actually experienced highly negative portrayals and elevated levels of visibility.

Brosius and Bathelt (1994) compared the effects on personal, and perceived public, opinion of baseline information in media accounts of issues and the use of exemplars, or illustrative individual cases. They found, not surprisingly, a variant of the old saw that a picture is worth a thousand words, i.e., that exemplars had a strong effect on the perceived distribution of public opinion and a moderate effect on personal opinion regarding the issue in question. In a similar vein, Gibson and Zillmann (1993) found that print news stories that included direct quotations—in this instance challenging the safety of amusement parks—had a greater impact on readers than those containing indirect testimony (i.e., paraphrasing) or no testimony whatsoever.

Ehrenberg (1974) examined the impact of repetitive advertising on brand preferences of consumers in the context of an awareness-trial-reinforcement model, and concluded that advertising could reinforce existing brand loyalties, but could not drive significant change in brand preferences or even generate new ones. As he put it (46), "Real conversion from virgin ignorance to full-blooded long-term commitment does not happen often." Spears, Brown, and Dacin (2006) proposed a so-called Unique Corporate Association Value (UCAV) approach, by which they sought to quantify the perceptions that various stakeholders hold of a given corporation, a key datum in assessing such stakeholder relationships.

Laidler-Kylander, Quelch, and Simonin (2007) applied the lessons of branding directly to NGOs, both advocacy and relief organizations, which they saw as commanding exceptionally high levels of trust and brand valuations, in the international system. Mapping NGOs in two dimensions by their function (relief-advocacy) and their scope (national-international), the authors suggested that branding in this environment has three key roles—reflecting the mission of the organization, building trust, and connecting with multiple stakeholders—that can, if developed strategically, add measurably to the influence and effectiveness of these organizations. In the process, they distinguish between the two types of NGOs, as well as between the for-profit and nonprofit sectors, with respect to their brand-building requirements. Whitmore (2007) provided a case study of nation-state rebranding, detailing efforts to "show a resurgent Russia in a multi-polar world, a world in which Russia is confident." (2) He saw this campaign as likely to extend to, and intensify before, the 2014 Winter Olympics in Sochi.

Codes of conduct and international standards regimes are expressions of commitment to moral behavior that can have substantial symbolic power when integrated into an IIC. Grant and Taylor (2004) examined the evolution of a regulatory framework, known as the Kimberley Process, to govern and ultimately end the trade in so-called "conflict diamonds," those that are traded illicitly to finance insurgencies and other conflicts. In the post-Cold War period, this issue emerged as a major focus of international NGO activity, which became organized into a series of transnational advocacy coalitions whose influence, the authors observed, accessed the international governance agenda in ways consistent with Keck and Sikkink's (1998) boomerang model (see below). Bartley (2007a) argued that such transnational systems of private regulation of corporate labor and environmental practices arising from political conflicts involving states, NGOs and other actors, i.e., certification associations based in codes of conduct, have emerged as important non-market-based institutional byproducts of globalization, as, for example, in the forest products and apparel industries. Bartley (2007b) used the case of forest certification to illustrate how foundations use their grant-making to establish a whole new field of activity, populate it with social movement organizations, and leverage the resultant protest activity to advance their goals. Seidman (2005) reflected on the development of corporate codes of conduct and of international regimes for monitoring and enforcement, concluding that such efforts have limitations, and benefit from the active engagement governments and their regulatory systems—another validation of Keck and Sikkink's (1998) boomerang model.

Johns (2001), a former parliamentarian and government minister in Australia, has proposed a code of conduct for NGOs based on the principle of transparency to which many of them subscribe, and on the content of codes of business or governmental behavior which they advocate. His argument is that NGOs are exercising increasing influence in the halls of government and commerce, claiming to represent and in some measure substituting for the public, and that, as a result, they should be obligated to disclose information regarding their internal governance, including organic documents; their representativeness, including membership, leadership selection process, and international affiliations; their finances, including sources and applications of funds; their fund-raising claims; and the nature of any claims they may make to policy-relevant expertise.

Literature on the Framing of Fear, Guilt, and the Perception of Risk

Kahneman and Tversky (1979) set out what they termed "prospect theory"—a stochastic model by which people choose among decision options that entail risk. The theory comprises two stages, termed editing and evaluation. In the first, or editing, stage, the options are organized and reformulated in ways that simplify choice. In the second, or evaluation, stage, the prospect demonstrating the highest positive value is selected. They suggested that this model could be applied to a variety of public policy issues, but that decision weights could be affected by such factors as the perceived likelihood of occurrence of a given risk-related event, or any associated ambiguity or vagueness. Flynn, Slovic, and Mertz (1993) examined the differences between the assessments of nuclear industry experts and the general public of the risk associated with a high-level radioactive waste repository. They found, not only that the experts and the public differed in their perceptions of the seriousness of the associated risk, but that they actually employed substantially different conceptual frameworks to arrive at them. Not surprisingly, the public assessment was much more negative; it focused on such hazards as danger, death and destruction. The experts were generally more positive, and even where negative focused on such alternative constraints as cost, delays, seismic challenges, and political controversy.

Roser and Thompson (1995) examined the use of fear appeals in converting low-involvement audiences into active publics. They found that even a message that conveyed a threat (in this instance environmental) but provided no cues regarding how to reduce it resulted in increased audience involvement, perceived risk, and even personal efficacy. Witte (1998), writing on the use of fear appeals in health-related public information campaigns, presented a model integrating perceived threat, fear, and efficacy, and set forth a series of twelve propositions arising from these relationships. For example, she argued that, when the perceived threat is low, regardless of the level of perceived efficacy, fear-appeal messages will simply not be processed, but under conditions of high efficacy, increases in the perception of threat will lead to high degrees of message acceptance. Witte concludes that a communicator can arouse fear to gain compliance with a desired behavior, but only where the individuals in question view themselves as having the ability to respond as recommended by the persuader. Lupia and Menning (2009) developed a model to demonstrate that the effectiveness of fear appeals used by politicians to advance their policy interests is not unlimited, but rather, is conditioned by the psychological profile of the public, which may either facilitate or impede arousal.

Kasperson and his colleagues (Kasperson et al, 1988; Kasperson and Kasperson, 1996) recognized that the effects of risk on society and on the institutions charged with managing it are impacted by the way the perception of risk is processed, and that its passage through various institutions adds dimensions of social meaning that become fundamentally associated with the risk. This can produce either an amplification of the apparent risk or its attenuation, depending on definitional components that are social constructs rather than direct elements of the underlying risk itself. Their model of this process (Kasperson and Kasperson, 1996: 97), shown below in slightly modified form, also suggests the interactions among individual, social, societal, institutional, and governmental actors that underlie much of the strategic decision-making in campaigns.

Bakir (2005) found this framework useful in context of a qualitative case study (Greenpeace-Shell-*Brent Spar*) in characterizing and evaluating Greenpeace's strategy.

Slovic, Finucane, Peters, and McGregor (2004) pointed to two different ways that individuals process risk, both of which must be taken into account in risk communication. The analytic system of risk processing relies on normative rules, probability assessments, logic, and the like to calculate expectations. It is relatively slow and effortful, and requires relatively detailed data. The experiential system, on the other hand, is intuitive and somewhat automatic, operating quickly and easily, and on minimal information. These systems operate in parallel and interact with one another, which has implications for the strategist who seeks either to exploit or to mitigate perceptions of risk. Savadori et al (2004), in a study of risk perceptions associated with several biotechnology applications, found substantial differences between experts (in this case professors and graduate students in biology at an Italian university) and the general public (represented here by persons with no formal training in biology). Specifically, they found that the public assigns consistently higher levels of risk to both food and medical applications than do experts, with variations attributable to potential harm and benefits, scientific knowledge, and familiarity in the case of food, and to potential harm alone for medical applications. Experts differentiated

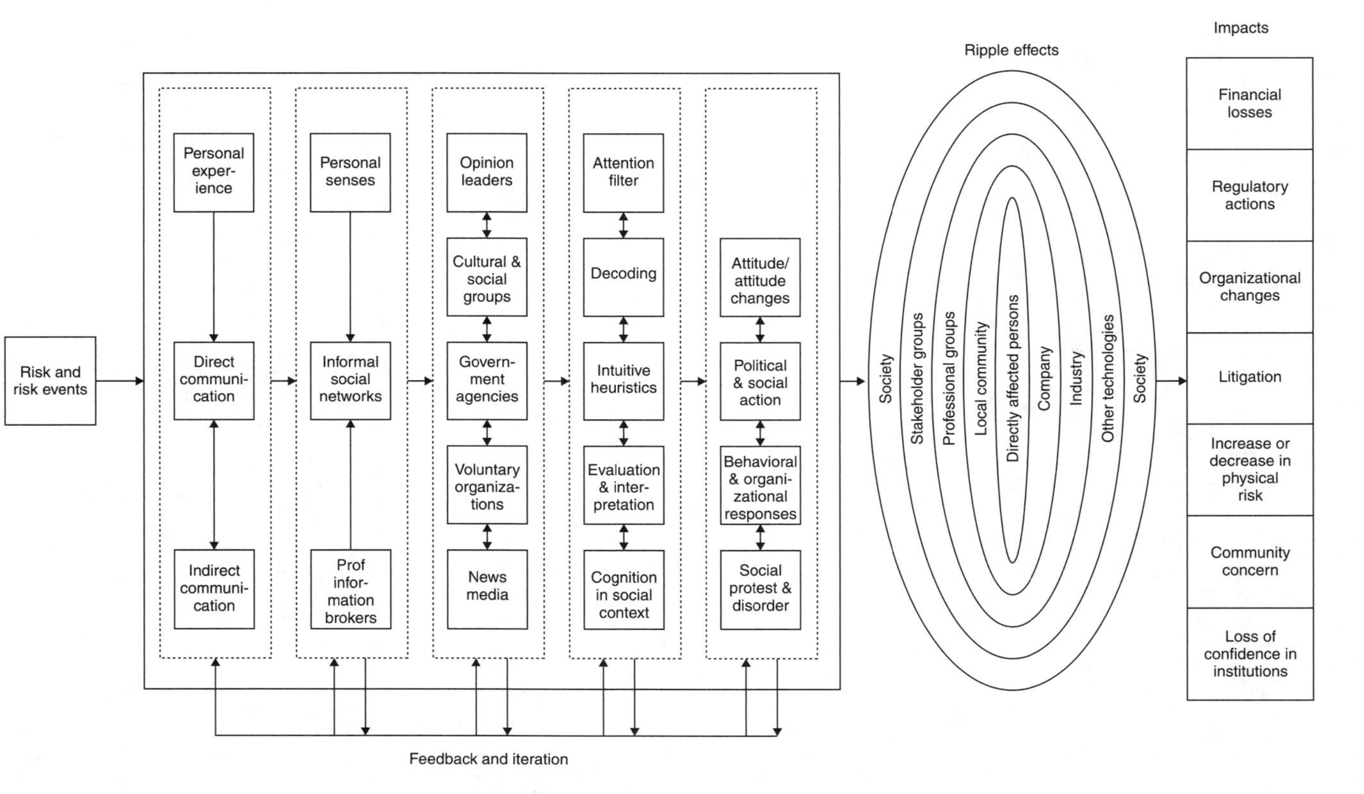

Figure B.2 Social Amplification and Attenuation of Risk.

among the food-related applications based on potential harm and benefits, and among medical applications based on potential harm, the number and type of people exposed, and scientific knowledge.

Building primarily on the work of Slovic, and of Kahneman and Tversky, Gardner (2008) provided an especially accessible treatment of the underlying science of fear and the processing by individuals of information related to it. He identified several explanatory heuristics, or "rules," including:

- the anchoring rule—based on intuition rather than reason, the tendency to fix on recently available information (a number, a recent event) to shape one's decision-making,
- the rule of typical things—again based mainly on intuition, the tendency to see the world through the lens of existing stereotypes and expectations as to how things are,
- the example rule—also known as the availability heuristic, is an assumption that the easier it is to recall an example of something, the more common that thing itself must be, and
- the good-bad rule—or the affect heuristic, by which snap intuitive judgments about the risk or reward of something guide subsequent decisions and actions.

Gardner provided numerous links between these rules of thumb and the use of fear appeals with respect to terrorism, crime, nuclear energy and other issues. Mlodinow (2008), whose work is also grounded in part in that of Kahneman and Tversky, examined a number of similar questions from a somewhat different perspective, namely that of how individuals understand and deal with randomness and the associated uncertainty.

Nohrstedt and Tassew (1993) provided an annotated bibliography of research on media coverage of risks, disasters, and crises organized around three basic perspectives on communication: injection, or linear, unidirectional communication between sender and receiver; tuning, or communication that is adjusted by the sender to accommodate attitudes, perceptions, or other attributes of the receiver; and dialogue, or communication that incorporates interaction between the sender and receiver.

O'Keefe (2000) surveyed the research literature on the use of guilt to produce persuasion. He found evidence that more explicit guilt appeals arouse more guilt than do less explicit appeals, but that the latter appeals are actually more persuasive. Of particular interest in the present context, however, might be O'Keefe's summary of research showing that appeals based on claims of hypocrisy, which is to say, a special case of inconsistency or imbalance in which reminders that the target's of persuasion have espoused preferred values in the past but have failed to act on them, may be especially effective in advocacy situations where the attitude or behavior in question is salient.

Literature on News Management and the Norms of Journalism

Molotch and Lester (1974) argued that news is a constructed reality, and its content is the product of "practical, purposive, and creative activities on the part of news promoters" interacting with journalists (termed by the authors "news assemblers") and audiences. They identified four classes of news events, including routines, accidents, scandals, and serendipitous events, each presenting different challenges to those who would control the news and to those who consume it. News, in their view, is a means by which those who hold power control the experiences of those who do not. In a subsequent case study (Molotch and Lester, 1975) of coverage of the 1969 Santa Barbara oil spill, a seminal event in the rebirth of the environmental movement, the authors determined that federal officials and corporate spokespersons had much greater upstream access to this "accidental" news than did local officials or conservationists, with the result that symbolic and pro-establishment topics and those with national as opposed to local implications prevailed.

In one of the earliest studies of newsroom decision-making, Tunstall (1971) explored the sociology of one corner of the culture of journalism, the expectations, behaviors, and professional interactions of specialized correspondents, and in the process opened several lines of inquiry that would soon be pursued by others. Tuchman (1973) focused on the core challenge of creating predictable workplace routines where the objective is to cover unexpected events. He posited several types of news—hard news, spot news, developing news, and continuing news—finding regularities in each classification that help to reduce the variability of the raw material from which news is constructed. Indeed, 1973 was a sort of kick-off year for studies of the biorhythms of the newsroom, as Epstein (1973) and Sigal (1973) both published significant entries. Epstein examined news routines at the major television networks, while Sigal focused on the interface between reporters and newsmakers in the form of foreign policy decision makers. Of interest here is Sigal's identification of four bargaining games that reporters and officials play—internal bargaining between reporters and their news organizations (e.g., for space and time), bargaining among reporters on a given beat (e.g., get the story first, but don't be the only one with it), bargaining between the reporter and the sources (trading information and implied knowledge), and bargaining among the sources as they strive to control the news—the collective result of which is the daily dose of news content. Journalist/sociologist Bernard Roshco (1975) followed shortly afterward with a similar analysis, albeit one grounded in the argument that media content is primarily reflective of the relationship between the media and other social institutions, a relationship that is serviced through news routines. Gans (1979) focused on the values, professional standards, and external pressures that guided journalists shaping the news. Bennett (1996a, though first published in 1983) carried much of this analysis to its logical conclusion, suggesting that the world of politics defined by the news is illusory, a social construction that amounted to little more than a façade. He characterized the news as being personalized, dramatized, fragmented, and normalized—biases arising from the requirements of the news-making process rather from events themselves. News and image management, in this view, is a natural outgrowth of a fundamental socio-political process. He later (1996b) posited five rules for journalists representing politics in the news—building a storyline, indexing sources and viewpoints based on the scale and content (and boundaries) of conflicts among key governmental or other powerful players, following the trail of power as a means to expand a story beyond its normal limits, basing the story in familiar elements of the extant political culture, and leveraging any credible, spontaneous images that may arise to challenge establishment boundaries on the storyline. Johnson-Cartee (2005) explored in detail the social construction of news, and particularly news narratives, and its transference into the construction of a broader political reality, with an emphasis on news rituals and standardized frames.

Earlier (1990), in a work of particular interest to the strategist, Bennett had posited an "indexing hypothesis" according to which news content tends to be "indexed" to the range and dynamics of debate among official sources, and is not driven by public opinion. He then measured the frequency, direction, and sourcing of all stories in four years of *New York Times* coverage of the Nicaraguan Contras, finding substantial support for this notion. Jha (2007) provided a *de facto* test of this hypothesis over time, finding that journalists covering the anti-globalization protests in 1999 were more likely than those covering the anti-war protests of 1967 to rely on official sources, the availability of alternative sources, research and analysis via the Internet in the more recent case notwithstanding.

Building on Bennett (1996a, 1996b), Ryfe (2006) identified two distinct classes of rules that explain the similarity of content across news organizations. A constitutive rule tells us what something is, while a regulative rule tells us something about it. That news is story-based defines (in part) what it is; that reporters should rely heavily on official sources establishes a rule for the creation of those stories. These rules establish assumptions or expectations about the news that create a sort of regression toward the mean in journalistic behavior, with the effect that independent journalists or news organizations acting independently tend to produce the same result, which is to say, similar news. Wittebols (1996) studied news coverage of protest on U.S. and Canadian television, finding that the extent and tone of coverage of domestic protest is guided by the extent of related debate among policy elites, while coverage of protests in other countries generally corresponds with the home government's foreign policy vis-à-vis the country in question.

Rada (1977) illustrated the use of staged events, provocative language, venue escalation (local to national), violation of sanctuary spaces (e.g., demonstrating outside spaces for which permits have been obtained or in spaces where such displays are not normal or generally allowed, such as a building lobby), by which a small, minority-based union local was able to force the media to cover its strike. Ultimately, the strike succeeded only when the union recruited a celebrity (Cesar Chavez) to its cause, and when it successfully pressured the struck manufacturer's principal customer to press for a resolution—in effect an early application of power structure analysis. Livingston and Bennett (2003) studied the dynamics of event-driven news, or that which arises spontaneously from events, as opposed to that generated by elites operating within institutional settings. Historically, they argued, such naturally-occurring news has represented a small minority of stories, with most news being, in effect, manufactured, or at the very least controlled, by elites. New technologies that can empower non-institutional story initiators and/or give journalists themselves greater access to previously tightly-managed events seemed to threaten the dominance of officialdom in defining events for the public. In this test focusing on international news, however, the authors found that, even as new technology opened up a wider range of stories and sources, journalists routinely turned to official sources for validation, which suggests that the indexing process previously described by Bennett (1990, 1996a) still sets the boundaries of what constitutes news.

DeFleur (1970) challenged the myth structure of news-making from a structural perspective, treating the media as a social system. Most notable is his schematic drawing of this system (166), which illustrates such structural components as legislative and regulatory bodies, advertising and market research agencies, the production and distribution systems, and the audience, and their interconnection through the exchange of financial, political, and ideational resources among them. Donohue, Tichenor, and Olien (1972) employed a similar social systems perspective to the mass media, focusing in their case more on function than on structures, with the primary function being information control, primarily in the form of gate-keeping. Herman and Chomsky (1988) took on the myth of the media—that news organizations are hardnosed and single-minded in their pursuit of truth—from an ideological perspective, arguing that the media are actually defenders of privilege, including their own. This fundamental social conservatism, they said, marginalizes dissent, producing asymmetries in media access that mirror larger power asymmetries in society as a whole. They suggested that the best way to understand the media was as agents of propaganda.

Manheim (2008) proposed a typology of journalistic forms based on two dimensions, hunter-gather versus cultivation, and basic versus enriched. This produced four distinct classes of journalistic practice: basic hunter-gatherer, which he characterized as fact-centered and assignment driven; basic cultivation, or news that is source-centered and beat-driven; enhanced hunter-gatherer, which incorporates investigative and explanatory journalism; and enhanced cultivation, or "enterprise" journalism that is reporter-defined. Each form of news poses a different challenge to the strategist. For news that is fact-centered, which he argued is the most common form, the challenge is to control the facts; for news that is source-centered, control access to the source; and for news that is explanatory, control the explanation. Enterprise news is the most difficult form to control, but also the least common.

Soley (1992) illuminated the use and influence of policy experts who are used by journalists (or on their own initiative) to contextualize and explain the news. He found these experts to constitute a distinct class of influentials, nurtured in part by think tanks and universities (see Dye, 2002, on these relationships), but a class containing its own elite of seemingly generalized experts who are called upon, in a sense, based as much or more on their own iconic identities as on their particular issue-specific expertise. Flynn, Slovic, and Mertz (1993), as noted elsewhere, suggested by implication that this reliance on experts can create an interpretive gulf between the media and their audiences. Steele (1995), in a study of experts appearing in media coverage of the Persian Gulf War, found that news organizations that used experts to help interpret events selected sources that reflected the professional ideology of journalists, particularly those who emphasized the players, policies, and predictions of what would happen next, as opposed to alternative interpretive frames.

Setting an interesting benchmark for change, Dennis (1991) argued that, at that point in time, environmental activists did not understand or appreciate the significance of the conventions, ground rules, traditions, or institutional culture of the news media, while the complexity of environmental issues, interacting with those systemic factors, led to coverage that was fragmented and generally uninteresting, while Gottleib (1991) suggested that the movement itself, with its greatest energy evident at the grassroots level and not fully reflected in its top-level organizations, was not yet positioned to advance these issues. Miller and Reichert (2000) argued that, because contentious stakeholders in environmental disputes have tended to compete within the media not by changing positions or offering new facts, but by altering the frames they advance, the strategy of the environmental interests could be advanced by examining these frame transitions.

Writing from the perspective of those who are likely to be targets of IICs and related outside attention, Messick (1999) focused on the tactics of concealment and obfuscation within organizations, either to conceal information or to create false impressions. He was concerned not about trade secrets or other generally legitimate proprietary information, but about what he termed "dirty secrets," knowledge about real or potential wrongdoing that must be concealed from competitors, regulators, adversarial attorneys, the media, and the general public, not to mention from likely protagonists in a campaign. Examples might include criminal behavior, other forms of illegality, false or deceitful records or practices, or harmful products or deeds, to name but a few. It is easy to see why such information might have particular value in the context of an IIC. Among the strategies he delineated were confidentiality or non-disclosure agreements; expansive classification schemes or definitions of just what constitutes confidential information, or just what might be covered under attorney-client privilege where litigation is involved; what he termed patterned amnesia, or the inability by the organization to recall certain critical information; and the use of smoke machines, or procedures and strategies that are designed to generate doubt, suspicion, or uncertainty about the existence of dirty secrets.

Finally we note that Jamieson and Campbell (2001) have provided a comprehensive overview of the structures and processes of the media, including advertising, as components of campaign strategy.

Literature on Digital Media

Perhaps the broadest, and one of the most insightful, looks at the effects of technological change on political life is provided by Bimber (2003), who identified a series of four information revolutions in American politics, of which the current era of information abundance is the most recent. He saw this as a period of leveling, in effect, in which the "traditional boundaries, resources, and structures of organizations have less influence over who has facility with political information and communication and who does not . . . As a result, processes of political intermediation, organizing and mobilizing appear to be changing" (229).

Though computer-based media had been available for many years before, it was around 1995, with the development of the World Wide Web, that the Internet first emerged as a viable factor in politics, and its emergence as a potent force, while now widely recognized, continues to evolve. As a result, scholarship on this topic typically has a very short half-life. Still, we can point to some notable efforts. Davis (1999), for example, provided an early and useful survey of political uses of the Internet, most notable in our context, perhaps, for its concluding chapters on virtual citizenry and the Internet as a forum for political participation. Tom Price (2000) reviewed some of the ways this new style of activism was manifesting itself with respect to the business community, both directly and through public policy initiatives. Within a short time, as noted by Rheingold (2002), new and important technology-based forms of activism had emerged. So-called "smart mobs," for example, could be mobilized on short notice, either via the Internet, extensive electronic mail networks, or even cell phones and text messaging, to generate swarms of activists at a physical location or a virtual one. Chadwick (2006) provided an especially thorough survey of the interplay between politics and the Internet, including but not limited to democratic norms and practices, the mobilization of interests and social movements, changes in the nature of governing, and new challenges with respect to surveillance, privacy, and security, as well as to the economics and governance of the Internet itself.

Writing before the emergence of the World Wide Web, Myers (1994) identified several characteristics of computer networks and communications that had the potential to enhance social activism. At the time, the principal ways that social movements employed computers for communication included email, information clearinghouses, and electronic bulletin boards. These computer applications were found to have an attractive speed-to-cost ratio, the ability to replicate information accurately across thousands of nodes, and substantial potential for interactivity. In the context of social movements *per se*, Myers saw the technology as enhancing the micro-social environment of geographically dispersed movements, providing means for message control much greater than those afforded by traditional news management efforts, creating the ability to generate virtual density for a given movement, and forming and coordinating coalitions. At the time of his writing, the principal constraints on achieving these benefits were the high cost and limited availability of, and the limited facility of activists with, computers and computer networks. Today, of course, those constraints no longer apply, and the effects Myers predicted have only been amplified by subsequent developments in both hardware and software.

Through a series of interviews with activists, Pickerill (2001) examined the use of the Internet by environmental activists in the UK, focusing on five issues: problems associated with Internet access by activists, the risks of Internet surveillance of activism, the potential of the Internet as a mobilizing force, the development of online tactics, and the potential environmental harm posed by computer technology itself. She found that activists were better able to control the content and distribution of their messages and reach a far wider audience, all at a lower cost than through traditional media; were able, through nonhierarchical forms of organizing, to avoid containment by either states or multinational corporations; to increase the cohesion of their movement both by reinforcing movement networks in the physical world and through engaging in virtual actions; to employ "swarming" and other new tactics; and to communicate and to act more quickly and more frequently, unconstrained by geographical boundaries and distances; all while maintaining a pragmatic view of the effects of their reliance on this technology.

Subramani and Rajagopalan (2003) proposed a typology for determining the influence of viral marketing in online social networks based on two dimensions, whether the influencer (i.e., each individual forwarding the information) is passive or actively persuasive, and whether the network externalities, or the added benefits arising from broad adoption of the marketing object, are high or low. In the passive–low configuration, for example, awareness is created and benefits are signaled; the viral influence is basically informational. In the active–high configuration, on the other hand, influencers are, in the authors' terms, motivated evangelists, and their influence is primarily normative. Their conclusion: viral marketers should recognize that influencers are not their *de facto* agents, but are knowledgeable helpers within a given social network. Explicit efforts to co-opt them are likely to prove counterproductive.

Micheletti and Stolle (2004) examined 3655 emails generated in a 2001 "culture jam"—in effect a pseudo-event challenging the company on its self-expressed values—targeting Nike on the issue of sweatshop labor as part of a larger campaign that was by then in its tenth year. The core event was a request by a campaigner that Nike produce a pair of customized shoes with the name "sweatshop" on them. The resulting email exchange, which the activist shared with a few friends, spread virally to an estimated 11 million people around the world, producing the unsolicited responses studied by the authors. They concluded that traditional examinations of social movements were increasingly outmoded because, with their tendency to focus on formal organizations and governmental institutions, they overlooked the emerging, viral, and less institutionalized phenomenon of "discursive political consumerism," facilitated by new media, that treats the marketplace as a political arena in which to target not only corporations, but also lifestyles and social values.

Feldner and Meisenbach (2007) studied the use of a website, SaveDisney.com, to challenge the legitimacy of a major corporation, but not by the traditional type of corporate critic. Rather, the challengers were former insiders, including Roy Disney and another former director, who formed an alliance of shareholders to challenge management on a matter of corporate governance. The campaign employed general themes of transparency and empowerment centered on a highly interactive website, and succeeded in forcing the resignation of the company's CEO.

Karpf (2008) provided a four-part typology of blogging by activists on the Internet, using the dimensions of the underlying software platforms (open or closed authorship) and the source of the blog's reputation (personal or institutional), then mapped the top twenty-five progressive and conservative blogs into the resulting two-dimensional space.

Baker (2008) has a rather different take on the utilization of new technologies, focusing not on the Internet, but on the ever-increasing capability of commercial, political, and other actors to mine databases that themselves contain ever richer and deeper data on more and more people. It's a theme that Waller (2003) began to explore with respect to commercial data system development, but Baker's treatment is more complete and more nuanced, though it ends with a similar conclusion: those who understand and control all the data—a technological elite he labels the "Numerati"—exercise the real power in contemporary society. Zarsky (2006) offered a similar argument, but from the perspective of the end-user. In an examination of online information collection, with particular emphasis on the user-specific tailoring of online advertising and marketing materials (cf. Leizerov, 2000, discussed elsewhere), he agreed that these methods were more effective than traditional forms of targeting, but argued that they can be unfair and highly manipulative.

If data-driven new-media campaigns and strategies have become ubiquitous, and if, as those like Baker (2008) would argue, the manipulation of data and media is a step toward the manipulation of the people who provide and use them, is there not then a danger that those citizens are facilitating processes through which they themselves are being "managed"? That is the question addressed by Howard (2006), who described the transformation of campaign organizations into what he terms the "hypermedia campaign," or one in which information technologies have been so thoroughly integrated into the organization that it has come to be organized around them, rather than around more traditional campaign functions. Though Howard wrote primarily in the context of electoral campaigns, much of his analysis is more generally applicable to the world of IICs.

Literature on Propaganda and Information Operations

It is not my purpose here to review the full, and extensive, literature on propaganda and its study. But neither should we overlook the lineal intellectual ties between propaganda, on the one hand, and either persuasion or the more general strategy of the information and influence campaign, on the other. The Institute for Propaganda Analysis (1937) offered an early, and now classic, delineation of seven basic propaganda techniques, including name calling (negative labeling), glittering generalities (the deliberate use of ambiguity and abstract terms), transfer (of the perceived properties of some favorably viewed object to a new object being promoted), testimonial (providing social support for a message through endorsements by individuals possessing high credibility with the intended audience), plain folks (emphasizing shared status or interests with the audience), card stacking (selective use of information, or outright deception, to provide a one-sided view), and band wagon (an appeal to join the crowd and, by extension, avoid being left out). Fleming (1995) evaluated these techniques in the context of six basic principles of general semantics, concluding that all seven are classic violations of these principles.

As ably chronicled by Glander (2000) in his insightful history of the rise of mass communication research, and illustrated by numerous scholars and practitioners over the past century from Harold Lasswell (1927) and Edward Bernays (1928) onward (see, for example, Buitenhuis's (1989) examination of the use of literature as propaganda; Hovland, Lumsdaine, and Sheffield's (1949) generalizations based on studies of Army training and propaganda efforts; the four working papers by Hideya Kumata and Wilbur Schramm in Institute of Communications Research (1955) detailing the differing approaches practiced in Japan, Nazi Germany, Great Britain, and the Soviet Union; Qualter's (1962) treatise on the connections between propaganda and psychological warfare; Packard's (1957) conspiratorial opus on the psychological seduction of consumers; Brown's (1963) essay on persuasive techniques ranging from propaganda through religious conversion to brainwashing; Ellul's (1965) exposition on the success-critical factors and the effects of propaganda in attitude formation; Combs and Nimmo's (1993) assertion that propaganda is, in their phrase, "inextricable woven into the fabric of our civilization" by virtue of the contemporary ubiquity of marketing and other persuasive communications, or Marlin's (2002) riff on this latter point (and on Ellul), using the widespread daily experience of propaganda as a pad from which to launch a relatively philosophical disquisition on the many ethical questions that such efforts raise), the study and application of propaganda and of the persuasive effects of mass communication have been inextricably interwoven over many years.

In some of the earliest work on this topic, Hoffer (1942) argued that the best constraint on propaganda is not counter-propaganda, but education, both as to the topic of the propaganda and as to its existence *per se*. Alfred McClung Lee (1944, 1945) focused on the role of the protagonist's interest in the assessment of propaganda, offering five more or less distinct approaches to propaganda analysis, or perhaps more correctly, five levels of analysis: societal, social psychological, communicatory, psychological, and technical. Each addresses different questions or concerns. At the societal level, for example, the focus may be on the struggle between contesting points of view and their advocates, while at the social psychological level questions arise regarding the particular folkways, mores, perceptions and sentiments at which appeals are directed. Communicatory analysis centers on channel characteristics, financing, and even regulatory regimes, while that at the psychological level might emphasize the personality types that are targeted or potentially susceptible to influence. The technical approach, in Lee's analysis, focuses on propaganda techniques, of which he offers a fairly self-explicating inventory similar to that advanced a few years earlier by the Institute for Propaganda Analysis (1937): issue selection, card-stacking, simplification, name calling, glittering generalities, transfer, testimonial, plain folks, band wagon, hot potato, and stalling.

Ettinger (1946) was perhaps the first scholar to examine systematically U.S.-directed propaganda efforts using the mandatory foreign-agent registration data maintained by the Department of Justice, though today we would judge his analysis to be highly subjective. He noted the importance assigned to American public opinion because of the nation's disproportionate international influence, and the "unchecked" availability of the U.S. public to manipulation by foreign governments. Included in Ettinger's analysis were examples of large-scale campaigns, publicity stunts, and appeals to the self-interest of the audience.

Davison (1971) saw the news media as primary targets and instruments of propaganda, the ingenuity, volume and complexity of which he saw increasing with each new development in communications technology. The objectives of these efforts were four in number: mobilizing hatred against an enemy, preserving the friendship of allies, preserving the friendship and procuring the cooperation of neutrals, and demoralizing the enemy. While these are primarily conflict-related goals, they have obvious parallels in applications to IIC settings. Davison's analysis also included an examination of the monetary costs of contemporaneous international propaganda—high in absolute terms, but relatively modest as instruments of public policy go—as well as thumbnails of early propaganda efforts by Alexander the Great, Frederick II of the Holy Roman Empire, and Napoleon, among others.

White (1971) provided criteria for marking the moral boundary between persuasion and propaganda. On the side of the line he deemed "inherently legitimate": getting and keeping attention, establishing and maintaining rapport, building credibility, appealing to emotions, and action involvement, or persuading by encouraging the subject to engage in pro-message behaviors. On the other side of the line: lying, innuendo, presenting opinion as fact, deliberate omission, and implied obviousness, or "speaking as if [the propagandist's] own version of reality were already established," as in the deliberate use of nouns, labels, and other language constructed within that reality (33). Similarly, John L. Martin (1971) proposed a distinction between two classes of propaganda, persuasive communication and facilitative communication, and argued that by far the lion's share of international propaganda is of the latter type, the purpose of which is simply to open channels of communication with a potential audience. He further distinguished between such propaganda having an effect and being effective, a distinction that is mirrored in our own discussion of IICs. Effectiveness, argued Martin, requires adoption of an articulable objective, prediction of a desired effect, control of the message and its delivery, and an outcome that matches intent. In a subsequent work (Martin, 1982), he characterized the use of disinformation in propaganda, which he saw as comprising two stages, creation of a forgery or fabrication followed by a publicity campaign to use the result to psychological advantage. Martin argued that this technique would only be used where the real facts or trends were disadvantageous to the initiating party.

Walton (1997) identified ten defining characteristics of propaganda, including a structure as dialogue between a proponent, usually active, and a respondent, usually passive, that is often, but not always, asymmetrical; message content that amounts to an argument; possessing a purposive quality or goal direction; an element of agency, in which the proponent represents an organized interest; indifference to logical reasoning; one-sided argumentation; compliance-seeking as a central objective; claiming justification based on the value of the result (e.g., elimination of fear or threat); the use of pejorative language that creates positive feelings toward the view that is advocated and negative feelings toward all other views; and, implicitly or explicitly, the elements of a quarrel with good guys (us) and bad guys (them). Many of these elements tend to be present in IIC discourse.

Gough (2003), in a paper prepared for the U.S. Army War College, provided a history of American efforts to exercise strategic influence, finding that the periods of greatest success shared certain characteristics, among them permanence of organization, assignment of specific roles and responsibilities to all agencies involved in the effort, top-level interest and guidance, full-time staffing, and access to key policy-makers. In sum, the efforts were judged to have proven most efficacious where the U.S. government has committed the infrastructure required to sustain them and, in contrast, to have proven least efficacious where it has not done so. Beavers (2005) emphasized the doctrinal need for the military, which engages in both activities, to distinguish between information operations, on the one hand, and perception management, on the other—if only to preserve its credibility in the former. Corman, Trethewey, and Goodall (2007) argued that message-based strategies were doomed to failure in the war of global ideas, and that an alternative relation-based and iterative model, one that inherently recognized the interactive nature of global communication, would be more likely to succeed.

In a RAND Corporation analysis aimed at formulating a U.S. strategy employing information and influence campaign techniques to reduce the threat posed by Islamic terrorism, Cragin and Gerwehr (2005) provided a brief but relatively comprehensive overview of approaches and an extensive bibliography of related intellectual resources. Set in the context of military psychological operations, as opposed to information operations—a significant difference of perspective in government-speak—the analysis focused on the objectives of compliance ("believe what you want, but do what we say"), conformity ("do what your context suggests is appropriate"), and conversion ("believe what we say, then behave accordingly") among key audiences including communities of varying sympathies and value.

Jessee (2006) argued that the terrorist group Al Qaeda, having adopted tactics used earlier by the IRA and the Italian Mafia, and routinely by many national governments, is the most effective contemporary non-state actor in employing denial and deception to advance its strategic ends. Denial in this context refers to channel blocking—eliminating channels of information through which an adversary (or, one might add, an intermediary) could independently obtain information; deception refers to actions that cause an adversary (or intermediary) to believe something is true when it is false. Jessee found that Al Qaeda routinely builds denial and deception into its tactics in such diverse areas as banking, travel and documents, donor relations and charities, communication, framing of events, and Internet activity, and provides instruction in both techniques as part of its operational training materials and practices. Torres, Jordán, and Horsburgh (2006) analyzed more than 2000 documents issued by the global jihadist movement between 1996 and 2005 in a study of propaganda and public communication techniques. The overwhelming majority of these were distributed via the Internet, particularly toward the end of the series. The authors identified three stages of development in jihadist communication strategy: reliance on traditional media (manifestos, video documentaries, audio-video recordings of leaders) and personalization (e.g., Osama bin Laden), until September 11, 2001; focus on the "compensations" of terror, from then until spring 2003; and decentralization and increased focus on the Internet, thereafter. They conclude that communication designed to achieve specific objectives is increasingly being integrated, and is evolving, as a component of jihadist strategy.

In an evolving series of operations manuals (United States Department of the Army, 2001; United States Joint Command, 2002; United States Joint Staff, 2006), the U.S. military has set out its doctrine on information operations, a portion of which relates to the formulation and implementation of communication strategies of the sort we have discussed here. Much of the focus in these highly detailed documents is on the projection of soft power, and on the emergent challenges posed by new communications technologies, both of which have the potential to redistribute power and reduce asymmetries (and thus reduce the value of traditional military superiority). Ward (2003) provided an interesting variation on this theme by emphasizing not information operations *per se*, but rather, strategic *influence* operations. His focus was thus less on process than on objectives and outcomes. To some extent, this development was foreshadowed by Kriesel (1985), who provided an overview of the role of psychological operations in U.S. national strategy. One of the unusual elements of this essay was a table listing an array of more than two dozen areas of psychological action, including, among others, agit-prop, campaign of truth, ideological warfare, international communication, international information, international propaganda, nerve warfare (threat), perception management, political advocacy, public diplomacy, persuasive communications, thought war, war of ideas, and war of words (74).

Hutchinson (2006), noting the distinction between information, on the one hand, and its associated vehicle, information technology, on the other, observed that information warfare has evolved from a set of technologically oriented tactics aimed at superiority of command and control to a set of content-oriented tactics designed to exercise influence in conflict situations. In the process, the manipulation of information, including, in his view, deception, has become an essential aspect of conflict.

Not all propaganda necessarily constitutes lies and deception, nor is all lying and deception necessarily propaganda. Nevertheless, the two sets of notions are clearly and frequently linked. So let us note here as well Huff's (1954) classic and enduring treatment of the use of statistical techniques to alter and create meaning, Bok's (1999) book on lying, of which she tends to disapprove, and Miller and Stiff's (1993) more systematic assessment of deceptive communication in general, including a listing of fifteen common forms of advertising deception that merits a summary here. They take the form of implied conclusions, and include:

- the proof implication—the mere existence of surveys or studies is used to imply supportive results;
- the demonstration implication—a claim is demonstrated absent controls or genuine testing;

- the reasonable basis implication—the assumption that claims about future performance are grounded in fact;
- the no qualification implication—claims are broadly stated with no indication of any limitations;
- the ineffective qualification implication—qualifications are stated, but are buried in the text or format of the message;
- the uniqueness implication—claims suggest that certain attributes are found only in this product;
- the halo implication—a valid claim to superiority in one aspect of a product leads consumers to generalize superiority to other aspects where it may not exist;
- the confusing resemblance implication—use of a particular word or phrase that is similar to a familiar and popular one and leads to misplaced favorable psychological connections;
- the ordinary meaning implication—words or phrases with ordinary meanings are used in ways that really reference different meanings;
- the contrast implication—a product is contrasted with a competing product to which it is superior on a given attribute, leading consumers to assume the advantageous comparison carries over to all attributes;
- the endorsement implication—messages center on celebrities or other consumers claiming satisfaction, suggesting that this will be a shared experience;
- the expertise implication—an endorser's genuine expertise in one field is applied to an unrelated product, and may be perceived as more generalized than warranted;
- the significance implication—a message states a true but insignificant fact, the emphasis on which makes it appear significant;
- product-specific implications—truthful claims that foster unjustified beliefs about broader product advantages; and
- the puffery implication—messages contain nonfactual opinion statements that are acknowledged as such, but nevertheless enhance perceptions of the product (8–9).

It takes exactly zero stretching of the imagination to see the relevance of this list to persuasive communications well beyond the realm of product advertising. Miller and Stiff also examine the situations in which deceptive communication is most likely to occur and the form it is likely to take in each, the verbal cues and nonverbal correlates of deception, and the factors that influence one's ability to detect the veracity of a source.

Literature on International Communication and Public Diplomacy

Merritt (1980) called for replacement of the propaganda model of international persuasive communications with a more complex one based on a strategy of structural communication wherein the communicator proactively controls the setting in which people acquire their perspectives, predispositions, and behaviors, then steps back and lets nature take its course. In their study of strategies of public diplomacy directed at the United States by other governments, Manheim and Albritton (1984) developed one such alternative, a two-dimensional model of public relations effectiveness, positing four classes of initial positioning—high visibility/negative valence, low visibility/negative valence, low visibility/positive valence, and high visibility/positive valence—each requiring a different communication strategy. They then tested this model using case studies of news coverage of seven nations during the year before and the year after each hired a public relations consultant. The model proved to be robust, leading to the subsequent development of a more extensive model of agenda dynamics (Manheim 1987).

McNelly and Izcaray (1986), in a study of urban adults in Venezuela, found that news exposure does not predict knowledge of the countries covered there, but that it has a positive effect on favorable attitudes toward those countries and on judging them to be successful. Salwen and Matera (1992), in a local case study, looked at the linkage between media mentions of foreign nations and audience learning, finding that audience members were aware of the level of coverage of particular nations, but were not influenced in their assessments of various countries as friends or enemies of the United States. Kiousis and Wu (2008) undertook a more comprehensive examination of public relations effects on national image projection incorporating measurement of public opinion. They found, with Manheim and Albritton, that public relations efforts were indeed associated with reductions in negative news portrayals, and were able as well to establish a relationship between media salience and public salience and attitudes regarding foreign nations. Suman Lee (2007) examined public relations efforts in the United States on the part of ninety-seven countries, finding this activity to be a significant predictor of prominence in U.S. news coverage. In an innovative follow-up study, Lee and Yoon (2010) treated nations as business enterprises, and examined the return on investment experienced by 152 countries that engaged in such activity in the United States during the period 1997–2003. They found these efforts to have "robust explanatory power" with respect to such indicators as trade, direct investment, and tourism.

In the course of discussing the special challenges to the study of political communication in the international system, Davison and George (1953) provided a structural guide to outbound international information flows that is still informative today.

Raymond Cohen (1987) examined the role of staging and performance in diplomatic communication, including such elements as selecting and controlling the setting, costuming, props, body language and gestures, role-playing, and scripting.

Manheim and Albritton (1987) examined an effort by the government of Southern Rhodesia (now Zimbabwe) to improve its image in the U.S. media in the face of a widely popular insurgency by means of news management, finding that these efforts did result in image gains as defined by their (1984) model of public relations effects.

Kunczik (1997) examined the means by which nations cultivate their international images, with particular emphasis on the use of public relations techniques as distinct from propaganda techniques. Manheim (1994a), reprising and extending some earlier work, looked specifically at the role of public relations consultants employed by other governments in efforts to influence U.S. foreign policy through strategic public diplomacy. In a related study (1994b) of efforts to generate support in the United States for the 1990 Gulf War, he found that these efforts could be highly successful when they occur in a supportive political environment. More generally, Nye (2004) positioned what he termed "soft power" as an alternative to coercion or payment to obtain one's objectives, using instead the power of attraction, of getting others to do a protagonist's bidding because they are attracted to its culture, political ideas and policies. In this framework, if I may be permitted to extend Nye's argument further than he does, a country, a corporation, or even an NGO can possess soft power, and the more it has, the fewer physical resources are required to achieve its ends. The quest to maximize and exploit soft power is thus a central focus of international public diplomacy, and a principal benefit of success.

Gilboa (2000) posited six ways in which the media play a role in contemporary diplomacy. In three of these—secret, closed-door, and open diplomacy—the media are essentially channels through which information is (potentially) to be distributed to the public. Here the operative strategic questions pertain to the nature and extent of any controls that are to be imposed on that process or any efforts that are to be undertaken to gain advantage through it. The other three—public diplomacy, media diplomacy, and media-brokered diplomacy—describe situations in which the media are employed by the parties as channels to communicate with one another. Livingston (1999) pointed to the continuing, rapid evolution of information gathering, transmission, and dissemination technologies that would both empower and challenge media institutions in their coverage of international affairs, and that had at least some potential to displace diplomacy.

Sheafer and Gabay (2009) examined the strategic contest between Israel and the Palestinians to determine the dominant frames in international discourse regarding Israeli disengagement from Gaza and the Palestinian elections during the period 2005–2006, illustrating through such devices as mapping the portrayals of legitimacy of the two sides in numerous media the fundamentally competitive nature of these campaigns, and in the process providing a model for such competitive analyses.

Cull (1995) took a much broader historical view in his exploration of the strategies employed in Great Britain's propaganda campaign of the 1930s and 1940s designed to discredit neutrality and bring the United States into the war. A similar historical sensitivity is reflected in his monograph (Cull, 2009) on strategies in public diplomacy, which he characterizes as comprising five approaches or elements—listening, advocacy, cultural diplomacy, exchange diplomacy, and international broadcasting, sometimes accompanied by psychological warfare.

The editors and contributors to Odugbemi and Jacobson (2008) took a relatively unique perspective on communication and campaigns in the international system. This volume was commissioned and published by The World Bank with an eye toward improving governance regimes, especially in the developing world. The general approach they advanced was, first, creating a political space for public engagement on issues of governance, then obtaining the support of middle managers in the public sector, identifying stakeholders and building broad coalitions of pro-change influentials, reshaping public opinion through framing and ICT, then leveraging this new public support into demands for good governance.

Literature on Social Movements, Advocacy Networks and NGOs

Having begun (in the social sciences) in sociology as a conceptual approach to understanding the relationships of individuals with others in their social groups and settings, social network analysis has emerged as an important area of research at the institutional level and, not coincidentally, in communication and political science as well. Social network analysis has the virtue of illustrating complex relationships in an easily grasped spatial form, supporting relatively sophisticated statistical analyses based in matrix algebra and other tools (Knoke and Kuklinski, 1982; Pattison 1993), and opening up whole new avenues of conceptual development (Knoke, 1990; Monge and Contractor, 2003). Much of the development and utility of this literature is summarized in highly readable form by Watts (2003), an engineer turned sociologist, who used the development of his own career and interests as a lens through which to view inquiry into networked phenomena. Castells (1997, 2000) used the concept of social networks, and the power of identification with them, to posit a fundamental transformation of contemporary society *per se*. With that as background, let us turn our attention next to the application of some of these ideas, both conceptually and in practice, to the analysis of networks as they come into play in social movements, national and transnational coalitions, and, of course, IICs.

Gamson (1975) provided an early statement of resource mobilization theory, one of the leading approaches to understanding social movements. The idea here is that the actions of such groups are not extremist (or for that matter, pluralist) in character so much as that they are simply political in the broad sense of the word. Their actions are governed by the articulated interests of the group, prevailing standards of (social) justice, the resources controlled by the group and its members, the resources controlled by other interests (especially government), and the costs of mobilization and collective action. In effect, Protests R Us. Using more than fifty historical case studies of protest groups over a century and a half (1800–1945), Gamson illustrated the utility of this framework. McCarthy and Zald (1977) suggested that the most useful way to examine social movement organizations (SMOs) is from this resource mobilization perspective—by focusing on how and from where they draw their financial and other support. This led the authors naturally to a focus on media, authorities, and other parties, as well as the interactions among social movement organizations. Their point, however, like their analysis, went well beyond a structural description, for the implication of their argument is that such organizations are forced to compete for relatively scarce resources, both with other social movement organizations operating in the same policy arena (what sociologists term the same "social movement industry," or SMI) and with those in other SMIs as well, and that they are best understood in terms of how, and how well, they do so. Indeed, writing a few years later (Zald and McCarthy, 1980) they noted that social movements are seldom unified. Rather, they tend to be comprised of SMOs that are:

> . . .linked to various segments of supporting constituencies (both institutional and individual), competing amongst themselves for resources and symbolic leadership, sharing facilities and resources at other times, developing stable and many times differentiated functions, occasionally merging into *ad hoc* coalitions, and occasionally engaging in all-out war against each other. (2)

Focusing then on SMIs, or those organizations operating within a given sector, such as environmentalists or animal rights activists, they set forth a series of hypotheses suggesting, for example, that such factors as the segment-specific competition for resources, the ideology and legitimacy of the SMOs in question, the degree of overlap among their constituencies and leadership, experience with alliances, and factionalism will determine the patterns of SMO behavior and, by extension, their potential effectiveness.

Evan (1981) and his contributors, in an early and still unique volume, examined the roles and influence of international scientific and professional associations as transnational actors to address the question of whether, as Francis Bacon asserted, knowledge truly is power. The consensus was that these expertise-based NGOs were not yet as influential in the global policy arena as they might become, in large measure because to that time they had worked principally through intergovernmental organizations, but that this weakness could be addressed through taking greater advantage of national-level affiliate structures and through the formation of higher-order coalitions that could act independently in the international system.

Young (1991) noted the rapid increase in the number of international advocacy NGOs focusing on a range of issues from poverty and disease to world peace. Writing in the pre-web era, he noted the challenges posed to such groups by language and cultural differences, political separation, interference with freedom of exchange across national boundaries, and the costs of long-distance travel and communication. He argued that the most successful NGOs would be those that best addressed these challenges, which he thought could best be accomplished through decentralized and federated structures. Though Young's analysis turned out to be more time-bound than some others, he did anticipate the development of technological solutions to many of these challenges, and predicted their adoption would increase international NGO effectiveness. Writing with colleagues just a few years later (Young, Koenig, Najam, and Fisher, 1999), he looked again at international NGO structures and, based on fifteen case studies, concluded that the federation form of organization appeared best able to advance group interests. With respect to advocacy, for example, a global federation possesses inherent legitimacy that provides entrée to major corporations, IGOs, and multilateral forums; provides leverage to national-level affiliates to promote their own national agendas; and adds weight to efforts to advance standard-setting and similar policy initiatives (335).

P.J. Simmons (1998) identified four ways in which NGOs influence governments, multilateral institutions, and corporations, including the setting of agendas, negotiating outcomes, conferring legitimacy, and implementing solutions to policy problems. He proposed a framework for understanding these organizations based on their goals, membership, funding, and activities, and proffered a series of questions by which a given NGO might be categorized. These included:

- What is the group's ultimate goal (e.g., change societal norms, improve understanding, influence agendas or policies, implement policies or solve problems where government action is lacking)?
- Who benefits (e.g., the public interest in general or on a narrow issue, private interests, interests of the unrepresented, such as future generations)?
- Who belongs (e.g., individuals, organizations)?
- What is the group's geographic range (e.g., community, sub-national, national, regional, transnational)?
- Who runs the organization (e.g., volunteers, experts, professionals)?
- How are they selected (e.g., invited, elected, appointed, managerial)?
- What is the group's source of funds (e.g., dues, donations, foundation grants, government grants or contracts, intergovernmental organizations)?

- What is the group's function (e.g., advocacy, information gathering and analysis, information dissemination, generation of ideas and recommendations, monitoring or watchdog, service delivery, financing and grant-making)?
- Who are the group's targets (e.g., the public, consumers, governments, intergovernmental organizations, non-state actors, private sector actors)? (85)

One can see in this listing a number of the attributes we have incorporated into our main discussion of the formulation of campaign strategy.

Smith, Pagnucco, and Lopez (1998) surveyed more than a hundred transnational human rights organizations, finding, among other things, that 64 percent had taken as a primary goal the setting of international standards and 53 percent attached similarly high importance to monitoring and enforcement of such standards as exist. Other principal areas of activity included lobbying, participation in UN-sponsored and other international meetings, promoting national implementation of international human rights initiatives, educating the general public as well as government officials on human rights issues, supporting international human rights campaigns initiated by other groups, and organizing and mobilizing citizens through letter writing, demonstrations, and boycotts of their own. More than two-thirds of these groups indicated that their principle challenge was raising funds to support their activities. In a related study, Smith (2004), arguing that the end of the Cold War opened up a broad new multilateral space for transnational organizing, surveyed the size, focus, geographic reach, and organizational structures of transnational social movement organizations during this period across the full range of issues. She concluded that the rate of growth actually slowed in the 1990s; that human rights and environmental issues prevailed as they had before, but that economic issues had grown in importance and more groups had adopted multiple- rather than single-issue agendas; and that the newest groups tended to be organized within the global north or south rather than across that boundary. Viewed through the somewhat longer lens of 1973–2000, substantial growth was still evident in the share of this space occupied by environmental groups, which grew in number from seventeen to 167. Organizations with a combined global justice/peace/environment agenda grew from seven to 109 during the same period. Of particular interest here, Smith also found that transnational organizations had become less centralized over these three decades, with the percentage employing coalition structures rising from twenty-five to sixty while the percentage employing more centralized federation structures dropped from fifty to eighteen. Warkentin (2001) examined the emergence of a genuinely transnational civil society facilitated by the development of the Internet, using that framework to profile three environmental NGOs (Earth Island Institute, Rainforest Action Network, and Greenpeace), three developmental NGOs (JustAct, Womankind Worldwide, and Oxfam), and two online resource networks (Institute for Global Communications and OneWorld).

Keck and Sikkink (1998) developed the "boomerang model" of international NGO influence that we discussed in Chapter 5, illustrating its workings with networks of activists addressing human rights, the environment, and violence against women. The first scholarly treatment of transnational advocacy networks, a term they coined, this book has been particularly influential, with respect both to the attention it has drawn to the topic and the affirmation of their model in subsequent works. The following years saw, for example, publication of several related anthologies, most notably Potter (2002), Smith and Johnston (2002), Della Porta and Tarrow (2005), and Bandy and Smith (2005a). Among the highlights of these several volumes: Smythe and Smith's (2002) analysis of what they characterized as an "associational revolution" in which new technology and the development of advocacy networks challenged the traditional control over international relations exercised by governments, which the authors, in turn, challenged to adapt by quoting (196) an old Cornish proverb that says, "The tongueless man gets his land took."; Cooper's (2002) case study of the strategic use of information and communication technologies (ICT) in Greenpeace's achievement of control over issue framing in a dispute over French nuclear testing; Caniglia's (2002) assessment of the influence of alliance formation between environmental advocacy organizations and policy elites, most notably agencies of the United Nations; Maney's (2002) delineation of more than a dozen propositions relating to the effects of system-level political and economic process variables to the opportunities for transnational protest; Nepstad's (2002) study of the use of narrative to generate collective identity and cross-border solidarity in the U.S.–Central American peace movement, particularly through the life (and death, by assassination) story of Salvadoran archbishop Oscar Romero, which she found to be emotionally engaging, melodramatic, resonant with dominant transnational values (in this case, those of the Church), and a model for action; Reimann's (2002) argument that the changing dynamics of the international system and the growing legitimacy and influence of transnational advocacy networks allowed greater latitude of action for Japanese environmental NGOs and facilitated their participation in the 1997 Kyoto round of climate negotiations; Smith's (2002) reprise of the 1999 Battle of Seattle and its implications for the globalization of resistance movements, notable in part for its delineation (216) of the tactics employed, among them the cultivation of affinity groups, transnational organization of the participants, framing (including the borrowing of such official templates as "Global People's Assembly" and "People's Tribunal"), and several forms of electronic activism; Faber's (2005) analysis of the extension of the transnational environmental justice movement into the United States in the context of three competing frames—identity politics (cultural oppression as the source of injustice), radical/liberal democratic politics (political domination, as by corporations and the imperial north, as the source of injustice), and socialist politics (economic exploitation as the source of injustice); Bandy and Smith's (2005b) listing of the factors that facilitate and impede the smooth and effective working of transnational movement networks; Johnson and McCarthy's (2005) detailed analysis of the temporal development of environmental movement organizations in the United States and internationally during the period 1945–2000; Sikkink's (2005) reminder that, even though most scholars and activists alike tend to view international institutions as targets of campaigns, as objects to be against, these structures can also be centers of opportunity to be exploited, particularly in campaigns directed at states; and Tarrow and McAdam's (2005) treatment of scale shift, or the expansion of contention to higher levels as multiple localized actions merge into broader clusters.

Separately, Tarrow (2005) explored this notion of scale shift in much greater detail, picking up as well on Sikkink's recognition of the international system as an opportunity structure. One contributor to the Della Porta and Tarrow volume, Bennett (2005), has suggested that transnational advocacy has entered a post-Keck-and-Sikkink world, a "second generation" of activism characterized by tensions between direct action networks and more centralized NGOs in which the latter have lost their dominant role, instead becoming embedded in loosely interconnected global networks, even as those networks are newly empowered by new social technologies.

Gready (2004) considered the threats posed by, and the potential utility of, boomerangs as they impact on human rights and related initiatives. He identified three classes of boomerangs, including advocacy, campaign strategy, and security boomerangs (by which he meant the globalization of such risks as violence, poverty, exploitation, and exclusion). The distinction between the first two of these, which are most relevant to our interests here, is unclear and probably inconsequential in context. Gready's main argument was that, for those interested in advancing human rights, the boomerang dynamic cuts both ways. Having considered this interactive global dynamic, he then extended his analysis to traditional national borders, which highlight what he termed "the considerable residual importance of the state" (345), but which, in his view, are being redrawn and violently reinforced to preserve supra-state boundaries between global haves and have-nots. Bloodgood and Clough (2008) employed agent-based modeling and simulation to assess the relative significance of several determinants of NGO effectiveness, finding, among other results, that the networking associated with the boomerang model can have some unexpected consequences, including competitive pressures among NGOs working on different sides of an issue. Bullert (1999) had earlier made a similar point, noting emergent differences of opinion within the anti-sweatshop movement in the 1990s regarding target selection and, more to the point, cross-cutting among coalitions formed around sweatshops and trade with China. Bennett, Breunig, and Givens (2008), in a case study of U.S. anti-war demonstrations, found evidence that individual social activists are developing new, cross-networked forms of engagement in which they—and not churches, unions, and other traditional institutions—serve as central nodes and as linkages between otherwise distinct networks.

Tarrow (2001) examined the convergence of scholarship on social movements and international relations, which he saw as being driven by grassroots insurgencies like that in Chiapas that sought global support, the internationalization of protest events like the 1999 Battle in Seattle, the success achieved by some transnational coalitions against states, and the activism of international NGOs centered on IGOs and on treaty negotiations. Tarrow argued that many such scholarly analyses did a poor job of specifying the differences among social movements, NGOs, and transnational advocacy networks, and of parsing their various relationships with states and international organizations. He saw the establishment of mass-based transnational social movements as particularly challenging, and argued that such movements differ significantly from international NGOs or activist networks in their dealings with states and international institutions. Diani and McAdam (2003) and their contributors examined the role of networks in social movements in countries around the world. In their respective concluding essays to this anthology, McAdam argued that social network analysis can contribute to an understanding of the dynamics, as well as the structures, of social movements by focusing, for instance, on the mechanisms of network formation, member recruitment, and network growth over time, while Diani called for a more comprehensive form of network analysis incorporating multiple levels of relationships, the diverse qualities of linkages, temporal aspects of network development, and a greater focus on the attributes of members that may facilitate network development.

Yanacopulos (2005) examined NGOs as "strategic organizations that form coalitions in order to influence other actors, particularly international financial institutions" (93). In doing so, she distinguished such coalitions, or strategic alliances, from other types of NGO networks in that they are created to deal with broad issues, operate over extended time periods, and involve greater levels of shared commitment from the members. Based on three case studies, she found that coalitions that met her criteria do indeed act strategically, and that they are sensitive to changing resource levels (funding, legitimacy, information) in their environments. Yanacopulos concluded by arguing that such coalitions are especially well suited to waging coordinated campaigns that can be conducted in multiple countries, at multiple levels, and aimed at high-order or more general issues or values. DeMars (2005) argued that NGOs are best understood, not in terms of their principles, but in terms of their partnerships in transnational networks, through which they have the opportunity to institutionalize conflict and reshape states. In a series of propositions, DeMars effectively creates a primer of NGO activism, the main elements of which are:

- NGOs are private actors pursuing public objectives;
- NGOs bind themselves to societal and political partners in several countries;
- NGOs carry and channel the agendas of their partners, in the process becoming institutional loci of cooperation and conflict among those agendas;
- NGOs operate autonomously from their partners;
- NGOs form networks that facilitate the transnational movement of norms, resources, information, and political responsibility;
- NGO networks institutionalize international conflict; and
- NGO networks are present throughout the international system, where they influence states and other actors. (pp. 34–61 passim).

The book is notable as well for its extensive listing of international advocacy NGOs (188–194).

Shaffer (2000) also examined coalition behavior among NGOs, finding in a survey of the executive directors of ninety-two environmental organizations that the groups most likely to participate in coalitions were those with professional leadership cadres that maintained socially networked relationships with the leaders of other groups, those with high levels of membership activity, and those that employed inside advocacy tactics. That said, however, he also noted that every organization in the survey engaged in coalition behavior at some level.

While NGOs have emerged as a common focus of strategic analysis in recent years, similar studies of IGO communications are less common. An exception is Feld and Wildgen (1982), who examined the communication strategy employed by NATO and its reflection in media coverage of the alliance.

Literature on the Use of Information and Communication Technology (ICT) to Build and Sustain Networks

Ayres (1999) saw the Internet as both a substitute for street-level activism and a facilitator of such activism on a global scale. The Internet promotes diffusion of protest ideas and tactics, he argued, but poses a danger that activism will be based on unreliable and unverifiable information. Agre (2002) posited an "amplification model" as an alternative to what he saw as an excess of technical determinism. In his view, technology enhances organizational capabilities to form or foster social networks and to forge information-sharing communities. Bennett (2003) saw the Internet as contributing to global activism aimed at corporations, and trade and development regimes, not just by speeding communication, reducing its costs, and transcending geographic barriers, but by binding together loosely structured and widely dispersed networks of activists, strengthening their sense of shared identity, and facilitating the organization of issues and actors.

Diani (2000) argued that computer-mediated communication (chiefly email) was likely to augment the mobilization of existing social movement communities, particularly transnational networks of elite professional campaigners, but was unlikely to forge new interconnections among prospective members or groups where none already existed. In a case study examining the opposition to the Multilateral Agreement on Investment, a component of the 1990s move toward international economic integration, Deibert (2000) found that the Internet greatly enhanced the efforts of citizen networks, comprising perhaps as many as 600 NGOs in seventy countries, by facilitating communication and coordination, by publicizing both the issue and the activists' interpretation of it, and as a mechanism for generating direct pressure, as through website-based emails to policymakers.

Leizerov (2000) conducted a detailed study of the tactical use of the Internet by privacy advocates in a 1999 dispute with Intel arising from the incorporation of a personal identifier in its chips that could be read by websites to verify the identity of users. He identified five strategic dimensions of social and political protest—time, space, force, mind, and culture—and a number of advantages available to anti-corporate activists via the Internet. Among these were the ease of cyber-protest, improvement on the free-rider problem, freedom from the constraints of any larger public agenda, immediacy, the ability to pose challenges to the target, the informality of alliance structures and decentralization of leadership, the low cost of operations, and the ease of access to the media, which use the Internet for sourcing.

Van De Donk, Loader, and Nixon (2004), in an edited volume, considered the ways in which the adoption by activists' of new information and communication technologies might seriously challenge traditional forms of political participation. The transnational, many-to-many, communication capabilities of the Internet, they argued, had the potential to circumvent the indexing of traditional media based on the range of official voices, while electronic mail and other online applications might simultaneously facilitate organization-building and coordination of action. (On this latter point see, for example, Rheingold (2002).) Several case studies (Cardoso and Neto (2004) on the pro-East Timor movement in Portugal; Edwards (2004) on the Dutch women's movement) and more broadly conceptual analyses (Rosenkrands (2004) on anti-corporate websites; Rucht (2004) on the adaptation of social movements using new media to address the weaknesses in their coverage by traditional media) illustrated this phenomenon. Van Aelst and Walgrave (2004) integrated the two perspectives in their analysis of the Internet's role in the development of the anti-globalization movement. In a later study, Smith, Costello, and Brecher (2009) identified five factors contributing to the growing influence of digital media in movement building: facilitating the formation of groups through the use of social networking tools; scaling up the distribution of information, even as it can be more effectively targeted to specialized audiences; inherent interactivity, and hence, engagement; destruction of communication hierarchies; and low cost and ease of use.

One of the most pervasive elements of many digital media is the use of distributed reputation systems, which is to say, the public ranking or evaluation of materials, contributors, reviews, commentary, news accounts and the like. Contributing to such ratings has emerged as a primary manifestation of interactivity in these media, and as such, can provide both a source of information and a mechanism of engagement for social movement organizations, advocacy groups, or other NGOs and civil society organizations. Karpf (2009) provided an analytical scheme for characterizing and evaluating these systems, and some anecdotal data on their use by strategists at one such organization, Move On.

Peizer (2006) used his extensive experience developing technology systems for social change for the Open Society Institute and elsewhere both as case studies and as a baseline for identifying ways that NGOs can take advantage of such technological developments—and the challenges of doing so successfully. One of the greatest challenges to taking full advantage of these capabilities, he noted, can be the internal culture and dynamics of NGOs themselves, where decision-making structures, personal interests, and even stakeholder relationships can be put into play, and thus threatened, by technological initiatives. The potential payoffs, however, he argued, are manifold and can be well worth the effort.

One emergent network of particular interest here is Indymedia, a global network of alternative, activist media distributed through the Internet. Pickard (2006) used the occasion of a 2002 funding crisis within the network to contextualize some issues that pertain to the maintenance of this and other activist networks. The crisis involved the question of how Indymedia could both accept funding from Ford or other foundations and still remain, well, indy. He found a degree of disconnect among the network's ideology, its technological capabilities, and its financial and organizational sustainability.

Literature on Communication and Networks in Insurgencies and Terrorism

Schmid and DeGraaf (1982) made a compelling, and at the time a novel, case for understanding acts of insurgent and terrorist violence as a form of communication in which the type of act, the target, the setting, the timing, and other attributes comprised a message being communicated to some opposing force. Their argument was nicely illustrated by Livingston (1994). Reflecting subsequent conceptual developments, Norris, Kern, and Just (2003) provided a similar, but far more nuanced, collection of essays arguing the importance of the framing of terrorism in the media. In the introduction to the volume, they defined terrorism as "the systematic use of coercive intimidation against civilians for political goals" (6). While we tend to picture this phenomenon purely in terms of physical acts of violence, the authors' definition opens up a much broader vista, and one that is focused more on psychological effects than on the acts themselves. For them, it provides a rationale for considering the importance of framing, but for us it points to but one of the reasons that terrorists engage in IICs, one product set of which may be advancing their preferred frames.

Arquilla and Ronfeldt (1996), in a RAND Corporation consulting report prepared for the Pentagon, developed the concept of "netwar," or a form of conflict "involving measures short of war, in which the protagonists use—indeed, depend on using—network forms of organization, doctrine, strategy, and communication. These protagonists generally consist of dispersed, often small groups who agree to communicate, coordinate, and act in an internetted manner . . ." (5). As the latter portion of this definition suggests, their argument arose in the context of then-emerging forms of cyber warfare. In a subsequent (Ronfeldt, Arquilla, Fuller, and Fuller, 1998) study of the Zapatista rebellion in Mexico, however, they extended it to incorporate what they termed "social netwar," in this case the formation of a network of civil society NGOs that rose to the defense of, and helped to legitimize, globalize, protect, and empower, what had been a domestic insurgency. In a later edited volume (Arquilla and Ronfeldt, 2001), the RAND team extended this idea of social netwar to examine a variety of terrorist, criminal, and anarchist networks, as well as activists supporting such causes as democracy in Burma, protest against the World Trade Organization, and environmental reform.

Cleaver (1998) studied international support of the Zapatista rebellion in Chiapas, Mexico, concluding that, in contrast to the reliance on traditional forms of communication within Mexico itself, the development of global support for the rebellion, and its influence, was greatly facilitated by computer-based communication, websites, and existing online communities of activists who could rapidly mobilize and coordinate their themes and actions. This support network was drawn together in large part by the adoption on the part of the Zapatistas of an enemy they could share in common with external activists: so-called neo-liberalism—a theory of governance favoring market-based outcomes, privatization, deregulation, and free trade, all anathema to the advocacy groups that emerged as a pro-Zapatista coalition. Schulz (1998) examined opportunity structures, network capacity, and "communication praxis" (akin to reality construction) as each contributed to the success of the Zapatista rebellion in Chiapas. He found the opportunity structure at the outset of the conflict to hold little promise, while the insurgency's network capacity, in contrast, was well developed because the Zapatistas were able to connect with existing and extensive domestic and international networks of NGOs that had formed around the recent negotiations on the North American Free Trade

Agreement. This provided them with access to audiences and resources, and as a result, with the opportunity to define their movement outside the customary frame for indigenous Mexican agrarian reform movements so long as their definition appealed to their networked civil society partners. Thus, notes Schulz, "The Zapatistas represent a new kind of guerilla in that their goal is not to impose themselves as a new sovereign but to strengthen civil society vis-à-vis the state . . ." (598). Another perspective is provided by Russell (2001), who compared "news" generated by the Zapatistas themselves and their allies with that generated by traditional news media.

Bob (2005) analyzed the ways in which insurgent movements—in this case the Ogoni in Nigeria and the Zapatistas in Mexico—employed marketing techniques to gain access to, and the support of, international NGO networks. A significant key to success, Bob found in this path-breaking analysis, is to frame the insurgent movement so as to match closely the goals, culture, tactics, ethics, and organizational needs of the would-be sponsor NGOs. Hammes (2005) argued that modern insurgencies are designed as communication campaigns, the objective of which is to convince enemy political leaders that their goals either cannot be achieved, or that the cost of doing so would be prohibitive. He characterizes this "fourth-generation" warfare as involving transnational, national, and sub-national organizations and networks, and differentiated messaging aimed at breaking the opponent's will. Asal, Nussbaum and Harrington (2007) argued that terrorist groups function just like transnational advocacy networks, citing the examples of Al Qaeda and the Tamil Tigers in Sri Lanka. In addition to the boomerang model, they noted, common tactics include information politics, leverage politics, symbolic politics, and accountability politics. "One can better understand the strategies of transnational terrorist groups by understanding that they are following a set of repertories that has been proved useful by many other nongovernmental organizations" (34). Similarly, Brachman (2006) argued that Al Qaeda has transformed itself into a social movement by leveraging new communication and information technologies, and suggested that the most important of its tactics might be the most mundane, such as web forums or even *jihadi* video games. He characterized the Qaeda strategy as "weaponizing the Internet."

Though not dealing with terrorism or insurgency, Walker (2002) applied the social netwar framework to the study of industrial conflict, studying labor union campaigns against four multinational employers. He argued that netwar established a new style of global campaigning that could be expected to increase in frequency and importance.

Literature on Campaign and Communication Strategies in General

We begin our inventory of the literature on strategy *per se* with some classics. The earliest known book on strategy, dating back some 2100 years, and the best known as well, is Sun-Tzu's classic, *The Art of War* (the 1993 Huang translation listed in Appendix C is a good one). Sun Tzu requires a good deal of contextual interpretation to be fully relevant to the development of IIC strategy, but if one takes the text conceptually rather than literally, it still speaks to us of a systematic approach to situational analysis and decision-making that has self-evident contemporary implications.

We have already made reference in the main text to another classic, Alinsky's (1971) *Rules for Radicals*, but no bibliographic inventory can be complete without a more pointed reference. This is arguably the very first and most essential reading for any would-be campaign strategist. His thirteen tactical "rules":

1. Power is not only what you have, but what the enemy thinks you have.
2. Never go outside the experience of your people.
3. Whenever possible go outside the experience of the enemy.
4. Make the enemy live up to their own book of rules.
5. Ridicule is man's most potent weapon.
6. A good tactic is one that your people enjoy.
7. A tactic that drags on too long becomes a drag.
8. Keep the pressure on.
9. The threat is usually more terrifying than the thing itself.
10. The major premise for tactics is the development of operations that will maintain a constant pressure upon the opposition.
11. If you push a negative hard and deep enough it will break through into its counter-side.
12. The price of a successful attack is a constructive alternative.
13. Pick the target, freeze it, personalize it, and polarize it (126–130, passim).

Beyond his discussion of these tactical matters and of the ethical issues we have addressed earlier, Alinsky provided insights into the guiding philosophy and perspectives behind (his) activism that do not appear elsewhere in the literature.

Finally in this first broad grouping, and as noteworthy in its way, is the work of Thomas Schelling's (1963, see also 1978) book, *The Strategy of Conflict*, which examines conflict situations and the strategy required to deal with them using the tools of game theory and mathematical models. Together these several books suggest the possible dimensions of a truly strategic mind.

Not surprisingly, there is an extensive how-to literature providing tactical and strategic advice on many aspects of campaigning. For general strategic advice, see Bobo, Kendall, and Max (1996), AFL-CIO (1981,1985, 2000), Communications Workers of America (1993), Oppenheimer and Lakey (1964), Service Employees International Union (nd), and Shaw (1996). For advice regarding media strategies in the context of campaigns, see Gregory,

Caldwell, Avni, and Harding (2005), Ryan (1991), and Salzman (2003). On the tactics of sit-ins, see Offner (2010). Of particular note here is Ganzi, Seymour, and Buffett (1998), an analysis published by the World Resources Institute, that provided a highly detailed strategic analysis of the organization, resource flows, and weighted stakeholder relationships in eight separate sectors of the financial services industry, and identified points of leverage in each sector that could be employed to advantage by environmental advocates. That industry has subsequently been targeted by a wide range of activists over issues ranging from executive compensation and mortgage-lending policies to labor and workplace issues. The Coalition for the International Criminal Court, an advocacy coalition comprised of religious groups, human rights advocates, and associations of lawyers, has provided guidelines (2003) for NGO media strategies that include such elements as the development of core messaging, framing, packaging and timing.

Though hardly an example of the activist literature on campaign strategy, Robert Simmons (1990) did provide a detailed approach to managing communication campaigns that imparted a great deal of potentially salient advice with respect to such matters as organizational structure, planning, problem definition, audience segmentation, campaign research, message design, and budgeting—in sum, the nuts and bolts issues that tend to be left out or minimized in the advocacy literature *per se*. Similarly, Webster, Phalen, and Lichty (2000) provided a systematic guide to audience research, which, together with Helen Katz's (2003) treatise on media buying for advertising, provide detailed technical guidance that can be used to great advantage in media-based IICs.

And there is, of course, a parallel literature providing advice to campaign targets, primarily corporations, on how best to defend themselves. Typical of the genre, though by no means alone, are Dezenhall (1999), Peters (1999), and Sitrick (1998). Deegan (2001) and Nichols (2001) are noteworthy in the present context for their focus on managing relations (or confrontations) with activist groups. Nancy Flynn (2006), though not writing in a campaign defense context *per se*, provides useful guidance regarding the rules of engagement for online blogs.

Suchman (1995), as noted earlier, provided an important taxonomic analysis of legitimacy and of various potential strategies for developing, maintaining, or, when necessary, restoring it. Legitimacy is the acceptance on the part of a given audience that a particular actor—in our context this could be a protagonist, an intermediary, or a target—is generally seen to be acting properly toward pro-social objectives within an established set of values, norms, and expectations. It can, in Suchman's terms, be pragmatic in form, arising from the self-interest of key stakeholders; moral, reflecting a normative acceptance of the actor and its behaviors; or cognitive, or, in effect, taken for granted. Within this framework, he proposed a series of strategic mechanisms for gaining and maintaining legitimacy, and for restoring it when lost or damaged.

Corporate campaigns are an important subclass of information and influence campaigns. These are campaigns employed by unions to pressure employers in organizing or contract disputes, and occasionally on policy or governance matters. Jarley and Maranto (1990) studied 28 campaigns conducted by labor unions in the period 1976–1988, when corporate campaign tactics were first being developed and deployed. They found that campaigns in support of union organizing were the most likely to succeed, followed by those designed to advance bargaining. Campaigns in support of strikes generally failed. In the authors' view, the generalizable determinants of success included conflict escalation, sensitivity of the target company to its public image, strategic use of the available regulatory bodies, vigorous support from the national leadership of the campaigning union, and the availability of favorable economic trade-offs to the target company that would follow upon a resolution of the dispute. Perry (1987) and Manheim (2001) have provided overviews and analyses of the strategies employed in these campaigns, including numerous examples drawn primarily from the United States. There is, as well, a rich case study literature focusing on specific campaigns. Examples include Ashby and Hawking (2009), Brisbin (2002), Getman (1998), Juravich and Bronfenbrenner (1999), and Rosenblum (1998). LaBotz (1991) blended analysis and case studies with tactical and strategic guidance for those conducting labor-based campaigns. Bronfenbrenner (2007) compiled several case studies of cross-border campaigns.

Broad and Cavanaugh (1997) provided one of the earliest comprehensive analyses of *anti*-corporate campaigns (essentially the same as corporate campaigns, but conducted by advocates other than unions) built around the theme of accountability, delineating a very useful framework incorporating as the main foci targets, initiators, strategic goals, instrumentalities of accountability, and geographic scope. Their discussion included such leverage points as codes of conduct, international agreements and structures, and private finance.

Lange (1993) summarized the ebb and flow in an information campaign pitting environmental groups against the timber industry in a conflict over old-growth timber and the spotted owl. He found that the two competing sides of the campaign systematically played off of one another, consistently mirroring one another's strategies and tactics, which included framing and reframing the issue, selecting relatively extreme evidence from studies and experts to support its own claims and refute those of the opponent, vilification (enemy construction) and ennobling, simplification and dramatization, and lobbying and litigating. Lange characterized this process as spiral-like, and emphasized the seemingly inescapable intertwining of competing forces and their respective initiatives. Huxham and Sumner (1999) conducted a post-mortem of sorts on the 1995 Greenpeace campaign that forced Shell Oil to cancel the planned disposal of its *Brent Spar* oil platform in the North Sea, and on the journalistic and academic critiques of that campaign. Of particular interest here is their summary of those critiques, which, according to the authors, characterized Greenpeace's campaign and Shell's response as a series of juxtaposed approaches, including (1) appealing to public opinion versus consulting with experts, (2) emphasizing ignorance versus emphasizing knowledge, (3) broad framing of the risk analysis, incorporating political and social considerations, versus narrow framing of the risk analysis, (4) broad symbolic and political goals versus narrow business goals and regulatory compliance, (5) emotion versus rationality, (6) openness versus secrecy, and (7) suspicion of government and regulatory bodies versus trust in government.

Bullert (1999) noted the central role played by strategic communication professionals in the development of the environmental, human rights, labor rights, and sweatshop issues that came together in the so-called "Battle of Seattle" protest aimed at the 1999 meeting of the World Trade Organization.

Carroll and Ratner (1999) studied the media strategies of three Canadian social movement organizations to deal with asymmetrical and dependent power relationships—in this case between themselves and the mainstream media—focusing on what the organizations in question regarded as the potential blocking, distortion, or facilitation of their ideas and issues. They found that the asymmetries were reduced by the sheer universality of the SMO messages, albeit within limits, but that the risks of undesirable framing arising from them endured. Moyer (2001) identified eight stages of development for social movements, each of which he examined from the perspectives of the movement itself, the relevant power-holders, the public, and the related goals, pitfalls, and crises. Of particular interest here is the sixth stage, which constitutes outreach to majority public opinion. Among the elements in play at this stage are large-scale efforts at public education and conversion, redefinition of the problem to show how it affects all segments of society, building a broad-based organizational structure, engaging with mainstream political and social institutions such as legislative bodies and the courts, engaging in direct action, and developing citizen involvement programs. The objectives here are to treat the general public, rather than the power-holders who are the ultimate target, as the key audience and to maintain the issue on the public agenda. This can be aided by the exploitation of focusing events when they occur (64–75). Pitt, Loehr, and Malviva (nd) studied the use of evidence by NGOs in three international campaigns, finding that campaign effectiveness may well turn on the relevance, reliability, audience suitability, and successful communication of this informational resource. Specifically, the authors found that the public is more responsive to easily understood and highly politicized messages, while policy-makers are more responsive to technical, solution-oriented information.

Ereaut and Segnit (2006), in a strategic communication plan on climate change prepared for the Institute for Public Policy Research in the UK, identified several rhetorical themes that were generating what they deemed public confusion on the issue, including alarmism on the part of climate-change advocates that can be seen as excluding the possibility of addressing the issue successfully, an activist focus on small actions that can be undertaken by individuals but that are so routine and lacking in drama that they may fade into wallpaper, and, on the other side, a tendency to mock and dismiss the unfathomable scale of (alarmist) advocacy claims. To address these concerns, the authors recommended that discourse on the issue be shaped to create the impression among the general public that related scientific disagreements have been resolved in favor of a self-evident consensus, and that, because the ongoing debate does not advance the cause of climate change, this frame be used to terminate the debate.

Most IICs are designed to bring about change, whether in attitude, behavior, policy, status, or some other thing. There is value to the strategist, then, in understanding the nature of change itself. Chin and Benne (1969) offered some guidance in this direction by classifying change-directed strategies. Their principal categories (and related strategies) included empirical–rational strategies (research and dissemination of knowledge through education, personnel selection and replacement, applied research linked to systems for diffusion of the results, utopian thinking and extrapolation of alternative futures, and using language to reorganize perceptions), normative re-educative strategies (improving the problem-solving capabilities of the system, fostering the intellectual growth of key personnel), and power-coercive strategies (nonviolent protest, using political institutions to achieve change, and manipulating and/or changing the composition of elites). Though they wrote in the context of intra-organizational change, their framework clearly has broader applications.

McCornack (1992) advanced what he termed information manipulation theory, an argument that persons engaged in interpersonal communication have certain expectations regarding the quantity, quality, manner, and relevance of information, and that any of these expectations can be exploited by a communicator as a means to achieve verbal deception. McCornack et al (1992) tested this argument empirically, finding that the amount, veracity, relevance, and clarity of messages can all influence perceived message deceptiveness.

Nothhaft and Wehmeier (2007) argued that public relations strategies centered on such notions as building trust or constructing images are generally simplistic, overlooking the complexity of the public and the dynamism of social systems. They proposed a more advanced approach based in socio-cybernetics. Rather than the traditional emphasis on direct, persuasive communication, such an approach instead would center on creating and maintaining conditions that favor the development of the desired outcome, which they term "cultivating" an image as opposed to constructing one. Merritt (1980) anticipated this development in the international arena.

DeVreese and Elenbaas (2008) found that exposure to news coverage of strategy frames, which is to say, a focus on strategy *per se*, contributed to higher levels of political cynicism, and that this effect was greatest among more knowledgeable individuals. Though their study focused on expressly political actors, its conclusions would seem to be applicable to IIC protagonists (or targets) more generally. Sellers (2010), in a richly detailed analysis of news management by Members of Congress and their leaders, found these efforts to play a central role, not only in advancing the policy agendas of one or the other party, but in the reinvigoration of the political parties themselves.

Kelman (1969), in the course of a discussion of the ethical dilemmas associated with using social scientific knowledge to manipulate human behavior, recommended three steps to mitigate this manipulation: increasing awareness of the manipulation, building protections against, and resistance to, the manipulation; and developing new alternative choices for the target of the manipulation. Though he intended these steps to be self-imposed by the strategist, they can also be seen as pointing the way toward the development of counter-manipulation, e.g., counter-campaign strategies, and are, in fact, reflected in our discussion of approaches to defense.

Literature on Social Marketing and Related Strategies

Johnson (1971), employing a form of spatial analysis emphasizing consumer (broadly defined) preferences, perceived attributes of the products (or policy choices) on offer, and assessments of the similarity or dissimilarity of the options, offered an early and illuminating perspective on the application of marketing concepts and techniques, most notably market segmentation, to the political realm. The contributors to Newman (1999) explored the many dimensions of what has come to be called political marketing, though they did so almost without exception in the context of electoral campaigns. One relatively taxonomic essay (Butler and Collins, 1999), however, did offer a conceptual structure of somewhat broader value. In the course of distinguishing between political and other forms of marketing, these authors pointed to such properties as the "mutability" of the "purchase", i.e., the fact that it might be altered or transformed, or have some unanticipated consequence in the post-purchase setting; the periodic character of the marketplace; and the central role played by the affirmation of social and ideological identifications.

Kotler and Levy (1969) proposed extending traditional marketing principles to the marketing of non-business organizations, persons, and ideas. They identified several core concepts—product definition, target audience definition, customer behavior analysis, multi-channel communication, integrated planning, and others—that they believed could be employed pro-socially. Later, Fox and Kotler (1980) reviewed the first decade of the application of marketing techniques to advancing social causes, focusing generally on public information campaigns, mainly in the field of public health. Pointing to successful efforts in family planning and heart disease prevention, they highlighted the value of establishing phased, specific objectives for the campaign over time, clearly defining audience segments, using research and pretesting to develop clear and salient messages, scheduling sufficient frequency of messages over a long period of time, stimulating interpersonal communication to increase the range of campaign channels, and evaluating the progress of the campaign over time. They also identified several barriers to success in social marketing campaigns that set them apart from commercial marketing efforts, among them the absence of solid and reliable data on the market itself, public pressure to reach the entire public rather than key segments, opposition on the part of key constituencies to certain types of appeals, limitations on the skills, resources, and infrastructure of the sponsoring cause groups, and the difficulty of isolating the effects of the campaign for purposes of evaluation.

Kotler, Roberto and Lee (2002) then literally wrote the book on the use of marketing techniques to advance social causes, setting out in detail the techniques for broadly based strategic marketing initiatives paralleling those employed in commerce. Andreasen (2006) had a very different, though generally complementary, take on the topic, focusing his analysis on creating and framing the public agenda and working through structures of allies that closely resemble the networks we have described here. Of particular interest is his identification of the motives that might lead corporations to sign on as campaign allies. These include participation as damage control, as a means to achieve some non-campaign-related end, as a one-time activity to increase sales or profits, or because a given initiative fits with the long-term interests of the company. Understanding these or other motives of a potential campaign intermediary can be very important to the recruitment efforts of a protagonist. Andreasen also notes that, even though it is typically organizations that are being recruited as campaign allies, it is always individuals within those organizations who make the related decisions. To an extent these perspectives are merged in Andreasen and Kotler (2003), who apply the techniques of strategic marketing to nonprofit organizations, aka, NGOs. Kotler was the sole author of this book's first edition, so it retains the systematic, taxonomic approach typical of his extensive writings, but evidence of Andreasen's sense of context is present here as well. Of particular interest, simply as a touch point, is the application of a stakeholder-based approach, as illustrated (75) in a graphic depicting the multiple publics to which the American Cancer Society must attend.

Manheim and Pratt (1986) noted that, even as they increased the levels of attention and resources they devoted to proactive social-responsibility programs in the United States and abroad, corporations were failing to communicate effectively the significance of these efforts, and thus not maximizing their social-capital returns. Vogel (2005) looked specifically at the business case for corporate social responsibility, finding that the "market for virtue" is not universal, and that certain types of firms operating in certain markets will find these practices to have greater economic value than some others. Werder (2008) tested the influence of corporate social responsibility initiatives on public perceptions of Starbucks, finding that these efforts did influence salient beliefs about the company, but did not influence company-related attitudes or behavioral intentions.

Literature on Stakeholders and Stakeholder-Based Strategies

Any discussion of stakeholder-based analysis necessarily begins with R. Edward Freeman's (1984) seminal book, *Strategic Management: A Stakeholder Approach*, which introduced into management scholarship in a highly taxonomic and systematic manner on the affirmative side some of the same ideas that were percolating upward at the time among anti-corporate activists (power structure analysis) as potential points of attack, namely that the key to the success of a business firm (or, arguably, any other organization) is the successful management of its diverse relationships. Freeman's map of generic stakeholder relationships (55), for example, and its specification into a detailed map of the relationships surrounding a hypothetical major oil company (122), could easily be mistaken for the maps employed by corporate antagonists, and his analysis of mediated relationships between indirect stakeholders and the firm, together with his discussion of coalition strategies, while presented proactively and in the context of advancing socially responsible behavior, are directly analogous to the uses of networking and intermediaries we explored in the main body of the present volume. As he points out from the outset, the stakeholder concept did not originate with Freeman. But that does not diminish the significance of this book.

In a review of related literature, Donaldson and Preston (1995) distinguished among three aspects of the stakeholder theory of the corporation: descriptive accuracy, instrumental power, and normative validity. They concluded that the three were both significant and mutually supportive, and that the underlying theoretical construct was more robust than traditional economic theory in explaining corporate behavior. Mitchell, Agle, and Wood (1997), as noted in Chapter 5, argued that the key to developing a robust theory of stakeholder identification and salience is found in three stakeholder attributes—power, legitimacy, and urgency—which they saw as variable in degree, socially constructed (i.e., based on shared perception as opposed to objective reality), and exercised either willfully or inadvertently. The essence of the argument is that these key attributes are most significant when they overlap, but that differences in the nature and extent of any overlap are highly consequential. Altogether they generated eight general classes of stakeholders, suggesting in the process those that will exercise the greatest leverage on the target.

Among the most common targets of stakeholder-based strategies are corporations, either in efforts to influence their own practices, where they are the ultimate targets of the campaign, or to manipulate them into exercising their often considerable leverage on governments and public policy, where they serve as potent intermediaries. Vogel (1978) provided an early and insightful analysis of these challenges to the business community, identifying many of the actors, actions and foci that have since emerged as commonplace, among them the politicizing of the corporation, the emphasis on transparency, the emergence of shareholder-based activism, internationalization, and the use of codes of conduct. A quarter-century later, these efforts to pressure corporations had, in some cases, morphed into something quite different, an ideological attack on the corporate form of organization *per se* (see Danaher and Mark, 2003).

A more common evolution, however, was a growing focus on the marketplace and consumerism as particular points of corporate *and governmental* vulnerability to influence. Friedman (1999) offered a remarkable summary and analysis of a common tactic, the economic boycott, as employed by consumers, minorities, religious groups, environmentalists, and labor. Bennett (2001) argued that the traditional boycott, though the point of origin, was only the beginning of a new consumer-driven politics arising from institutional fragmentation offset by new niche marketing capabilities, by a greater acceptance of personal choice in social identities and the frames this makes available to activists, and by a growing focus, driven by globalization and the declining power of national institutions, on trade regimes, development agencies, and multinational corporations. This theme found voice in Micheletti, Follesdal, and Stolle's (2004) collection of essays on political consumerism. Cashore, Auld, and Newsom (2004), for example, looked at the development of forest certification, a form of industry-wide code of conduct enforcement, by environmentalists. Also included were updates by Bennett (2004) and Friedman (2004) of their earlier analyses. Bennett identified four patterns of global consumer activism that bring together several themes in this inventory of literature: the permanence of interest-based campaigns, the organization of global activists in the form of decentralized networks, the emergence of the Internet as a *de facto* organizational structure, and the influence of new media on old, which is to say the transference of content and even news-making norms from the open and unfettered Internet to the more tightly controlled mass media.

Jones (2005) applied the stakeholder model of the firm to the notion of brand equity. His model (23), reproduced here with stakeholder-specific thematic appeals indicated, is similar to that employed by the power-structure analysts, both in form and in content.

Barnett (2007) argued that the business case for CSR must take account of the path-dependent nature of stakeholder relationships, which he saw as

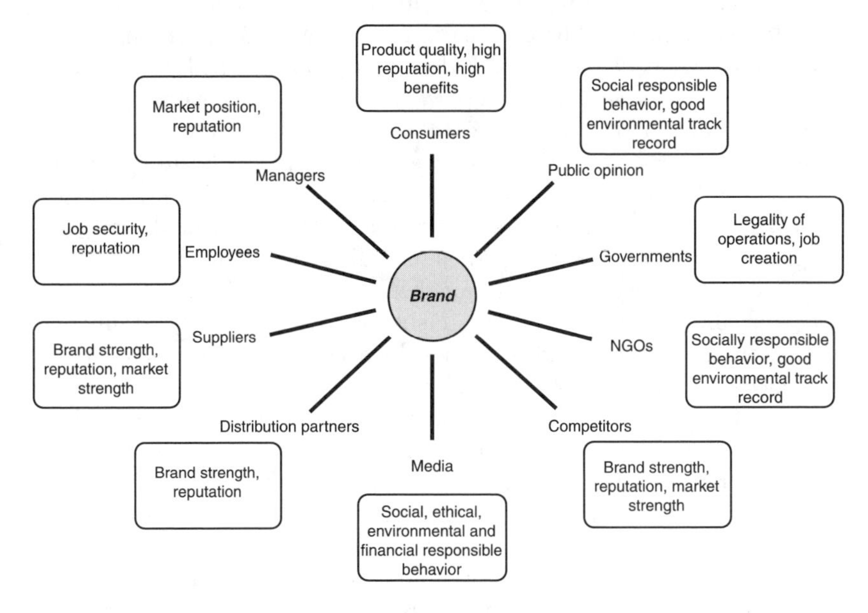

Figure B.3 Daisy Wheel Model of Brand Equities.

providing a filter of sorts in the form of the influence capacity of stakeholders and their motivation as derived from the financial performance of the company in question. Bonini, Court, and Marchi (2009) argued that companies need to develop an understanding of their reputations that mirrors the interests of their key stakeholders, and of the ways that their products or services, operations, supply chain, and other attributes interact with those interests. In effect, they proposed an approach to reputation management grounded in the basic ideas of market segmentation.

Hall (1992) analyzed the strategic value of intangible resources to a corporation. In a survey of CEOs, he found, not surprisingly, that the reputation of the company and its products were the most highly prized of these assets. Interestingly, public knowledge of the company ranked near the bottom in terms of relative importance. Fernández, Montes, and Vázquez (2000), writing in the context of investor decision-making, suggested that companies be evaluated strategically in terms of their intangible resources, which include human capital in the form of institutional knowledge, organizational capital (norms, routines, culture), technological capital (proprietary information), and relational capital (reputation, brands, distribution channels, long-term relationships, loyalty). These soft resources are useful to the strategist for assessing and potentially leveraging the relationship between a company and its shareholders, but are either directly applicable or at the least suggestive as criteria for evaluating other potential stakeholder pressure points as well.

Drucker (1976) identified public employee pension systems as emerging vehicles of influence, directly on the corporate sector through their increasing ownership share, and indirectly on politics. Rifkin and Barber (1978) saw this growing pension power as a source of increasing power for organized labor if the unions could harness their substantial potential influence on pension fund management and policies. Building on this foundation, and as noted elsewhere, Ganzi, Seymour, and Buffett (1998), provided a highly detailed strategic analysis of the stakeholder relationships in eight separate sectors of the financial services industry, and identified points of leverage in each sector that could be employed to advantage by environmental advocates. Fung, Hebb, and Rogers (2001) documented the extent of pension fund growth, which at the time of their writing exceeded $7 trillion in the United States, and pointed to strategies for advancing labor's economic and political agenda by using the resultant leverage. Manheim (2005a, 2005b) examined the implementation of some of these strategies during the 2003 proxy season. Chakrabarti (2004), in a study of shareholder activism on the part of unions that employed both case studies and a regression analysis of votes on shareholder resolutions submitted by unions, found that union influence is enhanced through coalition-building with other institutional shareholders, and especially when leveraged through a firm (Institutional Shareholder Services) that provided influential proxy-voting advice to a wide array of institutions other than unions. Price (2006) examined pressure tactics directed at corporate directors and what he saw as the benefits and challenges of responses grounded in cooperation with the activists.

Bhattacharya and Sen (2003) focused on the relationship between companies and consumers, and more particularly on the centrality to that relationship of consumers' identification with the company *per se*. They asserted that such identification is "active, selective, and volitional," and posited several ways in, and conditions under, which it may affect corporate behavior and standing. Cardador and Pratt (2006) picked up this argument, finding parallels between its treatment in the literatures of marketing and of management. Their analysis focused on three bases of identification: relationships, behaviors, and symbols. Einwiller, Fedorikhin, Johnson, and Kamins (2006) looked specifically at the interaction between consumer identification with a company and negative publicity about that company. They found that those with a stronger sense of identification were more resistant than others to moderately negative publicity, but that even strong identifiers were adversely affected by intensely negative publicity.

The relationship between corporations and their regulators is a complex one, and by no means unidirectional. Gordon and Hafer (2005), for example, looked at the use of signaling by corporations to their regulators of their willingness to resist intrusions, where the signaling in question took the form of political contributions. Using plant-level inspection data from the Nuclear Regulatory Commission and political expenditures by firms in that industry, they found evidence that large political donors are less compliant than smaller donors, and are monitored less. The authors also found indications that companies with publicly observable operating problems may reduce their political expenditures. The operative mechanism here is the dependency of regulatory agencies on legislative and budgetary support from elected officials, so in effect, the companies are communicating with their regulators through the key stakeholders of the latter.

Suman and Rossman (2000) brought together more than a dozen activists, attorneys, and industry representatives in a series of essays exploring the relationship between the advocacy community and the entertainment industry. Though the book offers few deep insights, it does suggest some of the opportunities and limitations of entertainment-directed tactics from several important perspectives.

Stakeholder influence can be hierarchical in nature. For example, Jacobs and Page (2005), in a study of constituency influence in foreign policy-making, found that U.S. foreign policy is most heavily influenced by internationally-oriented business leaders, and thence in descending order by policy experts, labor, and the general public, whose influence appears to be limited and episodic.

Fombrun and his colleagues (Fombrun, Gardberg, and Sever, 2000; Gardberg and Fombrun, 2002) undertook to develop a consistent metric, which they termed the Reputation Quotient, or RQ, to quantify the assessment of corporate reputations across various classes of stakeholders, and to validate and extend this measurement scale internationally. Principal RQ evaluative dimensions include the company's emotional appeal, products and services, vision and leadership, workplace environment, social and environmental responsibility, and financial performance.

MacMillan, Money, Downing and Hillenbrand (2004; see also Money and Hillenbrand, 2006) proposed a more comprehensive and more directly strategic stakeholder-based model, termed SPIRIT (Stakeholder Performance Indicator, Relationship Improvement Tool), as a mechanism for identifying the drivers of corporate reputation and employing them to generate desired outcomes. Among the reputation drivers identified in the model are the stakeholder's direct experience of the corporation's behavior (communications, products or services), their indirect experience of the corporation (as, for example, through media or third-party commentary), their behavioral support of the business (commitment, cooperation, subversion, or the like), and their emotional attachment to the corporation (e.g., trust, positive affect). These factors are used to evaluate the likely positive or negative outcomes of business strategies.

Literature on Vulnerabilities and Their Sources

Manheim (1990) showed how governments in unstable political systems rendered themselves far more vulnerable to pressure from both domestic and foreign activists by seeking and winning sponsorship of the Olympic Games. Sponsorship imposed on these governments extensive requirements for infrastructure development and rising expectations (and sometimes explicit commitments) for political reform, all in an ever-increasing glare of global media attention. It also left them open to allegations that they were failing to live up to the Olympic ideal. This dynamic added leverage to what otherwise might have proven obscure embarrassments arising from protest and other forms of reform activism, and empowered previously weak reform movements.

For some actors, vulnerabilities are structured into their social position itself. Tyler (1997), for example, noted the disconnect between the communications advice commonly offered to corporations during periods of crisis that they (or their executives) should accept responsibility and apologize for misdeeds, on the one hand, and the realities of legal liability that can be increased by such actions, on the other. The result tends to be equivocation or ambiguity in any statements that are issued, which can leave the public and other stakeholders dissatisfied, and executives frustrated and humiliated.

Weil (2005), in advancing a "strategic choice framework" to guide decision-making by union leaders, provided in the process a structural basis on which to evaluate the strength (or weakness) of a given union according to its positioning on two dimensions, external leverage and internal organizational capacity. The first derives from the environment in which the union operates, and takes into account such elements as the structure of the industries where it operates and of the associated labor markets, the nature and role of technology in those industries, and the relevant regulatory structures. The second includes such factors as the union's leadership and staffing, its recruitment processes, and its methods for allocating and deploying resources—all aspects of what we have termed infrastructure. Weil concluded that in general unions that seek to strengthen themselves must do so by increasing their organizational capacities first, and only then by seeking to enhance their leverage.

Bartley and Child (2009) examined the factors that open corporations to campaigns of naming and shaming. Those that are leaders in globalization are most likely to be targeted, these authors found in a study focusing on the apparel and shoe industries, but a strong secondary determinant is reputation, and more particularly the extent of a company's dependence on maintaining a good one. Large companies with branded consumer products and patterns of globalization, they suggested, are the most vulnerable.

Bremmer (2006), and Bremmer and Keat (2009), address risk, not in the context of thematic appeals as we have elsewhere in this review essay, but rather as a real attribute of economic and political systems. The first of these volumes posits a two-dimensional space in which to array political systems based on their degrees of openness and stability, respectively. The result is a "J Curve"—essentially a curvilinear relationship between the two attributes, with the implication that the least open systems (those at the left end of the distribution) will confront potentially existential challenges to their stability as they increase their openness, while those toward the right—the relatively open systems, will actually become *more* stable as they become even more open. Openness here refers in part to the extent to which a given country is integrated into the international system (e.g., through travel, communication, media access, foreign direct investment), and in part to the free flow of ideas and information within its borders. The principal challenge to stability occurs when closed systems reach a critical point of openness or, in the alternative, when open systems close themselves off to such a degree that they become destabilized. The second volume focuses on the nature and extent of political risk, and on mechanisms for anticipating and responding to it. Both books are written primarily for investors (the authors are associated with a global risk consultancy), but together, and taken in the present context, they provide some very useful tools for assessing the vulnerabilities of state-level or other systemic targets.

Generic Literature Reviews

Finally, the strategist can benefit from a selective reading of the extensive reviews of campaign-relevant literatures in the many scholarly "handbooks" that have been published over the years in various specialized fields of inquiry. A few of the more useful examples include Knutson (1973), Pool and Schramm (1973), Nimmo and Sanders (1981), Swanson and Nimmo (1990), and Kaid (2004).

Notes

1 Adam Hochschild (2005) provided an extraordinarily comprehensive analysis of the British anti-slave trade movement and its activities. The analysis here draws heavily on his account of those activities, and, to a lesser extent on Metaxas (2007), who assigned a more central role in the campaign to Mr. Wilberforce.

2 This discussion of Edison's campaign against alternating current draws its facts largely from Mark Essig's (2003, passim) excellent chronicle, supplemented with additional detail and insight provided by Maury Klein (2008: 256–278). The interpretation of those facts in the present context is my own.

3 This summary of the anti-sweatshop campaign is based on, and extends, a discussion in Manheim (2001: 71–74).

Appendix C A Bibliography for IIC Strategy (Including Sources Cited)

Abelson, Robert P. (1959) "Modes of Resolution of Belief Dilemmas," in *Journal of Conflict Resolution* 3: 343–352.

AFL-CIO (1981) *Manual of Corporate Investigation*. Washington, DC.

——. (1985) *Developing New Tactics: Winning with Coordinated Corporate Campaigns*. Washington, DC.

——. (2000) *The Campaign Guide: Organizing the Construction Industry*. Washington, DC.

Agre, Philip E. (2002) "Real-Time Politics: The Internet and the Political Process," in *The Information Society* 18: 311–331.

Ajzen, Icek, and Martin Fishbein (1980) *Understanding Attitudes and Predicting Social Behavior*. Upper Saddle River, NJ: Prentice-Hall.

Albrecht, Terrance L., and Mara B. Adelman (1987) *Communicating Social Support*. Thousand Oaks, CA: Sage.

Albritton, Robert B., and Jarol B. Manheim (1983) "News of Rhodesia: The Impact of a Public Relations Campaign," in *Journalism Quarterly* 60: 622–628.

Alinsky, Saul D. (1971) *Rules for Radicals: A Pragmatic Primer for Realistic Radicals*. New York: Random House.

Allan, Stuart, Barbara Adam, and Cynthia Carter, eds. (2000) *Environmental Risk and the Media*. London: Routledge.

Allport, Gordon W., and Leo J. Postman (1946–1947) "An Analysis of Rumor," in *Public Opinion Quarterly* 10: 501–517.

Anderson, Lynn R., and Martin Fishbein (1965) "Prediction of Attitude from the Number, Strength, and Evaluative Aspect of Beliefs About the Attitude Object: A Comparison of Summation and Congruity Theories," in *Journal of Personality and Social Psychology* 2: 437–443.

Anderson, Lynn R., and William J. McGuire (1965) "Prior Reassurance of Group Consensus as a Factor in Producing Resistance to Persuasion," in *Sociometry* 28: 44–56.

Andreasen, Alan R. (2006) *Social Marketing in the 21st Century*. Thousand Oaks, CA: Sage Publications.

Andreasen, Alan R., and Philip Kotler (2003) *Strategic Marketing for Nonprofit Organizations*, sixth edition. Upper Saddle River, NJ: Prentice-Hall.

Arquilla, John, and David Ronfeldt (1996) *The Advent of Netwar*. Santa Monica, CA: RAND.

——, eds. (2001) *Networks and Netwars: The Future of Terror, Crime, and Militancy*. Santa Monica, CA: RAND Corporation.

Asal, Victor, Brian Nussbaum, and D. William Harrington. (2007) "Terrorism as Transnational Advocacy: An Organizational and Tactical Analysis," in *Studies in Conflict and Terrorism* 30: 15–39.

Ashby, Steven K., and C.J. Hawking (2009) *Staley: The Fight for a New American Labor Movement*. Urbana, IL: University of Illinois Press.

Au, Wagner James (2007) "International Union Protesters Converge on IBM: Company refuses comment, strike leaders claim success, 1850 total attendance (including bananas and geometric dissenters)," in *New World Notes* (September 27). Found online at http://nwn.blogs.com/nwn/2007/09/international-u.html.

Ayres, Jeffrey M. (1999) "From the Streets to the Internet: The Cyber-Diffusion of Contention," in *Annals of the American Academy of Political and Social Science* 566: 132–143.

Baker, Stephen (2008) *The Numerati*. Boston, MA: Houghton Mifflin.

Bakir, Vian (2005) "Greenpeace v. Shell: Media Exploitation and the Social Amplification of Risk Framework (SARF)," in *Journal of Risk Research* 8: 679–691.

——. (2006) "Policy Agenda Setting and Risk Communication: Greenpeace, Shell, and Issues of Trust," in *Harvard International Journal of Press/Politics* 11: 67–88.

Bandy, Joe, and Jackie Smith, eds. (2005) *Coalitions Across Borders: Transnational Protest and the Neoliberal Order*. Lanham, MD: Rowman & Littlefield.

——. (2005) "Factors Affecting Conflict and Cooperation in Transnational Movement Networks," in Joe Bandy and Jackie Smith, eds. *Coalitions Across Borders: Transnational Protest and the Neoliberal Order*, 231–252. Lanham, MD: Rowman & Littlefield.

Barnett, Michael (2007) "Stakeholder Influence Capacity and the Variability of Financial Returns to Corporate Social Responsibility," in *Academy of Management Review* 32: 794–816.

Bartley, Tim (2007a) "Institutional Emergence in an Era of Globalization: The Rise of Transnational Private Regulation of Labor and Environmental Conditions," in *American Journal of Sociology* 113: 297–351.

——. (2007b) "How Foundations Shape Social Movements: The Construction of an Organizational Field and the Rise of Forest Certification," in *Social Problems* 54: 229–255.

Bartley, Tim, and Curtis Child (2009) "Shaming the Corporation: Globalization, Reputation, and the Dynamics of Anti–Corporate Movements," Working Paper, Department of Sociology, Indiana University. Found online at http://www.indiana.edu/~tbsoc/SM-corps-sub.pdf, December 22, 2009. An earlier version of this paper was presented at the Annual Meeting of the American Sociological Association, New York City, August 2007.

Bauer, Raymond A. (1964) "The Obstinate Audience: The Influence Process from the Point of View of Social Communication," in *American Psychologist* 19: 319–328.

Beavers, Garry J. (2005) "Defining the Information Campaign," in *Military Review* (November–December): 80–82.

Beder, Sharon (2002) "Environmentalists Help Manage Corporate Reputation: Changing Perceptions not Behaviour," in *Ecopolitics* 1: 60–72.

Bem, Daryl J. (1970) *Beliefs, Attitudes, and Human Affairs*. Belmont, CA: Brooks/Cole.

Benford, R.D., and D.A. Snow (2000) "Framing Processes and Social Movements: An Overview and Assessment," in *Annual Review of Sociology* 26: 611–639.

Bennett, W. Lance (1990) "Toward a Theory of Press–State Relations," in *Journal of Communication* 40: 103–125.

——. (1996a) *News: The Politics of Illusion*, third edition. White Plains, NY: Longman.

——. (1996b) "An Introduction to Journalism Norms and Representations of Politics," in *Political Communication* 13: 373–384.

——. (2001) "Consumerism and Global Citizenship: Lifestyle Politics, Permanent Campaigns, and International Regimes of Democratic Accountability," paper presented at the International Seminar on Political Consumerism, Stockholm University, Stockholm, Sweden.

——. (2003) "Communicating Global Activism: Strengths and Vulnerabilities of Networked Politics," in *Information, Communication and Society* 6: 143–168.

——. (2004) "Branded Political Communication: Lifestyle Politics, Logo Campaigns, and the Rise of Global Citizenship," in Michele Micheletti, Andreas Follesdal, and Dietlind Stolle, eds. *Politics, Products, and Markets: Exploring Political Consumerism Past and Present*, 101–126. New Brunswick, NJ: Transaction Books.

——. (2005) "Social Movements Beyond Borders: Understanding Two Eras of Transnational Activism," in Donatella Della Porta and Sidney Tarrow, eds. *Transnational Protest and Global Activism*, 203–226. Lanham, MD: Rowman & Littlefield.

Bennett, W. Lance, Christian Breunig, and Terri Givens (2008)"Communication and Political Mobilization: Digital Media and the Organization of Anti-Iraq War Demonstrations in the U.S.," in *Political Communication* 25: 269–289.

Bennett, W. Lance, and Regina G. Lawrence (1995) "News Icons and the Mainstreaming of Social Change," in *Journal of Communication* 45: 20–39.

Bennett, W. Lance, and Jarol B. Manheim (2001) "The Big Spin: Strategic Communication and the Transformation of Pluralist Democracy," in W. Lance Bennett and Robert M. Entman, eds., *Mediated Politics: Communication in the Future of Democracy*, 279–298. New York: Cambridge University Press.

——. (2006) "The One-Step Flow of Communication," in *Annals of the American Association for Political and Social Research* 608: 213–232.

Berg, John C., ed. (2003) *Teamsters and Turtles? U.S. Progressive Political Movements in the 21st Century*. Oxford, UK: Rowman & Littlefield.

Berger, Bruce K. (2001) "Private Issues and Public Policy: Locating the Corporate Agenda in Agenda-Setting Theory," in *Journal of Public Relations Research* 13: 91–126.

Berger, Peter L., and Thomas Luckman (1966) *The Social Construction of Reality: A Treatise in the Sociology of Knowledge*. New York: Doubleday.

Berlo, David K., James B. Lemert, and Robert J. Mertz (1969–1970) "Dimensions for Evaluating the Acceptability of Message Sources," in *Public Opinion Quarterly* 33: 563–576.

Bernays, Edward (1928) *Propaganda*. New York: H. Liveright.

Bhattacharya, C.B., and S. Sen (2003) "Consumer–Company Identification: A Framework for Understanding Consumers' Relationships with Companies," in *Journal of Marketing* 67: 76–88.

Bimber, Bruce (2003) *Information and American Democracy: Technology in the Evolution of Political Power*. Cambridge: Cambridge University Press.

Bitzer, Lloyd (1980) "Functional Communication: A Situational Perspective," in Eugene E. White, ed. *Rhetoric in Transition: Studies in the Nature and Uses of Rhetoric*, 21–38. University Park, PA: Pennsylvania State University Press.

Bloodgood, Elizabeth, and Emily Clough (2008) "NGOs in International Affairs: An Agent-Based Model and the Boomerang Effect," paper presented at the Annual Conference of the International Studies Association, San Francisco, CA.

Bob, Clifford (2005) *The Marketing of Rebellion: Insurgents, Media, and International Activism*. Cambridge: Cambridge University Press.

Bobo, Kim, Jackie Kendall, and Steve Max (1996) *Organizing for Social Change: A Manual for Activists in the 1990s*, second edition. Santa Ana, CA: Seven Locks Press.

Bok, Sissela (1999) *Lying: Moral Choice in Public and Private Life*, third edition. New York: Vintage.

Boninger, David S., Jon A. Krosnick, and Matthew K. Berent (1995) "Origins of Attitude Importance: Self-Interest, Social Identification, and Value Relevance," in *Journal of Personality and Social Psychology* 68: 61–80.

Bonini, Sheila, David Court, and Alberto Marchi (2009) "Rebuilding Corporate Reputations," in *McKinsey Quarterly* as accessed June 2, 2009, at http://www.mckinseyquarterly.com/PDFDownload.aspx?ar=2367: 1–8.

Boorstin, Daniel J. (1961) *The Image: A Guide to Pseudo-Events in America*. New York: Harper & Row.

Boulding, Kenneth E. (1969) *The Image: Knowledge in Life and Society*. Ann Arbor: University of Michigan Press.

Boulianne, Shelley (2009) "Does Internet Use Affect Engagement? A Meta-Analysis of Research," in *Political Communication* 26: 193–211.

Bowers, John W., Donovan J. Ochs, and Richard J. Jensen (1993) *The Rhetoric of Agitation and Control*, second edition. Long Grove, IL: Waveland Press.

Brachman, Jarret M. (2006) "High-Tech Terror: Al-Qaeda's Use of New Technology," in *The Fletcher Forum of World Affairs* 30: 149–164.

Brandeis, Louis D. (1914). *Other People's Money: And How the Bankers Use It*. New York: F.A. Stokes.

Brashers, Dale (2001) "Communication and Uncertainty Management," in *Journal of Communication* 51: 477–497.

Bremmer, Ian (2006) *The J. Curve: A New Way to Understand Why Nations Rise and Fall*. New York: Simon & Schuster.

Bremmer, Ian, and Preston Keat (2009) *The Fat Tail: The Power of Political Knowledge for Strategic Investing*. New York: Oxford University Press.

Briñol, Pablo, Derek D. Rucker, Zakary L. Tormala, and Richard E. Petty (2004) "Individual Differences in Resistance to Persuasion: The Role of Beliefs and Meta-Beliefs," in Eric S. Knowles and Jay A. Linn, eds. *Resistance and Persuasion*, 83–104. Mahwah, NJ: Lawrence Erlbaum Associates.

Brisbin, Richard A., Jr. (2002) *A Strike Like No Other Strike: Law & Resistance During the Pittston Coal Strike of 1989–1990*. Baltimore, MD: Johns Hopkins University Press.

Broad, Robin, and John Cavanaugh (1997) "The Corporate Accountability Movement: Lessons and Opportunities." Washington, DC: World Resources Institute.

Bronfenbrenner, Kate (2007) *Global Unions: Challenging Transnational Capitalism through Cross-Border Campaigns*. Ithaca: Cornell University Press.

Brosius, Hans-Bernd, and Anke Bathelt (1994) "The Utility of Exemplars in Persuasive Communications," in *Communication Research* 21: 48–78.

Brown, J.A.C. (1963) *Techniques of Persuasion: From Propaganda to Brainwashing*. London: Cox & Wyman.

Bryant, Jennings, and Dolf Zillmann, eds. (1994) *Media Effects: Advances in Theory and Research*. Hillsdale, NJ: Lawrence Erlbaum Associates.

Buitenhuis, Peter (1989) *The Great War of Words: Literature as Propaganda 1914–1918 and After*. London: B.T. Batsford.

Bullert, B.J. (1999) "Strategic Public Relations, Sweatshops and the Making of a Global Movement," Working Paper #2000-14. Cambridge, MA: Shorenstein Center, Harvard University.

Burke, Kenneth (1966) *Language as Symbolic Action*. Berkeley, CA: University of California Press.

——. (1984) *Permanence and Change*. Berkeley, CA: University of California Press.

Bustillo, Miguel (2010) "Consultant Sues Worker Over Article," in *Wall Street Journal* (June 19): B5.

Butler, Patrick, and Neil Collins (1999). "A Conceptual Framework for Political Marketing," in Bruce I. Newman, ed., *Handbook of Political Marketing*, 55–72. Thousand Oaks, CA: Sage.

Caniglia, Beth Schaefer (2002) "Elite Alliances and Transnational Environmental Movement Organizations," in Jackie Smith and Hank Johnston, eds. *Globalization and Resistance: Transnational Dimensions of Social Movements*, 153–172. Oxford, England: Rowman & Littlefield.

Cantril, Hadley (1940) *The Invasion from Mars: A Study in the Psychology of Panic*. Princeton, NJ: Princeton University Press.

Cardador, M.T., and M.G. Pratt (2006) "Identification Management and Its Bases: Bridging management and Marketing Perspectives through a Focus on Affiliation Dimensions," in *Journal of the Academy of Marketing Science* 34: 174–184.

Cardoso, Gustavo, and Pedro Pereira Neto (2004) "Mass Media Driven Mobilization and Online Protest: ICTs and the Pro-East Timor Movement in Portugal," in Wim Van De Donk, Brian D. Loader, Paul G. Nixon, and Dieter Rucht, eds. *Cyberprotest: New Media, Citizens and Social Movements*, 147–163. London: Routledge.

Carroll, William K., and R.S. Ratner (1999) "Media Strategies and Political Projects: A Comparative Study of Social Movements," in *Canadian Journal of Sociology* 24: 1–34.

Cartwright, Dorwin, and Frank Harary (1956) "Structural Balance: A Generalization of Heider's Theory," in *Psychological Review* 63: 277–293.

Cashore, Benjamin, Graeme Auld, and Deanna Newsom (2004) "Legitimizing Political Consumerism: The Case of Forest Certification in North America and Europe," in Michele Micheletti, Andreas Follesdal, and Dietlind Stolle, eds. *Politics, Products, and Markets: Exploring Political Consumerism Past and Present*, 181–202. New Brunswick, NJ: Transaction Books.

Castells, Manuel (1997) *The Power of Identity*. Oxford, England: Blackwell Publishers.

——. (2000) *The Rise of the Network Society*, second edition. Oxford, England: Blackwell Publishers.

Chadwick, Andrew (2006) *Internet Politics: States, Citizens, and New Communication Technologies*. New York: Oxford University Press.

Chaffee, Steven H. (1972) "The Interpersonal Context of Mass Communication," in F. Gerald Kline and Phillip J. Tichenor, eds. *Current Perspectives in Mass Communication Research*, 95–120. Beverly Hills, CA: Sage.

Chaiken, Shelly, and Alice H. Eagly (1983) "Communication Modality as a Determinant of Persuasion: The Role of Communicator Salience," in *Journal of Personality and Social Psychology* 45: 241–256.

Chakrabarti, Monami (2004) "Labor and Corporate Governance: Initial Lessons from Shareholder Activism," in *Working USA: The Journal of Labor and Society* 8: 45–69.

Chaudhuri, Arjun, and Ross Buck (1995) "Affect, Reason, and Persuasion: Advertising Strategies that Predict Affective and Analytic-Cognitive Responses," in *Human Communication Research* 21: 422–441.

Chelimsky, Eleanor (1985) "Budget Cuts, Data and Evaluation," in *Society* 22: 65–73.

Chin, Robert, and Kenneth D. Benne (1969) "General Strategies for Effecting Changes in Human Systems," in Warren G. Bennis, Kenneth D. Benne, and Robert Chin, eds. *The Planning of Change*, second edition, 32–59. New York: Holt, Rinehart and Winston.

Chong, Dennis (1996) "Creating Common Frames of Reference on Political Issues," in Diana C. Mutz, Paul M. Sniderman, and Richard A. Brody, eds. *Political Persuasion and Attitude Change*, 195–224. Ann Arbor: University of Michigan Press.

Chong, Dennis, and James N. Druckman (2007a) "A Theory of Framing and Opinion Formation in Competitive Elite Environments," in *Journal of Communication* 57: 99–118.

——. (2007b) "Framing Public Opinion in Competitive Democracies," in *American Political Science Review* 101: 637–655.

Clawson, Dan (2003) *The Next Upsurge: Labor and the New Social Movements*. Ithaca, NY: Cornell University Press.

Cleaver, Harry (1998) "The Zapatistas and the International Circulation of Struggle—Lessons Suggested and Problems Raised," paper presented at the INET'98 Conference, Geneva, Switzerland, accessed June 3, 2009, at http://libcom.org/library/zapatistas-international-circulation-struggle-cleaver.

Coalition for the International Criminal Court (2003) "NGO Media Outreach: Using the Media as an Advocacy Tool," accessed May 26, 2009, at http://www.iccnow.org/documents/CICC_MediaOutreachManual_Sep03.pdf.

Cohen, Arthur R. (1960) "Attitudinal Consequences of Induced Discrepancies Between Cognitions and Behavior," in *Public Opinion Quarterly* 24: 297–318.

Cohen, Bernard (1963) *The Press and Foreign Policy*. Princeton, NJ: Princeton University Press.

Cohen, Raymond (1987) *Theatre of Power: The Art of Diplomatic Signaling*. London: Longman.

Colvin, Gregory L. (1993) *Fiscal Sponsorship: 6 Ways to Do It Right*. San Francisco: Study Center Press.

Combs, James E. (1980) *Dimensions of Political Drama*. Santa Monica, CA: Goodyear.

Combs, James E., and Dan Nimmo (1993) *The New Propaganda: The Dictatorship of Palaver in Contemporary Politics*. New York: Longman.

Communications Workers of America (1993) *Mobilizing for the 90s*, second edition. Washington, DC.

Converse, Philip E. (1964) "The Nature of Belief Systems in Mass Publics," in David Apter, ed., *Ideology and Discontent*. New York: Free Press.

Cook, Fay Lomax, Tom R. Tyler, Edward G. Goetz, Margaret T. Gordon, David Protess, Donna R. Leff, and Harvey L. Molotch (1983) "Media and Agenda Setting: Effects on the Public, Interest Group Leaders, Policy Makers, and Policy," in *Public Opinion Quarterly* 47: 16–35.

Cook, Terrence E. (1980) "Political Justifications: The Use of Standards in Political Appeals," in *Journal of Politics* 42: 511–537.

Cooper, Andrew F. (2002) "Snap-Shots of an Emergent Cyber-Diplomacy: The Greenpeace Campaign Against French Nuclear Testing and the Spain-Canada 'Fish War,'" in Even H. Potter, ed. *Cyber-Diplomacy: Managing Foreign Policy in the Twenty-First Century*. Montreal: McGill-Queens University Press: 128–150.

Corman, Steven R., Angela Trethewey, and Bud Goodall. (2007) "A 21st Century Model for Communication in the Global War of Ideas: From Simplistic Influence to Pragmatic Complexity," Report #0701, Consortium for Strategic Communication, Arizona State University, Tempe, AZ.

Corrado, Michele (2002) "The Role of Survey Research in International Campaigns: What Can Be Learnt From Case Studies?" in Hans-Dieter Klingemann and Andrea Römmele, eds. *Public Information Campaigns & Opinion Research: A Handbook for the Student & Practitioner*. London: Sage: 125–146.

Cragin, Kim, and Scott Gerwehr (2005) *Dissuading Terror: Strategic Influence and the Struggle Against Terrorism*. Santa Monica, CA: RAND.

Crossen, Cynthia (2006) "'Cognitive Dissonance' Became a Milestone in 1950s Psychology," *The Wall Street Journal* (December 4): B1.

Cull, Nicholas J. (1995) *Selling War: The British Propaganda Campaign Against American "Neutrality" in World War II*. New York: Oxford University Press.

——. (2009) *Public Diplomacy: Lessons from the Past*. Los Angeles, CA: Figueroa Press.

Dahl, Robert (1961) *Who Governs?* New Haven, CT: Yale University Press.

Danaher, Kevin, and Jason Mark (2003) *Insurrection: Citizen Challenges to Corporate Power*. New York: Routledge.

Danes, Jeffrey E., and John E. Hunter (1980) "Designing Persuasive Communication Campaigns: A Multimessage Communication Model," in *Journal of Consumer Research* 7: 67–77.

Davenport, Christian (2010) "In choosing its battle names, the military must know its target audience," in *Washington Post* (March 20): A1.

Davis, Richard (1999) *The Web of Politics: The Internet's Impact on the American Political System*. New York: Oxford University Press.

Davison, W. Phillips (1958) "The Public Opinion Process," in *Public Opinion Quarterly* 22: 91–106.

——. (1971) "Some Trends in International Propaganda," in *Annals of the American Academy of Political and Social Science* 398: 1–13.

——. (1983) "The Third Person Effect in Communication," in *Public Opinion Quarterly*: 47: 1–15.

Davison, W. Phillips, and Alexander L. George (1953) "An Outline for the Study of International Political Communications," in *Public Opinion Quarterly* 16: 501–511.

Dearing, James W., and Everett M. Rogers (1996) *Agenda-Setting*. Thousand Oaks, CA: Sage.

Deegan, Denise (2001) *Managing Activism: A Guide to Dealing with Activists and Pressure Groups*. London: Institute of Public Relations and Kogan Page Ltd.

DeFleur, Melvin L. (1970) *Theories of Mass Communication*, second edition. New York: David McKay.

DeFleur, Melvin, Lucinda Davenport, Mary Cronin, and Margaret DeFleur (1992) "Audience Recall of News Stories Presented by Newspaper, Computer, Television and Radio," in *Journalism Quarterly* 69: 1010-1-22.

Deibert, Ronald J. (2000) "International Plug 'n Play? Citizen Activism, the Internet, and Global Public Policy," in *International Studies Perspectives* 1: 255–272.

Della Porta, Donatella, and Sidney Tarrow, eds. (2005) *Transnational Protest and Global Activism*. Lanham, MD: Rowman & Littlefield.

DeLuca, Kevin (2005) *Image Politics: The New Rhetoric of Environmental Activism*. Mahwah, NJ: Lawrence Erlbaum Associates.

DeMars, William E. (2005) *NGOs and Transnational Networks: Wild Cards in World Politics*. London: Pluto Press.

Dennis, Everette E. (1991) "In Context: Environmentalism in the System of News," in Craig L. LaMay and Everette E. Dennis, eds., *Media and the Environment*, 55–64. Washington, DC: Freedom Forum Media Studies Center.

Deutsch, Karl W. (1963) *The Nerves of Government: Models of Political Communication and Control*. Glencoe, IL: Free Press.

Devine, Patricia G., and Edward R. Hirst (1989) "Message Strategies and Information Campaigns: A Social-Psychological Analysis," in Charles T. Salmon, ed., *Information Campaigns: Balancing Social Values and Social Change*, 229–258. Thousand Oaks, CA: Sage.

DeVreese, Claes H., and Matthijs Elenbaas (2008) "Media in the Game of Politics: Effects of Strategic Metacoverage on Political Cynicism," in *International Journal of Press/Politics* 13: 285–309.

Dezenhall, Eric (1999) *Nail 'em: Confronting High-Profile Attacks on Celebrities and Businesses*. Amherst, NY: Prometheus.

Diani, Mario (2000) "Social Movement Networks Virtual and Real," in *Information, Communication & Society* 3: 386–401.

Diani, Mario, and Doug McAdam, eds. (2003) *Social Movements and Networks: Relational Approaches to Collective Action*. Oxford: Oxford University Press.

Dolnick, Edward (2008). *The Forger's Spell: A True Story of Vermeer, Nazis, and the Greatest Hoax of the Twentieth Century*. New York: Harper Collins.

Domhoff, G. William, ed. (1980) *Power Structure Research*. Beverly Hills, CA: Sage Publications.

——. (2009) *Who Rules America: Challenges to Corporate and Class Dominance*, sixth edition. New York: McGraw-Hill.

Donaldson, Thomas, and Lee E. Preston (1995) "The Stakeholder Theory of the Corporation: Concepts, Evidence, and Implications, in *Academy of Management Review* 20: 65–91.

Donohue, George A., Philip J. Tichenor, and Clarise N. Olien (1972) "Gatekeeping: Mass Media Systems and Information Control," in F. Gerald Kline and Phillip J. Tichenor, eds. *Current Perspectives in Mass Communication Research*, 41–69. Beverly Hills, CA: Sage.

Doob, Leonard W. (1947) "The Behavior of Attitudes," in *Psychological Review* 54: 135–156.

Downs, Anthony (1972) "Up and Down with Ecology: The Issue–Attention Cycle," in *The Public Interest* 28: 38–50.

Drucker, Peter E. (1976) *The Unseen Revolution: How Pension Fund Socialism Came to America*. New York: Harper & Row.

Druckman, James N. (2001) "Using Credible Advice to Overcome Framing Effects," in *Journal of Law, Economics & Organization* 17: 62–82.

——. (2004) "Political Preference Formation: Competition, Deliberation, and the (Ir)relevance of Framing Effects," in *American Political Science Review* 98: 671–686.

Druckman, James N., and Kjersten R. Nelson (2003) "Framing and Deliberation: Conversations Limit Elite Influence," in *American Journal of Political Science* 47: 729–745.

Duke, Lynne (2005) "The Man Who Made Kathie Lee Cry," in *The Washington Post* (July 31).

Dye, Thomas R. (2002) *Who's Running America: The Bush Restoration*, seventh edition. Englewood Cliffs, NJ: Prentice-Hall.

Edelman, Murray (1964) *The Symbolic Uses of Politics*. Urbana: University of Illinois Press.

——. (1971) *Politics as Symbolic Action: Mass Arousal & Quiescence*. Chicago: Markham Publishing.

——. (1988) *Constructing the Political Spectacle*. Chicago: University of Chicago Press.

——. (1993) "Contestable Categories and Public Opinion," in *Political Communication* 10: 231–242.

Edwards, Arthur (2004) "The Dutch Women's Movement Online: Internet and the Organizational Infrastructure of a Social Movement," in Wim Van De Donk, Brian D. Loader, Paul G. Nixon, and Dieter Rucht, eds. *Cyberprotest: New Media, Citizens and Social Movements*, 183–206. London: Routledge.

Eggen, Dan (2010) "How Interest Groups Behind Healthcare Legislation Are Finances Is Often Unclear," in *The Washington Post* (January 7): A1.

Ehrenberg, Andrew S.C. (1974) "Repetitive Advertising and the Consumer," in *Journal of Advertising Research* 14: 25–34.

Einwiller, S.A., A. Fedorikhin, A.R. Johnson, and M.A. Kamins (2006) "Enough is Enough! When Identification No Longer Prevents Negative Corporate Associations," in *Journal of the Academy of Marketing Science* 34: 185–194.

Eisenberg, E.M. (1984) "Ambiguity as Strategy in Organizational Communication," in *Communication Monographs* 51: 227–242.

Elder, Charles D., and Roger W. Cobb (1983) *The Political Uses of Symbols*. New York: Longman.

Elder, Randy W., Ruth A. Shults, David A. Sleet, James J. Nichols, Robert S. Thompson, and Warda Rajab (2004) "Effectiveness of Mass Media Campaigns for Reducing Drinking and Driving and Alcohol-Involved Crashes," in *American Journal of Preventative Medicine* 27: 57–65.

Ellul, Jacques (1965) *Propaganda: The Formation of Men's Attitudes*. New York: Alfred A. Knopf.

Entman, Robert M. (1993) "Framing: Toward Clarification of a Fractured Paradigm," *Journal of Communication* 43: 51–58.

——. (2003) "Cascading Activation: Contesting the White House's Frame After 9/11," in *Political Communication* 20: 415–432.

——. (2004) *Projections of Power: Framing News, Public Opinion, and U.S. Foreign Policy*. Chicago: University of Chicago Press.

——. (2008) "Theorizing Mediated Public Diplomacy: The U.S. Case," in *International Journal of Press/Politics* 13: 87–102.

Epstein, Edward Jay (1973) *News From Nowhere: Television and the News*. New York: Vintage Books.

Ereaut, Gill, and Nat Segnit (2006) *Warm Words: How Are We Telling the Climate Story and Can We Tell it Better?* London: Institute for Public Policy Research.

Essig, Mark (2003) *Edison & the Electric Chair: A Story of Light and Death*. New York: Walker & Company.

Ettinger, Karl E. (1946) "Foreign Propaganda in America," in *Public Opinion Quarterly* 10: 329–342.

Evan, William M., ed. (1981) *Knowledge and Power in a Global Society*. Beverly Hills, CA: Sage.

Eveland, William P., Jr., Andrew F. Hayes, Dhavan V. Shah, and Nojin Kwak (2005) "Understanding the Relationship Between Communication and Political Knowledge: A Model Comparison Approach Using Panel Data," in *Political Communication* 22: 423–446.

Faber, Daniel (2005) "Building a Transnational Environmental Justice Movement: Obstacles and Opportunities in the Age of Globalization," in Joe Bandy and Jackie Smith, eds. *Coalitions Across Borders: Transnational Protest and the Neoliberal Order*, 43–68. Lanham, MD: Rowman & Littlefield.

Fast, William R. (2002) *Knowledge Strategies: Balancing Ends, Ways and Means in the Information Age*. Washington, DC: Institute for National Strategic Studies, National Defense University.

Feld, Werner J., and John K. Wildgen (1982) "The Public Image of NATO in the United States," in *Political Communication and Persuasion* 2: 65–85.

Feldner, Sarah Bonewits, and Rebecca J. Meisenbach (2007) "SaveDisney.Com and Activist Challenges: A Habermasian Perspective on Corporate Legitimacy," in *International Journal of Strategic Communication* 1:2-7-226.

Fernandez, Esteban, José M. Montes, and Camilo J. Vázquez (2000) "Typology and Strategic Analysis of Intangible Resources: A Resource-Based Approach," in *Technovation* 20: 81–92.

Festinger, Leon (1957) *A Theory of Cognitive Dissonance*. Stanford, CA: Stanford University Press.

——, ed. (1964) *Conflict, Decision, and Dissonance*. London: Tavistock.

Fishbein, Martin (1967a) "A Behavior Theory Approach to the Relations Between Beliefs About an Object and the Attitude Toward the Object," in Martin Fishbein, ed., *Readings in Attitude Theory and Measurement*, pp. 389–400. New York: John Wiley.

——. (1967b) "A Consideration of Beliefs and Their Role in Attitude Measurement," in Martin Fishbein, ed., *Readings in Attitude Theory and Measurement*, pp. 257–266. New York: John Wiley.

Fleming, Charles A. (1995) "Understanding Propaganda from a General Semantics Perspective," in *A Review of General Semantics* 52: 3–13.

Flynn, J., Paul Slovic, and C.K. Mertz (1993). "Decidedly Different: Expert and Public Views of Risks from a Radioactive Waste Repository," in *Risk Analysis*, 13, 643–648.

Flynn, Nancy (2006) *Blog Rules: A Business Guide to Managing Policy, Public Relations, and Legal Issues*. New York: American Management Association.

Fombrun, C., N.A. Gardberg, and J.M. Sever (2000) "The Reputation Quotient: A Multiple Stakeholder Measure of Corporate Reputation," *Journal of Brand Management* 7: 241–255.

Fox, Karen F.A., and Philip Kotler (1980) "The Marketing of Social Causes: The First Ten Years," *Journal of Marketing* 44: 24–33.

Freedman, Anne E., and P.E. Freedman (1975) *The Psychology of Political Control*. New York: St. Martin's Press.

Freeman, R. Edward (1984) *Strategic Management: A Stakeholder Approach*. Boston: Pitman Publishing.

Friedman, Monroe (1999) *Consumer Boycotts: Effecting Change Through the Marketplace and the Media*. New York: Routledge.

——— . (2004) "Using Consumer Boycotts to Stimulate Corporate Policy Changes: Marketplace, Media, and Moral Considerations," in Michele Micheletti, Andreas

Follesdal, and Dietlind Stolle, eds. *Politics, Products, and Markets: Exploring Political Consumerism Past and Present*, 45–82. New Brunswick, NJ: Transaction Books.

Fung, Archon, Tessa Hebb, and Joel Rogers, eds. (2001) *Working Capital: The Power of Labor's Pensions*. Ithaca: Cornell University Press.

Funkhouser, G. Ray, and Eugene F. Shaw (1990) "How Synthetic Experience Shapes Social Reality," in *Journal of Communication* 40: 75–87.

Gamson, William A. (1975) *The Strategy of Social Protest*. Homewood, IL: Dorsey Press.

Gamson, William A., and A. Modigliani (1989) "Media Discourse and Public Opinion on Nuclear Power: A Constructionist Approach," in *American Journal of Sociology* 95:1–37.

Gans, Herbert J. (1979) *Deciding What's News: A Study of CBS Evening News, NBC Nightly News, Newsweek and Time*. New York: Vintage Books.

Ganzi, John, Frances Seymour, and Sandy Buffet (1998) *Leverage for the Environment: A Guide to the Private Financial Services Industry*. Washington: World Resources Institute.

Gardberg, Naomi A., and Charles F. Fombrun (2002) "The Global Reputation Quotient Project: First Steps Towards a Cross–Nationally Valid Measure of Corporate Reputation," *Corporate Reputation Review* 4: 303–307.

Gardner, Bruce (1983) "Fact and Fiction in the Public Data Budget Crunch," *Journal of Agricultural Economics* 65: 882–888.

Gardner, Daniel (2008) *The Science of Fear: How the Culture of Fear Manipulates Your Brain*. London: Penguin Books.

Getman, Julius (1998) *The Betrayal of Local 14: Paperworkers, Politics, & Permanent Replacements*. Ithaca, NY: Cornell University Press.

Gibson, Rhonda, and Dolf Zillmann (1993) "The Impact of Quotation in News Reports on Issue Perception," in *Journalism Quarterly* 70: 793–800.

Giffard, C. Anthony, and Nancy K. Rivenburgh (2000) "News Agencies, National Images, and Global Media Events," in *Journalism Quarterly* 77: 8–21.

Gilboa, Eytan (2000) "Mass Communication and Diplomacy: A Theoretical Framework," in *Communication Theory* 10: 275–309.

Gilens, Martin (2001) "Political Ignorance and Collective Policy Preferences," in *American Political Science Review* 95: 379–396.

Glander, Timothy (2000) *Origins of Mass Communications Research During the American Cold War: Educational Effects and Contemporary Implications* Mahwah, NJ: Lawrence Erlbaum Associates.

Goldhaber, Michael D. (2009) "A Win for Wiwa, a Win for Shell, a Win for Corporate Human Rights," in *The American Lawyer* (June 11).

Gordon, Sanford C., and Catherine Hafer (2005) "Flexing Muscle: Corporate Political Expenditures as Signals to the Bureaucracy," *American Political Science Review* 99: 245–261.

Gottleib, Robert (1991) "An Odd Assortment of Allies: American Environmentalism in the 1990s," in Craig L. LaMay and Everette E. Dennis, eds., *Media and the Environment*, 43–54. Washington, DC: Freedom Forum Media Studies Center.

Gough, Susan L. (2003) *The Evolution of Strategic Influence*. Carlisle Barracks, PA: U.S. Army War College.

Graber, Doris A. (1976) *Verbal Behavior and Politics*. Urbana: University of Illinois Press.

——. (1981) "Political Languages," in Dan Nimmo and Keith R. Sanders, eds., *Handbook of Political Communication*, 195–223. Beverly Hills, CA: Sage.

——. (1984) *Processing the News: How People Tame the Information Tide*. New York: Longman.

——. (2001) *Processing Politics: Learning from Television in the Internet Age*. Chicago: University of Chicago Press.

Grant, Andrew J., and Ian Taylor (2004) "Global Governance and Conflict Diamonds: The Kimberley Process and the Quest for Clean Gems," in *Round Table* 93: 385–401.

Gray, Jonathan (2001) "Striking Social Dramas, Image Events, and Meme Warfare: Performance and Social Activism—Past, Present, and Future," in *Text and Performance Quarterly* 21: 64–75.

Gready, Paul (2004) "Conceptualizing Globalisation and Human Rights: Boomerangs and Borders," in *International Journal of Human Rights* 8: 345–354.

Greenberg, Donald W. (1985) "Staging Media Events to Achieve Legitimacy: A Case Study of Britain's Friends of the Earth," in *Political Communication and Persuasion* 2: 347–362.

Greer, Jed, and Kavaljit Singh (1995) *TNCs and India: An Activists' Guide to Research and Campaign on Transnational Corporations*. New Delhi: Public Interest Research Group.

Gregory, Sam, Gillian Caldwell, Ronit Avni, and Thomas Harding, eds. (2005) *Video for Change: A Guide for Advocacy and Activism*. London: Pluto Press.

Grunig, James E. (1989) "Publics, Audiences, and Market Segments: Segmentation Principles for Campaigns," in Charles T. Salmon, ed., *Information Campaigns: Balancing Social Values and Social Change*, 199–228. Thousand Oaks, CA: Sage.

Grupp, Fred W., Jr. (1971) "Personal Satisfaction Derived from Membership in the John Birch Society," in *Western Political Quarterly* 24: 79–83.

Hall, Edward T. (1971) *Beyond Culture*. New York: Anchor/Doubleday.

Hall, R. (1992) "The Strategic Analysis of Intangible Resources," in *Strategic Management Journal* 13: 135–144.

Hallahan, Kirk (1999) "Seven Models of Framing: Implications for Public Relations," in *Journal of Public Relations Research* 11: 205–242.

Hamilton, Mark A. (1997) "The Phase-Interfaced Omnistructure Underlying the Processing of Persuasive Messages," in George A. Barnett and Franklin J. Boster, eds., *Progress in Communication Sciences, Volume XIII*. Greenwich, CT: Ablex: 1–42.

Hammes, Thomas X. (2005) "Insurgency: Modern Warfare Evolves into a Fourth generation," in *Strategic Forum*, #214: 1–7. Institute for National Strategic Studies, National Defense University, Washington, DC.

Hansen, Anders (1991) "The Media and the Social Construction of the Environment," in *Media, Culture and Society* 13: 443–458.

——. (2000) "Claims-Making and Framing in British Newspaper Coverage of the 'Brent Spar' Controversy," in Stuart Allan, Barbara Adam, and Cynthia Carter, eds. (2000) *Environmental Risk and the Media*, 55–72. London: Routledge.

Heider, Fritz (1946) "Attitudes and Cognitive Organization," in *Journal of Psychology* 21: 107–112.

Henry, Gary T., and Craig S. Gordon (2001) "Tracking Issue Attention: Specifying the Dynamics of the Public Agenda," in *Public Opinion Quarterly* 65: 157–177.

Herman, Edward S., and Noam Chomsky (1988) *Manufacturing Consent: The Political Economy of the Mass Media*. New York: Pantheon Books.

Hilgartner, Stephen, and Charles L. Bosk (1988) "The Rise and Fall of Social Problems: A Public Arenas Model," in *American Journal of Sociology* 94: 53–78.

Hochschild, Adam (2005) *Bury the Chains: Prophets and Rebels in the Fight to Free an Empire's Slaves.* Boston: Houghton Mifflin.

Hoffer, Charles R. (1942) "A Sociological Analysis of Propaganda," *Social Forces* 20: 445–448.

Holbrook, Allyson L., Matthew K. Berent, Jon A. Krosnick, Penny S. Visser, and David S. Boninger (2005) "Attitude Importance and the Accumulation of Attitude-Relevant Knowledge in Memory," in *Journal of Personality and Social Psychology* 88: 749–769.

Holmström, Susanne, Jesper Falkheimer, and Astrid Gade Nielsen (2010) "Legitimacy and Strategic Communication in Globalization: The Cartoon Crisis and Other Legitimacy Conflicts," in *International Journal of Strategic Communication* 4: 1–18.

Holsti, Ole R. (1967) "Cognitive Dynamics and Images of the Enemy," in *Journal of International Affairs* 21: 16–39.

Hovland, Carl I., Arthur A. Lumsdaine, and Fred D. Sheffield (1949) *Experiments in Mass Communication*. Princeton, NJ: Princeton University Press.

Hovland, Carl I., and Walter Weiss (1951–1952) "The Influence of Source Credibility on Communication Effectiveness," in *Public Opinion Quarterly* 15: 635–650.

Howard, Philip (2006) *New Media Campaigns and the Managed Citizen*. New York: Cambridge University Press.

Hsu, Spencer S. (2007) "FEMA Official Apologizes for Staged Briefing with Fake Reporters," *Washington Post* (October 27): A3.

Huff, Darrell (1954) *How to Lie with Statistics*. New York: W.W. Norton.

Hutchinson, William (2006) "Information Warfare and Deception," in *Informing Science* 9: 213–223.

Huxham, Mark, and David Sumner (1999) "Emotion, Science, and Rationality: The Case of the *Brent Spar*," in *Environmental Values* 8: 349–368.

Hyman, Herbert H., and Paul B. Sheatsley (1947) "Some Reasons Why Information Campaigns Fail," in *Public Opinion Quarterly* 11: 412–423.

Ihlen, Øyvind, and Mike Nitz (2008) "Framing Contests in Environmental Disputes: Paying Attention to Media and Cultural Master Frames," in *International Journal of Strategic Communication* 2: 1–18.

Institute for Propaganda Analysis (1937) "How to Detect Propaganda," in *Propaganda Analysis* 1: 1–4.

Institute of Communications Research (1955) *Four Working Papers on Propaganda Theory*. Urbana, IL: University of Illinois.

International Advocacy Non-Governmental Organisations Workshop (2006) *International Non Governmental Organisations' Accountability Charter*. Johannesburg, South Africa.

Iyengar, Shanto (1991) *Is Anyone Responsible? How Television Frames Political Issues*. Chicago: University of Chicago Press.

Iyengar, Shanto, and Donald R. Kinder (1987) *News That Matters: Television and American Opinion*. Chicago: University of Chicago Press.

Jacobs, Lawrence R., and Benjamin I. Page (2005) "Who Influences U.S. Foreign Policy?" in *American Political Science Review* 99: 107–135.

Jamieson, Kathleen Hall, and Karlyn Kohrs Campbell (2001) *The Interplay of Influence: News, Advertising, Politics, and the Mass Media*, fifth edition. Belmont, CA: Wadsworth.

Jarley, Paul, and Cheryl Maranto (1990) "Union Corporate Campaigns: An Assessment," in *Industrial and Labor Relations Review* 43: 505–524.

Jessee, Davin D. (2006) "Tactical Means, Strategic Ends: Al Qaeda's Use of Denial and Deception, " in *Terrorism and Political Violence* 18: 367–388.

Jha, Sonora (2007) "Exploring Internet Influence on the Coverage of Social Protest: Content Analysis Comparing protest Coverage in 1967 and 1999," in *Journalism and Mass Communication Quarterly* 84: 40–57.

Johns, Gary (2001) "Protocols with NGOs: The Need to Know," in *IPA Backgrounder* 13: 1–16.

Johnson, Eric, and John D. McCarthy (2005) "The Sequencing of Transnational and Social Movement Mobilization: The Organizational Mobilization of the Global and U.S. Environmental Movements," in Donatella Della Porta and Sidney Tarrow, eds. *Transnational Protest and Global Activism*, 71–93. Lanham, MD: Rowman & Littlefield.

Johnson, Richard M. (1971) "Market Segmentation: A Strategic Management Tool," in *Journal of Marketing Research* 8: 13–19.

Johnson-Cartee, Karen S. (2004) *News Narratives and News Framing: Constructing Political Reality*. Lanham, MD: Rowman & Littlefield.

Jones, Richard (2005) "Finding Sources of Brand Value: Developing a Stakeholder Model of Brand Equity," in *Journal of Brand Management* 13: 10–32.

Juravitch, Tom, and Kate Bronfenbrenner (1999) *Ravenswood: The Steelworkers' Victory and the Revival of American Labor*. Ithaca, NY: Cornell University Press.

Kahneman, Daniel (2003) "A Perspective on Judgment and Choice: Mapping Bounded Rationality," in *American Psychologist* 58: 697–720.

Kahneman, Daniel, and Amos Tversky (1979) "Prospect Theory: An Analysis of Decision Under Risk," in *Econometrica* 47: 263–291.

Kaid, Lynda Lee, ed. (2004) *Handbook of Political Communication Research*. Mahwah, NJ: Lawrence Erlbaum Associates.

Kane, Paul (2009) "'Jane Roe' Arrested at Supreme Court Hearing," in *Washington Post* (July 13).

Kaplowitz, Stan A., and Edward L. Fink (1997) "Message Discrepancy and Persuasion," in George A. Barnett and Franklin J. Boster, eds., *Progress in Communication Sciences, Volume XIII*. Greenwich, CT: Ablex: 75–106.

Karpf, David (2008) "Understanding Blogspace," in *Journal of Information Technology & Politics* 5: 369–385.

——. (2009) "Why Bowl Alone When You Can Flashmob the Bowling Alley? Implications of the Mobile Web for Online-Offline Reputation Systems," paper presented at the WebSci'09 Conference, Athens, Greece.

Kasperson, Roger E., and Jeanne X. Kasperson (1996) "Social Amplification and Attenuation of Risk," in *Annals of the American Academy of Political and Social Science* 545: 95–105.

Kasperson, Roger E., Ortwin Renn, Paul Slovic, Halina S. Brown, Jacque Emel, Robert Goble, Jeanne X. Kasperson, and Samuel Ratick (1988) "The Social Amplification of Risk: A Conceptual Framework," in *Risk Analysis* 8: 177–187.

Katz, Daniel (1960) "The Functional Approach to the Study of Attitudes," in *Public Opinion Quarterly* 24: 163–204.

Katz, Elihu (1961) "The Social Itinerary of Technical Change: Two Studies of the Diffusion of Innovation," in *Human Organization* 20: 70–82.

Katz, Elihu, and Paul F. Lazarsfeld (1955) *Personal Influence: The Part Played by People in Mass Communications*. New York: Free Press.

Katz, Elihu, Jay G. Blumler, and Michael Gurevitch (1973) "Uses and Gratifications Research," in *Public Opinion Quarterly* 37: 509–523.

Katz, Helen (2003) *The Media Handbook: A Complete Guide to Advertising, Media Selection, Planning, Research, and Buying*. Mahwah, NJ: Lawrence Erlbaum Associates.

Keck, Margaret E., and Kathryn Sikkink (1998) *Activists Beyond Borders: Advocacy Networks in International Politics*. Ithaca: Cornell University Press.

Kelly, George A. (1963) "The Expert as Historical Actor," in *Daedalus* 92: 529–548.

Kelman, Herbert C. (1958) "Compliance, Identification, and Internalization: Three Processes of Attitude Change," in *Journal of Conflict Resolution* 2: 51–60.

——. (1961) "Processes of Opinion Change," in *Public Opinion Quarterly* 25: 57–78.

——. (1969) "Manipulation of Human Behavior: An Ethical Dilemma for the Social Scientist," in Warren G. Bennis, Kenneth D. Benne, and Robert Chin, eds. *The Planning of Change*, second edition, 582–595. New York: Holt, Rinehart and Winston.

Kiesler, Charles A., Barry E. Collins, and Norman Miller (1969) *Attitude Change: A Critical Analysis of Theoretical Approaches*. New York: John Wiley.

Kiousis, Spiro, and Xu Wu (2008) "International Agenda-Building and Agenda-Setting: Exploring the Influence of Public Relations Counsel on US News media and Public Perceptions of Foreign Nations," in *International Communication Gazette* 70: 58–75.

Klein, Maury (2008) *The Power Makers: Steam, Electricity, and the Men Who Invented Modern America*. New York: Bloomsbury Press.

Klingemann, Hans-Dieter, and Andrea Römmele, eds. (2002) *Public Information Campaigns & Opinion Research: A Handbook for the Student & Practitioner*. London: Sage.

Knoke, David (1990) *Political Networks: The Structural Perspective.* Cambridge: Cambridge University Press.

Knoke, David, and James H. Kuklinski (1982) *Network Analysis.* Beverly Hills, CA: Sage Publications.

Knowles, Eric S., and Jay A. Linn, eds. (2004a) *Resistance and Persuasion.* Mahwah, NJ: Lawrence Erlbaum Associates.

——. (2004b) "Approach-Avoidance Model of Persuasion: Alpha and Omega Strategies for Change," in Eric S. Knowles and Jay A. Linn, eds. *Resistance and Persuasion*, 117–148. Mahwah, NJ: Lawrence Erlbaum Associates.

Knutson, Jeanne. N, ed. (1973) *Handbook of Political Psychology.* San Francisco, CA: Jossey-Bass.

Koster, Josh, and Tyler Davis (2010) "Nanotargeted Pressure: How digital ads helped turn CNN's Lou Dobbs problem into a PR nightmare," in *Politics Magazine* 287 (February), found online at http://www.politicsmagazine.com/magazine-issues/february-2010-the-case-study-issue.

Kotler, Philip, and Sidney J. Levy (1969) "Broadening the Concept of Marketing," in *Journal of Marketing* 33: 10–15.

Kotler, Philip, Ned Roberto, and Nancy Lee (2002) *Social Marketing: Improving the Quality of Life*, second edition. Thousand Oaks, CA: Sage Publications.

Kraus, Sidney, and Richard M. Perloff, eds. (1985) *Mass Media and Political Thought: An Information Processing Approach.* Beverly Hills, CA: Sage.

Kraus, Sidney, Dennis Davis, Gladys Engel Lang, and Kurt Lang (1975) "Critical Events Analysis," in Steven H. Chaffee, ed., *Political Communication: Issues and Strategies for Research.* Beverly Hills: Sage: 195–216.

Kriesel, Melvin E. (1985) "Psychological Operations: A Strategic View," in National Defense University, *Essays on Strategy: Selections from the 1984 Joint Chiefs of Staff Essay Competition*, 53–103.

Krosnik, Jon A. (1988) "Attitude Importance and Attitude Change," in *Journal of Experimental Social Psychology* 24: 240–255.

Krosnick, Jon A., and Donald R. Kinder. (1990) "Altering the Foundations of Support for the President Through Priming," in *American Political Science Review* 84: 497–512.

Krugman, Edward P., ed. (2008) *Consumer Behavior and Advertising Involvement: Selected Works of Herbert E. Krugman.* New York: Routledge.

Krugman, Herbert E. (1964) "Some Applications of Pupil Measurement," in *Journal of Marketing Research* 28: 15–19.

——. (1965) "The Impact of Television Advertising: Learning Without Involvement," *Public Opinion Quarterly* 29: 349–356.

——. (1966) "The Measurement of Advertising Involvement," *Public Opinion Quarterly* 30: 583–596.

——. (1971) "Brain Wave Measures of Media Involvement," *Journal of Advertising Research* 11: 3–10.

——. (1977) "Memory Without Recall, Exposure Without Perception," in *Journal of Advertising Research* 17: 7–12.

Krugman, Herbert E., and Eugene L. Hartley (1970) "Passive Learning from Television," *Public Opinion Quarterly* 34: 184–190.

Kunczik, Michael (1997) *Images of Nations and International Public Relations.* Mahwah, NJ: Lawrence Erlbaum Associates.

LaBotz, Dan (1991) *A Troublemaker's Handbook: How to Fight Back Where You Work—and Win!* Detroit: Labor Notes.

Laidler-Kylander, Nathalie, John A. Quelch, and Bernard L. Simonin (2007) "Building and Valuing Global Brands in the Nonprofit Sector," in *NonProfit Management & Leadership* 17: 253–277.

Lane, Robert E., and David O. Sears (1964) *Public Opinion*. Englewood Cliffs, NJ: Prentice-Hall.

Lange, Jonathan (1993) "The Logic of Competing Information Campaigns: Conflict over Old Growth and the Spotted Owl," in *Communication Monographs* 60.

Lanzetta, John T., Denis G. Sullivan, Roger D. Masters, and Gregory J. McHugo (1985) "Emotional and Cognitive Responses to Televised Images of Political Leaders," in Sidney Kraus and Richard M. Perloff, eds., *Mass Media and Political Thought: An Information Processing Approach*, 85–116. Beverly Hills, CA: Sage.

Lasswell, Harold D. (1927) *Propaganda Technique in the World War*. New York: Knopf.

LeBaron, Michelle (2003) "Communication Tools for Understanding Cultural Differences," in Guy Burgess and Heidi Burgess, eds. *Beyond Intractability*. Conflict Resolution Consortium, University of Colorado, Boulder. Published online at http://www.beyondintractability.org/essay/communication_tools/.

Lee, Alfred McClung (1944) "Interest Criteria in Propaganda Analysis," in *American Sociological Review* 10: 282–288.

——. (1945) "The Analysis of Propaganda: A Clinical Summary," in *American Journal of Sociology* 51: 126–135.

Lee, Suman (2007) "International Public Relations as a Predictor of Prominence of US News Coverage," in *Public Relations Review* 33: 158–165.

Lee, Suman, and Youngmin Yoon (2010) "Return on Investment (ROI) of International Public Relations: A Country-Level Analysis," in *Public Relations Review* 36: 15–20.

Leizerov, Sagi (2000) "Privacy Advocacy Groups versus Intel: A Case Study of How Social Movements are Tactically Using the Internet to Fight Corporations," in *Social Science Computer Review* 18: 461–483.

Lemert, James B. (1981) *Does Mass Communication Change Public Opinion After All? A New Approach to Effects Analysis*. Chicago: Nelson-Hall.

Levin, Kenneth D., Diana R. Nichols, and Blair T. Johnson (2000) "Involvement and Persuasion: Attitude Functions for the Motivated Processor," in Gregory R. Maio and James M. Olson, eds. *Why We Evaluate: Functions of Attitude*: 163–194. Mahwah, NJ: Lawrence Erlbaum Associates.

Lewin, Kurt (1936) *Principles of Topological Psychology*. New York: McGraw Hill.

Lippmann, Walter (1922) *Public Opinion*. New York: Harcourt Brace.

Lipsky, Michael (1968) "Protest as a Political Resource," in *American Political Science Review* 62: 1144–1158.

Livingston, Steven (1994) *The Terrorism Spectacle*. Boulder, CO: Westview Press.

——. (1999) "The New Information Environment and Diplomacy," paper presented at the Annual Meeting of the International Studies Association, Washington, DC.

Livingston, Steven, and W. Lance Bennett (2003) "Gatekeeping, Indexing, and Live-Event News: Is Technology Altering the Construction of News?" in *Political Communication* 20: 363–380.

Lundy, Lisa K. (2006) "Effect of Framing on Cognitive Processing in Public Relations," in *Public Relations Review* 32: 295–301.

Luntz, Frank (2007) *Words That Work: It's Not What You Say, It's What People Hear*. New York: Hyperion.

Lupia, Arthur, and Jesse O. Menning (2009) "When Can Politicians Scare Citizens Into Supporting Bad Policies?," in *American Journal of Political Science* 53: 90–106.

MacFarquhar, Neil (2007) "At State Dept., Blog Team Joins Muslim Debate," in *New York Times* (September 22).

Machiavelli, Niccolò (1992) *The Prince*. Translated by W.K. Marriott. New York: Alfred A. Knopf.

MacMillan, Keith, Kevin Money, Steve Downing, and Carola Hillenbrand (2004) "Giving Your Organization SPIRIT: An Overview and Call to Action for Directors on Issues of Corporate Governance, Corporate reputation and Corporate Responsibility," in *Journal of General Management* 30: 15–42.

Maio, Gregory R., and James M. Olson, eds. (2000a) *Why We Evaluate: Functions of Attitude*. Mahwah, NJ: Lawrence Erlbaum Associates.

——. (2000b) "What is a Value-Expressive Attitude?" in Gregory R. Maio and James M. Olson, eds. *Why We Evaluate: Functions of Attitude*: 249–270. Mahwah, NJ: Lawrence Erlbaum Associates.

Maney, Gregory M. (2002) "Transnational Structures and Protest: Linking Theories and Assessing Evidence," in Jackie Smith and Hank Johnston, eds., *Globalization and Resistance: Transnational Dimensions of Social Movements*, 31–50. Oxford, England: Rowman & Littlefield.

Manheim, Jarol B. (1976) "Can Democracy Survive Television?" in *Journal of Communication* 26: 84–90.

——. (1987) "A Model of Agenda Dynamics," in Margaret L. McLaughlin, ed. *Communication Yearbook 10*. Beverly Hills, CA: Sage Publications, pp. 499–516.

——, (1990) "Rites of Passage: The 1988 Seoul Olympics as Public Diplomacy," in *Political Research Quarterly* 43: 279–295.

——. (1991) *All of the People, All the Time: Strategic Communication in American Politics*. Armonk, NY: M.E. Sharpe.

——. (1994a) *Strategic Public Diplomacy and American Foreign Policy: The Evolution of Influence*. New York: Oxford University Press.

——. (1994b) "Strategic Public Diplomacy: Managing Kuwait's Image During the Gulf Conflict," in W. Lance Bennett and David Paletz, eds. *Taken By Storm: The Media, Public Opinion, and Foreign Policy in the Gulf War*, 131–148. Chicago: University of Chicago Press.

——. (2000) *Corporate Conduct Unbecoming: Codes of Conduct and Anti-Corporate Strategy*. St. Michaels, MD: Tred Avon Institute Press.

——. (2001) *The Death of a Thousand Cuts: Corporate Campaigns and the Attack on the Corporation*. Mahwah, NJ: Lawrence Erlbaum Associates.

——. (2004) *Biz-War and the Out-of-Power Elite: The Progressive Attack on the Corporation*. Mahwah, NJ: Lawrence Erlbaum Associates.

——. (2005a) *Power Failure, Power Surge: Union Pension Fund Activism and the Publicly Held Corporation*. Washington: HR Policy Association.

——. (2005b) "The Strategic Use of Social Responsibility Investing," in Jon Entine, ed., *Pension Fund Politics: The Dangers of Socially Responsible Investing*, 81–101. Washington: American Enterprise Institute.

——. (2008) "The News Shapers: Strategic Communication as a Third Force in Newsmaking," in Doris A. Graber, Denis McQuail, and Pippa Norris, eds. *The Politics of News, The News of Politics*, second ed., 98–116. Washington: CQ Press.

Manheim, Jarol B., and Robert B. Albritton (1984) "Changing National Images: International Public Relations and Media Agenda Setting," in *American Political Science Review* 78: 641–654.

——. (1987) "Insurgent Violence versus Image Management: The Struggle for National Images in Southern Africa," in *British Journal of Political Science* 17:201–218.

Manheim, Jarol B., and Cornelius B. Pratt (1986) "Communicating Corporate Social Responsibility," in *Public Relations Review* 12: 9–18.

Margolis, Michael, and Gary A. Mauser, eds. (1989) *Manipulating Public Opinion: Essays on Public Opinion as a Dependent Variable*. Pacific Grove, CA: Brooks Cole.

Marlin, Randal (2002) *Propaganda & the Ethics of Persuasion*. Peterborough, Ontario, Canada: Broadview Press.

Martel, Myles (1983) *Political Campaign Debates: Images, Strategies, and Tactics*. New York: Longman.

Martin, Christopher R. (2004) *Framed: Labor and the Corporate Media*. Ithaca, New York: Cornell University Press.

Martin, L. John (1971) "Effectiveness of International Propaganda," in *Annals of the American Academy of Political and Social Science* 398: 61–70.

——. (1982) "Disinformation: An Instrumentality in the Propaganda Arsenal," in *Political Communication and Persuasion* 2: 47–64.

Martin, Paul S. (2008) "The Mass Media as Sentinel: Why Bad News About Issues is Good News for Participation," in *Political Communication* 25: 180–193.

McCarthy, John D., and Mayer N. Zald (1977) "Resource Mobilization and Social Movements: A Partial Theory," in *American Journal of Sociology* 82: 1212–1241.

McCombs, Maxwell D. (2004) *Setting the Agenda: The Mass Media and Public Opinion*. Cambridge, England: Polity Press.

McCombs, Maxwell D., and Donald E. Shaw (1972) "The Agenda-Setting Function of Mass Media," *Public Opinion Quarterly* 36: 176–187.

McCormick, John P. (2001) "Machiavellian Democracy: Controlling Elites with Ferocious Populism," in *American Political Science Review* 95: 297–313.

McCornack, Steven A. (1992) "Information Manipulation Theory," in *Communication Monographs* 59: 1–16.

McCornack, Steven A., Timothy R. Levine, Kathleen Solowcsuk, Helen I. Torres, and Dedra M. Campbell (1992) "When the Alteration of Information is Viewed as Deception: An Empirical Test of Information Manipulation Theory," in *Communication Monographs* 59: 17–29.

McGuire, William J. (1961) "Resistance to persuasion conferred by active and passive prior refutation of the same and alternative counterarguments," in *Journal of Abnormal and Social Psychology* 63: 326–332.

——. (1976) "Some Internal Psychological Factors Influencing Consumer Choice," in *Journal of Consumer Research* 2: 303–319.

——. (1989) "Theoretical Foundations of Campaigns," in Ronald E. Rice and Charles K. Atkins, eds., *Public Communication Campaigns*, second edition (Newbury Park, CA: Sage Publications), pp. 43–65.

McGuire, William J., and Demetrios Papageorgis (1962) "Effectiveness of Forewarning in Developing Resistance to Persuasion," in *Public Opinion Quarterly* 26: 24–34.

McLeod, Jack M., and Benjamin H. Detenber (1999) "Framing Effects of Television Coverage of Social Protest," in *Journal of Communication* 49: 3–23.

McNelly, John T., and Fausto Izcaray (1986) "International News Exposure and Images of Nations," in *Journalism Quarterly* 63: 546–553.

Mendelsohn, Harold (1973) "Some Reasons Why Information Campaigns Can Succeed," *Public Opinion Quarterly* 37: 50–65.

Menn, Joseph (2010a) "Hackers Target Friends of Google Workers," in *Financial Times* (January 25).

——. (2010b) "Cyberattack Threat to US Groups," in *Financial Times* (January 25).

Merritt, Richard L. (1980) "Transforming International Communications Strategies," in *Political Communication and Persuasion* 1: 5–42.

Messick, David M. (1999) "Dirty Secrets: Strategic Uses of Ignorance and Uncertainty," in L.L. Thompson, J.M. Levine and D.M. Messick, eds.. *Shared Cognition in Organizations: The Management of Knowledge*, 71–88. Mahwah, NJ: Lawrence Erlbaum Associates.

Metaxas, Eric (2007) *Amazing Grace: William Wilberforce and the Heroic Campaign to End Slavery*. New York: Harper Collins.

Meyer, David S., and Joshua Gamson (1995) "The Challenge of Cultural Elites: Celebrities and Social Movements," in *Sociological Inquiry* 62: 181–206.

Micheletti, Michele, Andreas Follesdal, and Dietlind Stolle, eds. (2004) *Politics, Products, and Markets: Exploring Political Consumerism Past and Present*. New Brunswick, NJ: Transaction Books.

Micheletti, Michele, and Dietlind Stolle (2004) "A Case of Discursive Political Consumerism: The Nike E-mail Exchange," in *Political Consumerism: Its Motivations, Power, and Conditions in the Nordic Countries and Elsewhere*. Proceedings of the Second International Seminar on Political Consumerism, Oslo August 26–29, 2004: 255–290.

Miller, Gerald R., and James B. Stiff (1993) *Deceptive Communication*. Newbury Park, CA: Sage.

Miller, M. Mark, and Bonnie Parnell Riechert (2000) "Interest Group Strategies and Journalistic Norms," in Stuart Allan, Barbara Adam, and Cynthia Carter, eds. (2000) *Environmental Risk and the Media*, 45–54. London: Routledge.

Mills, C. Wright (1956) *The Power Elite*. New York: Oxford University Press.

Mitchell, Ronald K., Bradley R. Agle, and Donna J. Wood (1997) "Toward a Theory of Stakeholder Identification and Salience: Defining the Principle of Who and What Really Counts," *Academy of Management Review* 22: 853–886.

Mlodinow, Leonard (2008) *The Drunkard's Walk: How Randomness Rules Our Lives*. New York: Vintage Books.

Molotch, Harvey, and Marilyn Lester (1974) "News as Purposive Behavior: On the Strategic Use of Routine Events, Accidents, and Scandals," in *American Sociological Review* 39: 101–112.

——. (1975) "Accidental News: The Great Oil Spill as Local Occurrence and National Event," in *American Journal of Sociology* 81: 235–260.

Mondak, Jeffrey J., Diana C. Mutz, and Robert Huckfeldt (1996) "Persuasion in Context: The Multilevel Structure of Economic Evaluations," in Diana C. Mutz, Paul M. Sniderman, and Richard A. Brody, eds. *Political Persuasion and Attitude Change*, 249–266. Ann Arbor: University of Michigan Press.

Money, Kevin, and Carola Hillenbrand (2006) "Using Reputation Measurement to Create Value: An Analysis and Integration of Existing Measures," in *Journal of General Management* 32: 1–12.

Monge, Peter R., and Noshir S. Contractor (2003) *Theories of Communication Networks*. New York: Oxford University Press.

Morin, Arthur L. (1994) "Regulating the Flow of Data: OMB and the Control of Government Information," in *Public Administration Review* 54: 434–443.

Morris, Harvey (2010a) "US lobbyists push for tough laws on Iran," in *Financial Times* (February 28), found online at http://www.ft.com/cms/s/0/ff151e5a-2490-11df-8be0-00144feab49a.html.

——. (2010b) "Caterpillar bows to pressure and severs its trading links with Iran," in *Financial Times* (March 1), found online at http://www.ft.com/cms/s/0/30d15d3c-24d2-11df-8be0-00144feab49a.html.

——. (2010c) "Activists target KPMG over Iran ties," in *Financial Times* (March 14), found online at http://www.ft.com/cms/s/0/38e9be40-2fd3-11df-9153-00144feabdc0.html.

——. (2010d) "KPMG severs Iran ties," in *Financial Times* (April 2), found online at http://www.ft.com/cms/s/0/2f514e22-3e77-11df-a706-00144feabdc0.html.

Moyer, Bill (2001) *Doing Democracy: The MAP Model for Organizing Social Movements*. Gabriola Island, BC, Canada: New Society Publishers.

Mueller, Claus (1973) *The Politics of Communication: A Study in the Political Sociology of Language, Socialization, and Legitimation*. Oxford, UK: Oxford University Press.

Mutz, Diana C. (2006) *Hearing the Other Side: Deliberative Versus Participatory Democracy*. New York: Cambridge University Press.

Mutz, Diana C., and Byron Reeves (2005) "The New Videomalaise: Effects of Televised Incivility on Political Trust," in *American Political Science Review* 99: 1–15.

Myers, Daniel J. (1994) "Communication Technology and Social Movements: Contributions of Computer Networks to Activism," in *Social Science Computer Review* 12: 250–260.

Nelson, Thomas E., Zoe Oxley, and Rosalee A. Clawson (1997) "Toward a Psychology of Framing Effects," *Political Behavior* 19: 221–247.

Nepstad, Sharon Erickson (2002) "Creating Transnational Solidarity: The Use of Narrative in the U.S.–Central America Peace Movement," in Jackie Smith and Hank Johnston, eds. *Globalization and Resistance: Transnational Dimensions of Social Movements* 133–149. Oxford, England: Rowman & Littlefield.

Neuman, W. Russell, Marion R. Just, and Ann N. Crigler, eds. (1992) *Common Knowledge: News and the Construction of Political Meaning*. Chicago: University of Chicago Press.

Newman, Bruce I., ed. (1999) *Handbook of Political Marketing*. Thousand Oaks, CA: Sage.

Nichols, Nick (2001) *Rules for Corporate Warriors: How to Fight and Survive Attack Group Shakedowns*. Bellevue, WA: Free Enterprise Press.

Nimmo, Dan (1974) *Popular Images of Politics*. Englewood Cliffs, NJ: Prentice-Hall.

Nimmo, Dan D., and Keith R. Sanders, eds. (1981) *Handbook of Political Communication*. Beverly Hills, CA: Sage.

Noelle-Neumann, Elizabeth (1974) "The Spiral of Silence," in *Journal of Communication* 24: 43–51.

Nohrstedt, Stig Arne, and Admassu Tassew (1993) "Communication and Crisis: An Inventory of Current Research", in *Psykologiskt Försvar Rapport* 163. Stockholm, Sweden.

Norris, Pippa, Montague Kern, and Marion Just, eds. (2003) *Framing Terrorism: The News Media, the Government and the Public*. London: Routledge.

North American Congress on Latin America (1970) *NACLA Research Methodology Guide*. New York.

Nothhaft, Howard, and Stefan Wehmeier (2007) "Coping with Complexity: Sociocybernetics as a Framework for Communication Management," in *International Journal of Strategic Communication* 1: 151–168.

Nye, Joseph S., Jr. (2004) *Soft Power: The Means to Success in World Politics*. New York: Public Affairs.

Odugbemi, Sina, and Thomas Jacobson, eds. (2008) *Governance Reform: Citizens, Stakeholders, and Voice*. Washington, DC: World Bank.

Offner, Amy (2010) "Winning a Sit-In," in *Labor Notes* (January 4). Found online at http://labornotes.org/print/blogs/2010/01/winning-sit.

O'Keefe, Daniel J. (2000) "Guilt and Social Influence," in M.E. Roloff, ed. *Communication Yearbook 23*: 67–101. Thousand Oaks, CA: Sage.

——, ed. (2002) *Persuasion: Theory and Research*, second edition. Thousand Oaks, CA: Sage Publications.

Oppenheimer, Martin, and George Lakey (1964) *A Manual for Direct Action*. Chicago: Quadrangle Books.

Osgood, Charles E. (1960) "Cognitive Dynamics in the Conduct of Human Affairs," in *Public Opinion Quarterly* 24: 341–365.

Osgood, Charles E., and Percy H. Tannenbaum (1955) "The Principle of Congruity in the Prediction of Attitude Change," in *Psychological Review* 62: 42–55.

Packard, Vance. (1957) *The Hidden Persuaders*. New York: David McKay.

Pan, Zhongdang, and Gerald M. Kosicki (1993) "Framing Analysis: An Approach to News Discourse," in *Political Communication* 10: 55–75.

Pattison, Philippa (1993) *Algebraic Models for Social Networks*. Cambridge: Cambridge University Press.

Payne, Rodger A. (2001) "Persuasion, Frames, and Norm Construction," *European Journal of International Relations* 7: 37–61.

Peizer, Jonathan (2006) *The Dynamics of Technology for Social Change*. New York: iUniverse.

Perloff, Richard M. (2003) *The Dynamics of Persuasion: Communication and Attitudes in the 21st Century*, second edition. Mahwah, NJ: Lawrence Erlbaum Associates.

Perry, Charles R. (1987) *Union Corporate Campaigns*. Philadelphia: The Wharton School of the University of Pennsylvania.

Peters, Glen (1999) *Waltzing With the Raptors: A Practical Roadmap to Protecting Your Company's Reputation*. New York: John Wiley.

Petty, Richard E., and John T. Cacioppo (1986) "The Elaboration Likelihood Model of Persuasion," in Leonard Berkowitz, ed., *Advances in Experimental Social Psychology* 19: 123–205. New York: Academic Press.

Petty, Richard E., and Joseph R. Priester (1994) "Mass Media Attitude Change: Implications of the Elaboration Likelihood Model of Persuasion," in Jennings Bryant and Dolf Zillman, eds. *Media Effects: Advances in Theory and Research*, 91–122. Hillsdale, NJ: Lawrence Erlbaum Associates.

Petty, Richard E., S. Christian Wheeler, and George Y. Bizer (2000) "Attitude Functions and Persuasion: An Elaboration Likelihood Approach to Matched Versus Mismatched Messages," in Gregory R. Maio and James M. Olson, eds. *Why We Evaluate: Functions of Attitude*: 133–162. Mahwah, NJ: Lawrence Erlbaum Associates.

Pfau, Michael (1997) "The Inoculation Model of Resistance to Persuasion," in George A. Barnett and Franklin J. Boster, eds., *Progress in Communication Sciences, Volume XIII*. Greenwich, CT: Ablex: 133–172.

Pickard, Victor W. (2006) "United Yet Autonomous: Indymedia and the Struggle to Sustain a Radical Democratic Network," in *Media, Culture & Society* 28: 315–336.

Pickerill, Jenny (2001) "Environmental Internet Activism in Britain," in *Peace Review* 13: 365–370.

Pitt, Catherine, Caroline Loehr, and Alankar Malviva (nd) "Campaigns, Evidence, and Policy Influence: Lessons from International NGOs," *Research and Policy in Development*. London: Overseas Development Institute.

Polgreen, Lydia (2008) "Oil Field Operation Suspended After Attack by Nigerian Rebels," in *New York Times* (June 20).

Pollay, Richard W. (1989) "Campaigns, Change, and Culture: On the Polluting Potential of Persuasion," in Charles T. Salmon, ed., *Information Campaigns: Balancing Social Values and Social Change* 185–196. Thousand Oaks, CA: Sage.

Pool, Ithiel de Sola, and Wilbur Schramm, eds. (1973) *Handbook of Communication*. Chicago, IL: Rand McNally.

Potter, Evan H. (2002) *Cyber-Diplomacy: Managing Foreign Policy in the Twenty-First Century*. Montreal: McGill-Queen's University Press.

Price, Tom (2000) *Cyber Activism: Advocacy Groups and the Internet*. Washington, DC: Foundation for Public Affairs.

——. (2006) *Activists in the Boardroom: How Advocacy Groups Seek to Shape Corporate Behavior*. Washington, DC: Foundation for Public Affairs.

Price, Vincent, and David Tewksbury. (1997) "News Values and Public Opinion: A Theoretical Account of Media Priming and Framing," in George Barnett and Franklin J. Boster, eds. *Progress in Communication Sciences*. Greenwich, CT: Ablex: 173–212.

Pride, Richard A. (1995) "How Activists and Media Frame Social Problems: Critical Events Versus Performance Trends for Schools," in *Political Communication* 12: 5–26.

Putnam, Robert D. (2000) *Bowling Alone: The Collapse and Revival of American Community*. New York: Simon & Schuster.

Qualter, T.H. (1962) *Propaganda and Psychological Warfare*. New York: Random House.

Rada, Stephen E. (1977) "Manipulating the Media: A Case of a Chicano Strike in Texas," in *Journalism Quarterly* 54: 109–113.

Rakow, Lana F. (1989) "Information and Power: Toward a Critical Theory of Information Campaigns," in Charles T. Salmon, ed., *Information Campaigns: Balancing Social Values and Social Change*, 164–184. Thousand Oaks, CA: Sage.

Ray, Michael L. (1973) "Marketing Communication and the Hierarchy of Effects," in Peter Clarke, ed. *New Models for Mass Communication Research*, 147–176. Beverly Hills, CA: Sage.

Reber, Bryan H., and Bruce K. Berger (2005) "Framing Analysis of Activist Rhetoric: How the Sierra Club Succeeds or Fails at Creating Salient Messages," in *Public Relations Review* 31: 185–195.

Reimann, Kim D. (2002) "Building Networks from the Outside In: Japanese NGOs and the Kyoto Climate Change Conference," in Jackie Smith and Hank Johnston, eds. *Globalization and Resistance: Transnational Dimensions of Social Movements*, 173–187. Oxford, England: Rowman & Littlefield.

Rheingold, Howard (2002) *Smart Mobs: The Next Social Revolution*. Cambridge, MA: Perseus.

Rice, Ronald E., and Charles K. Atkin, eds. (1989) *Public Communication Campaigns*, second edition. Newbury Park, CA: Sage Publications.

——. (1994) "Principles of Successful Public Information Campaigns," in Jennings Bryant and Dolf Zillman, eds. *Media Effects: Advances in Theory and Research*, 365–388. Hillsdale, NJ: Lawrence Erlbaum Associates.

Rifkin, Jeremy, and Randy Barber (1978) *The North Will Rise Again: Pensions, Politics and Power in the 1980s*. Boston: Beacon Press.

Rigg, Malcolm (2002) "The Importance of Research in Planning and Developing Communications Campaigns: The UK Government Home Office Smoke Alarms Campaign," in Hans-Dieter Klingemann and Andrea Römmele, eds. *Public Information Campaigns & Opinion Research: A Handbook for the Student & Practitioner*, 52–60. London: Sage.

Riker, William H. (1986) *The Art of Political Manipulation*. New Haven, CT: Yale University Press.

——. (1996) *The Strategy of Rhetoric: Campaigning for the American Constitution*. New Haven, CT: Yale University Press.

Rogers, Everett M. (1962) *Diffusion of Innovations*. New York: Free Press.

Rokeach, Milton (1972) *Beliefs, Attitudes, and Values*. San Francisco: Jossey-Bass.

Ronfeldt, David, John Arquilla, Graham E. Fuller and Melissa Fuller (1998) *The Zapatista Social Netwar in Mexico*. Santa Monica, CA: RAND Corporation.

Rosenberg, Milton J. (1960) "A Structural Theory of Attitude Dynamics," in *Public Opinion Quarterly* 24: 319–340

Rosenblum, Jonathan D. (1998) *Copper Crucible: How the Arizona Miners' Strike of 1983 Recast Labor-Management Relations in America*, second edition. Ithaca, NY: Cornell University Press.

Rosenkrands, Jacob (2004) "Politicizing *Homo economicus*: Analysis of Anti-corporate Websites," in Wim Van De Donk, Brian D. Loader, Paul G. Nixon, and Dieter Rucht, eds. *Cyberprotest: New Media, Citizens and Social Movements*, 57–76. London: Routledge.

Roser, Connie, and Margaret Thompson (1995) "Fear Appeals and the Formation of Active Publics," in *Journal of Communication* 45: 103–121.

Roshco, Bernard (1975) *Newsmaking*. Chicago: University of Chicago Press.

Roth, Alex (2009) "FedEx and UPS Clash Over Legislation," in *The Wall Street Journal* (July 20), found online at http://online.wsj.com/article/SB124804725157963745.html.

Rubin, Alan M. (1994) "Media Uses and Effects: A Uses-and-Gratifications Perspective," in Jennings Bryant and Dolf Zillman, eds. *Media Effects: Advances in Theory and Research*, 417–436. Hillsdale, NJ: Lawrence Erlbaum Associates.

Rubin, Alissa (2010) "Taliban Overhaul Image in Bid to Win Allies," in *New York Times* (January 21).

Rucht, Dieter (2004) "The Quadruple 'A': Media Strategies of Protest Movements Since the 1960s," in Wim Van De Donk, Brian D. Loader, Paul G. Nixon, and Dieter Rucht, eds. *Cyberprotest: New Media, Citizens and Social Movements*, 29–56. London: Routledge.

Russell, Adrienne (2001) "Chiapas and the New News: Internet and Newspaper Coverage of a Broken Cease-Fire," in *Journalism* 2: 197–220.

Ryan, Charlotte (1991) *Prime Time Activism: Media Strategies for Grassroots Organizing*. Boston: South End Press.

Ryfe, David M. (2006) "The Nature of News Rules," in *Political Communication* 23: 203–214.

Salmon, Charles T., ed. (1989a) *Information Campaigns: Balancing Social Values and Social Change*. Thousand Oaks, CA: Sage.

——. (1989b) "Campaigns for Social 'Improvement': An Overview of Values, Rationales, and Impacts," in Charles T. Salmon, ed., *Information Campaigns: Balancing Social Values and Social Change*, 19–53. Thousand Oaks, CA: Sage.

Salmon, Charles T., L.A. Post, and Robin E. Christensen (2003) "Mobilizing Public Will for Social Change," Paper prepared for the Communications Consortium Media Center, Washington, DC.

Salwen, Michael B., and Frances R. Matera (1992) "Public Salience of Foreign Nations," in *Journalism Quarterly* 69: 623–632.

Salzman, Jason (2003) *Making the News: A Guide for Activists and Nonprofits*. Boulder, CO: Westview Press.

Savadori, Lucia, Stefania Savio, Eraldo Nicotra, Rino Rumiati, Melissa Finucane, and Paul Slovic (2004) "Expert and Public Perception of Risk from Biotechnology," in *Risk Analysis* 24: 1289–1299.

Schein, Edgar H. (1969) "The Mechanisms of Change," in Warren G. Bennis, Kenneth D. Benne, and Robert Chin, eds. *The Planning of Change*, second edition, 98–107. New York: Holt, Rinehart and Winston.

Schelling, Thomas C. (1963) *The Strategy of Conflict*. New York: Galaxy Books.

——. (1978) *Micromotives and Macrobehavior*. New York: W.W. Norton.

Scheufele, Dietram A. (1999) "Framing as a Theory of Media Effects," in *Journal of Communication* 49 (1): 103–122.

Scheufele, Dietram A., and Patricia Moy (2000) "Twenty-Five Years of the Spiral of Silence: A Conceptual Review and Empirical Outlook," in *International Journal of Public Opinion Research* 12: 3–28.

Scheufele, Dietram A., and David Tewksbury (2007) "Framing, Agenda Setting, and Priming: The Evolution of Three Media Effects Models," in *Journal of Communication* 57: 9–20.

Schmid, Alex P., and Janny DeGraaf (1982) *Violence as Communication: Insurgent Terrorism and the Western News Media*. Beverly Hills, CA: Sage.

Schopenhauer, Arthur (1970). *Essays and Aphorisms*. London: Penguin Books.

Schultz, Don E., Stanley I. Tannenbaum, and Robert F. Lauterborn (1993) *Integrated Marketing Communication*. Lincolnwood, IL: NTC Business Books.

Schulz, Markus S. (1998) "Collective Action Across Borders: Opportunity Structures, Network Capacities, and Communicative Praxis in the Age of Advanced Globalization," in *Sociological Perspectives* 41: 587–616.

Scott, Robert Lee, and Donald K. Smith (1969) "The Rhetoric of Confrontation," in *Quarterly Journal of Speech* 55: 1–8.

Sears, David O., and Jonathan L. Freedman (1971) "Selective Exposure to Information: A Critical Review," in *Public Opinion Quarterly* 31: 545–553.

Seidman, Gay W. (2005) "Monitoring Multinationals: Corporate Codes of Conduct," in Joe Bandy and Jackie Smith, eds. *Coalitions Across Borders: Transnational Protest and the Neoliberal Order*, 163–183. Lanham, MD: Rowman & Littlefield.

Sellers, Patrick (2010) *Cycles of Spin: Strategic Communication in the U.S. Congress.* Cambridge: Cambridge University Press.

Service Employees International Union (nd) *Contract Campaign Manual.* Washington, DC.

Shaffer, Martin B. (2000) "Coalition Work among Environmental Groups: Who Participates?" in *Research in Social Movements, Conflict and Change* 22: 111–126.

Shavitt, Sharon, and Michelle R. Nelson (2000) "The Social-Identity Function in Person Perception: Communicated Meanings of Product Preferences," in Gregory R. Maio and James M. Olson, eds. *Why We Evaluate: Functions of Attitude*: 37–58. Mahwah, NJ: Lawrence Erlbaum Associates.

Shaw, Randy. (1996) *The Activist's Handbook: A Primer for the 1990s and Beyond.* Berkeley: University of California Press.

Sheafer, Tamir, and Itay Gabay (2009) "Mediated Public Diplomacy: A Strategic Contest over International Agenda Building and Frame Building," *Political Communication* 26: 447–467.

Sherif, Carolyn W., and Muzafer Sherif (1967) "The Social Judgment-Involvement Approach to Attitude and Attitude Change," in Muzafer Sherif, ed., *Social Interaction*, 342–352. Chicago: Aldine.

Sherman, S., D. Mackie, and D. Driscoll (1990) "Priming and the Differential Use of Dimensions in Evaluation," in *Personality and Social Psychology Bulletin* 16: 405–418.

Shoemaker, Pamela J., and Stephen D. Reese (1991) *Mediating the Message: Theories of Influences on Mass Media Content.* New York: Longman.

Sigal, Leon (1973) *Reporters and Officials: The Organization and Politics of Newsmaking.* Lexington, MA: D.C. Heath.

Sikkink, Kathryn (2005) "Patterns of Dynamic Multilevel Governance and the Insider–Outsider Coalition," in Donatella Della Porta and Sidney Tarrow, eds. *Transnational Protest and Global Activism*, 151–173. Lanham, MD: Rowman & Littlefield.

Simmons, P.J. (1998) "Learning to Live with NGOs," in *Foreign Policy* 112: 82–96.

Simmons, Robert E. (1990) *Communication Campaign Management: A Systems Approach.* New York: Longman.

Sitrick, Michael S. (1998) *Spin: How to Turn the Power of the Press to Your Advantage.* Washington, DC: Regnery Publishing.

Slovic, Paul, Melissa L. Finucane, Ellen Peters, and Donald G. McGregor (2004) "Risk as Analysis and Risk as Feelings: Some Thoughts about Affect, Reason, Risk, and Rationality," in *Risk Analysis* 24: 311–322.

Smith, Brendan, Tim Costello, and Jeremy Brecher (2009) "Social Movements 2.0," in *The Nation* (January 15).

Smith, Grant W. (1998) "The Political Impact of Name Sounds," in *Communication Monographs* 65: 154–172.

Smith, Jackie (2002) "Globalizing Resistance: The Battle of Seattle and the Future of Social Movements," in Jackie Smith and Hank Johnston, eds. *Globalization and Resistance: Transnational Dimensions of Social Movements*, 207–227. Oxford, England: Rowman & Littlefield.

——. (2004) "Exploring Connections Between Global Integration and Political Mobilization," in *Journal of World-Systems Research* 10: 254–285.

Smith, Jackie, and Hank Johnston, eds. (2002) *Globalization and Resistance: Transnational Dimensions of Social Movements*. Oxford, England: Rowman & Littlefield.

Smith, Jackie, Ron Pagnucco, and George Lopez (1998) "Globalizing Human Rights: The Work of Transnational Human Rights NGOs in the 1990s," in *Human Rights Quarterly* 20: 379–412.

Smith, M. Brewster (1968) "A Map for the Analysis of Personality and Politics," in *Journal of Social Issues* 24: 15–28.

Smythe, Elizabeth, and Peter J. Smith (2002) "New Technologies and Networks of Resistance," in Even H. Potter, ed. *Cyber-Diplomacy: Managing Foreign Policy in the Twenty-First Century*. Montreal: McGill-Queens University Press: 48–82.

Snow, David A., E. Burke Rochford, Jr., Steven K. Worden, and Robert D. Benford (1986) "Frame Alignment Processes, Micromobilization, and Movement Participation," in *American Sociological Review* 51: 464–481.

Soley, Lawrence C. (1992) *The News Shapers: The Sources Who Explain the News*. Westport, CT: Praeger.

Sparks, Glenn G. (2002) *Media Effects Research: A Basic Overview*. Belmont, CA: Wadsworth.

Spears, Nancy, Tom J. Brown, and Peter A. Dacin (2006) "Assessing the Corporate Brand: The Unique Corporate Association Valence (UCAV) Approach," in *Journal of Brand Management* 14: 5–19.

Steele, Janet (1995) "Experts and the Operational Bias of Television News: The Case of the Persian Gulf War," *Journalism and Mass Communication Quarterly* 72: 799–812.

Stone, Brad, and Noam Cohen (2009) "Social Networks Spread Iranian Defiance Online," *New York Times* (June 16).

Subramani, Mani R., and Balaji Rajagopalan (2003) "Knowledge-Sharing and Influence in Online Social Networks via Viral Marketing," in *Communications of the Association for Computing Machinery* 46: 300–307.

Suchman, Mark C. (1995) "Managing Legitimacy: Strategic and Institutional Approaches," in *Academy of Management Review* 20: 571–610.

Suman, Michael, and Gabriel Rossman, eds. (2000) *Advocacy Groups and the Entertainment Industry*. Westport, CT: Praeger.

Sun Tzu (1993) *The Art of War*. Translated by J.H. Huang. New York: William Morrow.

Swanson, David L., and Dan Nimmo, eds. (1990) *New Directions in Political Communication: A Resource Book*. Newbury Park, CA: Sage.

Tanaka, Yasumasa (1971) "Psychological Factors in International Persuasion," in *Annals of the American Academy of Political and Social Science* 398: 50–60.

Tannenbaum, Percy H. (1955) "The Indexing Process in Communication," in *Public Opinion Quarterly* 19: 292–302.

Tarrow, Sidney (2001) "Transnational Politics: Contention and Institutions in International Politics," *Annual Review of Political Science* 4: 1–20.

——. (2005) *The New Transnational Activism*. Cambridge: Cambridge University Press.

Tarrow, Sidney, and Doug McAdam (2005) "Scale Shift in Transnational Contention," in Donatella Della Porta and Sidney Tarrow, eds. *Transnational Protest and Global Activism*, 121–147. Lanham, MD: Rowman & Littlefield.

Thompson, Erik P., Arie W. Kruglanski, and Scott Spiegel (2000) "Attitudes as Knowledge Structures and Persuasion as a Specific Case of Subjective Knowledge Acquisition," in Gregory R. Maio and James M. Olson, eds. *Why We Evaluate: Functions of Attitude*: 59–96. Mahwah, NJ: Lawrence Erlbaum Associates.

Thrall, A. Trevor, Jaime Lollio-Fakhreddine, Jon Berent, Lana Donnelly, Wes Herrin, Zachary Paquette, Rebecca Wenglinski, and Amy Wyatt (2008) "Star Power: Celebrity Advocacy and the Evolution of the Public Sphere," in *International Journal of Press/Politics* 13: 362–385.

Tichenor, Philip J., G.A. Donohue, and C.N. Olien (1970) "Mass Media Flow and Differential Growth in Knowledge," in *Public Opinion Quarterly* 34: 159–170.

Tichenor, Philip J., Jane M. Rodenkirchen, Clarice N. Olien, and George A. Donohue (1973) "Community Issues, Conflict, and Public Affairs Knowledge," in Peter Clarke, ed. *New Models for Mass Communication Research*, 45–80. Beverly Hills, CA: Sage.

Torres, Manual R., Javier Jordán, and Nicola Horsburgh (2006) "Analysis and Evolution of the Global Jihadist Movement Propaganda," in *Journal of Terrorism and Political Violence* 18: 399–421.

Tuchman, Gaye (1973) "Making News by Doing Work: Routinizing the Unexpected," in *American Journal of Sociology* 79: 110–131.

Tunstall, Jeremy (1971) *Journalists at Work. Specialist Correspondents: Their News Organizations, News Sources, and Competitor Colleagues*. Beverly Hills, CA: Sage.

Tversky, Amos, and Daniel Kahneman (1981) "The Framing of Decisions and the Psychology of Choice," in *Science* 211: 453–458.

Tyler, Lisa (1997) "Liability Means Never Having to Say You're Sorry: Corporate Guilt, legal Constraints, and Defensiveness in Corporate Communication," in *Management Communication Quarterly* 11: 51–73.

United States Department of the Army (2001) "Information Superiority," in *Field Manual No. FM 3-0,* 11-1—11-24. Washington, DC.

United States Department of Defense (2001) *Report of the Defense Science Board Task Force in Managed Information Dissemination*. Washington, DC: Office of the Under Secretary of Defense for Acquisition, Technology and Logistics.

United States Joint Command, Control and Information Warfare School, National Defense University (2002) *Information Operations: The Hard Reality of Soft Power.* Washington, DC.

United States Joint Staff (2006) *Information Operations*, Joint Publication 3–13. Washington, DC: U.S. Department of Defense.

Van Aelst, Peter, and Stefaan Walgrave (2004) "New Media, New Movements? The Role of the Internet in Shaping the 'Anti-Globalization' Movement," in Wim Van De Donk, Brian D. Loader, Paul G. Nixon, and Dieter Rucht, eds. *Cyberprotest: New Media, Citizens and Social Movements*, 97–122. London: Routledge.

Van De Donk, Wim, Brian D. Loader, Paul G. Nixon, and Dieter Rucht, eds. (2004) *Cyberprotest: New Media, Citizens and Social Movements*. London: Routledge.

Vidal, John (2002) "Anti-GM Warrior Melchett Joins PR Firm That Advised Monsanto," in *The Guardian* (January 8).

Vogel, David (1978) *Lobbying the Corporation: Citizen Challenges to Business Authority*. New York: Basic Books.

——. (2005) *The Market for Virtue: The Potential Limits of Corporate Social Responsibility*. Washington: Brookings Institution.

Voltmer, Katrin, and Andrea Römmele (2002) "Information and Communication Campaigns: Linking Theory to Practice," in Hans-Dieter Klingemann and Andrea Römmele, eds. *Public Information Campaigns & Opinion Research: A Handbook for the Student & Practitioner*, 9–20. London: Sage.

Walker, Steve (2002) "To Picket Just Click It! Social Netwar and Industrial Conflict in a Global Economy," Working Paper IMRIP 2002-1, School of Information Management, Leeds Metropolitan University. Found online at http://www.leedsmet.ac.uk/inn/2002-1.pdf.

Waller, Angie (2003) *Data Mining the Amazon*. N.P.

Walton, Douglas (1997) "What Is Propaganda, and What Exactly Is Wrong with It?" in *Public Affairs Quarterly* 11: 383–413.

Ward, Brad M. (2003) "Strategic Influence Operations—The Information Connection." Carlisle, PA: U.S. Army War College.

Warkentin, Craig (2001) *Reshaping World Politics: NGOs, the Internet, and Global Civil Society*. Lanhan, MD: Rowman & Littlefield.

Watson, Goodwin (1969) "Resistance to Change," in Warren G. Bennis, Kenneth D. Benne, and Robert Chin, eds. *The Planning of Change*, second edition, 488–498. New York: Holt, Rinehart and Winston.

Watts, Duncan J. (2003) *Six Degrees: The Science of a Connected Age*. New York: W.W. Norton.

Webster, James G., Patricia Phalen, and Lawrence W. Lichty (2000) *Ratings Analysis: The Theory and Practice of Audience Research*, second ed. Mahwah, NJ: Lawrence Erlbaum Associates.

Wegener, Duane T., Richard E. Petty, Natalie D. Smoak, and Leandre R. Fabrigar (2004) "Multiple Routes to Resisting Attitude Change," in Eric S. Knowles and Jay A. Linn, eds. *Resistance and Persuasion*, 13–38. Mahwah, NJ: Lawrence Erlbaum Associates.

Weil, David (2005) "A Strategic Choice Framework for Union Decision-Making," in *WorkingUSA: The Journal of Labor and Society* 8: 327–347.

Weiss, Janet A., and Mary Tschirhart (1994) "Public Information Campaigns as Policy Instruments," in *Journal of Policy Analysis and Management* 13: 82–119.

Werder, Kelly Page (2008) "The Effect of Doing Good: An Experimental Analysis of the Influence of Corporate Social Responsibility Initiatives on Beliefs, Attitudes, and Behavioral Intention," in *International Journal of Strategic Communication* 2: 115–135.

White, Ralph K. (1971) "Propaganda: Morally Questionable and Morally Unquestionable Techniques," in *Annals of the American Academy of Political and Social Science* 398: 26–35.

Whitmore, Brian (2007) "Spinning the Kremlin: Russia's New Agitprop," *Radio Free Europe/Radio Liberty*, November 5: 1–6.

Wiebe, G.D. (1951–1952) "Merchandising Commodities and Citizenship on Television," *Public Opinion Quarterly* 15: 679–691.

Willnat, Lars (1997) "Agenda Setting and Priming: Conceptual Links and Differences," in Maxwell McCombs, Donald L. Shaw, and David Weaver, eds.

Communication and Democracy: Exploring the Intellectual Frontiers in Agenda-Setting Theory, 51–66. Mahwah, NJ: Lawrence Erlbaum Associates.

Witte, Kim (1998) "Fear as Motivator, Fear as Inhibitor: Using the Extended Parallel Process Model to Explain Fear Appeal Successes and Failures," in P.A. Anderson and L.K. Guerrero, eds.. *The Handbook of Communication and Emotion: Research, Theory, Applications, and Contexts*, 423–450. San Diego, CA: Academic Press.

Wittebols, James (1996) "News From the Noninstitutional World: U.S. and Canadian Television News Coverage of Social Protest," in *Political Communication* 13: 345–361.

Wolfsfeld, Gadi (1997) *Media and Political Conflict: News from the Middle East*. Cambridge: Cambridge University Press.

Yanacopulos, Helen (2005) "The Strategies That Bind: NGO Coalitions and Their Influence," in *Global Networks* 5: 93–110.

Young, Dennis R. (1991) "The Structural Imperatives of International Advocacy Associations," in *Human Relations* 44: 921–941.

Young, Dennis R., Bonnie L. Koenig, Adil Najam, and Julie Fisher (1999) "Strategy and Structure in Managing Global Associations," in *Voluntas: International Journal of Voluntary and Nonprofit Organizations* 10: 323–343.

Zajonc, Robert B. (2001) "Mere Exposure: A Gateway to the Subliminal," in *Current Directions in Psychological Science* 10: 224–228.

Zald, Mayer N., and John D. McCarthy (1980) "Social Movement Industries: Competition and Cooperation among Movement Organizations," in *Research in Social Movements, Conflict and Change* 3: 1–20.

Zaller, John R. (1992) *The Nature and Origins of Mass Opinion*. Cambridge: Cambridge University Press.

——. (1996) "The Myth of Massive Media Impact Revived: New Support for a Discredited Idea," in Diana C. Mutz, Paul M. Sniderman, and Richard A. Brody, eds. *Political Persuasion and Attitude Change*, 17–78. Ann Arbor: University of Michigan Press.

Zarsky, Tal (2006) "Online Privacy, Tailoring, and Persuasion," in Katherine Strandburg and Daniela Stan Raicu, eds., *Privacy and Technologies of Identity: A Cross-Disciplinary Conversation*, 209–224. Berlin: Springer.

Zielske, Hubert A. (1959) "The Remembering and Forgetting of Advertising," in *Journal of Marketing* 23: 239–243.

Zielske, Hubert A., and Walter A. Henry (1980) "Remembering and Forgetting Television Ads," in *Journal of Advertising Research* 20: 7–13.

Zillmann, Dolf, and Hans-Bernd Brosius (2000) *Exemplification in Communication: The Influence of Case Reports on the Perception of Issues*. Mahwah, NJ: Lawrence Erlbaum Associates.

Zimbardo, Philip, Mark Snyder, James Thomas, Alice Gold, and Sharon Gurwitz (1970) "Modifying the Impact of Persuasive Communications with External Distraction," in *Journal of Personality and Social Psychology* 16: 669–680.

Zimmerman, Ann (2010) "Rival Chains Secretly Fund Opposition to Wal-Mart," *Wall Street Journal* (June 7): A1.

Author Index

Abelson, Robert P. 210, 275
Adam, Barbara 275, 286, 293
Adelman, Mara B. 210, 275
Agle, Bradley R. 93, 267, 293
Agre, Philip E. 255, 275
Ajzen, Icek 212, 275
Albrecht, Terrance L. 210, 275
Albritton, Robert B. 30, 246, 247, 275, 292
Alinsky, Saul D. ix, 38, 46, 146, 177–8, 260, 275
Allan, Stuart 275, 286, 293
Allport, Gordon W. 206, 275
Anderson, Lynn R. 212, 215, 275, 303
Andreasen, Alan R. 194, 266, 275
Arquilla, John 112, 125, 258, 275, 297
Asal, Victor 259, 275
Ashby, Steven K. 194, 262, 275
Atkin, Charles K. 199, 292, 297
Au, Wagner James 49, 275
Auld, Graeme 268, 278
Avni, Ronit 194, 261, 285
Ayres, Jeffrey M. 255, 275

Baker, Stephen 239, 275
Bakir, Vian 194, 220, 230, 275
Bandy, Joe 194, 252, 253, 275, 283, 299
Barber, Randy 270, 297
Barnett, Michael 268, 275
Bartley, Tim 228, 272, 275
Bathelt, Anke 227, 278
Bauer, Raymond A. 200, 275
Beavers, Garry J. 243, 275
Beder, Sharon 161, 275
Bem, Daryl J. 199, 275
Benford, R.D. 222, 225, 275, 300
Benne, Kenneth D. 264, 279, 288, 298, 302
Bennett, W. Lance 197, 200, 226, 233, 234, 235, 253, 254, 255, 268, 276, 290, 291
Berent, Jon 301
Berent, Matthew K. 211, 277, 286
Berg, John C. 194, 276
Berger, Bruce K. 220, 224, 276, 297
Berger, Peter L. 207, 276
Berlo, David K. 200, 276
Bernays, Edward 240, 276
Bhattacharya, C.B. 270, 276
Bimber, Bruce 237, 276
Bitzer, Lloyd 208, 277
Bizer, George W. 212, 296
Bloodgood, Elizabeth 253, 277
Blumler, Jay G. 202, 288
Bob, Clifford 85, 130, 194, 259, 277
Bobo, Kim 194, 260, 277
Bok, Sissela 244, 277
Boninger, David S. 211, 277, 286
Bonini, Sheila 195, 269, 277
Boorstin, Daniel J. 207, 277
Bosk, Charles L. 217, 286
Boulding, Kenneth E. 207, 277
Boulianne, Shelley 203, 277
Bowers, John W. 206, 277
Brachman, Jarrett M. 259, 277
Brandeis, Louis D. 153, 277
Brashers, Dale 222, 277
Brecher, Jeremy 49, 54, 256, 299
Bremmer, Ian 272, 277
Breunig, Christian 254, 276
Briñol, Pablo 216, 277
Brisbin, Richard 194, 262, 277
Broad, Robin 262, 277
Bronfenbrenner, Kate 194, 262, 277, 287
Brosius, Hans-Bernd 203, 227, 278, 303
Brown, Halina S. 288
Brown, J.A.C. 240, 278
Brown, Tom J. 228, 300

Bryant, Jennings 200, 278, 295, 297
Buck, Ross 214, 267, 279
Buffett, Sandy 261, 270
Buitenhuis, Peter 240, 278
Bullert, B.J. 194, 226, 253, 263, 278
Burke, Kenneth 204, 278, 300
Bustillo, Miguel 132, 278
Butler, Patrick 265, 278

Cacioppo, John T. 75, 212, 295
Caldwell, Gillian 194, 261, 285
Campbell, Dedra M. 237, 287, 292
Caniglia, Beth Schaefer 252, 278
Cantril, Hadley 195, 278
Cardador, M.T. 270, 278
Cardoso, Gustavo 256, 278
Carroll, William K. 263, 278
Carter, Cynthia 274, 286, 293
Cartwright, Dorwin 209, 278
Cashore, Benjamin 268, 278
Castells, Manuel 248, 278
Cavanaugh, John 262, 277
Chadwick, Andrew 237, 279
Chaffee, Steven H. 200, 279, 289
Chaiken, Shelly 200, 279
Chakrabarti, Monami 270, 279
Chaudhuri, Arjun 214, 279
Chelimsky, Eleanor 60, 279
Child, Curtis 272, 275
Chin, Robert 264, 279, 288, 298, 302
Chomsky, Noam 216, 235, 286
Chong, Dennis 218, 223, 279
Christensen, Robin E. 220, 298
Clawson, Dan 194, 279
Clawson, Rosalie A. 223, 294
Cleaver, Harry 112, 258, 279
Clough, Emily 253, 277
Cobb, Roger W. 205, 282
Cohen, Arthur R. 209, 279
Cohen, Bernard 218, 279
Cohen, Noam 49, 300
Cohen, Raymond 207, 246, 279
Collins, Barry E. 164, 209, 278
Collins, Neil 265, 278
Colvin, Gregory L. 197, 279
Combs, James E. 207, 240, 279
Contractor, Noshir S. 248, 294
Converse, Philip E. 212, 280
Cook, Fay Lomax 219, 280
Cook, Terrence E. 211, 280
Cooper, Andrew F. 252, 280
Corman, Steven R. 170, 243, 280
Corrado, Michele 189, 280
Costello, Tim 49, 54, 256, 299
Court, David 195, 269, 277
Cragin, Kim 243, 280
Crigler, Ann N. 219, 294
Cronin, Mary 203, 281
Crossen, Cynthia 73, 280
Cull, Nicholas J. 70–1, 248, 280

Dacin, Peter A. 228, 300
Dahl, Robert 197, 280
Danaher, Kevin 24, 268, 280
Danes, Jeffrey E. 212, 280
Davenport, Christian 59, 280
Davenport, Lucinda 203, 281
Davis, Dennis 227, 289
Davis, Richard 237, 280
Davis, Tyler 96, 289
Davison, W. Phillips 217, 218, 241, 246, 280
Dearing, James W. 219, 281
Deegan, Denise 195, 261, 281
DeFleur, Margaret 203, 281
DeFleur, Melvin L. 203, 235, 281
DeGraaf, Janny 257, 298
Deibert, Ronald J. 256, 281
Della Porta, Donatella 252, 253, 276, 281, 287, 299, 301
DeLuca, Kevin 208, 281
DeMars, William E. 254, 281
Dennis, Everette E. 236, 281, 285
Detenber, Benjamin H. 224, 292
Deutsch, Karl W. 196, 281
Devine, Patricia G. 198, 281
DeVreese, Claes H. 265, 281
Dezenhall, Eric 195, 261, 281
Diani, Mario 254, 256, 281
Dolnick, Edward 153, 281
Domhoff, G. William 196, 281
Donaldson, Thomas 267, 281
Donnelly, Lana 301
Donohue, George A. 202, 208, 235, 281, 301
Doob, Leonard W. 213, 282
Downing, Steve 271, 291
Downs, Anthony 217, 282
Driscoll, D. 225, 299
Drucker, Peter E. 270, 282
Druckman, James N. 223, 279, 282
Duke, Lynne 102, 282
Dye, Thomas R. 196, 236, 282

Eagly, Alice 200, 279
Edelman, Murray 44–5, 57, 204, 205, 206, 226, 282
Edwards, Arthur 256, 282

Eggen, Dan 27, 282
Ehrenberg, Andrew S. 227, 282
Einwiller, S.A. 270, 282
Eisenberg, E.M. 206, 282
Elder, Charles D. 205, 282
Elder, Randy W. 199, 282
Elenbaas, Matthijs 265, 281
Ellul, Jacques 38, 240, 241, 282
Emel, Jacques 288
Entman, Robert M. 220, 222, 276, 282
Epstein, Edward J. 233, 283
Ereaut, Gill 263, 283
Essig, Mark 6, 7, 17n2, 283
Ettinger, Karl E. 195, 241, 283
Evan, William M. 249, 283
Eveland, William P. 208, 283

Faber, Daniel 252, 283
Fabrigar, Leandre R. 216, 302
Falkheimer, Jesper 206, 286
Fast, William R. 208, 283
Fedorikhin, A. 270, 282
Feld, Werner J. 255, 283
Feldner, Sarah Bonewits 239, 283
Fernandez, Esteban 269, 283
Festinger, Leon 71, 73, 209, 283
Fink, Edward L. 211, 288
Finucane, Melissa 230, 298, 299
Fishbein, Martin 69, 212, 274, 283
Fleming, Charles A. 240, 283
Flynn, J. 229, 236, 283
Flynn, Nancy 261, 284
Follesdal, Andreas 268, 276, 278, 284, 293
Fombrun, Charles F. 271, 284
Fox, Karen F.A. 194, 265, 284
Freedman, Anne E. 196, 284
Freedman, Jonathan L. 214, 299
Freedman, P.E. 196, 284
Freeman, R. Edward 91, 156–7, 267, 284
Friedman, Monroe 268, 284
Fuller, Graham E. 112, 125, 258, 297
Fuller, Melissa 112, 225, 258, 297
Fung, Archon 270, 284
Funkhouser, G. Ray 208, 285

Gabay, Itay 247, 299
Gamson, Joshua 226, 293
Gamson, William A. 221, 248, 249, 284
Gans, Herbert 233, 284
Ganzi, John 92, 194, 261, 270, 284
Gardberg, N.A. 271, 284
Gardner, Bruce 60, 284
Gardner, Daniel 232, 284
George, Alexander L. 246, 280
Gerwehr, Scott 243, 280
Getman, Julius 194, 262, 284
Gibson, Rhonda 227, 284
Giffard, Anthony C. 227, 284
Gilboa, Eytan 247, 284
Gilens, Martin 208, 284
Givens, Terri 254, 276
Glander, Timothy 195, 240, 285
Goble, Robert 288
Goetz, Edward G. 280
Gold, Alice 303
Goldhaber, Michael D. 131, 285
Goodall, Bud 170, 243, 280
Gordon, Craig S. 217, 286
Gordon, Margaret T. 280
Gordon, Sanford C. 270, 285
Gottleib, Robert 236, 285
Gough, Susan L. 242, 285
Graber, Doris A. 203, 204, 205, 285, 291
Grant, Andrew J. 194, 228, 285
Gray, Jonathan 207, 285
Gready, Paul 253, 285
Greenberg, Donald W. 207, 285
Greer, Jed 194, 285
Gregory, Sam 194, 260, 285
Grunig, James E. 199, 285
Grupp, Fred W., Jr. 209, 285
Gurevitch, Michael 202, 288
Gurwitz, Sharon 303

Hafer, Catherine 270, 285
Hall, Edward T. 204, 285
Hall, R. 269, 285
Hallahan, Kirk 222, 285
Hamilton, Mark A. 214, 286
Hammes, Thomas X. 259, 286
Hansen, Anders 224, 286
Harary, Frank 209, 278
Harding, Thomas 194, 261, 285
Harrington, D. William 259, 275
Hartley, Eugene L. 194, 201, 289
Hawking, C.J. 194, 262, 275
Hayes, Andrew F. 208, 283
Hebb, Tessa 270, 284
Heider, Fritz 209, 278, 286
Henry, Gary T. 217, 286
Henry, Walter A. 194, 213, 303
Herman, Edward S. 216, 235, 286
Herrin, Wes 301
Hilgartner, Stephen 217, 286
Hillenbrand, Carola 271, 291, 293
Hirst, Edward R. 198, 281
Hochschild, Adam 17n1, 286

Hoffer, Charles R. 195, 241, 286
Holbrook, Allyson L. 211, 286
Holmström, Susanne 206, 286
Holsti, Ole R. 226, 286
Horsburgh, Nicola 243, 301
Hovland, Carl I. 195, 200, 240, 286
Howard, Philip 240, 286
Hsu, Spencer S. 179, 286
Huckfeldt, Robert 218, 293
Huff, Darrell 244, 286
Hunter, John E. 212, 280
Hutchinson, William 244, 286
Huxham, Mark 262, 286
Hyman, Herbert H. 65, 195, 198, 286

Ihlen, Øyvind 224, 287
Iyengar, Shanto 219, 221, 287
Izcaray, Fausto 246, 293

Jacobs, Lawrence R. 271, 287
Jacobson, Thomas 248, 295
Jamieson, Kathleen Hall 237, 287
Jarley, Paul 194, 262, 287
Jensen, Richard J. 206, 277
Jessee, Davin D. 243, 287
Jha, Sonora 234, 287
Johns, Gary 175, 229, 287
Johnson, A.R. 270, 282
Johnson, Blair T. 290, 212
Johnson, Eric 253, 287
Johnson, Richard M. 265, 287
Johnson-Cartee, Karen S. 234, 287
Johnston, Hank 252, 278, 291, 294, 297, 299, 300
Jones, Richard 268, 287
Jordán, Javier 243, 301
Juravitch, Tom 194, 287
Just, Marion R. 219, 257, 294, 295

Kahneman Daniel 215, 221, 229, 232, 287, 301
Kaid, Lynda Lee 273, 287
Kamins, M.A. 270, 282
Kane, Paul 103, 287
Kaplowitz, Stan A. 211, 288
Karpf, David 239, 257, 288
Kasperson, Jeanne X. 230, 288
Kasperson, Roger E. 230, 288
Katz, Daniel 76–7, 211, 288
Katz, Elihu 200, 201, 202, 288
Katz, Helen 261, 288
Keat, Preston 272, 277
Keck, Margaret E. 107–8, 228, 229, 252, 253, 288
Kelly, George 208, 288
Kelman, Herbert C. 170, 213, 265, 288
Kendall, Jackie 194, 260, 277
Kern, Montague 237, 295
Kiesler, Charles A. 164, 209, 288
Kinder, Donald R. 219, 224, 287, 289
Kiousis, Spiro 246, 288
Klein, Maury 9, 10, 17n1, 288
Klingemann, Hans Dieter 199, 280, 288, 297, 302
Knoke, David 248, 289
Knowles, Eric S. 216, 277, 289, 302
Knutson, Jeanne N. 273, 289
Kohrs, Karlyn 287
Kosicki, Gerald M. 223, 295
Koster, Josh 96, 289
Kotler, Philip 194, 265, 266, 274, 284, 289
Kraus, Sidney 227, 289, 290
Kriesel, Melvin E. 244, 289
Krosnick, Jon A. 210, 211, 224, 277, 286, 289
Kruglanski, Arie W. 211, 301
Krugman, Edward P. 47, 194, 202, 289
Krugman, Herbert E. 47–8, 75, 194, 201, 202, 289
Kuklinski, James H. 248, 289
Kunczik, Michael 247, 289
Kwak, Nojin 208, 283

LaBotz, Dan 195, 262, 290
Laidler-Kylander, Nathalie 228, 290
Lakey, George 195, 260, 295
Lane, Robert E. 216, 290
Lang, Gladys Engel 227, 289
Lang, Kurt 227, 289
Lange, Jonathan 262, 290
Lanzetta, John T. 202, 290
Lasswell, Harold D. 240, 290
Lauterborn, Robert F. 194, 298
Lawrence, Regina G. 226, 276
Lazarsfeld, Paul F. 200, 288
LeBaron, Michelle 205, 290
Lee, Alfred McClung 195, 241, 290
Lee, Nancy 194, 266, 289
Lee, Suman 246, 290
Leff, Donna R. 280
Leizerov, Sagi 239, 256, 290
Lemert, James B. 200, 217, 276, 290
Lester, Marilyn 18, 233, 293
Levin, Kenneth D. 212, 290
Levine, Timothy R. 292
Levy, Sidney 194, 265, 289
Lewin, Kurt 209, 214, 290

Lichty, Lawrence W. 261, 302
Linn, Jay A. 216, 277, 289, 302
Lippmann, Walter 216, 290
Lipsky, Michael 196–7, 290
Livingston, Steven 235, 247, 257, 290
Loader, Brian D. 256, 278, 282, 297, 298, 301
Loehr, Caroline 263, 296
Lollio-Fakhreddine, Jaime 301
Lopez, George 251, 300
Luckman, Thomas 207, 276
Lumsdaine, Arthur A. 195, 240, 286
Lundy, Lisa K. 221, 290
Luntz, Frank 195, 291
Lupia, Arthur 230, 291

McAdam, Doug 253, 254, 281, 301
McCarthy, John D. 249, 253, 387, 292, 303
McCombs, Maxwell D. 218, 219, 221, 292, 302
McCormick, John P. 196, 292
McCornack, Steven A. 264, 292
MacFarquhar, Neil 44, 291
McGregor, Donald G. 230, 299
McGuire, William J. 40, 42–3, 163–4, 199, 213, 215, 274, 292
Machiavelli, Niccolò ix, 196, 291, 292
McHugo, Gregory J. 202, 290
Mackie, D. 225, 299
McLeod, Jack M. 224, 292
MacMillan, Keith 271, 291
McNelly, John T. 246, 293
Maio, Gregory R. 77, 211, 290, 291, 296, 299, 301
Malviva, Alankar 263, 296
Maney, Gregory M. 252, 291
Manheim, Jarol B. 17n3, 30, 45, 46, 80, 99, 100, 197, 200, 202, 219, 227, 235, 246, 247, 262, 266, 270, 271, 274, 276, 291, 292
Maranto, Cheryl 194, 262, 287
Marchi, Alberto 195, 269, 277
Margolis, Michael 203, 292
Mark, Jason 24, 268, 280
Marlin, Randal 241, 292
Martel, Myles 207, 292
Martin, Christopher L. 224, 292
Martin, L. John 242, 292
Martin, Paul S. 225, 292
Masters, Roger D. 202, 290
Matera, Francis R. 246, 298
Mauser, Gary A. 203, 292
Max, Steve 194, 260, 277
Meisenbach, Rebecca J. 239, 283
Mendelsohn, Harold 198, 293
Menn, Joseph 90, 293
Menning, Jesse O. 230, 291
Merritt, Richard L. 245, 264, 293
Mertz, C.K. 229, 236, 283
Mertz, Robert J. 200, 276
Messick, David M. 236, 293
Metaxas, Eric 17, 293
Meyer, David S. 226, 293
Micheletti, Michele 239, 268, 276, 278, 284, 293
Miller, Gerald R. 244, 245, 293
Miller, M. Mark 236, 293
Miller, Norman 164, 209, 288
Mills, C. Wright 196–7, 293
Mitchell, Ronald K. 93, 267, 293
Mlodinow, Leonard 232, 293
Modigliani, A. 221, 284
Molotch, Harvey L. 18, 233, 280, 293
Mondak, Jeffrey J. 218, 293
Money, Kevin 271, 291, 293
Monge, Peter R. 248, 294
Montes, José M. 269, 283
Morin, Arthur L. 60, 294
Morris, Harvey 34, 294
Moy, Patricia 218, 298
Moyer, Bill 195, 263, 294
Mueller, Claus 206, 294
Mutz, Diana C. 203, 218, 279, 293, 294, 303
Myers, Daniel J. 237, 238, 294

Nelson, Kjersten R. 223, 282
Nelson, Michelle R. 211, 299
Nelson, Thomas E. 223, 294
Nepstad, Sharon Erickson 252, 294
Neto, Pedro Pereira 256, 278
Neuman, W. Russell 218, 219, 294
Newman, Bruce I. 265, 278, 294
Newsom, Deanna 268, 278
Nichols, Diana R. 212, 290
Nichols, James J. 199, 282
Nichols, Nick 195, 261, 294
Nicotra, Eraldo 298
Nielsen, Astrid Gade 206, 286
Nimmo, Dan 208, 240, 273, 279, 285, 294, 300
Nitz, Mike 224, 287
Nixon, Paul G. 256, 278, 282, 297, 298, 301
Noelle-Neumann, Elizabeth 218, 294
Nohrstedt, Stig Arne 232, 295
Norris, Pippa 257, 291, 295

Nothhaft, Howard 265, 295
Nussbaum, Brian 259, 275
Nye, Joseph S., Jr. 247, 295

Ochs, Donovan J. 206, 277
Odugbemi, Sina 248, 295
Offner, Amy 104, 261, 295
O'Keefe, Daniel 69, 79, 209, 232, 295
Olien, Clarise N. 202, 208, 235, 281, 301
Olson, James M. 77, 211, 290, 291, 296, 299, 301
Oppenheimer, Martin 195, 260, 295
Osgood, Charles E. 210, 295
Oxley, Zoe 223, 294

Packard, Vance 240, 295
Page, Benjamin I. 271, 287
Pagnucco, Ron 251, 300
Pan, Zhongdang 223, 295
Papageorgis, Demetrios 215, 292
Paquette, Zachary 129, 301
Pattison, Philippa 248, 295
Payne, Rodger A. 221, 295
Peizer, Jonathan 257, 295
Perloff, Richard M. 209, 289, 290, 295
Perry, Charles R. 262, 295
Peters, Ellen 230, 299
Peters, Glen 195, 261, 295
Petty, Richard E. 75, 211, 212, 213, 216, 277, 295, 296, 302
Pfau, Michael 216, 296
Phalen, Patricia 261, 302
Pickard, Victor W. 257, 296
Pickerill, Jenny 238, 296
Pitt, Catherine 263, 296
Polgreen, Lydia 131, 296
Pollay, Richard W. 198, 296
Pool, Ithiel de Sola 273, 296
Post, L.A. 220, 298
Postman, Leo J. 206, 274
Potter, Evan H. 252, 280, 296, 300
Pratt, Cornelius B. 266, 292
Pratt, M.G. 270, 278
Preston, Lee E. 267, 281
Price, Tom 237, 270, 296
Price, Vincent 225, 296
Pride, Richard A. 227, 296
Priester, Joseph R. 213, 295
Protess, David 280
Putnam, Robert D. 202, 203, 296

Qualter, T.H. 240, 296
Quelch, John A. 228, 290

Rada, Stephen E. 234, 296
Rajab, Warda 199, 282
Rajagopalan, Balaji 238, 300
Rakow, Lana F. 198, 296
Ratick, Samuel 288
Ratner, R.S. 263, 278
Ray, Michael L. 202, 296
Reber, Bryan H. 224, 297
Reese, Stephen D. 200, 299
Reimann, Kim D. 252, 297
Renn, Ortwin 288
Rheingold, Howard 237, 256, 297
Rice, Ronald E. 199, 292, 297
Riechert, Bonnie Parnell 293
Rifkin, Jeremy 270, 297
Rigg, Malcolm 199, 297
Riker, William H. 18, 204, 297
Rivenburgh, Nancy K. 227, 284
Roberto, Ned 194, 266, 289
Rodenkirchen, Jane M. 202, 301
Rogers, Everett M. 83, 201, 219, 281, 297
Rogers, Joel 270, 284
Rokeach, Milton 212, 213, 297
Römmele, Andrea 195, 199, 280, 288, 297, 302
Ronfeldt, David 85, 122, 125, 258, 274, 297
Rosenberg, Milton J. 210, 297
Rosenblum, Jonathan D. 194, 262, 297
Rosenkrands, Jacob 256, 297
Roser, Connie 229, 297
Roshco, Bernard 233, 297
Rossman, Gabriel 271, 300
Roth, Alex 37, 297
Rubin, Alan M. 202, 297
Rubin, Alissa 126, 297
Rucht, Dieter 256, 278, 282, 297, 298, 301
Rucker, Derek D. 216, 277
Rumiati, Rino 298
Russell, Adrienne 259, 298
Ryan, Charlotte 195, 261, 298
Ryfe, David M. 234, 298

Salmon, Charles T. 198, 220, 281, 285, 296, 298
Salwen, Michael B. 246, 298
Salzman, Jason 195, 261, 298
Savadori, Lucia 230, 299
Savio, Stefania 298
Schein, Edgar H. 213, 298
Schelling, Thomas C. 260, 298
Scheufele, Dietram A. 218, 225, 298
Schmid, Alex P. 257, 298

Schopenhauer, Arthur 153, 298
Schramm, Wilbur 240, 273, 296
Schultz, Don E. 194, 298
Schulz, Markus S. 112, 258–9, 298
Scott, Robert Lee 206, 298
Sears, David O. 214, 216, 290, 299
Segnit, Nat 263, 283
Seidman, Gay W. 228, 299
Sellers, Patrick 265, 299
Sen, S. 270, 276
Sever, J.M. 271, 284
Seymour, Frances 92, 194, 261, 270, 284
Shaffer, Martin B. 255, 299
Shah, Dhavan V. 145, 283
Shavitt, Sharon 211, 299
Shaw, Donald E. 218, 219, 292
Shaw, Eugene F. 208, 284
Shaw, Randy 195, 260, 299
Sheafer, Tamir 247, 299
Sheatsley, Paul B. 65, 195, 198, 286
Sheffield, Fred D. 195, 240, 286
Sherif, Carolyn W. 74, 211, 299
Sherif, Muzafer 74, 211, 299
Sherman, S. 225, 299
Shoemaker, Pamela J. 200, 299
Shults, Ruth 199, 282
Sigal, Leon 233, 299
Sikkink, Kathryn 107–8, 228, 229, 252, 253, 288, 299
Simmons, P.J. 250, 299
Simmons, Robert E. 261, 299
Simonin, Bernard 228, 290
Singh, Kavaljit 194, 285
Sitrick, Michael S.29, 195, 261, 299
Sleet, David A. 199, 282
Slovic, Paul 229, 230, 232, 236, 283, 288, 298, 299
Smith, Brendan 49, 54, 256, 299
Smith, Donald K. 206, 298
Smith, Grant W. 205–6, 299
Smith, Jackie 194, 251, 252, 253, 275, 278, 283, 291, 294, 297, 299, 300
Smith, M. Brewster 214, 300
Smith, Peter J. 252, 300
Smoak, Natalie D. 216, 302
Smythe, Elizabeth 252, 300
Snow, David A. 222, 225, 275, 300
Snyder, Mark 303
Soley, Lawrence C. 236, 300
Solowcsuk, Kathleen 292
Sparks, Glenn G. 200, 300
Spears, Nancy 228, 300
Spiegel, Scott 211, 301
Steele, Janet 236, 300
Stiff, James B. 244, 245, 293
Stolle, Dietland 239, 268, 276, 278, 284, 293
Stone, Brad 49, 300
Subramani, Mani R. 238, 300
Suchman, Mark C. 23, 261, 300
Sullivan, Denis G. 202, 290
Suman, Michael 271, 300
Sumner, David 262, 286
Sun Tzu ix, 153, 155, 260, 300
Swanson, David L. 273, 300

Tanaka, Yasumasa 215, 300
Tannenbaum, Percy H. 210, 220, 295, 300
Tannenbaum, Stanley I. 194, 298
Tarrow, Sidney 252, 253, 254, 276, 281, 287, 299, 300, 301
Tassew, Admassu 232, 295
Taylor, Ian 194, 228, 285
Tewksbury, David 225, 296, 298
Thomas, James 303
Thompson, Erik P. 211, 301
Thompson, Margaret 229, 297
Thompson, Robert S. 199, 282
Thrall, A. Trevor 226, 301
Tichenor, J. Philip 202, 208, 235, 279, 281, 301
Tormala, Zakary L. 216, 277
Torres, Helen I. 292
Torres, Manual R. 243, 301
Trethewey, Angela 243, 280
Tschirart, Mary 199, 302
Tuchman, Gaye 233, 301
Tunstall, Jeremy 233, 301
Tversky, Amos 215, 221, 229, 232, 287, 301
Tyler, Lisa 272, 301
Tyler, Tom R. 280

Van Aelst, Peter 256, 301
Van De Donk, Wim 256, 278, 282, 297, 298, 301
Vázquez, Camilo J. 269, 283
Vidal, John 161, 301
Visser, Penny S. 286
Vogel, David 267, 268, 302
Voltmer, Katrin 195, 199, 302

Walgrave, Stefaan 256, 301
Walker, Steve 259, 283, 302
Waller, Angie 239, 302
Walton, Douglas 242, 302
Ward, Brad M. 244, 302

Warkentin, Craig 251, 302
Watson, Goodwin 215, 302
Watts, Duncan J. 85, 120, 123, 248, 302
Webster, James G. 261, 302
Wegener, Duane T. 216, 302
Wehmeier, Stefan 264, 295
Weil, David 272, 302
Weiss, Janet A. 199, 302
Weiss, Walter 200, 286
Wenglinski, Rebecca 301
Werder, Kelly Page 267, 302
Wheeler, S. Christian 212, 296
White, Ralph K. 242, 302
Whitmore, Brian 228, 302
Wiebe, G.D. 198, 303
Wildgen, John K. 255, 283
Willnat, Lars 219, 302
Witte, Kim 229–30, 303
Wittebols, James 234, 303
Wolfsfeld, Gadi 203, 303
Wood, Donna J. 93, 267, 293
Wu, Xu 246, 288
Wyatt, Amy 301

Yanacopulos, Helen 254, 303
Yoon, Yungmin 246, 290
Young, Dennis R. 250, 303

Zajonc, Robert B. 214, 303
Zald, Mayer N. 249, 292, 303
Zaller, John R. 203, 216, 217, 303
Zarsky, Tal 239, 303
Zielske, Hubert A. 62, 194, 213, 303
Zillmann, Dolf 200, 203, 227, 278, 284, 295, 297, 303
Zimbardo, Philip 214, 303
Zimmerman, Ann 132, 303

Subject Index

60 Plus Association 27

Accenture 102
Adidas 12, 14
advertising 36–7, 46, 47, 48, 49–50, 62, 66, 96, 103, 104, 163, 194, 213, 214, 227, 235, 239, 244–5, 261
  recall of, temporal sequencing 62, 213
AFL-CIO 12–13, 104, 194, 260
agenda dynamics 80–2, 87–8, 219–20, 246
  cognitive space, dimensions of 81–2
  content-cognition interactions 81–2
  decision-making space, dimensions of 87–8
  dimensionality of spaces in 80–2
  information space, dimensions of 80–1
  strategic implications of 82, 88
agenda setting 58, 63, 79, 82, 218–21, 225
Ahmadinejad, Mahmoud 49, 145–6
Al Qaeda 243, 259
Alien Torts Claims Act 106, 131
Allianz 34
Amazing Grace 4
ambiguity (*see* language)
America's Voice 95–6
American Council on Science and Health 27
Amnesty International 112–13, 130
Annan, Kofi 109
anti-corporate campaigns (*see also* corporate campaigns) 146, 256, 262, 267
anti-slavery campaign 3–6
  components 4–5
  as first social justice movement 3–4
  outcome 5–6
  strategy and tactics 4–5
anti-sweatshop campaign 11–16, 64, 102–3, 226, 239, 253, 263
  components 12–16
  objectives 11–12, 13
  strategy and tactics 14–16
applied research, role in IICs 194–5
Aristotle 38, 43, 45
Association for Progressive Communications 112–13
Astroturf campaigns 28, 105
AT&T 102
attention (*see also* distraction) 16, 30, 40, 42, 58, 63, 67, 73, 88, 101, 102, 104, 111, 112, 131, 139, 142, 146, 167, 178, 186, 199, 202, 205, 207, 214, 217, 218–19, 220, 225, 226, 227, 242, 266
audiences (*see also* public opinion) 19, 21, 22, 30, 38–9, 40, 43–5, 47–63, 73–4, 79, 96, 137–9, 145, 151, 162, 164, 186, 189–93 *passim*, 199, 200, 201–2, 203, 207, 208, 214, 215, 219, 220–3, 225, 229, 233, 236, 238, 240–3 *passim*, 246, 257, 259, 261, 263, 265–6
  access to 96
  engagement of 22, 23, 40, 47–8, 200, 201–2, 229
  persuasion of 23, 38–9, 43–5, 56–63, 69, 79, 151, 162, 164, 189–193 *passim*, 200, 246
  properties of 21, 22
  segmentation of 14, 19, 48, 49, 50–1, 52–6, 208, 261, 265–6
    attitudinal 54–5
    behavioral 55
    demographic 14, 53
    digital media and 54

geographic 53
and market structures 52–3
psychographic 55

Bacon, Sir Francis 249
Ballinger, Jeff 12–15
basic research, role in IICs 194–5
Battle in Seattle 252, 254, 263
belief systems 67–9
boomerang model 107, 109, 228–9, 252–3, 259
boycotts 5, 15, 86, 103, 251, 268
Brandeis, Louis D. 153
branding 70, 190–1, 228–9, 268–9, 272
Brent Spar 220, 224, 230, 262
Brown, Harold 9–10
Bureau of the Census 60
Bureau of Economic Analysis 60
Bureau of Justice Statistics 60
Burson Marsteller 161

campaign intermediaries 12, 22, 23, 25–7, 33, 47, 50, 59, 88, 95, 96–122 *passim*, 123, 127, 128, 130, 131–4, 136–40, 141–3, 145, 148, 151, 157–60, 162, 164, 166, 167, 172, 175, 181, 185, 187–8, 196, 199, 224, 241, 259, 266, 267, 268
allies as 12, 22, 25–7, 33, 59, 96, 100, 101, 104, 106, 107–8, 111, 116–18, 120, 127, 129, 133, 147, 160, 162, 172, 181, 187, 224, 241, 259, 266
attributes of 25–31, 100, 113, 117–18, 133–4, 151, 187, 267
coalitions 15, 18, 22, 37, 95–6, 104, 106, 110, 112, 114–15, 206, 228, 238, 249–55 *passim*, 258, 261, 267, 270
interconnections and campaign architecture 35–6, 96–8, 113–22, 134, 157–61, 188
journalists as 26, 28–9, 48–50, 179, 219, 223, 225, 233–6 *passim*
media as 11–15 *passim*, 18, 23, 25–6, 28–31, 33, 47–63, 70–1, 80–1, 85, 95–6, 104, 100, 112, 114, 122, 126, 131, 141, 159, 161, 162, 164, 171, 178, 180, 186–8, 192, 195, 196, 197–208 *passim*, 213, 214, 217–27 *passim*, 231–49 *passim*, 255–73 *passim*
networks of 47, 105–22, 123–40, 150–1, 157–61, 167–8, 172, 180, 186–8, 196, 208, 209, 217, 238, 248–59, 266, 267–71
role of 88–99, 107–8, 113–20
selection and use as function of protagonist's attributes 123–40, 151, 157–62, 167–8
strategic considerations regarding 120–2, 123–40, 142–3, 145, 148, 157–62, 167–8, 196–7, 199
surrogates as 11, 25–6, 96–7, 100, 106, 132, 133, 136–7, 162
types of 25–6
campaign protagonists 8, 19, 22–8, 31, 32–5, 37, 38, 42–7, 85, 87–9, 93–8, 100–22 *passim*, 123–51 *passim*, 155–69 *passim*, 173–80 *passim*, 185–8, 236, 241, 247, 258, 261, 266
attributes of 25, 32–5, 42, 100, 113, 123–40, 151, 180, 187
strategic implications of 32–7, 126–40
examples of 3, 124, 135
freedom of action of 126, 172
identity of interest with target 124, 127, 131, 133, 135
infrastructure of 77, 121, 124, 126, 135
legitimacy of 22–4, 43, 96, 100, 121, 123–40 *passim*, 145, 157, 161, 180, 188, 261
portrayal of 22–4
resources of 35–7, 89, 95, 100, 119, 120–1, 124–35, 155–8, 161, 180, 247, 265–6
transparency of 23, 121, 124–37, 175
visibility of 28, 95–6, 121, 124–37, 157
campaign strategy 16–17, 19–22, 22–37, 38–40, 42–64, 65, 74–5, 85–122, 123–40, 142, 150–1, 180–1, 191, 194, 204–8, 217, 220–32, 233–7, 248–59, 263–4
conceptual grounding of 16–17, 42–64
defined 21–2
driven by protagonist's attributes 42, 100, 113, 123–40
elements of 22–8
issue management 23–4, 32, 43, 58–60, 63, 74–5, 100–6 *passim*, 142, 150–1, 181, 191, 217, 254
and framing 220–32
networking as component 85–122, 123–40, 248–59

news management 28–30, 48–50, 233–7
positioning the media (*see also* frames and framing) 28–30
relationship management 95–9
rhetoric, role of 27, 38–40, 41, 42–3, 44, 65, 137–9, 204–8, 263–4
sophistication, degree of 16–17, 19, 20–1, 32–3, 49, 92–3, 180–1, 194
campaign tactics 4–5, 7–10, 14–16, 32–3, 38–64, 65–84, 100–7, 123–40, 144, 151, 236, 248, 243, 244, 252, 259, 260, 270, 271
Alinsky's rules 38, 46, 260
directed at advocacy groups 106
directed at civic groups 106
directed at community activists 106
directed at financial analysts 107
directed at industry analysts 107
directed at institutional shareholders 107
directed at investment community 106–7
directed at legal system 106
directed at legislators and/or the legislative process 104–5
directed at media 104
directed at NGOs 106
directed at the public in various roles 101–4
directed at regulators and/or the regulatory process 105
directed at religious groups 106
directed at the target 100–1
campaign targets 14, 15, 22, 25, 33, 45, 78–9, 86–8, 88–100, 100–1, 102–3, 118–19, 127, 129, 141–50, 150–1, 155–69, 186–8, 253–4, 261, 267–9, 271–3
attributes of 25, 45, 78–9, 86–8, 127, 141–50, 186–8
compartmentalized organization of 168
decision-making space of 86–8
defenses available to 155–69
managing perceptions 22, 25, 145–7, 150–1, 164
relationships with stakeholders 15, 33, 88–100, 118–19, 129, 142–3, 155–9, 186–8, 261, 267–9
selection criteria 14, 100, 143–50, 253–4
tactics directed at 100–1
vulnerabilities, potential 143–50, 271–3
association with risk 148
high transparency 147
high visibility 146–7
inherent structural weaknesses 149
instability 149
limited resources 149
low legitimacy 145–6
low transparency 147
negative perceptions 146
physical weakness 148–9
poor reputation 149
responsiveness 148
risk aversion 148
self-generated leverage 150, 102–3
cascading activation model 222
castellar defense 153–5, 167
Caterpillar 34
Catholic Healthcare West 46
celebrities 5, 95–6, 102–3, 104, 226, 235, 245
Center for Medicine in the Public Interest 27
Center for Union Facts 163
centralized statistical agencies (CESTAs) 60
Chavez, Cesar 235
Chong + Koster 95–6
Clarkson, Thomas 4–5
ClickZ 96
CNN/Time Warner 95–6
communication/persuasion matrix 40, 42
elements of communications in 42–56
effects of communications in 56–63
communications 18–19, 28, 42–7, 47–57, 56–63, 96, 100, 101–7 *passim*, 119–20, 129, 137–9, 143–4, 240
attention to 42
channels 42, 47–56
attributes of 47–8
and credibility 48–50
interactivity 47–8
message suitability 48
selection criteria 50–2
selection, effects of 49, 50, 76
strategic considerations 47–63, 162
effects 42, 56–63
agenda setting 58, 60–1
attitude change 42, 54, 55
behavior cueing 42
duration 62–3
emotional arousal 57
framing (*see also* frames and framing) 58–61
knowledge gain 57–8
personal or social gratification 56–7
primacy 63
recency 63

reinforcement 42
retention 42
exposure to 42
interaction with actions and relationships 137–9, 143–4
interest in 42
messages (*see also* frames and framing) 18–19, 28, 43–7, 47–50, 58–60, 96, 100, 119–20, 129, 240
campaigns as aggregations of 19
continuity 18–19, 58–60, 119–20, 129
core elements 43–4
credibility of 28, 48–50, 96, 100, 240
defining terms of debate 43
differentiation 44–5
interaction with channels 47–50
points of origin 46–7
stylistic elements 44–5
substantive elements 43–4
receivers (*see also* audience) 52–7
homogeneity versus heterogeneity of 52–3
sources (*see also* campaign intermediaries, campaign protagonists) 42–3
attributes of 42–3
number of 43
tactics directed at particular stakeholders 100–7 *passim*
coalitions 15, 18, 22, 37, 95–6, 104, 106, 110, 112–13, 113–16, 206, 228, 238, 248–55 *passim*, 258, 261, 267, 270
cognitive dissonance (*see* persuasion)
codes of conduct 16, 45, 101, 109, 125, 173–5, 211, 228–9, 262, 268
conflict diamonds 228
corporate campaigns (*see also* anti-corporate campaigns) 12–13, 262
Council on Economic Priorities (CEP) 109
critical events (*see* focusing events)
Croce, Benedetto 141
cybernetics 196, 264

Daimler 34
Darton, William 5
data mining 51, 52, 55, 186–8
DaVinci, Leonardo 151
De Saint-Exupéry, Antoine 152
deception 240, 243, 244–5, 264
Defense Science Board 189–93
diffusion of innovation 201
digital media (*see also* information and communications Technologies (ICT)) 44, 45, 48, 49, 50, 53–4, 57, 95–6, 171, 195, 237–40, 256–7
characteristics of 48, 50, 57, 238, 257
tactics employing 44, 49, 53–4, 95–6, 239–40
used to build and sustain advocacy networks 237–8, 256–7
Disney Corporation 239
Disney, Roy 239
distraction (*see also* attention) 58, 214, 226
distributed reputation systems 257
Dobbs, Lou 95–6
dramatization 29, 206–7, 234, 252, 262, 264

Einstein, Albert 1, 178, 183
electoral campaigns 19–20, 84–5
elites 21, 33, 162, 196, 203, 204, 205, 208, 219, 222, 234, 235, 252, 264
enemy construction 11, 14, 46, 226, 241, 258, 262
Energy Information Administration 60
Eni 34
environmentalists 3, 22, 90–3, 109, 130–1, 145, 161, 189, 208, 224, 228, 229, 233, 236, 238, 249, 251, 252, 253, 255, 258, 261, 262, 263, 268, 270, 271
campaigns by 22, 60–1, 92–3, 161, 165, 189, 238
Equiano, Olaudah 4
ethics 175–80, 259
events (*see* focusing events)
exemplification 203
experts 10, 132, 208, 229, 230, 236, 245, 250, 262–3, 271
exposure 50, 51, 211, 213, 214, 215, 217, 223
avoidance 50
repeated 214, 223
selective 211, 214, 215
timing of 51

Farah Manufacturing 12
Federal Emergency Management Agency (FEMA) 179
FedEx 36–7
focusing events 32, 121, 227, 263
forest certification (*see* codes of conduct)

frames and framing (*see also* media) 14, 32, 58–63, 81–2, 95, 100, 104, 111, 130–1, 139, 150, 155, 162–4, 166, 181, 218–32, 234, 236, 252–3, 258, 259, 263–4
bridging 225
competition 155, 221–4 *passim*, 252–3
control of 60–1, 252
defined 58–9
effects 59, 61–3, 186–8, 220–4 *passim*
modes of 222
of protest 224
of risk 220, 229–32, 263
salience in 80–1, 220–1, 223
stages of 61–2, 225, 229
standardized 234
tactics employing 100, 104, 130–1, 162–4, 264
Franklin, Benjamin 5, 38
Friends of the Earth 130

General Electric Corporation 10, 34, 47, 194
Giant Foods 132
Gifford, Kathie Lee 102–3
Global Exchange 24, 112–13
Global Fashion 102–3
Global Labor Strategies 54
global warming 60–1, 165, 263–4
Google 90
Greenpeace 130, 161, 175, 220, 224, 230, 251, 252, 262–3

Harvard Living Wage Campaign 103–4
Health Care for America Now 27
heresthetic 204
heuristics 203, 232
high-context communication 204–5
Holbrooke, Richard 34
Holmes, Oliver Wendell, Sr. 38
Honda 34
Hotel workers union 98–9
HSBC 34
human rights organizations 12, 112–13, 130, 251–3 *passim*, 261, 263
Human Rights Watch 130
Hurricane Katrina 179
hypermedia campaign 240

IBM 49
icons 14, 190, 226–7
images 13, 14, 45, 46–7, 59, 129, 164, 167, 190, 208, 216–17, 219–20, 221, 226–7, 234, 247
creation of 14, 208, 264
effect of 13, 208, 216–17
and framing 221
monitoring 167
national 227, 247
in the news 226–7, 234
patterns 219–20
role in campaign communications 45, 46–7, 59, 129, 164, 190
immigration policy 95–6
indexing hypothesis 234
Indonesia 12–15
Indymedia 257
information and communication technologies (ICT) (*see also* digital media) 252, 255–7
information and influence campaigns (IICs – *see also* campaign intermediaries, campaign protagonists, campaign strategy, campaign tactics, campaign targets, public information campaigns) 16–17, 18–37, 38–47, 53, 55, 56, 62–3, 65, 66, 68–9, 70–4, 77–9, 82, 83, 86, 88, 95–9, 100, 101, 103, 104, 105, 106, 107–8, 109, 110–11, 112–13, 114, 116–20, 121, 122, 126–40, 141–3, 143–7, 149, 151, 153–69, 170, 171–81, 185–93, 195, 198, 199, 202, 207, 209, 217, 221, 222, 227, 228, 229, 241–2, 244, 245–59, 261, 263, 265, 266, 268, 271
allies, role in 22, 25, 26, 33, 43, 46, 96, 101, 104, 106, 107, 111, 116–20, 127, 129, 133, 136, 147, 160, 162, 172, 181, 186–8, 241, 266
architecture of (*see also* networks, architecture) 35–6, 96, 134–40, 160
access points 160
protagonists' attributes highly determinative 126–40
role specialization in 96–7
argumentation and rhetoric in 38–47
character of 18–37
code of conduct for 173–5, 229
constraints on 173–81, 217
defense against 40, 146, 153–69, 195, 261, 265
analyzing network structures 155–9
components 155–66
deactivating or neutralizing intermediaries 157, 160

inducing resistance to persuasion 163–6
vulnerability reduction 155–7
counter-campaign 40, 162–3, 195, 265
grounded in theory 155–6
information management and control 165–6, 60–1
intelligence gathering in 155, 157–8, 167
reverse engineering 155–63
distinguished from public information campaigns 32–3
duration 21, 62–3, 127–9
dynamic of 95–9, 107–8, 134–40, 155, 253–4
effectiveness of 42, 70–1, 123, 143–4, 180, 186–8, 242, 246, 263
effects of 186–8
international dynamics 33, 103, 105, 106, 107, 107–8, 109, 112–13, 114, 123–31, 160, 175, 221, 222, 228, 229, 245–59, 263, 268
levels of complexity and sophistication 141–3
Level I, characterized 141–2
Level II, characterized 142
Level III, characterized 142–3
objectives 19–22 *passim*, 26–7, 33, 37, 39, 40, 45–7, 55, 68–9, 77–9, 86, 88, 95, 96, 98, 107, 110–11, 119, 122, 123, 126, 128, 134, 139, 143–4, 155–6, 166, 189–93 *passim*, 199, 261
outcomes 20–1, 35–6, 40, 42, 86, 128, 143–7, 185, 198, 227, 244, 250, 258, 271
power, role in (*see also* – power, power structure analysis) 32–7, 44–5
as relationship management 95–9
research in 25, 53, 56, 66, 70–4, 82, 95, 110, 121, 139, 165, 185–93
importance of 185
research questions raised in 186–8
types and methods used in 186–8
serendipity in 140
setting 25, 31–2, 36, 39, 40, 45, 65, 73, 78, 83, 88, 99, 100, 134, 149, 151, 172, 180, 185, 195, 202, 207, 209, 241–2, 245–6
significance of 171–3
and social science theory 16–17, 66, 194–273
style versus substance in 22–4
styles 126–40
breadth 127–8, 129
directness 127–8
duration 127–8
implications for tactics 131–40
intensity 127–8
policy focused 127–8
process focused 127–8
redundancy127–8
scale 127–8
self-focused, 127–8
specificity127–8
transparency 127–8, 129
types of 20–2
influence-centered 20–2
information-centered 20–2
ubiquity of 170, 180, 181, 241
information operations 77, 243–4
information processing 75, 196, 201, 214
Ingersoll Rand 34
innovation, diffusion of 201
Institute for Liberty 27
Institute for Public Policy Research 60–1, 263–4
Institutional Shareholder Services (ISS) 99, 270
institutional shareholders 98–9, 107, 270
tactics directed at 107
insurgencies 3, 20, 30, 124–6, 130–1, 150, 166, 170, 173, 228, 247, 254, 257–9
communication strategy of 189–90, 257–9
marketing of 130–1, 259
Intel 256
international communication (*see also* public diplomacy) 244, 245–8
international governmental organizations (IGOs) 124, 126, 250, 254, 255
Internet (*see* digital media)
Iran 49, 145–6
Iran-Contra Affair 224–5
issue-attention cycle, 217
issue management (*see* campaign strategy)
issue salience 45, 73, 74–5, 79, 80–2, 206, 211, 219–23 *passim*

J Curve 272–3
Johnson, Harvey E., Jr., Vice Admiral 179
Jones, Phil 165
journalists (*see* campaign intermediaries)
Just Say No 41

Kernaghan, Charles 102–3
Kimberley Process 228
Knight, Philip 11–14, 64, 223, 226
knowledge structures 180, 204–5, 207–8
KPMG 34

labor unions 3, 11–16, 27, 36, 131–2, 147–8, 157, 163, 254, 262, 270, 272
language (*see also* naming) 23, 43–5, 131, 204–8, 234–5, 264
  ambiguity in 206
  control of 43–5
  functions of 205
  power of 23, 45
  in propaganda 242
  role in campaigns 23, 43, 131, 206, 234–5, 264
  styles of 204
legitimacy 4, 13, 22–3, 24, 31, 34, 43, 48, 78, 93–4, 96, 100, 113, 121, 123–35 *passim*, 137, 139, 145–7, 157, 161–2, 170, 180, 188, 196, 205–7 *passim*, 239, 247, 250, 252, 254, 261, 267–8
  as attribute of stakeholders 93–4, 267–8
  defined 22–3, 261
  managing 23, 78, 96, 123–35 *passim*, 207, 239
lexicon (*see* language)
low-context communication 204–5
low-involvement learning 201–2

Mann, Michael 165
market segmentation (*see* audiences, segmentation of)
Marriott International 98–9
McCorvey, Norma 103
McFarland, Sean, General 59
McLuhan, Marshall 47
media (*see also* campaign intermediaries, communications) 50, 56–8, 61–3, 79, 82, 95, 122, 159, 164, 186–8, 195, 196–7, 199–203, 208, 213, 218–21, 225
  attributes of 50
  effects 56–8, 61–3, 79, 82, 195, 199–203, 208, 213, 218–21, 225
    agenda setting 58, 63, 79, 82, 218–21, 225
    diffusion 201
    duration 61–63, 213
    emotional arousal 57
    framing (*see* frames and framing)
    involvement and 201–2
    knowledge gain 57–8, 63, 208
    personal or social gratification 56–7, 63, 202
    primacy 61, 63
    recency 61, 63
  as objects of campaign strategy 23, 95–6, 159, 164, 196–7
  tactics directed at 104
Media Matters 95–6
Mexico 112–13, 258–9
moral imperative in campaigns 8, 11, 28, 43, 46, 100, 153, 167, 173, 178
Morland, George 5
motivation 26, 27, 39, 57, 71, 78, 93, 95, 105, 110, 111, 139, 164, 168, 181, 191, 198, 199, 210, 212, 213, 216, 223, 225, 238, 269
Moussavi, Mir Hussein 49
Movement for the Survival of the Ogoni People (MOSOP) 130–1
Multilateral Agreement on Investment (MAI) 256
Munich Re 34

naming (as a strategy – *see also* frames and framing, language, positioning) 9, 22, 23, 59, 104, 204, 206, 272
National Agricultural Statistics Service 60
National Center for Education Statistics 60
National Center for Health Statistics 60
National Council of Bishops 46
National Interfaith Committee for Worker Justice 46
National Labor Committee 102–3
netwar (*see* social netwar)
networks 47, 85–140, 150–1, 157–61, 167–8, 171, 172, 180, 186–8, 196, 208, 217, 238, 251, 254, 256, 266, 267–8
  architecture 113–16, 116–20, 157–9, 160, 180, 186–8
    all-channel network 114, 116
    chain network 114, 116
    circle network 114, 116
    start network 114, 116
  intermediaries in 47, 96, 107–8, 110–13, 117–22, 123, 127, 131–40, 150–1, 157–61, 167, 186–8, 196, 266, 267, 268

links in 110, 113–14, 116, 120, 168, 217, 254
members 113–14
nodes in 110, 113–14, 116, 168, 208, 217, 238, 254
pathways through 116–22, 172
multipath strategy 121
netwaves against the wall 121–2
path of greatest and most sustained pressure 121
path of least distance 120
path of least resistance 120–1
protagonist strengths and weakness, implications for networking 123–40
relationships in 93, 113–14, 267–8
bidirectional 114
intensity of 114
unidirectional 114
salience of 93, 267–8
role in IICs 85–140 *passim*
linear 119
mapping 113–20, 158–9, 167–8, 267
by function 114–15
by sequencing 116–20
temporal 119
strategic implications 120–22, 158–9
strategic requirements for managing 110–13, 116, 123–40, 158, 160
activation 110, 123–40, 158, 160
channel management 111
communication 113
control 111, 116
endorsement 113
expansion 111
focusing attention of members 111
funding 113
identification of prospective members 110
motivation of members 111
network formation 110
recruitment 110
relationship maintenance 110
New York State Death Penalty Commission 6–7, 9
news management (*see* campaign strategy)
Newton, John 4
Nigeria 130–1
Nike 11–16, 226, 229, 239
nongovernmental organizations (NGOs) 3, 12, 33, 34, 106–15, 124–5, 129, 130–1, 135, 149, 159, 168, 175, 217, 220, 228, 229, 247, 248–55, 255–7, 258, 259, 261, 263, 266
alliance formation by 254–5
attributes of 124–5, 168, 250–1
and advocacy networks 228–9
and boomerang model 107–8, 109, 228–9, 252–4
branding of 228
code of conduct for 175, 229
ICT use and network building by 255–7
as protagonists 124–5, 135, 247, 250–1
tactics directed at 106
North American Free Trade Agreement (NAFTA) 112, 258–9

Office of the Director of National Intelligence 179
Omar, Muhammad 125–6
Open Society Institute 257
Organization for Economic Cooperation and Development (OECD) 107

parsimony, principle of 120, 121, 151
Partnership to Improve Patient Care 27
personalization 95–6, 101, 102–3, 150, 171, 243
persuasion 21, 23, 25, 37, 38–47 *passim* 43, 50, 54–5, 56, 58, 63, 65, 66, 67–9, 69–79, 82, 100, 122, 141, 143, 148, 150, 162–3, 163–6, 186–8, 194, 198, 199, 202, 204, 209–16, 222, 223–4, 225, 226, 245, 267
affects 67–8, 74, 204, 212, 215, 225
and attitude change 54–5, 58, 63, 69–79, 82, 150, 162–3, 186–8, 194, 198, 202, 209–16, 223, 226
and behavior change 21, 37, 50, 63, 72, 100, 122, 143, 148, 202, 212, 213
attitude 58, 67–8, 72, 74, 204, 209–16 *passim*, 225
components 67–8, 72, 74, 204, 209–16 *passim*, 225
direction 58, 68, 210
integration into attitude clusters 68–9
intensity 68, 216
attitude change, theories and approaches 69–77, 82, 199, 202, 209–13, 223–4
balance theories 71, 209–10

belief-based approach 69–71, 212, 223–4
implications for persuasion 71
cognitive dissonance 71–4, 199, 202, 209–11
implications for persuasion 72
elaboration likelihood model 75–6, 211–13
implications for persuasion 76
function approach 76–7, 211–12
functions of attitudes 76, 211
implications for persuasion 77
social judgment-involvement approach 74–5, 82, 209, 211–12
implications for persuasion 74–5, 82
summative model (*see* belief-based approach)
attitude objects 67, 69
beliefs 23, 25, 43, 54, 56, 65, 67–9, 70–2, 78, 164, 209–16 *passim*, 222, 225, 245, 267
integration into belief systems 67–9
by strength of argument 38–47 *passim*
cognitions (*see* beliefs *in this heading*)
resistance to 39, 40, 66, 69, 72, 163–6, 210, 215–16
as component of campaign defense 163–6
inoculation 25, 163–4, 215–16
sources 40, 43, 72, 76, 78–9, 141, 210, 214, 223
attributes 43, 76, 78, 214
effects 43, 72, 210, 223
strategic questions 43, 78–9
regarding message content and objectives 78
regarding persuasive setting 78
regarding source(s) of persuasive messages 78
regarding target's access to channels 78
regarding target's availability for persuasion 78
regarding target's existing cognitive state 78
tactical choices 79
Petrobras 34
Pfizer Pharmaceuticals 27
Philbin, John P. 179
Pitt, William 4
pluralist theory of democracy 197
political consumerism (*see also* stakeholders) 239
Porter Novelli 27
positioning (*see also* frames and framing) 22, 24, 31, 72, 81, 87, 100, 118, 119, 124, 139, 151, 190, 246, 272
power 32–7
asymmetries as driving force in IICs 32–7
and stakeholder relationships (*see* power structure analysis)
power elite 196–7
power structure analysis 11, 88–95, 142, 155–7, 160–3, 196, 267
characterized 88–9
as defining characteristic of IICs 11, 93–5
source of differentiation across campaigns 94–5
source of regularities across campaigns 94–5
illustrated 89–92
as key to defending against IICs 155–7, 160–3
Presence Switzerland 70–1
Press for Change 12
priming (*see also* media) 218, 219, 225
propaganda 20, 38, 126, 195, 198, 235, 240–5, 247, 248
classification of techniques 240, 242
disinformation in 244–5
use by Al Qaeda 243–4
prospect theory 239
pseudo-events 121–2, 204, 207, 234, 239
psychological operations 77, 243, 244
public diplomacy 20, 126, 189, 222, 244, 245–8
public information campaigns (PICs) 20, 32–3, 141, 174, 198–9
public opinion (*see also* audiences, market segmentation, persuasion, media) 18, 26–8, 32, 39, 40–1, 44, 53–4, 57, 65, 79, 92–3, 96–8, 101–4, 106, 110, 146, 147, 148, 150–1, 170, 198, 199, 216–18, 220, 222, 227, 229–32, 252, 263
as campaign target 32, 199
creating appearance of support 26–8
demographic subsets 53–4
exploitation of 32, 217, 227, 263
frames of reference 218
as intermediary 23, 96–8, 101–4, 110, 148
issue-publics 147
mobilization of 40, 53–4, 65, 220, 222
recruitment of 222

spiral of silence 218
tactics directed at 27, 39, 40–1, 44, 57, 79, 92–3, 101–4, 106, 146, 148, 150–1, 170, 198, 229–32, 252
affinity-based appeals 102, 252
fear appeals 79, 101, 148, 229–32
mobilization 103, 106
values-based appeals 27, 39, 40–1, 44, 57, 92–3, 101–2, 146, 150–1, 198
third person effect 218

Reagan, Nancy 41
Reagan, Ronald 60, 225
reasoned action, theory of 212
Reebok 12, 14
reference publics 196–7
Reputation Quotient 271
resource mobilization theory 248–9
rhetoric 18, 27, 32, 38–9, 41, 43, 44, 65, 139, 146, 204–8 *passim*, 223, 264
risk 93, 102–3, 104, 106, 148, 150, 162, 181, 220, 230–2, 262–3, 272–3
aversion to 93, 148
celebrity, association with 102–3
communication 230
framing of 220, 230–2, 262–3
perception of, tactics employing 104, 106, 148, 150, 162, 230–2, 262–3
systemic risk 181, 272–2
Roe v. Wade 103
Roosevelt, Franklin D. 18
Ross, Dennis 34

SA8000 109
Safeway 132
Saint Consulting Group 131–2
salience 45, 73, 75, 79, 80–2, 93, 200, 206, 211, 213, 216, 219–23, 246, 267
SaveDisney 239
schema theory 203
Service Employees International Union (SEIU) 46
Sharp, Granville 4
Shell Oil Company 34, 130–1, 220, 230, 262–3
Siegfried, André 18
Siemens 34
sit-ins 103–4
smart mobs 237
Social Accountability International 109
social amplification and attenuation of risk framework 220–1
social judgment-involvement (*see* persuasion)
social marketing 20, 194, 198, 265–7
Social Movement Industries (SMIs) 249
Social Movement Organizations (SMOs) 228–9, 248–9, 251, 256, 257, 263
social movements 4, 11, 14, 162, 248–9, 256, 259, 263
social netwar 112–13, 258–9
social network analysis 186–8, 195, 248, 254
Society to Effect the Abolition of the Slave Trade 4, 14
Sodexho Marriott 98–9
soft power 145, 244, 247
Sotomayor, Sonia 103
South Africa 34
Southern Rhodesia 30, 34
Southwick, Alfred Porter 6–8
spiral of silence 218
Sri Lanka 259
Stakeholder Performance Indicator, Relationship Improvement Tool (SPIRIT) 271
stakeholder theory of the firm 156–7, 267
stakeholders (*see also* campaign intermediaries, campaign targets, power structure analysis) 15, 23, 33, 88–107, 116–22, 155–9, 267–9, 271
and brand equity 228, 268–9
as relational capital 269
consumers as 268
in foreign policy 271
management of relationships 95–9
role in campaigns 33, 98, 116–22, 155–9
salience of 93, 267–8
self-interest of 23, 98–9
shareholders as 93–4
tactics directed at 101–7
targeting of 15
Stevenson, Adlai 170
strategic choice framework 272
strategic influence operations 244
Students for a Democratic Society (SDS) 11
Supervalu 132
swarming 238
Switzerland 70–1
symbols 57, 76, 196, 204–5, 207, 221, 270

Taliban 125–6
Tamil Tigers 259
terrorist organizations 24, 33, 114, 124–6, 135, 170, 243, 257–9
  communication strategies 257–8
  as protagonists 124–6, 135
  as transnational advocacy networks 259
third parties (*see* campaign intermediaries)
third person effect (*see* public opinion)
topological psychology 209, 214
Total 34
Triangle Shirtwaist Factory fire 13
transnational advocacy networks (TANs) 106, 130–1, 228–9, 248–55 *passim*, 259
  influence of 228–9
  tactics employing 106, 259
two-step flow of communication hypothesis 200–1

United Against Nuclear Iran (UANI) 34
United Nations 107, 109, 124, 227, 252
United Nations Global Compact (UNGC) 109
United States Department of Defense 77, 244
United States Department of State 44
University of East Anglia 165
UPS 36–7
uses and gratifications (*see* media)

valence 80–2, 178, 246
  in agenda dynamics 80–2, 246
violence 30, 103, 257–8
  as communication 30, 257–8
  tactical use of 103
viral marketing 238
virtual strike 49
visibility 19–20, 21, 28, 80–2, 95–6, 121, 124, 126–31, 133, 134–7, 146–7, 157, 220, 227, 246
  as an attribute 21, 80–2, 124, 127, 133, 146–7
  as a strategy 19–20, 28, 95–6, 121, 126–31, 134–7, 157, 220, 227, 246
  in agenda dynamics 80–2
vulnerabilities assessment 271–3

Wal-Mart 102–3, 131–2
Wars, strategic naming of 59
Washington Post Test 178–9
Wedgwood, Josiah 5, 14
Westinghouse, George 6–11
Wilberforce, William 4
Woods, Tiger 102–3
Woolsey, James 34
World Economic Forum 109
World Resources Institute 92–3
Wyeth Pharmaceuticals 27

Zapatista rebellion 112–13, 125, 258–9